THE NORTHWOODS CONSPIRACY

BY

Ken Hudnall, J.D.

Omega Press
El Paso, Texas

Other Works by Ken Hudnall

FICTION

Manhattan Conspiracy
Blood On The Apple
Capital Crimes
Angel of Death

The Darkness Series
When Darkness Falls
Fear the Darkness

Even Paranoids Have Enemies

The Estate Sale Murders:
Deadman's Diary
Curse of the Dragon's Tooth

NON-FICTION

The Occult Connection
UFO's, Secret Societies and Ancient Gods
The Hidden Race

No Safe Haven: Homeland Insecurity

Spirits of the Border
The History and Mystery of El Paso Del Norte
The History and Mystery of Fort Bliss, Texas
The History and Mystery of the Rio Grande
The History and Mystery of New Mexico
The History and Mystery of Colorado

The Veterans Practical Primer: Getting Your Benefits

THE NORTHWOODS CONSPIRACY

All rights Reserved © 2006 By Ken Hudnall

No part of this books may be reproduced or transmitted in any form or by any means, graphic, electronic, or mechanical, including photocopying, recording, taping, or by any information storage retrieval system, without the written permission of the author.

OMEGA PRESS
An imprint of Omega Communications

For Information Address:

Omega Press
5823 N. Mesa, #823
El Paso, Texas 79912
Or
http://www.kenhudnall.com

FIRST EDITION

Printed in the United States of America

TABLE OF CONTENTS

PART ONE 7
- CHAPTER ONE 9
- CHAPTER TWO 13
- CHAPTER THREE 23

PART II 55
- CHAPTER FOUR 57
- CHAPTER FIVE 61
- CHAPTER SIX 67
- CHAPTER SEVEN 77
- CHAPTER EIGHT 97
- CHAPTER NINE 99
- CHAPTER TEN 103
- CHAPTER ELEVEN 109
- CHAPTER TWELVE 119
- CHAPTER THIRTEEN 125
- CHAPTER FOURTEEN 137
- CHAPTER FIFTEEN 145
- CHAPTER SIXTEEN 157
- CHAPTER SEVENTEEN 161
- CHAPTER EIGHTEEN 185
- CHAPTER NINETEEN 205
- CHAPTER TWENTY 221
- CHAPTER TWENTY-ONE 237
- CHAPTER TWENTY-TWO 255
- CHAPTER TWENTY-THREE 259
- CHAPTER TWENTY-FOUR 277
- CHAPTER TWENTY-FIVE 283
- CHAPTER TWENTY-SIX 287
- CHAPTER TWENTY-SEVEN 295
- CHAPTER TWENTY-EIGHT 299
- CHAPTER TWENTY-NINE 307
- CHAPTER THIRTY 317
- CHAPTER THIRTY-ONE 327
- INDEX 333

PART ONE

SMOKE AND MIRRORS

CHAPTER ONE
WHAT IS THE NORTHWOOD CONSPIRACY

"The hidden hand of the market will never work without a hidden fist -- McDonald's cannot flourish without McDonnell-Douglas, the designer of the F-15. And the hidden fist that keeps the world safe for Silicon Valley's technologies is called the US Army, Air Force, Navy and Marine Corps."
-- Thomas Friedman, "A Manifesto for the Fast World", New York Times Magazine, March 28, 1999

    This is a work of non-fiction. While the author has had to prove some of the points in this work through circumstantial evidence, there is no doubt that operating behind the scenes is a group that uses war and military power as a tool to keep their own personal business profits at a high level. It is these people who have been directly responsible for the utilization of the program that is referred to herein as The Northwood Conspiracy.

SETTING THE STAGE
    In this day and time, there has been much discussion about war and the threat of war. The Middle East has been a powder keg waiting to explode since the end of World War II. Now, with our invasion, the fuse has been lit; the only question remaining to be answered is how long the fuse might be.

    We in America have lived for generations with the firm belief that we are insulated from the effects of war due to the two oceans that separate us from the war zones in less settled parts of the world. However, now, our most basic beliefs have been shaken as the war we have watched in the news was brought home to us when the World Trade Center Towers were brought down in the worst attack against the American people ever carried out. Terrorism came to America.

    Once again, America was caught napping and subjected to a devastating attack that inflicted thousands of casualties on an innocent population. Now of course, the systems in place to serve and protect the American people immediately sprang into action, but the wound to our national pride was deep. The heroic acts of the New York City fire and police departments are a matter of record. There is no question that these men and women went far beyond the call of duty in their selfless acts of bravery. My question would be what led to the need for these men and women to risk their lives for their fellow man?

The reactions of the different branches of our government to the attack that took place on September 11, 2001 were certainly predictable. The Justice Department immediately moved toward instituting more stringent controls on our liberties. For the first time since the Civil War, government authorities arrested and incarcerated suspected terrorists without trial, and in some cases without even bringing charges. For some of these individuals the Writ of Habeas Corpus was suspended.

Since hijacked planes had been used in the attack on the Trade Center and the Pentagon, travel restrictions were immediately instituted by the Justice Department and for a period of time no planes, either commercial or private, were allowed to leave the ground. A new governmental department, called Homeland Security, was brought into being. A new, sweeping law, popularly called The Patriot Act, was written and enacted in record time. America had been attacked and was now reacting. In the national desire for revenge against the unknown attackers, however, certain things were overlooked in regard to this law that, I believe, deserved serious consideration.

WHO PROFITED

Criminal investigators spend years studying criminal behavior and getting to understand the perpetrators. Combating terrorism is not very different from combating crime; many of the same rules apply. When a crime has been committed, one of the first questions law enforcement personnel ask is who profited from this crime. Generally, the assumption is that the person or people that profited the most are the initial suspects. So in regard to the terrorist attack on the World Trade Center on September 11, 2001, let us first ask who profited by the cowardly attack?

The terrorist attack on the World Trade Center in September 11, 2001, was an event outside the understanding and experience of the majority of the American people. Only a few times in the history of this country have enemy forces been able to strike against our homeland. Most people have a hard time understanding what individual or group would carry out such dastardly acts and the response is to create stereotypes of what a terrorist looks or acts like.

Some people consider terrorists to be complete cowards whoa re afraid to face their enemies so they resort to these sneak attacks. Others consider terrorist to be unstoppable enemies who have a suicidal intent. Still others think about the Spy vs. Spy comic strip from Mad Magazine. Even our political leaders have referred to the terrorists as wearing diapers on their heads. All of these stereotypes fall short of the mark. However, no matter what side of the aisle someone is on, there seems to e absolutely no doubt that it was foreign terrorists who carried out this dastardly attack.

This having been said, however, just for the sake of argument, in the next few chapters, let's look at some of those groups that profited from the attack not only on the World Trade Center but in every war that the United States has fought. The reader might be surprised that some of those who actually profited from the deaths of so many innocent Americans.

ALWAYS A VICTIM

The vast majority of Americans are by nature isolationists who just desire to be left alone. However, once aroused the attacking forces quickly learn that they have a tiger by the tail. As a prime example, I give you the Japanese surprise attack on our fleet based at Pearl Harbor in 1941. We were almost beaten to the canvas at the sound of the bell, so to speak, and yet we wound up devastating the Japanese Homeland.

In almost every war we have fought as a nation, we reacted to being attacked by an enemy. The history books show that the American Revolution was started as a result of British attacks on the colonists and the War of 1812 was started as a result of the British impressing our seaman and stifling our trade. The war with Mexico came about as a result of Mexican aggression against American settlers, the American Civil War was started to free the slaves and the Spanish American War was a result of the dastardly sinking of the U.S.S. Maine. America was pulled in World War I as a result of German attacks on our shipping and our involvement in World War II came about as a result of the Japanese surprise attack on Pearl Harbor. The Korean War (or police action to use the proper name) began to free the South Koreans from the Communist aggression of the north and the Vietnam War was a result of the North Vietnamese attacking our ships in the Gulf of Tonkin. The first Gulf War was entered into in order to free Kuwait from Saddam's illegal invasion and the second Gulf War came about because Afghanistan and Iraq harbored terrorists and supported the activities of various Terroristic groups.

The unfortunate thing is that none of these simple reasons for American involvement in the various wars we have fought are true. The American people, time and again, have been maneuvered and manipulated into going to war in order to further the interests of a select group of powerful individuals who have always carefully stayed hidden in the shadows. Now it is time that these little known power players who have profited from so much death and destruction be brought out into the limelight.

CHAPTER TWO
OPERATION NORTHWOODS

"*It's inherent in [the] government's right, if necessary, to lie to save itself.*"
Arthur Sylvester, Assistant Secretary of Defense for Public Affairs.

    Americans as a whole are not enthusiastic about getting involved in the problems of other people, other countries, or other continents. We have long looked at the oceans that border our east and west coats as sufficient barriers to keep us out of the problems of other countries. As a result, America has not traditionally been openly militaristic and usually we refused to fight unless we were attacked. Certainly, the Central Intelligence Agency (CIA) has conducted enough wars to fill hundreds of books, but this was not the President ordering the United States Army to attack some other country and the only Americans involved were employees of the CIA.

    Frankly, it would take something major, such as a surprise attack, to get us to declare war on some other country. As examples I would point to the sinking of the Lousitania and the Zimmerman telegram that caused us to enter World War I; the attack on our fleet at Pearl Harbor that caused us to enter World War II; the Gulf of Tonkin incident that caused us to conduct the police action in Vietnam; the invasion of Kuwait that caused us to conduct Operation Desert Storm and the attacks on New York City by Al-Qaeda that caused us to invade Afghanistan and Iraq. These are normally proudly pointed to by our leaders as proof that American's military might is only used in a just cause, normally in defense of our country or to help some weaker ally against a stronger aggressor.

    This reluctance of the American people to fight has long been frustrating to those President's who felt the need to go empire building around the globe. In his new exposé of the National Security Agency entitled *Body of Secrets*, author James Bamford[1] highlights a set of proposals designed to get public support for an invasion of Cuba that were submitted President Kennedy by the Joint Chiefs of Staff. This set of proposals was codenamed **OPERATION NORTHWOODS**. This document, titled "Justification for U.S. Military

---

[1] Bamford, James, <u>Body of Secrets</u>, Anchor Books, New York, 2002.

Intervention in Cuba" was provided by the JCS to Secretary of Defense Robert McNamara on March 13, 1962, as the key component of Operation Northwoods. Written in response to a request from the Chief of the Cuba Project, Col. Edward Lansdale the Top Secret memorandum describes U.S. plans to covertly engineer various pretexts that would justify a U.S. invasion of Cuba. These proposals -- part of a secret anti-Castro program known as **Operation Mongoose** – included:

- Staging the assassinations of Cubans living in the United States,

- Developing a fake "Communist Cuban terror campaign in the Miami area, in other Florida cities and even in Washington,"

- Including "sink[ing] a boatload of Cuban refugees (real or simulated),"

- Faking a Cuban airforce attack on a civilian jetliner, and

- Concocting a "Remember the Maine" incident by blowing up a U.S. ship in Cuban waters and then blaming the incident on Cuban sabotage.

Bamford felt that Operation Northwoods "may be the most corrupt plan ever created by the U.S. government.[2]." This was nothing more than psychological warfare directed against the American people and it was suggested by the leaders of the nation's military. Excerpts from the declassified 1962 U.S. Joint Chiefs of Staff Memo: Operation Northwoods - Justification for U.S. Military Intervention in Cuba are included below.

TOP SECRET SPECIAL HANDLING NOFORN
THE JOINT CHIEFS OF STAFF
WASHINGTON 25, D.C.
13 March 1962
MEMORANDUM FOR THE SECRETARY OF DEFENSE

Subject: Justification for U.S. Military Intervention in Cuba (TS)

1. The Joint Chiefs of Staff have considered the attached Memorandum for the Chief of Operations, Cuba Project, which responds to a request of that office for brief but precise description of pretexts which would provide justification for US military intervention in Cuba.

2. The Joint Chiefs of Staff recommend that the proposed memorandum be forwarded as a preliminary submission suitable for planning purposes. It is assumed that there will be similar submissions from other agencies and that these

---

[2] See Also: Friendly Fire - Book: U.S. Military Drafted Plans to Terrorize U.S. Cities to Provoke War With Cuba, by David Ruppe, ABCNews.com, 5/1/01

inputs will be used as a basis for developing a time-phased plan. Individual projects can then be considered on a case-by-case basis.

3. Further, it is assumed that a single agency will be given the primary responsibility for developing military and para-military aspects of the basic plan. It is recommended that this responsibility for both overt and covert military operations be assigned the Joint Chiefs of Staff.

For the Joint Chiefs of Staff:

SYSTEMATICALLY REVIEWED,
BY JCS ON 21 May 84   [signed]
CLASSIFICATION CONTINUED

L. L. Lemnitzer
Chairman
Joint Chiefs of Staff

1 Enclosure
Memo for Chief of Operations, Cuba Project

RECOMMENDATIONS

8. It is recommended that:

    a. Enclosure A together with its attachments should be forwarded to the Secretary of Defense for approval and transmittal to the Chief of Operations, Cuba Project.

    b. This paper NOT be forwarded to commanders of unified or specified commands.

    c. This paper NOT be forwarded to US officers assigned to NATO activities.

    d. This paper NOT be forwarded to the Chairman, US Delegation, United Nations Military Staff Committee.

APPENDIX TO ENCLOSURE A

DRAFT
MEMORANDUM FOR THE SECRETARY OF DEFENSE

Subject: Justification for U.S. Military Intervention in Cuba (TS)

1. Reference is made to memorandum from Chief of Operations, Cuba project, for General Craig, subject: "Operation MONGOOSE", dated 5 March 1962,

which requested brief but precise description of pretexts which the Joint Chiefs of Staff consider would provide justifications for US military intervention in Cuba.

2. The projects listed in the enclosure hereto are forwarded as a preliminary submission suitable for planning purposes. It is assumed that there will be similar submissions from other agencies and that these inputs will be used as a basis for developing a time-phased plan. The individual projects can then be considered on a case-by-case basis.

3. This plan, incorporating projects selected from the attached suggestions, or from other sources, should be developed to focus all efforts on a specific ultimate objective which would provide adequate justification for US military intervention. Such a plan would enable a logical build-up of incidents to be combined with other seemingly unrelated events to camouflage the ultimate objective and create the necessary impression of Cuban rashness and irresponsibility on a large scale, directed at other countries as well as the United States. The plan would also properly integrate and time phase the courses of action to be pursued. The desired resultant from the execution of this plan would be to place the United States in the apparent position of suffering defensible grievances from a rash and irresponsible government of Cuba and to develop an inter- national image of a Cuban threat to peace in the Western Hemisphere.

4. Time is an important factor in resolution of the Cuban problem. Therefore, the plan should be so time-phased that projects would be operable within the next few months.

5. Inasmuch as the ultimate objective is overt military intervention, it is recommended that primary responsibility for developing military and para-military aspects of the plan for both overt and covert military operations be assigned the Joint Chiefs of Staff.

PRETEXTS TO JUSTIFY US MILITARY INTERVENTION IN CUBA
(Note: The courses of action which follow are a preliminary submission suitable only for planning purposes. They are arranged neither chronologically nor in ascending order. Together with similar inputs from other agencies, they are intended to provide a point of departure for the development of a single, integrated, time-phased plan. Such a plan would permit the evaluation of individual projects within the context of cumulative, correlated actions designed to lead inexorably to the objective of adequate justification for US military intervention in Cuba).

1. Since it would seem desirable to use legitimate provocation as the basis for US military intervention in Cuba a cover and deception plan to include requisite

preliminary actions such as has been developed in response to Task 33 c, could be executed as an initial effort to provoke Cuban reactions. Harassment plus deceptive actions to convince the Cubans of imminent invasion would be emphasized. Our military posture throughout execution of the plan will allow a rapid change from exercise to intervention if Cuban responses justifies.

2. A series of well coordinated incidents will be planned to take place in and around Guantanamo to give genuine appearance of being done by hostile Cuban forces.

   a. Incidents to establish a credible attack (not in chronological order):

   (1) Start rumors (many). Use clandestine radio.

   (2) Land friendly Cubans in uniform "over-the-fence" to stage attack on the base.

   (3) Capture Cuban (friendly) saboteurs inside the base.

   (4) Start riots near the entrance to the base (friendly Cubans).

   (5) Blow up ammunition inside the base; start fires.

   (6) Burn aircraft on airbase (sabotage).

   (7) Lob mortar shells from outside of base into base. Some damage to installations.

   (8) Capture assault teams approaching from the sea of vicinity of Guantanamo City.

   (9) Capture militia group which storms the base.

   (10) Sabotage ship in harbor; large fires -- napthalene.

   (11) Sink ship near harbor entrance. Conduct funerals for mock-victims (may be lieu of (10)).

   b. United States would respond by executing offensive operations to secure water and power supplies, destroying artillery and mortar emplacements which threaten the base.

   c. Commence large scale United States military operations.

3. A "Remember the Maine" incident could be arranged in several forms:

a. We could blow up a US ship in Guantanamo Bay and blame Cuba.

b. We could blow up a drone (unmanned) vessel anywhere in the Cuban waters. We could arrange to cause such incident in the vicinity of Havana or Santiago as a spectacular result of Cuban attack from the air or sea, or both. The presence of Cuban planes or ships merely investigating the intent of the vessel could be fairly compelling evidence that the ship was taken under attack. The nearness to Havana or Santiago would add credibility especially to those people that might have heard the blast or have seen the fire. The US could follow with an air/sea rescue operation covered by US fighters to "evacuate" remaining members of the non-existent crew. Casualty lists in US newspapers would cause a helpful wave of national indignation.

4. We could develop a Communist Cuba terror campaign in the Miami area, in other Florida cities and even in Washington. The terror campaign could be pointed at Cuban refugees seeking haven in the United States. We could sink a boatload of Cubans enroute to Florida (real or simulated). We could foster attempts on lives of Cuban refugees in the United States even to the extent of wounding in instances to be widely publicized. Exploding a few plastic bombs in carefully chosen spots, the arrest of Cuban agents and the release of prepared documents substantiating Cuban involvement also would be helpful in projecting the idea of an irresponsible government.

5. A "Cuban-based, Castro-supported" filibuster could be simulated against a neighboring Caribbean nation (in the vein of the 14th of June invasion of the Dominican Republic). We know that Castro is backing subversive efforts clandestinely against Haiti, Dominican Republic, Guatemala, and Nicaragua at present and possible others. These efforts can be magnified and additional ones contrived for exposure. For example, advantage can be taken of the sensitivity of the Dominican Air Force to intrusions within their national air space. "Cuban" B-26 or C-46 type aircraft could make cane-burning raids at night. Soviet Bloc incendiaries could be found. This could be coupled with "Cuban" messages to the Communist underground in the Dominican Republic and "Cuban" shipments of arms which would be found, or intercepted, on the beach.

6. Use of MIG type aircraft by US pilots could provide additional provocation. Harassment of civil air, attacks on surface shipping and destruction of US military drone aircraft by MIG type planes would be useful as complementary actions. An F-86 properly painted would convince air passengers that they saw a Cuban MIG, especially if the pilot of the transport were to announce such fact. The primary drawback to this suggestion appears to be the security risk inherent

in obtaining or modifying an aircraft. However, reasonable copies of the MIG could be purchased from US resources in about three months.

7. Hijacking attempts against civil air and surface craft should appear to continue as harassing measures condoned by the government of Cuba. Concurrently, genuine defections of Cuban civil and military air and surface craft should be encouraged.

8. It is possible to create an incident which will demonstrate convincingly that a Cuban aircraft has attacked and shot down a chartered civil airliner enroute from the United States to Jamaica, Guatemala, Panama or Venezuela. The destination would be chosen only to cause the flight plan route to cross Cuba. The passengers could be a group of college students off on a holiday or any grouping of persons with a common interest to support chartering a non-scheduled flight.

    a. An aircraft at Eglin AFB would be painted and numbered as an exact duplicate for a civil registered aircraft belonging to a CIA proprietary organization in the Miami area. At a designated time the duplicate would be substituted for the actual civil aircraft and would be loaded with the selected passengers, all boarded under carefully prepared aliases. The actual registered aircraft would be converted to a drone.

    b. Take off times of the drone aircraft and the actual aircraft will be scheduled to allow a rendezvous south of Florida. From the rendezvous point the passenger-carrying aircraft will descend to minimum altitude and go directly into an auxiliary field at Eglin AFB where arrangements will have been made to evacuate the passengers and return the aircraft to its original status. The drone aircraft meanwhile will continue to fly the filed flight plan. When over Cuba the drone will begin transmitting on the international distress frequency a "MAY DAY" message stating he is under attack by Cuban MIG aircraft. The transmission will be interrupted by the destruction of aircraft which will be triggered by radio signal. This will allow IACO radio stations in the Western Hemisphere to tell the US what has happened to the aircraft instead of the US trying to "sell" the incident.

9. It is possible to create an incident which will make it appear that Communist Cuban MIGs have destroyed a USAF aircraft over international waters in an unprovoked attack.

    a. Approximately 4 of 5 F-101 aircraft will be dispatched in trail from Homestead AFB, Florida, to the vicinity of Cuba. Their mission will be to reverse course and simulate fakir aircraft for an air defense exercise in southern Florida. These aircraft would conduct variations of these flights at frequent intervals. Crews would be briefed to remain at least 12 miles off the Cuban coast;

however, they would be required to carry live ammunition in the event that hostile actions were taken by the Cuban MIGs.

b. On one such flight, a pre-briefed pilot would fly tail-end Charley at considerable interval between aircraft. While near the Cuban Island this pilot would broadcast that he had been jumped by MIGs and was going down. No other calls would be made. The pilot would then fly directly west at extremely low altitude and land at a secure base, an Eglin auxiliary. The aircraft would be met by the proper people, quickly stored and given a new tail number. The pilot who had performed the mission under an alias, would resume his proper identity and return to his normal place of business. The pilot and aircraft would then have disappeared.

c. At precisely the same time that the aircraft was presumably shot down a submarine or small surface craft would disburse F-101 parts, parachute, etc., at approximately 15 to 20 miles off the Cuban coast and depart. The pilots retuning to Homestead would have a true story as far as they knew. Search ships and aircraft could be dispatched and parts of aircraft found.

ENCLOSURE B
FACTS BEARING ON THE PROBLEM

1. The Joint Chiefs of Staff have previously stated that US unilateral military intervention in Cuba can be undertaken in the event that the Cuban regime commits hostile acts against US forces or property which would serve as an incident upon which to base overt intervention.

2. The need for positive action in the event that current covert efforts to foster an internal Cuban rebellion are unsuccessful was indicated by the Joint Chiefs of Staff on 7 March 1962, as follows:

" - - - determination that a credible internal revolt is impossible of attainment during the next 9-10 months will require a decision by the United States to develop a Cuban "provocation" as justification for positive US military action."

3. It is understood that the Department of State also is preparing suggested courses of action to develop justification for US military intervention in Cuba.

The above excerpts are taken from the original 15-page US Government TOP SECRET document, "Chairman, Joint Chiefs of Staff, Justification for US Military Intervention in Cuba [including cover memoranda], March 13, 1962," available at the National Security Archive website in pdf format at the following link: http://www.gwu.edu/~nsarchiv/news/20010430/doc1.pdf (if you don't have it, download Adobe Acrobat Reader to view pdf formatted files).

THROUGH THE MIRROR

So here we have men at the senior levels of the military hierarchy seriously discussing instigating a war with a foreign power in order to further their own interests. In line with President Kennedy's instructions, the Joint Chiefs of Staff had previously stated that US unilateral military intervention in Cuba could be undertaken in the event that the Cuban regime committed hostile acts against US forces or property which would serve as an incident upon which to base overt intervention.

President Kennedy had no desire to get the United States into a shooting war with an enemy. Granted, the United States Military could have easily decimated the Cuban military forces and taken the country just as we have done in Iraq. However, Cuba's strongest ally was the Soviet Union, who would have taken a dim view of out invasion of Cuba. So it was stressed that we could act only if Cuba took the first aggressive action. Thus the concept that became Operation Northwood came into being -----Or did it?

After reading the Operation Northwood proposal, I began to read about our earlier conflicts, looking for similar activities that might infer that a similar program had been used earlier in American history. I really did not think that I would find it, but to my surprise, I found a number of correlations between earlier wars and the proposals in Operation Northwood. I also found references to a hidden group of powerful men who have been directing this country's actions since the beginning of the colonies. The membership of this august body would shock and surprise many.

After I finished my study, I have begun to feel that Operation Northwoods was just a formalization of a practice that has been ongoing since at least 1776 and perhaps earlier. Before someone jumps up screaming that I am being subversive and unpatriotic to make such suggestions, let me say that I believe that having served my country as an Infantry officer in the United States Army to the extent that I am now a 100% disabled veteran, entitled me to ask whatever questions I desire.

OUR GOVERNMENT WOULDN'T LIE TO US

During my college years, which happened to coincide with the beginnings of the Vietnam War, I continually heard people shouting "My Country – right or wrong – it is my country!" Tens of thousands of our best and brightest walked into the caldron of war and did not return. Most of those I associated with felt that it was a just war, because President Lyndon Johnson had gone on television, told us about the dastardly attack on our ship in the Gulf of Tonkin by the cowardly North Vietnamese. Congress passed the Tonkin Resolution and we went to war in Vietnam.

Today, some forty or so years later, it has now been revealed that the incident in the Gulf of Tonkin that led to a formal approval by Congress for military operations to be conducted in Vietnam never happened. As we will see in a later chapter, the Tonkin incident was manufactured by the highest levels of our government in order to influence public opinion into supporting the war that the President wanted to have in Vietnam. So the bottom line to this was that our own government lied to us in order to get approval to lead us into a war. Of course, the government will not ever admit that the administration lied in order to influence Congress, considering the lie to be as effective a weapon as a bomb.

In October of 1962, upon being caught in a direct and unambiguous lie regarding whether the Pentagon knew of any offensive weapons in Cuba, when in fact Defense Department officials were debating whether to invade the island in order to remove those very weapons, Arthur Sylvester, assistant secretary of defense for public affairs, made the audacious claim, "*It's inherent in [the] government's right, if necessary, to lie to save itself.*" Begging the question of just who the enemy was, Sylvester added, "*News generated by the actions of the government ... [are] part of the arsenal of weaponry that a president has.*"

So the government, much like modern religion, feels that it is acceptable to lie to the voters since it is being done in the name of a good cause. However, if a citizen lies to the government then the citizen goes to jail. If the government represents the people, this it would seem to me to be long for the government to lie to its constituents.

CHAPTER THREE
AMERICAN MILITARY OPERATIONS

"News generated by the actions of the government ... [are] part of the arsenal of weaponry that a president has." Arthur Sylvester, assistant secretary of defense for public affairs

I consider myself educated and well read. My library at home has in excess of 10,000 books and I have always read a book a day since childhood. Through my long association with the U.S. military, I have developed a number of contacts who have also kept me aware of various actions being planned or initiated. When I began my research into Americans military actions, I was aware of only a few, however, the more I researched the issue the more little known military actions I discovered. I also discovered a number of instances when American military might was used against American citizens in order to protect private industry.

These actions may be considered little in the grand scheme of things, but each one of these is the flexing of the military might of this country and is a direct reflection on the American people[3]. Another consideration is that in many of these little known operations people on both sides died, which, to them, makes each operation a large one, no matter how the policy makers saw it. The following is a partial list of U.S. military interventions from 1789 to 2005[4]. However, there are not enough trees in the forest to make enough paper to record

---

[3] I verified some of my findings through a smiliar list complied by Zoltan Grossman is an Assistant Professor of Geography at the University of Wisconsin- Eau Claire (Box 4004, Eau Claire, WI 54701 USA). His peace writings can be seen at http://www.uwec.edu/grossmzc/peace.html and he can be reached at zoltan@igc.org .

[4] Among sources used, beside news reports, are the Congressional Record (23 June 1969), 180 Landings by the U.S. Marine Corp History Division, Ege & Makhijani in Counterspy (July-Aug, 1982), "Instances of Use of United States Forces Abroad, 1798-1993" by Ellen C. Collier of the Library of Congress Congressional Research Service, and Ellsberg in Protest & Survive.

all of the following categories of actions, so I have opted not to show them, even though they too are the flexing of our military muscles:

- Mobilizations of the National Guard
- Offshore shows of naval strength
- Reinforcements of embassy personnel
- The use of non-Defense Department personnel (such as the Drug Enforcement Administration)
- Military exercises
- Non-combat mobilizations (such as replacing postal strikers)
- The permanent stationing of armed forces
- Covert actions where the U.S. did not play a command and control role
- The use of small hostage rescue units
- Most uses of proxy troops
- U.S. piloting of foreign warplanes
- Foreign disaster assistance
- Military training and advisory programs not involving direct combat
- Civic action programs and many other military activities.

The following are actual events where U.S. military personnel were used in what amounted to combat roles in order to carry out U.S. Government policies[5] in situations of conflict or potential conflict or for other than normal peacetime purposes. The instances differ greatly in number of forces, purpose, extent of hostilities, and legal authorization. Five of the instances are declared wars: the War of 1812, the Mexican War of 1846, the Spanish American War of 1898, World War I declared in 1917, and World War II declared in 1941.

Some of the instances were extended military engagements that might be considered undeclared wars. These include the Undeclared Naval War with France from 1798 to 1800; the First Barbary War from 1801 to 1805; the Second Barbary War of 1815; the Korean War of 1950-53; the Vietnam War from 1964 to 1973; and the Persian Gulf War of 1991. In some cases, such as the Persian Gulf War against Iraq, Congress authorized the military action although it did not declare war.

The majority of the instances listed were brief Marine or Navy actions prior to World War II to protect U.S. citizens or promote U.S. interests. A number were actions against pirates or bandits. Some were events, such as the stationing of Marines at an Embassy or legation, which later were considered normal

---

[5] Some of these events came from "Instances of Use of United States Forces Abroad, 1798 – 1993" by Ellen C. Collier, Specialist in U.S. Foreign Policy, Foreign Affairs and National Defense Division, Washington DC: Congressional Research Service -- Library of Congress -- October 7, 1993

peacetime practice. Covert actions, disaster relief, and routine alliance stationing and training exercises are not included here, nor are the Civil and Revolutionary Wars and the continual use of U.S. military units in the exploration, settlement, and pacification of the West.

INSTANCES OF USE OF UNITED STATES ARMED FORCES, 1798-2005

1798-1800 --   Undeclared Naval War with France. This contest included land actions, such as that in the Dominican Republic, city of Puerto Plata, where marines captured a French privateer under the guns of the forts.

1801-05 --   Tripoli. The First Barbary War included the USS George Washington and USS Philadelphia affairs and the Eaton Expedition, during which a few marines landed with United States Agent William Eaton to raise a force against Tripoli in an effort to free the crew of the Philadelphia. Tripoli declared war but not the United States.

1806 --   Mexico (Spanish territory). Capt. Z. M. Pike, with a platoon of troops, invaded Spanish territory at the headwaters of the Rio Grande on orders from Gen. James Wilkinson. He was made prisoner without resistance at a fort he constructed in present day Colorado, taken to Mexico, and later released after seizure of his papers.

1806-10 --   Gulf of Mexico. American gunboats operated from New Orleans against Spanish and French privateers off the Mississippi Delta, chiefly under Capt. John Shaw and Master Commandant David Porter.

1810 --   West Florida (Spanish territory). Gov. Claiborne of Louisiana, on orders of the President, occupied with troops, territory in dispute east of Mississippi as far as the Pearl River, later the eastern boundary of Louisiana. He was authorized to seize as far east as the Perdido River.

1812 --   Amelia Island and other parts of east Florida, then under Spain. Temporary possession was authorized by President Madison and by Congress, to prevent occupation by any other power; but possession was obtained by Gen. George Matthews in so irregular a manner that his measures were later disavowed by the President.

1812-15 -- War of 1812. On June 18, 1812, the United States declared war on the United Kingdom of Great Britain and Ireland. Among the issues leading to the war were British interception of neutral ships and blockades of the United States during British hostilities with France.

1813 -- West Florida (Spanish territory). On authority given by Congress, General Wilkinson seized Mobile Bay in April with 600 soldiers. A small Spanish garrison gave way. Thus U.S. advanced into disputed territory to the Perdido River, as projected in 1810. No fighting.

1813-14 -- Marguesas Islands. U.S. forces built a fort on the island of Nukahiva to protect three prize ships which had been captured from the British.

1814 -- Spanish Florida. Gen. Andrew Jackson took Pensacola and drove out the British with whom the United States was at war.

1814-25 -- Caribbean. Engagements between pirates and American ships or squadrons took place repeatedly, especially ashore and offshore about Cuba, Puerto Rico, Santo Domingo, and Yucatan. Three thousand pirate attacks on merchantmen were reported between 1815 and 1823. In 1822 Commodore James Biddle employed a squadron of two frigates, four sloops of war, two brigs, four schooners, and two gunboats in the West Indies.

1815 -- Algiers. The Second Barbary War was declared by the opponents but not by the United States. Congress authorized an expedition. A large fleet under Decatur attacked Algiers and obtained indemnities.

1815 -- Tripoli. After securing an agreement from Algiers, Decatur demonstrated with his squadron at Tunis and Tripoli, where he secured indemnities for offenses during the War of 1812.

1816 -- Spanish Florida. United States forces destroyed Nicholls Fort, called also Negro Fort, which harbored raiders making forays into United States territory.

1816-18 -- Spanish Florida - First Seminole War. The Seminole Indians, whose area was a resort for escaped slaves and border ruffians, were attacked by troops under Generals Jackson and Gaines and pursued into northern Florida. Spanish posts were attacked and occupied, British citizens executed. In 1819 the Floridas were ceded to the United States.

1817 -- Amelia Island (Spanish territory off Florida). Under orders of President Monroe, United States forces landed and expelled a group of smugglers, adventurers, and freebooters.

1818 -- Oregon. The USS Ontario, dispatched from Washington, landed at the Columbia River and in August took possession of Oregon territory. Britain had conceded sovereignty but Russia and Spain asserted claims to the area.

1820-23 -- Africa. Naval units raided the slave traffic pursuant to the 1819 Act of Congress.

1822 -- Cuba. United States naval forces suppressing piracy landed on the northwest coast of Cuba and burned a pirate station.

1823 -- Cuba. Brief landings in pursuit of pirates occurred April 8 near Escondido; April 16 near Cayo Blanco; July 11 at Siquapa Bay; July 21 at Cape Cruz; and October 23 at Camrioca.

1824 -- Cuba. In October the USS Porpoise landed bluejackets near Matanzas in pursuit of pirates. This was during the cruise authorized in 1822.

1824 -- Puerto Rico (Spanish territory). Commodore David Porter with a landing party attacked the town of Fajardo which had sheltered pirates and insulted American naval officers. He landed with 200 men in November and forced an apology. Commodore Porter was later court-martialed for overstepping his powers.

1825 -- Cuba. In March cooperating American and British forces landed at Sagua La Grande to capture pirates.

1827 -- Greece. In October and November landing parties hunted pirates on the islands of Argenteire, Miconi, and Androse.

1831-32 -- Falkland Islands. Captain Duncan of the USS Lexington investigated the capture of three American sealing vessels and sought to protect American interests.

1832 -- Sumatra - February 6 to 9. A naval force landed and stormed a fort to punish natives of the town of Quallah Battoo for plundering the American ship Friendship.

1833 -- Argentina - October 31 to November 15. A force was sent ashore at Buenos Aires to protect the interests of the United States and other countries during an insurrection.

1835-36 -- Peru - December 10, 1835, to January 24, 1836, and August 31 to December 7, 1836. Marines protected American interests in Callao and Lima during an attempted revolution.

1836 -- Mexico. General Gaines occupied Nacogdoches (Tex.), disputed territory, from July to December during the Texan war for independence, under orders to cross the "imaginary boundary line" if an Indian outbreak threatened.

1838-39 -- Sumatra - December 24, 1838, to January 4, 1839. A naval force landed to punish natives of the towns of Quallah Battoo and Muckie (Mukki) for depredations on American shipping.

1840 -- Fiji Islands - July. Naval forces landed to punish natives for attacking American exploring and surveying parties.

1841 -- Drummond Island, Kingsmill Group. A naval party landed to avenge the murder of a seaman by the natives.

1841 -- Samoa - February 24. A naval party landed and burned towns after the murder of an American seaman on Upolu Island.

1842 -- Mexico. Commodore T.A.C. Jones, in command of a squadron long cruising off California, occupied Monterey, Calif., on October 19, believing war had come. He discovered peace, withdrew, and saluted. A similar incident occurred a week later at San Diego.

1843 -- China. Sailors and marines from the St. Louis were landed after a clash between Americans and Chinese at the trading post in Canton.

1843 -- Africa -- November 29 to December 16. Four United States vessels demonstrated and landed various parties (one of 200 marines and sailors) to discourage piracy and the slave trade along the Ivory Coast, and to punish attacks by the natives on American seamen and shipping.

1844 -- Mexico. President Tyler deployed U.S. forces to protect Texas against Mexico, pending Senate approval of a treaty of annexation. (Later rejected.) He defended his action against a Senate resolution of inquiry.

1846-48 -- Mexican War. On May 13, 1846, the United States recognized the existence of a state of war with Mexico. After the annexation of Texas in 1845, the United States and Mexico failed to resolve a boundary dispute and President Polk said that it was necessary to deploy forces in Mexico to meet a threatened invasion.

1849 -- Smyrna. In July a naval force gained release of an American seized by Austrian officials.

1851 -- Turkey. After a massacre of foreigners (including Americans) at Jaffa in January, a demonstration by the Mediterranean Squadron was ordered along the Turkish (Levant) coast.

1851 -- Johanns Island (east of Africa) -- August. Forces from the U.S. sloop of war Dale exacted redress for the unlawful imprisonment of the captain of an American whaling brig.

1852-53 -- Argentina -- February 3 to 12, 1852; September 17, 1852 to April 1853. Marines were landed and maintained in Buenos Aires to protect American interests during a revolution.

1853 -- Nicaragua -- March 11 to 13. U.S. forces landed to protect American lives and interests during political disturbances.

1853-54 -- Japan. Commodore Perry and his expedition made a display of force leading to the "opening of Japan" and the Perry Expedition.

1853-54 -- Ryukyu and Bonin Islands. Commodore Perry on three visits before going to Japan and while waiting for a reply from Japan made a naval demonstration, landing marines twice, and secured a coaling concession from the ruler of Naha on Okinawa; he also demonstrated in the Bonin Islands with the purpose of securing facilities for commerce.

1854 -- China -- April 4 to June 15 to 17. American and English ships landed forces to protect American interests in and near Shanghai during Chinese civil strife.

1854 -- Nicaragua -- July 9 to 15. Naval forces bombarded and burned San Juan del Norte (Greytown) to avenge an insult to the American Minister to Nicaragua.

1855 -- China -- May 19 to 21. U.S. forces protected American interests in Shanghai and, from August 3 to 5 fought pirates near Hong Kong.

1855 -- Fiji Islands -- September 12 to November 4. An American naval force landed to seek reparations for depredations on American residents and seamen.

1855 -- Uruguay -- November 25 to 29. United States and European naval forces landed to protect American interests during an attempted revolution in Montevideo.

1856 -- Panama, Republic of New Grenada -- September 19 to 22. U.S. forces landed to protect American interests during an insurrection.

1856 -- China -- October 22 to December 6. U.S. forces landed to protect American interests at Canton during hostilities between the British and the Chinese, and to avenge an assault upon an unarmed boat displaying the United States flag.

1857 -- Nicaragua -- April to May, November to December. In May Commander C.H. Davis of the United States Navy, with some marines, received the surrender of William Walker, who had been attempting to get control of the country, and protected his men from the retaliation of native allies who had been fighting Walker. In November and December of the same year United States vessels Saratoga, Wabash, and Fulton opposed another attempt of William Walker on Nicaragua. Commodore Hiram Paulding's act of landing marines and compelling the removal of Walker to the United States, was tacitly disavowed by Secretary of State Lewis Cass, and Paulding was forced into retirement.

1858 -- Uruguay -- January 2 to 27. Forces from two United States warships landed to protect American property during a revolution in Montevideo.

1858 --	Fiji Islands -- October 6 to 16. A marine expedition chastised natives for the murder of two American citizens at Waya.
1858-59 --	Turkey. The Secretary of State requested a display of naval force along the Levant after a massacre of Americans at Jaffa and mistreatment elsewhere "to remind the authorities (of Turkey) of the power of the United States."
1859 --	Paraguay. Congress authorized a naval squadron to seek redress for an attack on a naval vessel in the Parana River during 1855. Apologies were made after a large display of force.
1859 --	Mexico. Two hundred United States soldiers crossed the Rio Grande in pursuit of the Mexican bandit Cortina.
1859 --	China -- July 31 to August 2. A naval force landed to protect American interests in Shanghai.
1860 --	Angola, Portuguese West Africa -- March 1. American residents at Kissembo called upon American and British ships to protect lives and property during problems with natives.
1860 --	Colombia, Bay of Panama -- September 27 to October 8. Naval forces landed to protect American interests during a revolution.
1863 --	Japan -- July 16. The USS Wyoming retaliated against a firing on the American vessel Pembroke at Shimonoseki.
1864 --	Japan -- July 14 to August 3. Naval forces protected the United States Minister to Japan when he visited Yedo to negotiate concerning some American claims against Japan, and to make his negotiations easier by impressing the Japanese with American power.
1864 --	Japan -- September 4 to 14. Naval forces of the United States, Great Britain, France, and the Netherlands compelled Japan and the Prince of Nagato in particular to permit the Straits of Shimonoseki to be used by foreign shipping in accordance with treaties already signed.
1865 --	Panama -- March 9 and 10. U.S. forces protected the lives and property of American residents during a revolution.

1866 -- Mexico. To protect American residents, General Sedgwick and 100 men in November obtained surrender of Matamoras. After 3 days he was ordered by U.S. Government to withdraw. His act was repudiated by the President.

1866 -- China. From June 20 to July 7, U.S. forces punished an assault on the American consul at Newchwang.

1867 -- Nicaragua. Marines occupied Managua and Leon.

1867 -- Formosa -- June 13. A naval force landed and burned a number of huts to punish the murder of the crew of a wrecked American vessel.

1868 -- Japan (Osaka, Hiolo, Nagasaki, Yokohama, and Negata) -- February 4 to 8, April 4 to May 12, June 12 and 13. U.S. forces were landed to protect American interests during the civil war in Japan over the abolition of the Shogunate and the restoration of the Mikado.

1868 -- Uruguay -- February 7 and 8, 19 to 26. U.S. forces protected foreign residents and the customhouse during an insurrection at Montevideo.

1868 -- Colombia -- April. U.S. forces protected passengers and treasure in transit at Aspinwall during the absence of local police or troops on the occasion of the death of the President of Colombia.

1870 -- Mexico -- June 17 and 18. U.S. forces destroyed the pirate ship Forward, which had been run aground about 40 miles up the Rio Tecapan.

1870 -- Hawaiian Islands -- September 21. U.S. forces placed the American flag at half mast upon the death of Queen Kalama, when the American consul at Honolulu would not assume responsibility for so doing.

1871 -- Korea -- June 10 to 12. A U.S. naval force attacked and captured five forts to punish natives for depredations on Americans, particularly for murdering the crew of the General Sherman and burning the schooner, and for later firing on other American small boats taking soundings up the Salee River.

1873 -- Colombia (Bay of Panama) -- May 7 to 22, September 23 to October 9. U.S. forces protected American interests during hostilities over possession of the government of the State of Panama.

1873 -- Mexico. United States troops crossed the Mexican border repeatedly in pursuit of cattle and other thieves. There were some reciprocal pursuits by Mexican troops into border territory. Mexico protested frequently. Notable cases were at Remolina in May 1873 and at Las Cuevas in 1875. Washington orders often supported these excursions. Agreements between Mexico and the United States, the first in 1882, finally legitimized such raids. They continued intermittently, with minor disputes, until 1896.

1874 -- Hawaiian Islands -- February 12 to 20. Detachments from American vessels were landed to preserve order and protect American lives and interests during the coronation of a new king.

1876 -- Mexico -- May 18. An American force was landed to police the town of Matamoras temporarily while it was without other government.

1882 -- Egypt -- July 14 to 18. American forces landed to protect American interests during warfare between British and Egyptians and looting of the city of Alexandria by Arabs.

1885 -- Panama (Colon) -- January 18 and 19. U.S. forces were used to guard the valuables in transit over the Panama Railroad, and the safes and vaults of the company during revolutionary activity. In March, April, and May in the cities of Colon and Panama, the forces helped reestablish freedom of transit during revolutionary activity.

1888 -- Korea -- June. A naval force was sent ashore to protect American residents in Seoul during unsettled political conditions, when an outbreak of the populace was expected.

1888 -- Haiti -- December 20. A display of force persuaded the Haitian Government to give up an American steamer which had been seized on the charge of breach of blockade.

1888--89 -- Samoa -- November 14, 1888, to March 20, 1889. U.S. forces were landed to protect American citizens and the consulate during a native civil war.

1889 -- Hawaiian Islands -- July 30 and 31. U.S. forces protected American interests at Honolulu during a revolution.

1890 **SOUTH DAKOTA** -U.S. Troops attacked 300 Lakota Indians at Wounded Knee when white officials became alarmed at the religious fervor and activism taking place within the Sioux Tribe as a result of the Ghost Dance and in December 1890 banned the Ghost Dance on Lakota reservations. When the rites continued, officials called in troops to Pine Ridge and Rosebud reservations in South Dakota. The military, led by veteran General Nelson Miles, geared itself for another campaign.

1890 -- Argentina. A naval party landed to protect U.S. consulate and legation in Buenos Aires.

1891 -- Haiti. U.S. forces sought to protect American lives and property on Navassa Island.

1891 -- Bering Strait -- July 2 to October 5. Naval forces sought to stop seal poaching.

1891 -- Chile -- August 28 to 30. U.S. forces protected the American consulate and the women and children who had taken refuge in it during a revolution in Valparaiso.

1892 **IDAHO** - Army troops were used to suppress a silver miners' strike.

1893 -- **HAWAII** -- January 16 to April 1. Marines were landed ostensibly to protect American lives and property, but many believed it was actually to promote a provisional government under Sanford B. Dole which overthrew the Kingdom. This action was disavowed by the United States.

1894 **CHICAGO** - Troops were used to breakup a rail strike, 34 were killed.

1894 --	Brazil -- January. A display of naval force was authorized in order to protect American commerce and shipping at Rio de Janeiro during a Brazilian civil war.
1894 --	Nicaragua -- July 6 to August 7. U.S. forces sought to protect American interests at Bluefields following a revolution.
1894-95 --	China. Marines were stationed at Tientsin and penetrated to Peking for protection purposes during the Sino--Japanese War.
1894-95 --	China. A naval vessel was beached and used as a fort at Newchwang for protection of American nationals.
1894-96 --	Korea -- July 24, 1894 to April 3, 1896. A guard of marines was sent to protect the American legation and American lives and interests at Seoul during and following the Sino-- Japanese War.
1895 --	Colombia -- March 8 to 9. U.S. forces protected American interests during an attack on the town of Bocas del Toro by a bandit chieftain.
1896 --	Nicaragua -- May 2 to 4. U.S. forces protected American interests in Corinto during political unrest.
1898 --	Nicaragua -- February 7 and 8. U.S. forces protected American lives and property at San Juan del Sur.
1898 -	**MINNESOTA** - Army troops battled members of the Chippewa Tribe at Leech Lake.
1898 --	The Spanish--American War. On April 25, 1898, the United States declared war with Spain. The war followed a Cuban insurrection against Spanish rule and the sinking of the U.S.S. Maine in the harbor at Havana.
1898--99 --	China -- November 5, 1898 to March 15, 1899. U.S. forces provided a guard for the legation at Peking and the consulate at Tientsin during contest between the Dowager Empress and her son.
1899-1901 -	**IDAHO** - Army troops occupied Coeur d'Alene mining region.
1899 --	Nicaragua. American and British naval forces were landed to protect national interests at San Juan del Norte, February 22 to

March 5th and at Bluefields a few weeks later in connection with the insurrection of Gen. Juan P. Reyes.

1899 -- Samoa -- February-May 15. American and British naval forces were landed to protect national interests and to take part in a bloody contention over the succession to the throne.

1899--1901 -- Philippine Islands. U.S. forces protected American interests following the war with Spain and conquered the islands by defeating the Filipinos in their war for independence.

1900 -- China -- May 24 to September 28. American troops participated in operations to protect foreign lives during the Boxer rising, particularly at Peking. For many years after this experience a permanent legation guard was maintained in Peking, and was strengthened at times as trouble threatened.

1901 - **OKLAHOMA** -Army troops battled the Creek Indian revolt.

1901 -- Colombia (State of Panama) -- November 20 to December 4. U.S. forces protected American property on the Isthmus and kept transit lines open during serious revolutionary disturbances.

1902 -- Colombia -- April 16 to 23. U.S. forces protected American lives and property at Bocas del Toro during a civil war.

1902 -- Colombia (State of Panama) -- September 17 to November 18. The United States placed armed guards on all trains crossing the Isthmus to keep the railroad line open, and stationed ships on both sides of Panama to prevent the landing of Colombian troops.

1903 -- Honduras -- March 23 to 30 or 31. U.S. forces protected the American consulate and the steamship wharf at Puerto Cortez during a period of revolutionary activity.

1903 -- Dominican Republic -- March 30 to April 21. A detachment of marines was landed to protect American interests in the city of Santo Domingo during a revolutionary outbreak.

1903 -- Syria -- September 7 to 12. U.S. forces protected the American consulate in Beirut when a local Moslem uprising was feared.

1903-04 -- Abyssinia. Twenty-five marines were sent to Abyssinia to protect the U.S. Consul General while he negotiated a treaty.

1903-14 -- Panama. U.S. forces sought to protect American interests and lives during and following the revolution for independence from Colombia over construction of the Isthmian Canal. With brief intermissions, United States Marines were stationed on the Isthmus from November 4, 1903, to January 21 1914 to guard American interests.

1904 -- Dominican Republic -- January 2 to February 11. American and British naval forces established an area in which no fighting would be allowed and protected American interests in Puerto Plata and Sosua and Santo Domingo City during revolutionary fighting.

1904 -- Tangier, Morocco. "We want either Perdicaris alive or Raisula dead." A squadron demonstrated to force release of a kidnapped American. Marine guard was landed to protect the consul general.

1904 -- Panama -- November 17 to 24. U.S. forces protected American lives and property at Ancon at the time of a threatened insurrection.

1904-05 -- Korea -- January 5, 1904, to November 11, 1905. A Marine guard was sent to protect the American legation in Seoul during the Russo-Japanese War.

1906-09 -- Cuba -- September 1906 to January 23, 1909. U.S. forces sought to restore order, protect foreigners, and establish a stable government after serious revolutionary activity.

1907 -- Honduras -- March 18 to June 8. To protect American interests during a war between Honduras and Nicaragua, troops were stationed in Trujillo, Ceiba, Puerto Cortez, San Pedro Laguna and Choloma.

1910 -- Nicaragua -- May 19 to September 4. U.S. forces protected American interests at Bluefields.

1911 -- Honduras -- January 26. American naval detachments were landed to protect American lives and interests during a civil war in Honduras.

1911 -- China. As the nationalist revolution approached, in October an ensign and 10 men tried to enter Wuchang to rescue missionaries but retired on being warned away and a small landing force guarded American private property and consulate at Hankow. A marine guard was established in November over the cable stations at Shanghai; landing forces were sent for protection in Nanking, Chinkiang, Taku and elsewhere.

1912 -- Honduras. A small force landed to prevent seizure by the government of an American-owned railroad at Puerto Cortez. The forces were withdrawn after the United States disapproved the action.

1912 -- Panama. Troops, on request of both political parties, supervised elections outside the Canal Zone.

1912 -- Cuba -- June 5 to August 5. U.S. forces protected American interests on the Province of Oriente, and in Havana.

1912 -- China -- August 24 to 26, on Kentucky Island, and August 26 to 30 at Camp Nicholson. U.S. forces protect Americans and American interests during revolutionary activity.

1912 -- Turkey -- November 18 to December 3. U.S. forces guarded the American legation at Constantinople during a Balkan War.

1912-25 -- Nicaragua -- August to November 1912. U.S. forces protected American interests during an attempted revolution. A small force, serving as a legation guard and seeking to promote peace and stability, remained until August 5, 1925.

1912-41 -- China. The disorders which began with the Kuomintang rebellion in 1912, which were redirected by the invasion of China by Japan and finally ended by war between Japan and the United States in 1941, led to demonstrations and landing parties for the protection of U.S. interests in China continuously and at many points from 1912 on to 1941. The guard at Peking and along the route to the sea was maintained until 1941. In 1927, the United States had 5,670 troops ashore in China and 44 naval vessels in its waters. In 1933 the United States had 3,027 armed men ashore. The protective action was generally based on treaties with China concluded from 1858 to 1901.

1913 --	Mexico -- September 5 to 7. A few marines landed at Ciaris Estero to aid in evacuating American citizens and others from the Yaqui Valley, made dangerous for foreigners by civil strife.
1914 --	Haiti -- January 29 to February 9, February 20 to 21, October 19. Intermittently U.S. naval forces protected American nationals in a time of rioting and revolution.
1914 -	**COLORADO** - Army troops are used to break up a miner's strike.
1914 --	Dominican Republic -- June and July. During a revolutionary movement, United States naval forces by gunfire stopped the bombardment of Puerto Plata, and by threat of force maintained Santo Domingo City as a neutral zone.
1914-17 --	Mexico. Undeclared Mexican--American hostilities followed the Dolphin affair and Villa's raids and included capture of Vera Cruz and later Pershing's expedition into northern Mexico.
1915-34 --	Haiti -- July 28, 1915, to August 15, 1934. U.S. forces maintained order during a period of chronic and threatened insurrection.
1916 --	China. American forces landed to quell a riot taking place on American property in Nanking.
1916-24 --	Dominican Republic -- May 1916 to September 1924. American naval forces maintained order during a period of chronic and threatened insurrection.
1917 --	China. American troops were landed at Chungking to protect American lives during a political crisis.
1917-18 --	World War I. On April 6, 1917, the United States declared war with Germany and on December 7, 1917, with Austria-Hungary. Entrance of the United States into the war was precipitated by Germany's submarine warfare against neutral shipping.
1917-22 --	Cuba. U.S. forces protected American interests during insurrection and subsequent unsettled conditions. Most of the Uni States armed forces left Cuba by August 1919, but two companies remained at Camaguey until February 1922.

1918-19 -- Mexico. After withdrawal of the Pershing expedition, U.S. troops entered Mexico in pursuit of bandits at least three times in 1918 and several times in 1919. In August 1918 American and Mexican troops fought at Nogales.

1918-20 -- Panama. U.S. forces were used for police duty according to treaty stipulations, at Chiriqui, during election disturbances and subsequent unrest.

1918-20 Soviet Russia. Marines were landed at and near Vladivostok in June and July to protect the American consulate and other points in the fighting between the Bolshevik troops and the Czech Army which had traversed Siberia from the western front. A joint proclamation of emergency government and neutrality was issued by the American, Japanese, British, French, and Czech commanders in July. In August 7,000 men were landed in Vladivostok and remained until January 1920, as part of an allied occupation force. In September 1918, 5,000 American troops joined the allied intervention force at Archangel and remained until June 1919. These operations were in response to the Bolshevik revolution in Russia and were partly supported by Czarist or Kerensky elements.

1919 -- Dalmatia. U.S. forces were landed at Trau at the request of Italian authorities to police order between the Italians and Serbs.

1919 -- Turkey. Marines from the USS Arizona were landed to guard the U.S. Consulate during the Greek occupation of Constantinople.

1919 -- Honduras -- September 8 to 12. A landing force was sent ashore to maintain order in a neutral zone during an attempted revolution.

1920 - **WEST VIRGINIA** –Troops are used against striking mineworkers.

1920 -- China -- March 14. A landing force was sent ashore for a few hours to protect lives during a disturbance at Kiukiang.

1920 -- Guatemala -- April 9 to 27. U.S. forces protected the American Legation and other American interests, such as the cable station, during a period of fighting between Unionists and the Government of Guatemala.

1920-22 --	Russia (Siberia) -- February 16, 1920, to November 19, 1922. A Marine guard was sent to protect the United States radio station and property on Russian Island, Bay of Vladivostok.
1921 --	Panama -- Costa Rica. American naval squadrons demonstrated in April on both sides of the Isthmus to prevent war between the two countries over a boundary dispute.
1922 --	Turkey -- September and October. A landing force was sent ashore with consent of both Greek and Turkish authorities, to protect American lives and property when the Turkish Nationalists entered Smyrna.
1922-23 --	China. Between April 1922 and November 1923 marines were landed five times to protect Americans during periods of unrest.
1924 --	Honduras -- February 28 to March 31, September 10 to 15. U.S. forces protected American lives and interests during election hostilities.
1924 --	China -- September. Marines were landed to protect Americans and other foreigners in Shanghai during Chinese factional hostilities.
1925 --	China -- January 15 to August 29. Fighting of Chinese factions accompanied by riots and demonstrations in Shanghai brought the landing of American forces to protect lives and property in the International Settlement.
1925 --	Honduras -- April 19 to 21. U.S. forces protected foreigners at La Ceiba during a political upheaval.
1925 --	Panama -- October 12 to 23. Strikes and rent riots led to the landing of about 600 American troops to keep order and protect American interests.
1926 --	China -- August and September. The Nationalist attack on Han brought the landing of American naval forces to protect American citizens. A small guard was maintained at the consulate general even after September 16, when the rest of the forces were withdrawn. Likewise, when Nation forces captured Kiukiang, naval forces were landed for the protection of foreigners November 4 to 6.

1926-33 -- Nicaragua -- May 7 to June 5, 1926; August 27, 1926, to January 1933. The coup d'etat of General Chamorro aroused revolutionary activities leading to the landing of American marines to protect the interests of United States. United States forces came and went intermittently until January 3, 1933. Their work included activity against the outlaw leader Sandino in 1928.

1927 -- China -- February. Fighting at Shanghai caused American naval forces and marines to be increased. In March a naval guard was stationed at American consulate at Nanking after Nationalist forces captured the city. American and British destroyers later used shell fire to protect Americans and other foreigners. Subsequently additional forces of marines and naval forces were stationed in the vicinity of Shanghai and Tientsin.

1932 - **WASHINGTON DC** - Army troops are used to stop WWI vet bonus protest.

1932 -- China. American forces were landed to protect American interests during the Japanese occupation of Shanghai.

1933 -- Cuba. During a revolution against President Gerardo Machada naval forces demonstrated but no landing was made.

1934 -- China. Marines landed at Foochow to protect the American Consulate.

1940 -- Newfoundland, Bermuda, St. Lucia, - Bahamas, Jamaica, Antigua, Trinidad, and British Guiana. Troops were sent to guard air and naval bases obtained by negotiation with Great Britain. These were sometimes called lend-lease bases.

1941 -- Greenland. Greenland was taken under protection of the United States in April.

1941 -- Netherlands (Dutch Guiana). In November the President ordered American troops to occupy Dutch Guiana, but by agreement with the Netherlands government in exile, Brazil cooperated to protect aluminum ore supply from the bauxite mines in Surinam.

1941 -- Iceland. Iceland was taken under the protection of the United States

1941 -- Germany. Sometime in the spring the President ordered the Navy to patrol ship lanes to Europe. By July U.S. warships were convoying and by September were attacking German submarines. In November, the Neutrality Act was partially repealed to protect U.S. military aid to Britain.

1941-45 -- World War II. - On December 8, 1941, the United States declared war with Japan, on December 11 with Germany and Italy, and on June 5, 1942, with Bulgaria, Hungary and Romania. The United States declared war against Japan after the surprise bombing of Pearl Harbor, and against Germany and Italy after those nations, under the dictators Hitler and Mussolini, declared war against the United States.

1943 - **DETROIT** - Army troops are used to put down a Black rebellion.

1945 -- China. In October 50,000 U.S. Marines were sent to North China to assist Chinese Nationalist authorities in disarming and repatriating the Japanese in China and in controlling ports, railroads, and airfields. This was in addition to approximately 60,000 U.S. forces remaining in China at the end of World War II.

1946 -- Trieste. President Truman ordered the augmentation of U.S. troops along the zonal occupation line and the reinforcement of air forces in northern Italy after Yugoslav forces shot down an unarmed U.S. Army transport plane flying over Venezia Giulia. Earlier U.S. naval units had been dispatched to the scene.

1948 -- Palestine. A marine consular guard was sent to Jerusalem to protect the U.S. Consul General.

1948 -- Berlin. After the Soviet Union established a land blockade of the U.S., British, and French sectors of Berlin on June 24, 1948, the United States and its allies airlifted supplies to Berlin until after the blockade was lifted in May 1949.

1948-49 -- China. Marines were dispatched to Nanking to protect the American Embassy when the city fell to Communist troops, and to Shanghai to aid in the protection and evacuation of Americans.

1950 - **PUERTO RICO** - Independence rebellion crushed in Ponce.

1950-53 --	Korean War. The United States responded to North Korean invasion of South Korea by going to its assistance, pursuant to United Nations Security Council resolutions.
1950-55 --	Formosa (Taiwan). In June 1950 at the beginning of the Korean War, President Truman ordered the U.S. Seventh Fleet to prevent Chinese Communist attacks upon Formosa and Chinese Nationalist operations against mainland China.
1954 -	Guatemala - CIA directs exile invasion after new gov't nationalized U.S. company lands using troops and bombers based in Nicaragua.
1954-55 --	China. Naval units evacuated U.S. civilians and military personnel from the Tachen Islands.
1956 --	Egypt. A Marine battalion evacuated U.S. nationals and other persons from Alexandria during the Suez crisis.
1958 --	Lebanon. Marines were landed in Lebanon at the invitation of its government to help protect against threatened insurrection supported from the outside.
1959-60 --	The Caribbean. 2d Marine Ground Task Force was deployed to protect U.S. nationals during the Cuban crisis.
1961 -	Cuba – CIA sponsored "Bay of Pigs" invasion of Cuba failed.
1962 --	Cuba. President Kennedy instituted a "quarantine" on the shipment of offensive missiles to Cuba from the Soviet Union. He also warned Soviet Union that the launching of any missile from Cuba against nations in the Western Hemisphere would bring about U.S. nuclear retaliation on the Soviet Union. A negotiated settlement was achieved in a few days.
1962 --	Thailand. The 3d Marine Expeditionary Unit landed on May 17, 1962 to support that country during the threat of Communist pressure from outside; by Jul 30 the 5000 marines had been withdrawn.
1962-75 --	Laos. From October 1962 until 1976, the United States played a role of military support in Laos.

1964 -- Congo. The United States sent four transport planes to provide airlift for Congolese troops during a rebellion and to transport Belgian paratroopers to rescue foreigners.

1964-73 -- Vietnam War. U.S. military advisers had been in South Vietnam a decade, and their numbers had been increased as the military position the Saigon government became weaker. After the attacks on U.S. destroyers in the Tonkin Gulf, President Johnson asked for a resolution expressing U.S. determination to support freedom and protect peace in Southeast Asia. Congress responded with the Tonkin Gulf Resolution, expressing support for "all necessary measures" the President might take to repel armed attacks against U.S. forces and prevent further aggression. Following this resolution, and following a Communist attack on a U.S. installation in central Vietnam, the United States escalated its participation in the war to a peak of 543 000 in April 1969.

1965 -- Dominican Republic. The United States intervened to protect lives and property during a Dominican revolt and sent more troops as fears grew that the revolutionary forces were coming increasingly under Communist control.

1967 - **DETROIT** - Army troops battled Blacks, 43 were killed.

1967 -- Congo. The United States sent three military transport aircraft with crews to provide the Congo central government with logistical support during a revolt.

1968 - **UNITED STATES** - After the assassination of Martin Luther King over 21,000 soldiers were deployed to various major cities.

1970 -- Cambodia. U.S. troops were ordered into Cambodia to clean out Communist sanctuaries from which Viet Cong and North Vietnamese attacked U.S and South Vietnamese forces in Vietnam. The object of this attack, which lasted from April 30 to June 30, was to ensure the continuing safe withdrawal of American forces from South Vietnam and to assist the program of Vietnamization.

1973 - **SOUTH DAKOTA** - Army personnel directed the Wounded Knee siege of the Lakota Sioux.

1974 -- Evacuation from Cyprus. United States naval forces evacuated U.S. civilians during hostilities between Turkish and Greek Cypriot forces.

1975 -- Evacuation from Vietnam. On April 3, 1975, President Ford reported U.S. naval vessels, helicopters, and Marines had been sent to assist in evacuation of refugees and U.S. nationals from Vietnam. (Note 3)

1975 -- Evacuation from Cambodia. On April 12, 1975, President Ford reported that he had ordered U.S. military forces to proceed with the planned evacuation of U.S. citizens from Cambodia.

1975 -- South Vietnam. On April 30 1975, President Ford reported that a force of 70 evacuation helicopters and 865 Marines had evacuated about 1,400 U.S. citizens and 5,500 third country nationals and South Vietnamese from landing zones near the U.S. Embassy in Saigon and the Tan Son Nhut Airfield.

1975 -- Mayaguez incident. On May 15, 1975, President Ford reported he had ordered military forces to retake the SS Mayaguez, a merchant vessel en route from Hong Kong to Thailand with U.S. citizen crew which was seized from Cambodian naval patrol boats in international waters and forced to proceed to a nearby island.

1976 -- Lebanon. On July 22 and 23, 1974, helicopters from five U.S. naval vessels evacuated approximately 250 Americans and Europeans from Lebanon during fighting between Lebanese factions after an overland convoy evacuation had been blocked by hostilities.

1976 -- Korea. Additional forces were sent to Korea after two American military personnel were killed while in the demilitarized zone between North and South Korea for the purpose of cutting down a tree.

1978 -- Zaire. From May 19 through June 1978, the United States utilized military transport aircraft to provide logistical support to Belgian and French rescue operations in Zaire.

1980 -- Iran. On April 26, 1980, President Carter reported the use of six U.S. transport planes and eight helicopters in an unsuccessful attempt to rescue American hostages being held in Iran.

1981 --	El Salvador. After a guerilla offensive against the government of El Salvador, additional U.S. military advisers were sent to El Salvador, bringing the total to approximately 55, to assist in training government forces in counterinsurgency.
1981 --	Libya. On August 19, 1981, U.S. planes based on the carrier Nimitz shot down two Libyan jets over the Gulf of Sidra after one of the Libyan jets had fired a heat-seeking missile. The United States periodically held freedom of navigation exercises in the Gulf of Sidra, claimed by Libya as territorial waters but considered international waters by the United States.
1982 --	Sinai. On March 19, 1982, President Reagan reported the deployment of military personnel and equipment to participate in the Multinational Force and Observers in the Sinai. Participation had been authorized by the Multinational Force and Observers Resolution, Public Law 97-132.
1982 --	Lebanon. On August 21, 1982, President Reagan reported the dispatch of 80 marines to serve in the multinational force to assist in the withdrawal of members of the Palestine Liberation force from Beirut. The Marines left Sept. 20, 1982.
1982 --	Lebanon. On September 29, 1982, President Reagan reported the deployment of 1200 marines to serve in a temporary multinational force to facilitate the restoration of Lebanese government sovereignty. On Sept. 29, 1983, Congress passed the Multinational Force in Lebanon Resolution (P.L. 98-119) authorizing the continued participation for eighteen months.
1983 --	Egypt. After a Libyan plane bombed a city in Sudan on March 18, 1983, and Sudan and Egypt appealed for assistance, the United States dispatched an AWACS electronic surveillance plane to Egypt.
1983-89 --	Honduras. In July 1983 the United States undertook a series of exercises in Honduras that some believed might lead to conflict with Nicaragua. On March 25, 1986, unarmed U.S. military helicopters and crewmen ferried Honduran troops to the Nicaraguan border to repel Nicaraguan troops.
1983 --	Chad. On August 8, 1983, President Reagan reported the deployment of two AWACS electronic surveillance planes and

eight F-15 fighter planes and ground logistical support forces to assist Chad against Libyan and rebel forces.

1983 -- Grenada. On October 25, 1983, President Reagan reported a landing on Grenada by Marines and Army airborne troops to protect lives and assist in the restoration of law and order and at the request of five members of the Organization of Eastern Caribbean States.

1984 -- Persian Gulf. On June 5, 1984, Saudi Arabian jet fighter planes, aided by intelligence from a U.S. AWACS electronic surveillance aircraft and fueled by a U.S. KC-10 tanker, shot down two Iranian fighter planes over an area of the Persian Gulf proclaimed as a protected zone for shipping.

1985 -- Italy. On October 10, 1985, U.S. Navy pilots intercepted an Egyptian airliner and forced it to land in Sicily. The airliner was carrying the hijackers of the Italian cruise ship Achille Lauro who had killed an American citizen during the hijacking.

1986 -- Libya. On March 26, 1986, President Reagan reported to Congress that, on March 24 and 25, U.S. forces, while engaged in freedom of navigation exercises around the Gulf of Sidra, had been attacked by Libyan missiles and the United States had responded with missiles.

1986 -- Libya. On April 16, 1986, President Reagan reported that U.S. air and naval forces had conducted bombing strikes on terrorist facilities and military installations in Libya.

1986 -- Bolivia. U.S. Army personnel and aircraft assisted Bolivia in anti-drug operations.

1987-88 -- Persian Gulf. After the Iran-Iraq War resulted in several military incidents in the Persian Gulf, the United States increased U.S. Navy forces operating in the Persian Gulf and adopted a policy of reflagging and escorting Kuwaiti oil tankers through the Gulf. President Reagan reported that U.S. ships had been fired upon or struck mines or taken other military action on September 23, October 10, and October 20, 1987 and April 19, July 4, and July 14, 1988. The United States gradually reduced its forces after a cease-fire between Iran and Iraq on August 20, 1988.

1988 -- Panama. In mid-March and April 1988, during a period of instability in Panama and as pressure grew for Panamanian military leader General Manuel Noriega to resign, the United States sent 1,000 troops to Panama, to "further safeguard the canal, U.S. lives, property and interests in the area." The forces supplemented 10,000 U.S. military personnel already in Panama.

1989 -- Libya. On January 4, 1989, two U.S. Navy F-14 aircraft based on USS John F. Kennedy shot down two Libyan jet fighters over the Mediterranean Sea about 70 miles north of Libya. The U.S. pilots said the Libyan planes had demonstrated hostile intentions.

1989 -- Panama. On May 11, 1989, in response to General Noriega's disregard of the results of the Panamanian election, President Bush ordered a brigade- sized force of approximately 1,900 troops to augment the estimated 11,000 U.S. forces already in the area.

1989 - **VIRGIN ISLANDS** - Troops were deployed in St. Croix to put down Black unrest after storm.

1989 -- Andean Initiative in War on Drugs. On September 15, 1989, President Bush announced that military and law enforcement assistance would be sent to help the Andean nations of Colombia, Bolivia, and Peru combat illicit drug producers and traffickers. By mid-September there were 50- 100 U.S. military advisers in Colombia in connection with transport and training in the use of military equipment, plus seven Special Forces teams of 2-12 persons to train troops in the three countries.

1989 -- Philippines. On December 2, 1989, President Bush reported that on December 1 U.S. fighter planes from Clark Air Base in the Philippines had assisted the Aquino government to repel a coup attempt. In addition, 100 marines were sent from the U.S. Navy base at Subic Bay to protect the U.S. Embassy in Manila.

1989 -- Panama. On December 21, 1989, President Bush reported that he had ordered U.S. military forces to Panama to protect the lives of American citizens and bring General Noriega to justice. By February 13, 1990, all the invasion forces had been withdrawn.

1990 -- Liberia. On August 6, 1990, President Bush reported that a reinforced rifle company had been sent to provide additional security to the U.S. Embassy in Monrovia, and that helicopter teams had evacuated U.S. citizens from Liberia.

1990 -- Saudi Arabia. On August 9, 1990, President Bush reported that he had ordered the forward deployment of substantial elements of the U.S. armed forces into the Persian Gulf region to help defend Saudi Arabia after the August 2 invasion of Kuwait by Iraq. On November 16, 1990, he reported the continued buildup of the forces to ensure an adequate offensive military option.

1991 -- Iraq. On January 18, 1991, President Bush reported that he had directed U.S. armed forces to commence combat operations on January 16 against Iraqi forces and military targets in Iraq and Kuwait, in conjunction with a coalition of allies and U.N. Security Council resolutions. On January 12 Congress had passed the Authorization for Use of Military Force against Iraq Resolution (P.L. 102-1). Combat operations were suspended on February 28, 1991.

1991 -- Iraq. On May 17, 1991, President Bush stated in a status report to Congress that the Iraqi repression of the Kurdish people had necessitated a limited introduction of U.S. forces into northern Iraq for emergency relief purposes.

1991 -- Zaire. On September 25-27, 1991, after widespread looting and rioting broke out in Kinshasa, U.S. Air Force C-141s transported 100 Belgian troops and equipment into Mnshasa. U.S. planes also carried 300 French troops into the Central African Republic and hauled back American citizens and third country nationals from locations outside Zaire.

1992 -- Sierra Leone. On May 3, 1992, U.S. military planes evacuated Americans from Sierra Leone, where military leaders had overthrown the government.

1992 -- Kuwait. On August 3, 1992, the United States began a series of military exercises in Kuwait, following Iraqi refusal to recognize a new border drawn up by the United Nations and refusal to cooperate with U.N. inspection teams.

1992 -- Iraq. On September 16, 1992 President Bush stated in a status report that he had ordered U.S. participation in the enforcement of a prohibition against Iraqi flights in a specified zone in southern Iraq, and aerial reconnaissance to monitor Iraqi compliance with the cease-fire resolution.

1992 – 1994	Yugoslavia- Naval, NATO, blockade of Serbia and Montenegro.
1992 --	Somalia. On December 10, 1992, President Bush reported that he had deployed U.S. armed forces to Somalia in response to a humanitarian crisis and a U.N. Security Council Resolution determining that the situation constituted a threat to international peace. This operation, called Operation Restore Hope, was part of a U.S.-led United Nations Unified Task Force (UNITAF) and came to an end on May 4, 1993. U.S. forces continued to participate in the successor United Nations Operation in Somalia (UNOSOM II), which the U.N. Security Council authorized to assist Somalia in political reconciliation and restoration of peace.
1992 -	**LOS ANGELES** – Army and Marine personnel were deployed against anti-police uprising.
1993 --	Iraq. On January 19, 1993, President Bush said in a status report that on December 27, 1992, U.S. aircraft shot down an Iraqi aircraft in the prohibited zone; on January 13 aircraft from the United States and coalition partners had attacked missile bases in southern Iraq; and further military actions had occured on January 17 and 18. Administration officials said the United States was deploying a battalion task force to Kuwait to underline the continuing U.S. commitment to Kuwaiti independence.
1993 --	Iraq. On January 21, 1993, shortly after his inauguration, President Clinton said the United States would continue the Bush policy on Iraq, and U.S. aircraft fired at targets in Iraq after pilots sensed Iraqi radar or anti-aircraft fire directed at them.
1993 --	Bosnia-Herzegovina. On February 28, 1993, the United States began an airdrop of relief supplies aimed at Muslims surrounded by Serbian forces in Bosnia.
1993 --	Bosnia-Herzegovina. On April 13, 1993, President Clinton reported U.S. forces were participating in a NATO air action to enforce a U.N. ban on all unauthorized military flights over Bosnia-Herzegovina.

1993 -- Iraq. In a status report on Iraq of May 24, President Clinton said that on April 9 and April 18 U.S. warplanes had bombed or fired missiles at Iraqi anti-aircraft sites which had tracked U.S. aircraft.

1993 -- Somalia. On June 10, 1993, President Clinton reported that in response to attacks against U.N. forces in Somalia by a factional leader, the U.S. Quick Reaction Force in the area had participated in military action to quell the violence. The quick reaction force was part of the U.S. contribution to a success On July 1, President Clinton reported further air and ground military operations on June 12 and June 17 aimed at neutralizing military capabilities that had impeded U.N. efforts to deliver humanitarian relief and promote national reconstruction, and additional instances occurred in the following months.

1993 -- Iraq. On June 28, 1993, President Clinton reported that on June 26 U.S. naval forces had launched missiles against the Iraqi Intelligence Service's headquarters in Baghdad in response to an unsuccessful attempt to assassinate former President Bush in Kuwait in April 1993.

1993 -- Iraq. In a status report of July 22, 1993, President Clinton said on June 19 a U.S. aircraft had fired a missile at an Iraqi anti-aircraft site displaying hostile intent. U.S. planes also bombed an Iraqi missile battery on August 19, 1993.

1993 -- Macedonia. On July 9, 1993, President Clinton reported the deployment of 350 U.S. armed forces to Macedonia to participate in the U.N. Protection Force to help maintain stability in the area of former Yugoslavia.

1994 - Haiti – Troops and a naval blockade were used against the military government; U.S. troops restored President Aristide to office three years after the military coup.

1996-97 Zaire (Congo)- U.S. Marines were stationed at the Rwandan Hutu refugee camps, in the same area where the Congo revolution began.

1997 - Liberia – U.S. troops came under fire during evacuation of foreigners.

1997 -	Albania - U. S. troops came under fire during evacuation of foreigners.
1998 -	Sudan - Missile attack launched against a pharmaceutical plant alleged to be "terrorist" nerve gas plant.
1998 -	Afghanistan - Missile attack launched on a former CIA training camps used by Islamic fundamentalist groups alleged to have attacked embassies.
1998 -	Iraq - Four days of intensive air strikes by U.S. forces after weapons inspectors allege Iraqi obstructions.
1999 -	Yugoslavia - Heavy NATO air strikes were launched after Serbia declined to withdraw from Kosovo. NATO occupation of Kosovo accomplished.
2000	Yemen - USS Cole bombed by terrorists.
2001 -	Macedonia - NATO forces deployed to move and disarm Albanian rebels.
2001 -	**NEW YORK CITY** – U.S. military reaction to hijacker attacks on New York City and Washington D.C. resulted in troops in all major airports.
2001 -	Afghanistan - Massive U.S. mobilization to overthrow Taliban, hunt Al Qaeda fighters, install Karzai regime. Forces also engaged in neighboring Pakistan.
2002	Yemen - Predator drone missile attack was launched against a group of Al Qaeda personnel, including a US citizen.
2002	Philippines - Training mission for Philippine military fighting Muslim Abu Sayyaf rebels evolves into US combat missions in Sulu Archipelago next to Mindanao.
2003 -	Colombia - US Special Forces sent to rebel zone to back up Colombian military protecting oil pipeline.
2003 -	Iraq - Second Gulf War launched for "regime change" in Baghdad. US, joined by UK and Australia, attacks from Kuwait, other Gulf states, and European and US bases.

It should be noted that a number of the actions outlined above are still ongoing, such as the Second Gulf War which shows no signs of ending any time soon. This brings the list as current as possible as of the time of this writing. It is also important for the purposes of this work that the reader also note that a large number of these military incursions were done in order to support U.S. trading efforts and some were done simply to support private corporations who had the influence to get the president's ear.

I believe that there exists a group of private citizens so wealthy and well connected that they are able to call upon military support to carry out their programs. I think that the actions of Halliburton that have taken place in Iraq go a long way toward proving my point.

PART II

HIDDEN HANDS

CHAPTER FOUR
THE NEW WORLD

This crusade, this war on terrorism, is going to take a long time.
- President Bush II, September 2001

As I have postulated, by all indications there is a private organization that has tremendous influence upon the various governments and this organization has taken a hand in various conflicts in order to carry out some grand scheme. Many times this hidden hand is obscured as a result of the victor not wanted to admit that except for this assistance, it could not have won its wars. History, upon which we base many of our preconceived notions, is not always reported truthfully.

As an example, as children, we were all inundated with "historical" information about the founding of this great land. The one that I remember the clearest was that Spanish Queen Isabel pawned her crown jewels to finance Columbus' journey to the new world. Christopher Columbus is pictured as the brave sea farer who believed that the world was round and offered to prove it. It was said that he so impressed the Queen that she took a personal hand in the matter and the famous voyage of discovery was the end result.

Actually, it took Columbus over eight years of petitioning and begging before he was able to gain the approval of the Spanish crown for his expedition. During this long period, naturally Colón (Columbus) made many friends at the Spanish Royal Court. One of these friends was a powerful financier named Luís de Santángel, who offered at some risk to himself to finance the 2 million maravedís needed for the journey. When the Spanish Crown finally took an interest in Colón's proposal, Queen Isabel offered some of her personal (not Crown) jewels as collateral to Santángel, to minimize his risk on the large loan needed by Columbus. Being a loyal Spaniard and wanting some leverage with the Queen, he wisely refused her magnanimous gesture. However, this is the basis of the story of Queen Isabella offering her jewels to finance the voyage.

When Colón sailed for the new world, he was backed not only by the Crown and Santángel (1.2 million maravedís), but, though history would have us believe that he was penniless, he also invested his own funds (approximately 250,000), and was backed by other noble friends at court. In fact, Colón was given only two vessels - the Niña and Pinta; he had to charter the Gallega - rechristened Santa María - on his own. He also carried maps that showed the path he should take across the uncharted seas; maps that history says very little about.

In all of the history taught in our schools about Christopher Columbus and the discovery of the new world, it is interesting to note that absolutely no mention was made about the fact that Christopher Columbus, himself, claimed that an ancient prophecy led him to discover the new world. About 1500 A.D. Columbus discussed this belief in one of the letter he wrote about America. In this letter he wrote: *"God made me the messenger of the new heaven and the new earth of which he spoke in the Apocalypse of St John after having spoken of it through the mouth of Isaiah; and he showed me the spot where to find it.*[6]*"*

Christopher Columbus also wrote a famous book, entitled the "Book of Prophecies[7]", containing over 200 biblical and patristic passages which he compiled, but how many people realize why he would write such a book? When Columbus made his case to win support from the Vatican and the Spanish monarchy, at the centre of his manifesto was a millennial prophecy about the destiny of the land that he would discover. A "New World" was to arise in the West to wage one last Crusade against the Arab powers of the Middle East. Have we now begun this last Crusade with the war in Iraq?

A war across such a vast distance, over thousands of miles of sea and land, would have seemed unlikely at the time of Colon. Yet, as the new Millennium dawned, soon after the Year 2000 AD, events were set in motion that would fulfill the prophecy. In researching the basis of Columbus' predictions, a serious examination of the mysterious influences[8] which, from behind the scenes, shape America and Western civilization was conducted. The findings support my theory.

Another example of how history is written by the victors is the story of the Spanish Armanda and the aborted invasion of England. History reports that the daring English sea captains were raiding Spanish ships for treasurers that were used for the benefit of England. In response, the Spanish Crown sent the Grand Armada to crush the English upstarts. The history of the mighty Spanish Armada, written primarily by the victors in this affair, the English, and a number of swashbuckling adventure movies made much of the fact that through courage and the power of good English ships, the underdog English Navy saved Great

---

[6] Prof Bryan F. Le Beau (1992). Christopher Columbus and the Matter of Religion. Omaha, Nebraska, USA: Center for the Study of Religion and Society (Newsletter [online]), Vol. 4, No. 1.
[7] Delno C. West & August Kling (Translation & commentary) (1991), The "Libro de las Profecias" of Christopher Columbus. Gainesville, USA: University of Florida Press.
[8] Knight C. et al. (2001). Hiram Key. USA: Fair Winds Press.

Britain from the wrath of the Spanish Armada - the greatest naval force in the world.

In actuality, most of what we are taught about the Armada comes only from English sources. These contemporary sources were, according to David Howarth[9] meager, but were embellished by nineteenth-century historians, who wrote at the peak of British Imperial Pride and made the Armada story into a national heroic tale which was far from true. The numerous small wars that led up to the Armada were actually caused by English attempts to disrupt the Spanish international trading monopoly from the New World. Since the Spanish had "discovered" the new world, they thought it only right that they have the monopoly on rape, plunder and murder. The Armada, Spain's attempt to protect its trading empire by crushing the English once and for all, was a disaster from the beginning.

The Spaniards of that day were the best soldiers in the world, but in naval maneuvers and in the use of heavy artillery they were far behind their English rivals. The worst blunder of all was committed after the death of the only naval commander of repute that Spain possessed, when King Philip appointed the Duke of Medina Sidonia - a man inexperienced in naval matters as the commander of the force that came to be known as the Armada.

The Armada left Lisbon on the 20th of May, 1588. It consisted of about 130 ships, and 30,493 men; but at least half of the Spanish ships were transports, and two-thirds of the men were soldiers not sailors. The English ships slipped past the Spanish fleet in the night, and cannonaded the rear of the fleet as it sailed up the English Channel. The next night some fire ships were drifted into the Armada as the tide flowed. The Spaniards, ready for this danger, slipped their cables, but nonetheless suffered some losses from collisions.

On the Monday following, the great battle took place off Gravelines, in which the Spaniards were entirely outclassed and defeated. It says much for their heroism that only one ship was reported captured; but three sank, four or five ran ashore, and the Duke of Medina Sidonia took the resolution of leading the much damaged remnant around the north of Scotland and Ireland, and so back to Spain. More and more Spanish ships were now lost in every storm. On the 13th of September, the Duke returned to Santander, having lost about half his fleet and about three-quarters of his men.

Great as were the effects of the failure of the Armada, they are nevertheless often exaggerated. The defeat no doubt set bounds on the previously unbridled expansion of Spain, and secured the power of her English rival. Yet it is a mistake to suppose that this change was immediate, obvious, or uniform - or entirely in favor of the English. Spain was still a world power and would remain so until the early 1900s.

---

[9] Howarth, David, <u>The Voyage of the Armada: The Spanish Story,</u> Viking, Penguin, New York, New York. 1981.

History has made much of the cruelty of the Spanish Conquistadors to the native populations of the new world, not bothering to report that the English were just as cruel in their search for riches, even to their own people. However, to the English, the Spanish were all that was evil about their world. English ship captains were encouraged to capture the treasure ships of the Spanish Crown under letters of marque issued by the English government, but only if the English Crown received a portion of the booty. In a number of cases, the English privateers were actually the aggressor, even though initially there was not a state of war between England and Spain. Of course, this continual raiding of the Spanish treasure ships by English privateers eventually led to the many wars that devastated the old world for a good number of years. All of this was brought about by sheer unadulterated greed on the part of both the Spanish as well as the English.

However, the bottom line to this conflict was that the Spanish appear to a have been defending themselves against the English incursions rather than attacking in an unprovoked fashion. This attacking a rival and then exploiting the rival's defensive actions as aggression, is certainly within keeping with the plan known today as Operation Northwoods.

CHAPTER FIVE
THE BREAKDOWN OF THE ESTABLISHED ORDER

"You may not believe in prophecy, but among the leaders of nations there are those who do." T. V. Acheson, 1999

    The established order of things, in so far as the average man in Europe was concerned was that each country was ruled by its own King, and/or Queen. In the dawn of history, these rulers actually ruled by Divine Right, that is they were the direct representatives of the gods, or God, depending on the country. Interestingly enough, the majority of the rulers of the various European countries were related, which made the numerous wars and disagreements of history nothing more than family squabbles. It was this familial relationship between rulers which resulted in the stability that the European people enjoyed. However, it was a barrier to the unfettered greed of the group that now operates like a puppet master with the countries of the world as the helpless pawns.
    There are a number of legends about how the major royal bloodlines of Europe came to be, including one that holds that the Merovingian bloodline[10] was actually descended from the literal children of Christ. Whatever may have been their origins, the Merovingian rulers hold a great interest for anyone trying to trace the royal lines of Europe. According to the Grande Chronique de France of Charles V, the Merovingians were descendants of the Salian Franks, but for whatever reason, even the subjects of the Merovingian Kings considered their

---

[10] The Merovingians were the early rulers of what is now France. The Merovingian rulers actually saved the Christian church from certain destructions. However, according to the history of this family, when the last Merovingian King refused to make Christianity the official religion of his kingdom, the leaders of the early Catholic Church conspired with the mayor of the palace to assassinate King Dagobert as he lay sleeping. The assassin was recognized by the church as the rightful heir to the throne, which gave rise to the Carolingian Dynasty.

bloodline to be holy. This dynasty takes its name from Merovech, the ancestor of Clovis.

The power of the first Merovingians was limited originally to the kingdoms of Cambrai, ruled by Clodio, and Tournai, governed by Childeric. Clovis (481-511), son of Childeric, soon extended his authority to all of Gaul. His conversion to Christianity under the influence of his wife, the Burgundian princess Clotilda, paved the way for the Gallo-Roman population to recognize and accept him as king and gave the Roman Catholic Church a much needed power base from which to combat its numerous enemies.

Divided among Clovis's four sons, who continued to expand its borders, the kingdom was united once again under Clotaire I (558-561). His sons in turn subdivided the legacy, but two of them, Chilperic I, king of Neustria wedded to Fredegund, and Sigibert I, king of Austrasia married to Brunhild, embarked on a long and savage conflict that lasted until Clotaire II (613-629) ascended the throne. His son, Dagobert I, reigned until 639. Dagobert's royal treasurer, Saint Eligius, established numerous religious houses and charitable institutions in his diocese of Noyon. Around this time mayors of the palace, who represented the interests of important landowners and royal officials, began to wield increasing power. Mayors of the palace exerted total control over the last Merovingians, impoverished and debauched figureheads known as rois fainéants ("do-nothing kings"), who were gradually supplanted by the Carolingians. The much-vaunted Trojan origins of the Franks are but a legend that dates back to the seventh century; it was developed by chroniclers of the Capetian era to enhance the monarchy's prestige.

The Carolingians

This Frankish dynasty succeeded the Merovingians and ruled over Gaul, western Germany, the Alps, and northern Italy from the mid-eighth century to the end of the tenth century. The Carolingians rose to power gradually over a long period of time, in the shadow of the Merovingian kings. As early as 687 Pepin of Heristal became mayor of the palace and held all Neustria in his sway. His illegitimate son, Charles Martel (685-741), mayor of the palace to Thierry IV, strengthened his power base and won fame by repulsing the Arabs at Poitiers in 732. Pepin the Short, his son, worked to consolidate the family's acquisitions, first alongside his brother Carloman, and later alone after his elder brother's abdication in 747.

Pepin then united Austrasia and Neustria to become the first Frankish king of the Carolingian line (elected at Soissons in 751). Anointed by Saint Boniface, Pepin assisted Pope Stephen II against the Lombards; from them he wrested the Exarchate of Ravenna and the Pentapolis, which he donated to the Church. His son Charles, better known as Charlemagne (742-814), was the true founder of the Carolingian empire, successively king of the Franks, king of the Lombards, then Emperor of the West. Charlemagne initially shared power with his brother Carloman, but when the latter died in 771 he inherited a disparate collection of land holdings where his authority had yet to be firmly established. Still, at his death in 814, what he left behind was a remarkably well organized and administered empire that stretched from the River Elbe to the Pyrenees.

Charlemagne's heir, Louis the Pious (778-840), proved incapable of maintaining unity owing to the quarrels of his sons. In 843 the Treaty of Verdun formalized the breakup of the empire: defeated at Fontenoy in 841, Lothair retained possession only of Italy and Lotharingia (Lorraine), a strip of land running from Provence to Frisia; his brother Louis received all of Germany, while Charles the Bald (823-877), the youngest son born of a second marriage, was allotted Francia occidentalis (western France). Two attempts to restore the empire, one led by Charles the Bald in 875 and another by his nephew, Charles the Fat in 885, both proved fruitless. Although art and culture continued to flourish, an inexorable decline had begun, accentuated by internal rifts and foreign threats (the Viking invasions). Thereafter each parcel of the former empire followed its separate destiny, and others would afterward take up the legacy.

The Capetians

The Capetian Dynasty was founded by Hugh Capet, elected king of France in 987 over the last legitimate pretender of the Carolingian line, Charles, Duke of Lower Lorraine. Originally conceded by election, kingship did not become hereditary among the Capetians until 1179. The Capetians initially controlled only the Duchy of France (Paris and Orleans), but owing to a shrewd and persistent policy of annexation their jurisdiction progressively extended to other regions: Artois, Vermandois, and Auvergne were incorporated into the kingdom under Philip Augustus (1180-1223), who also confiscated from the English monarch John Lackland the territories of Anjou (birthplace of the Plantagenet family), Maine, Normandy, Poitou, Saintonge, and Touraine. Capetian dominions further expanded to include the county of Toulouse under Philip III the Bold (1270-1285), and later Champagne, Angoumois, and the county of Lyons under Philip IV the Fair[11] (1285-1314). The direct Capetian line produced 14 monarchs, among them Saint Louis (1226-1270), then died out with Charles IV the Fair (1323-1328), the last of Philip IV the Fair's three sons. They were succeeded by the Valois branch of the Capetians, of which Charles V was the third to rule after Philip VI of Valois (1328-1350) and John II the Good (1350-1364). The Valois line endured until the death of Henry III in 1589. His successor, Henry IV (1589-1614) was the first Capetian king of the Bourbon line, which continued without interruption until Louis XVI was deposed in 1791.

It might also be mentioned that among all of the royal lines of Europe, the nobles of France enjoyed the rights, privileges and powers of absolute rulers until the time of the French Revolution. Unlike his peers in most Western

---

[11] Philip the Fair was the French King who orchestrated the destruction of the Templar Order.

European countries, a French nobleman enjoyed the absolute power of life and death over those living on his estates. As we shall see, it was also the French nobility that had aroused the ire of the shadow masters.

Knights Templar

Originally called "The Poor Fellow Soldiers of Christ and the Temple of Solomon", the name of this well known band of warriors was soon shortened to "The Knights Templar". The Templars were a monastic military order formed at the end of the First Crusade with the mandate of protecting Christian pilgrims on route to the Holy Land. Never before had a group of secular knights banded together and taken the monastic vows. In this sense they were the first of the Warrior Monks and eventually, the Pope decreed that only he could discipline this Order. The Templars fought along side King Richard I (Richard The Lion Hearted) and other Crusaders in the battles for the Holy Lands.

From humble beginnings of poverty when the order relied on alms from the traveling pilgrims, the Order would go on to have the backing of the Holy See and the collective European monarchies. Within two centuries they had become powerful enough to defy all but the Papal throne. Feared as warriors, respected for their charity and sought out for their wealth, there is no doubt that the Templar knights were the key players of the monastic fighting Orders[12].

In addition to their legendary fighting prowess, due to their vast wealth and surplus of materials the Templars essentially invented banking, as we know it. The church forbade the lending of money for interest, which they called usury. The Templars, being the clever sort they were, changed the manner in which loans were paid and were able to skirt the issue and finance even kings. This ability gave the order tremendous power and influence among secular rulers.

The Templars were destroyed, perhaps because of this wealth or fear of their seemingly limitless powers. In either case, the Order met with a rather untimely demise at the hands of the Pope and the King of France in 1307 and by 1314, "The Poor Fellow Soldiers of Christ and the Temple of Solomon" ceased to exist, at least officially.

Although originally a small group of nine knights, they quickly gained fame largely due to the backing of Bernard of Clairvaux and his "In Praise of the New Knighthood". Bernard at that time was often called the Second Pope and was the chief spokesman of Christendom. He is also the one responsible for helping to draw up the Order's rules of conduct.

In European political circles, they became very powerful and influential. This was because they were immune from any authority save that of the Papal Throne. (Pope Innocent II exempted the Templars from all authority except the Pope.) After the crusades were over, the knights returned to their Chapters throughout Europe and became known as moneylenders to the monarchs. In the process many historians believe they invented the Banking System.

---

[12] Howarth, Stephen, <u>The Knights Templar</u>, Barnes and Noble Books, New York. 1982

The secret meetings and rituals of the knights would eventually cause their downfall. The King of France, Philip the Fair used these rituals and meetings to his advantage to destroy the knights. The real reason for his crushing the Templars was that he felt threatened by their power and immunity. In 1307, Philip, who desperately needed funds, to support his war against England's Edward I made his move against the Knights Templar.

On October 13th, 1307[13], King Philip had all the Templars arrested on the grounds of heresy, since this was the only charge that would allow the seizing of their money and assets. The Templars were tortured and as a result, ridiculous confessions were given to end the torture. These confessions included:

- Trampling and spitting on the cross
- Homosexuality and Sodomy
- Worshipping of the Baphomet[14]

---

[13] October 13, 1307 fell on a Friday, which gave rise to the superstition that Friday the 13th is an unlucky day.

[14] Baphomet was said to be a skull that would talk to the leader of the Templars. This tale apparently came from **The Legend Of The Skull Of Sidon.**

It is well known that the order of the Templars were monastic in nature and therefore forbidden to have involvement with women (see Templar Rule of Order). The legend of the Skull of Sidon states that one Templar knight had a relationship with a woman who died. He dug up the woman's corpse and consummated their relationship resulting in a most grisly birth nine months later.

"A great lady of Maraclea was loved by a Templar, A Lord of Sidon; but she died in her youth, and on the night of her burial, this wicked lover crept to the grave, dug up her body and violated it. then a voice from the void bade him return in nine months time for he would find a son. He obeyed the injunction and at the appointed time he opened the grave again and found a head on the leg bones of the skeleton (skull and crossbones). The same voice bade him 'guard it well, for it would be the giver of all good things', and so he carried it away with him. It became his protecting genius, and he was able to defeat his enemies by merely showing them the magic head. In due course, it passed to the possession of the order."

This tale can be traced back to a twelfth century author named Walter Mapp, although the story at this time is not connected with the Templar Knights. However, at the time of their trials 1307-1314 CE it was well woven into the Templar legend. In fact it was called upon during the actual trials of the Templars.

Edward Burman in his book <u>Supremely Abominable Crimes</u> tells of an Antonio Sicci, an apostolic notary from Vercelli, Northern Italy. Sicci recounts to the inquisitors the tale of the Lord of Sidon which he claimed he learned while working for the order in the Holy Land. His accusation and recounting of the tale is similar to that quoted in Baigent and Leigh's book.

As unbelievable as this tale seems to modern eyes, it was easily bought during the period. The inquisitors and theologians would have picked up on the fact that the woman of the piece was Armenian by background. This they would have connected with the Armenian Church and its Paulician sects. The Paulicians and the Bogomils were practitioners of Catharism which the church had all but wiped out during the Albigensian Crusade. Since the church believed the Cathari to be practitioners of the Black Mass and

Philip was successful in ridding the Templars of their power and wealth and urged all fellow Christian leaders to do the same thing. On March 19th, 1314 the last Grand Master of the Knights Templar, Jacques de Molay was burned at the stake. De Molay is said to have cursed King Philip and Pope Clement, as he burned, asking both men to join him within a year. Whether he actually uttered the curse or if it is simply an apocryphal tale; what remains as fact is that Clement died only one month later and Philip IV seven months after that. Many have pointed to the coincidence of the time of their deaths as proof that the Templars assassinated both of these men, who they considered to be traitors.

It was, I believe, this betrayal of the Knights Templar that led to the complete and utter destruction of the Royal Families of Europe. The removal of the greatest stabilizing force on the scene, led to a number of wars and revolutions as others rushed to fill the vacuum left by the removal of the hereditary rulers. How this came about is the crux of what I call the Northwoods Conspiracy.

---

necromancy, the woman's Armenian background would make the story guilty by association.

CHAPTER SIX
THE KNIGHTS TEMPLAR

     A major player in the fall of the established order, and my nominee for the group that has pulled the world's strings for several hundred years, was the organization known to history as the Knights Templar. This order of warrior monks, who were to become one of the most powerful and controversial organizations in European medieval history, were actually known by a variety of names; the Poor Knights of Christ and the Temple of Solomon, la Milice du Christ or, more commonly, the Knights Templar. Detailed accounts of the founding of the order are non-existent and there is a body of oral history that holds that the order is much older than previously supposed, having operated under other names prior to operating openly on the stage of history. The main source of information regarding the order's founding used by historians are the documents written by Guillaume de Tyre some seventy years after the event, and while this is commonly accepted as the true account, alternative versions regarding the founding of this legendary band of warrior monks do exist, some of which are supported by documentation that makes them seem reasonably credible[15].

The Formation of the Order
     According to Guillaume de Tyre the Order was founded by a vassal of the Count of Champagne, a certain Hugh de Payen, acting in collaboration with André de Montbard, the uncle of Bernard of Clairvaux. In 1118, the two knights along with seven companions presented themselves to the younger brother of Godfroi de Bouillon who had accepted the title of King Baudoin I of Jerusalem[16].

---

[15] I am indebted to the Official International Website ORDO SUPREMUS MILITARIS TEMPLI HIEROSOLYMITANI®, The Magistral Grand Priory of The Holy Lands (Notre Dame, Saint Mary of Magdalene) for a good bit of the history of the Templars.
  http://www.ordotempli.org/history_of_the_knights_templar.htm
[16] During the time that the Crusaders held the Holy Land, a royal line was established to rule the holy city of Jerusalem. This royal line still exists today.

They announced to the monarch that it was their intention to found an order of warrior monks so that 'as far as their strength permitted, they should keep the roads and highways safe . . . with a special regard for the protection of pilgrims.' The new order took vows of personal poverty and chastity and swore to hold all their property in common.

History states that the king was so grateful to these penniless knights for coming to his aide that he granted them permanent quarters within an already overcrowded city. The mere fact that King Baudoin I had his pick of the cream of European nobility and did not need nine, allegedly, itinerant knights, should not cause us to doubt the public history of the Templars, no matter how strange it sounds. The quarters granted by King Baudoin I was far larger than that needed for just nine knights and included the area containing the stables of what was believed to be the original Temple of Solomon. Even so powerful a religious leader as the Patriarch of Jerusalem took an interest in the Templars, and officially granted the new order of penniless knights the right to wear the double barred Cross of Lorraine as their official insignia.

The original nine knights are generally believed to have been:

- Hugh de Payen, a vassal of Hugh de Champagne and a relative by marriage to the St. Clairs of Roslin.

- André de Montbard, the uncle of Bernard of Clairvaux and another vassal of Hugh de Champagne.

- Geoffroi de St Omer, a son of Hugh de St Omer.

- Payen de Montdidier, a relative of the ruling family of Flanders.

- Achambaud de St-Amand, another relative of the ruling house of Flanders.

- Geoffroi Bisol,

- Gondemare,

- Rosal,

- Godfroi.

Gondemar and Rosal were Cistercian monks who were now just transferring their allegiance from their original religious order to that of the Knights Templar. Many would simply see this transfer as one that took place between the monastic and the military arm of the same order, for the Cistercians and the Knights Templar were so closely linked by ties of blood, patronage and shared objectives that many Templar scholars believe that they were two arms from the same body. It is also exceedingly strange that a band of penniless knights, even ones of noble blood would be able to have an audience with the King of an embattled city and talk the king into giving them free room and board in return for a promise that they could not possibly keep.

I would have to believe that there were other forces at work that were not part of the accepted story. I also believed, based upon the historic military reputation of the Saracens at that point in history that nine knights, who allegedly did not even have enough horses for each one to have his own mount, would have not fared very well trying to protect the pilgrims on the roads to the holy city. So the question of why the Templars went to the Holy Land is one that has baffled scholars for centuries.

The position of Hugh de Champagne in this whole affair is also curious and confusing in the extreme. There is a letter to him from the Bishop of Chartres dated 1114, congratulating him on his intention to join la Milice du Christ, which is another name for the Knights Templar. He certainly took up a form of lay associate membership of the order in 1124 and thereby created a bizarre anomaly in feudal terms, for by joining the Order and swearing obedience to its Grand Master Hugh de Payen he came under the direct control of a man who in the normal social order of things was his own vassal.

There is a secret Templar archive in the principality of Seborga in northern Italy which has recently been discovered containing documents that demand further study. It is claimed that St Bernard of Clairvaux founded a monastery there in 1113, to protect a *'great secret'*. This monastery under the direction of its abbot, Edouard, contained two monks who had joined the order with Bernard, two knights who took the names of Gondemar and Rosal on their profession as monks. One document claims that in February 1117 Bernard came to this monastery released Gondemar and Rosal from their vows and then blessed these two warrior monks and their seven companions, prior to their departure to Jerusalem. This departure was not immediate and did not take place until November 1118. The seven companions of the two ex-Cistercians are listed as follows:

- André de Montbard,

- Count Hugh I de Champagne,

- Hugh de Payen,

- Payen de Montdidier,

- Geoffroi de Sainte-Omer,

- Archambaud de St Amand, and

- Geoffroi Bisol.

The document records that it was St. Bernard that nominated Hugh de Payen as the first grand master of the Poor Militia of Christ and that Hugh de Payen was consecrated in this position by the Abbot Edouard of Seborga. The act of nominating High de Payen as the grand master of this new order would seem to indicate that St. Bernard was in fact in command of this order, even though history holds that he was simply an advisor. This also shows the amount of power that St. Bernard commanded among his peers.

Whether or not Hugh de Champagne was directly involved in the actual founding of the Knights Templar is something of a mystery. Whatever the truth may prove to be, two things are certain. Firstly the count of Champagne was at the very least a prime mover behind the scenes even if he is not to be numbered among the original nine founding knights. Secondly, all those involved in both founding and promoting the Order were linked by a complex web of direct family relationships.

The main reason given to history for the founding of the Order, to protect the pilgrim routes in the Holy Land, does not bear any close examination whatsoever for the first ten or twelve years of the Order's existence. It would have been a physical impossibility for nine middle-aged knights to protect the dangerous route from Jaffa to Jerusalem from all the bandits and marauding infidels who believed that the pilgrims, who provided such easy pickings for Islamic raiders, were a gift from God.

Add to the impossibility of the mission that they had allegedly dedicated themselves to accomplishing are the recorded actions of the knights are the activities that occupied their time. In spite of their announced goal of protecting the roads, their actions make this an even more incredible scenario, for they did not patrol the dangerous roads of the Holy Land to protect the pilgrims, but spent nine years in the dangerous and demanding task of excavating and mining a series of tunnels under their quarters on the Temple Mount. These arduous tasks were completed with the patronage and open support of the King of Jerusalem.

Stables of Solomon

Let us take a moment to investigate the area granted to the Templars. The Stables of Solomon are located along the southern wall of the Temple Mount[17]. The construction of the southeastern part of The Temple Mount is artificially built of refillment works and arches. Located in this area are long underground halls, the most famous among them being Solomon's Stables and the Double and Triple gates. It is possible that similar arches exist to the west of [southern end of] the Temple Mount but there is currently no access to this area.

---

[17] The articles entitled Solomon's Stables by Tuvia Sagiv can be found at http://www.templemount.org/solstables.html

It is traditional to attribute this valuted construction to extensive reconstruction and leveling works that were carried out by Herod at the Temple Mount, however additional changes were carried out in this area at a later period.

Among other reasons, the object of building arches was to decrease the pressure on the supporting walls, and to elevate the platform above the bedrock. But others have argued that the reason for the [system of arches] was to overcome the problem of isolating [defilement of surface buildings] by the dead who might be buried below in "the graves in the depth."

Herod carried out extensive works in the Temple Mount therefore doubling it's surface area. These projects demanded much work mainly because

Figure 1: A view inside the Stables of Solomon.

of topographical difficulties in the south-east part of the Temple Mount. In this [southern] area the bedrock slopes down to the Kidron river 47 meters below the Temple Mount in elevation. Herod managed to overcome this problem by filling the area behind the walls with soil up to a height of 30 meters. Onto this leveled area were built vaults and pillars which supported the south-eastern court of the Temple Mount platform. The building of pillars in turn created underground halls some of which in time came to be known as "Solomon's Stables." The length of these stables is approximately (30 meters from east to west, and 60 meters from south to north). Their height is an estimated 9 meters and the floor is 12.5 meters lower than that of the Temple Mount court. This extensive construction work was supported by the Temple Mount wall which is approximately 47 meters in height. However, due to the covering and build up of refuse, the south-western corner of the wall can only be seen up to a height of 29 meters. The halls are a make up of decorated rows which are connected one to another by wide and rounded arches. These arches are 1 meter thick and made of a coarse stone and are partly of secondary use [reused masonry]. Some of these bear Herodian building characteristics of cut even margins and a flat central boss. It is assumed that most of the work was carried out by Moslems after the Moslem conquest.

The underground halls are made of 12 pillared avenues which differ from one another in length. The northern wall contains a gem stone, which may have been used as a gate's frame during the Second Temple period. Here and there can be seen traditionally decorated stones, which are typical of the Crusaders.

The surface [of the floor of the stables] slopes moderately from west to east. The surface of the south-eastern corner was raised during renovation work carried out at the site in 1890. As a result "The Singular Gate" (which is blocked), was covered up to the height of the upper arch.

From the Crusader period this area benaeth the southeastern platform of the Temple Mount [see map] has been named Solomon's Stables. The name has a mythical connection to Solomon which shows the great intensity and lasting impression that this place had upon the Crusaders. Solomon's Stables were connected to this king just as were the Golden Dome (associated by the Crusaders with Solomon's Temple), and El-Aksa (associated with Solomon's palace). However, the Arabs did not preserve the names "Solomon's palace" and "Solomon's temple" because they wanted to destroy any remnant of the Crusaders occupation of the site.

Due of the impressive construction of these stables and the mystique surrounding them, Solomon's stables are an important part of popular Muslim tradition. Their myth has it that there was a need for "the Jinn intervention" (a demon), so this demon carried the massive stones to their place. "This was carried out according to Solomon's order," it is said, because he "was known to rule over all the demons."

H. DeVogue tells of the great number of stones that the pilgrims customarily left at this location (Solomon's stables) "so as to dominate the Demons that the eastern imagination determined their place amongst these dark pillars."

From the Herodian period and until the 20th century there does not exist any clear information about this site. Most Muslim sources prior to the Crusader period relate almost entirely to the site called "Jesus' Cradle" [or, "the Cradle of Jesus"]. In the Crusader period the underground chambers were mostly used as stables for the Crusade knights, though as refrenced above, the area of Solomon's Stables was turned over to the Knights Templar. They most probably opened a special gate in the northern wall to let the horses enter in. The holes and notches in the arches used for tying up the horses and the troughs, (situated close to the northern wall), found here, prove that this location was used as stables.

According to Johanan from Wierberg in his account, "*at the descent from the road there is a large gate, through it one can enter to the Temple's court. On* the right, to the south is a temple which from what has been told, was built by Solomon. There, are large stables which can hold more than 2000 horses (two thousand), or 1500 camels. In this place the Templar knights own many large houses and a new church which has not been completed. They own much property and wealth here, and in other places."

Solomon's Stables were additionally mentioned by the Jewish pilgrim Benjamin from Tudela: "*and there in Jerusalem were stables in a house that belonged to Solomon, who built an extremely strong building from large stones, there was not to be seen such a building in the whole world.*"

Moji'r Al Din described this site at the end of the 15th century: "*Solomon's Stables...below the court area, under a plot of planted trees lies a large and beamed underground area named Solomon's Stables, this area stretches beneath most of the court, it seems that this building is from the days of Solomon....*"

Apparently this site was not generally used by the Moslems. They visited it only occasionally, this fact can be concluded from Felix Fabri's description who secretly entered it through an opening in the wall (the eastern wall) with the assistance of a Jewish guide, "*both the Jews and the Arabs state that the underground chambers were used as Solomon's stables, however it is accepted that here were stored the perfumes that Solomon received from the Queen of Sheba...*"

(I Kings 10:10). "*It is unacceptable that Solomon would stable horses so close to the Temple as this would be seen disrespectful. In addition, Solomon built elsewhere cities for chariots for the use of iron chariots, the horses and the horsemen. In Solomon's stables were many piles of stones. Our guide explained that the Jews place these stones, so that when the day comes for them to settle in the Land of Israel, these sites would be reserved for them...above the vaults lays an opening which through the Moslems throw all the dirt that they sweep from the Temple Mount...during our visit we were in great fear, for if the Muslims were to discover us, we would come to a bitter end. If it were not for our fear we would have climbed on the piles of dirt so as to reach up to the Court of The Temple Mount....and so, after we saw it all, we returned to the opening that we had entered through and circled Mount Moriah.*"

The Templar Excavations

History records that the Templars spent much of their time digging diligently into the base of the Temple Mount. The extensive tunnels originally mined by the Templars were re-excavated in 1867, by Lieutenant Warren of the Royal Engineers at the behest of The Palestine Exploration Fund[18]. Lieuteuant

---

[18] The Palestine Exploration Fund (PEF) was founded in 1865 by a group of distinguished academics and clergymen The purpose of the PEF is to promote research into the archaeology and history, manners and customs and culture, topography, geology

Warren recorded that the access tunnel descends vertically downwards for eighty feet through solid rock before radiating in a series of minor tunnels horizontally under the site of the ancient Temple of Solomon itself. Unfortunately, Lieutenant Warren failed to find the fabled hidden treasure of the Temple of Jerusalem, but in the tunnels excavated so laboriously by the Templars, they found a spur, remnants of a lance, a small Templar cross and the major part of a Templar sword. These artifacts are now preserved for posterity by the Templar archivist for Scotland, Robert Brydon of Edinburgh.

Also in his keeping is a letter from a certain Captain Parker who took part in Warren's excavation under the Temple and several subsequent ones. Parker wrote to Robert's grandfather in 1912 and told of how on one of these expeditions he had discovered *a secret room carved in the solid rock beneath the temple site with a passage leading from it to the Mosque of Omar.* Parker went on to describe how when he broke through the stonework at the end of the passage and found himself within the confines of the mosque, he had to flee to save himself from a small army of extremely angry and devout Muslims. Two questions arise from the nature and position of these Templar excavations. What treasures were the Knights Templar seeking beneath the Temple Mount? And how did they know precisely where to dig?

A Clue Perhaps?

On the exterior of Chartres Cathedral, by the north door, there is a carving on a pillar, which gives us an indication of the object sought by the burrowing Templars, representing the Ark of the Covenant, but in a rather strange context. The Ark is depicted as being transported on a wheeled vehicle. Legend recounts that the Ark of the Covenant had been secreted deep beneath the Temple in Jerusalem centuries before the fall of the city to the Romans. It had been hidden there to protect it from yet another invading army who had laid the city to waste. Hugh de Payen had been chosen by the leaders of the Early Church to lead the expedition mounted to locate the Ark and bring it back to Europe. This expedition was accomplished under the public cover of a band of religious knights who wanted to protect the roads of the Holy Land from Saracen Raiders.

Persistent legends recount that the Ark was then hidden for a considerable time deep beneath the crypt of Chartres Cathedral. The same legends also claim that the Templars found many other sacred artifacts from the old Jewish temple in the course of their investigations and that a considerable quantity of documentation was also located during the dig. While there has been much speculation as to the exact nature of these documents, a reasonable consensus is emerging that they contained scriptural scrolls, treatises on sacred

---

and natural sciences of the Levant the southern portion of which was conventionally named 'Palestine'.

geometry, and details of certain knowledge, art and science - the hidden wisdom

Figure 2: An interior view of the Cathedral of Chartres

of the ancient initiates of the Judaic/Egyptian tradition. Until very recently these legends received short shrift from academic historians, but that situation is undergoing considerable change.

In fact, one modern archeological discovery tends to support the speculative scenario that the Templars actually knew where to look for what has become known as the Templar Treasure and precisely what they were seeking. The Copper Scroll, one of the Dead Sea Scrolls discovered at Quamran, tends to confirm not only the objective of the Templar excavations but also, albeit indirectly, gives some credence to the bizarre concept of the transmission of hidden knowledge through the generations that led to the Templar's discoveries in Jerusalem.

CHAPTER SEVEN
THE REAL KING SOLOMON

Who Was King Solomon?
There is much history as well as legend surround the figure known to history as King Solomon. King Solomon (970-928 BCE) is arguably one of the best known Kings to have ruled early Israel. He was the son of David the founder of the Houe of David, considered one of the most royal lines to ever sit on the throne of Israel. Solomon's reign was marked by a constant tension between two conflicting orientations: faithfulness to the God of Israel and fulfillment of the Judaic religious precepts, against a propensity to yield to the pervasive foreign influences that penetrated the kingdom as a result of the obligation simposed by its grandiose nature[19].

The Davidic line, or Davidic Kingdom, known in Hebrew as Malchut Beit David ("Monarchy [of the] House of David") refers to the tracing of royal lineage by kings and major leaders in Jewish history to King David in Judaism. Upon being chosen and becoming king, the custom in the times of the Tanakh was to be anointed with olive oil by having it poured on the head. In David's case, this was done by the prophet Samuel. The anointing is called meshicha (meaning "pouring") in Hebrew and that is why a king (melekh or melech in Hebrew) is referred to as a Mashiach or Messiah or a Melech HaMashiach meaning "The Annointed King". The procedure of anointment, in David's case symbolized the descent of God's holiness (kedusha) upon the king and as a sign of a bond never to be broken.

The anointing of David by the Prophet Samuel was a sign that the monarchy was vouchsafed to David directly from God as confirmed in the Book of Samuel: The Books of Samuel, also referred to as [The Book of] Samuel , are (two) books in the Hebrew Bible (Judaisms Tanakh and originally writtten in Hebrew) and the Old Testament of Christianity. ...

"...Now he [David] was ruddy, and with beautiful eyes, and goodly to look upon. And the Lord said: *'Arise, anoint him; for this is he.'* Then Samuel [the prophet] took the horn of oil, and anointed him in the midst of his brethren;

---

[19] http://jeru.huji.ac.il/eb32l.htm

and the spirit of the Lord came mightily upon David from that day forward..."[20], and

"And Nathan said to the king:...*Thus says the Lord of hosts: I took you from the sheepcote, from following the sheep, that you should be prince over my people, over Israel. And I have been with you wherever you went, and have cut off all your enemies from before you; and I will make you a great name, like the name of the great ones that are in the earth... and I will cause you to rest from all your enemies. Moreover the Lord tells you that the Lord will make you a house....*Then David the king went in, and sat before the Lord...'now therefore let it please you to bless the house of your servant, that it may continue forever before you; for you, O Lord God, have spoken it; and through your blessing let the house of your servant be blessed forever*[21]*,'" and

"Then came all the tribes of Israel to David to Hebron, and spoke, saying: *'Behold, we are your bone and your flesh. In times past, when Saul was king over us, it was you that did lead out and bring in Israel; and the Lord said to you: You shalt feed my people Israel, and you shall be prince over Israel.'* So all the elders of Israel came to the king to Hebron; and King David made a covenant with them in Hebron before the Lord; and they anointed David king over Israel...[22]"

As well as in the Book of Chronicles: The Book of Chronicles is a book in the Hebrew Bible (also see Old Testament). ...

"...So all the elders of Israel came to the king to Hebron; and David made a covenant with them in Hebron before the Lord; and they anointed David king over Israel, according to the word of the Lord by the hand of Samuel...[23]", and

"...And these are the numbers of the heads of them that were armed for war, who came to David to Hebron, to turn the kingdom of Saul to him, according to the word of the Lord...All these, being men of war, that could order the battle array, came with a whole heart to Hebron, to make David king over all Israel; and all the rest also of Israel were of one heart to make David king.[24]"

Thus all subsequent monarchs in both the ancient first united Kingdom of Israel and the later Kingdom of Judah needed to show their direct descent from King David to validate their claim to the throne/s in order to rule over the Israelite and Jewish people/s in perpetuity. The Kingdom of Israel according to the Bible, was the nation formed around 1021BC from the descendants of Jacob, son of Isaac, who was given the name Israel, meaning Struggles With God. ... The Kingdom of Judah in the times of the Hebrew Bible, was the nation formed from the territories of the tribes of Judah, Simeon and Benjamin after the Kingdom of Israel was divided, and was named after Judah son...

---

[20] (I Samuel, 16:12-13, and (http://www.mechon-mamre.org/e/et/et08a16.htm)).

[21] (II Samuel, 7:1-29 (http://www.mechon-mamre.org/e/et/et08b07.htm)),

[22] (II Samuel, 5:1-3 (http://www.mechon-mamre.org/e/et/et08b05.htm)).

[23] (I Chronicles, 11:3 (http://www.mechon-mamre.org/e/et/et25a11.htm))

[24] (I Chronicles, 12:24;39 (http://www.mechon-mamre.org/e/et/et25a12.htm)).

In cases where this rule was broken, the verdict of history has not been kind according to classical understandings within traditional Judaism. Two important examples are:

After the death of King Solomon, son of David, the ten northern tribes of the Kingdom of Israel revolted against the Davidic line, refusing to accept Rehoboam son of Solomon and instead chose as king Jeroboam who was not a member of King David's family. The fate of this northern kingdom was sealed when they were eventually conquered by Assyria who exiled them completely until they became The Ten Lost Tribes.

The Hasmoneans, also known as the Maccabees, who were priests, (kohanim) from the Tribe of Levi, establshed a monarchy of their own in Judea following their revolt and war against the Greek Seleucid dynasty. The Hasmoneans were not connected to the Davidic line that is attached to the Tribe of Judah. The Levites had always been excluded from the Israelite monarchy. When the Maccabees assumed the throne in order to re-dedicate the defiled Second Temple, a cardinal rule was nevertheless broken, and it has been considered to be contributing to their own downfall, and part of the eventual downfall of Judea and when internal strife brought in Rome and resulted in the violent non-Jewish Herod the Great becoming king, and eventually ended with the destruction of the Second Temple by the Roman Empire according to scholars within Orthodox Judaism.

With the cessation of the Jewish monarchy following the destructions of both the Temple of Solomon[25] and the Second Temple, the line of the monarchy was always carefully preserved and guarded even though no kings such as David and his immediate descendants were alive. It was from that supposed Davidic line though that many great rabbis and "princes" of the people were claimed descent. Thus men such as the editor of the Mishnah, Rabbi Judah haNasi and his heirs were considered to be from the Davidic line, hence also the title "Nasi" meaning prince. Many of the heads of the Jewish communities in Babylon, the Reish Galuta were also described as being of the Davidic line.

The major undertaking of Solomon's reign - besides his almost complete success in preserving the kingdom which he inherited from his father King David - was the building of the magnificent Temple to the God of Israel on the summit of Mount Moriah, a project which his father, for various reasons, had not undertaken.

The resplendent Temple was an expression of the power that resided in Solomon's kingdom and of its beneficent foreign relations. The monumental sanctuary received the symbolic affirmation of the God to whom it was dedicated: "*the priests came out of the sanctuary for the cloud had filled the House of the Lord and the priests were not able to remain and perform the service*

---

[25] It was secrets hidden beneath the Temple that the Knights Tempalr gained their tremendous power.

because of the cloud, for the Presence of the Lord filled the House of the Lord... "(1 Kings 8:11).

Solomon also experienced a divine revelation in the form of a vision following the conclusion of the dedicatory service: "*I have heard the prayer and the supplication which you have offered to Me. I consecrate this House which you have built and I set My name there forever* "(1 Kings 9:3). The concentration of religious ritual in the Temple, together with the institutionalization of the biblical injunction regarding the pilgrimage festivals, transformed Jerusalem - despite its unpromising natural features - into an important political and commercial center during Solomon's reign.

At the same time, the king's earthly imperial rule involved him in the affairs of the surrounding peoples: "*Solomon allied himself by marriage with Pharaoh, king of Egypt. He married Pharaoh's daughter and brought her to the City of David*" (1 Kings 3:1), and built her a palace (1 Kings 7:8). This unique historical evidence of an Egyptian princess leaving her country to live in Israel attests both to Solomon's power and Egypt's temporary weakness. However, this marriage, and others he made with high-born foreigners for political expediency, inclined the king to the culture and religion of those peoples, causing him to neglect his own God: "*At that time Solomon built a shrine for Chemosh the abomination of Moab on the hill near Jerusalem, and one for Moloch the abomination of the Ammonites. And he did the same for all his foreign wives who offered and sacrificed to their gods*" (1 Kings 11:7-8). His reign was a time of religious tolerance which apparent his God did not like.

A strong impression was also made by the foreign dignitaries who visited Jerusalem, of whom the most famous is probably the Queen of Sheba. She had "*heard of Solomon's fame, through the name of the Lord, and she came to test him with hard questions. She arrived in Jerusalem with a very large retinue, with camels bearing spices, a great quantity of gold, and precious stones*" (1 Kings 10:1-2).

Maintaining the excessive splendor necessitated the use of forced labor on a vast scale (1 Kings 5:28). This, and the many palaces that Solomon built in the "miloh", the area that he prepared for this purpose on the slopes of Mount Moriah, including the palace for Pharaoh's daughter, turned the people against him"(1 Kings 12:3).

At a spiritual level, the pagan rituals that flourished at his encouragement seemed to dull the divine luster of his monarchy: "*And the Lord said to Solomon, Because you are guilty of this - you have not kept My covenant and the laws which I enjoined upon you - I will tear the kingdom away from you... But, for the sake of your father David, I will not do it in your lifetime; I will tear it away from your son*" (1 Kings 11:11-12). The united imperial kingdom of David and Solomon endured for only two generations. Around Solomon there sprang up the myth of extraordinary kingly splendor and superhuman wisdom.

There has been much written about the famed Temple of Solomon and the treasures that were kept within this Holiest of Holies. However, the Jerusalem

Temple of David's son, King Solomon, was something of an enigma until the 1970s. Prior to that, no physical evidence had been discovered in respect of the Temple itself - the House of Yahweh or House of the Lord, as it was more correctly called (1-Kings 3:1, 6:1).

The Old Testament book of 1-Kings 6:2-38 gives details of the construction, which was demolished by Nebuchadnezzar of Babylon 400 years later in 586 BC. A new, larger Temple was built on the same site by Prince Zerubbabel of Jerusalem from 535 BC, and this was later extended by the Seleucid Kings, the Hasmonaeans, and finally by King Herod the Great in the 1st century BC.

In his 1st-century Antiquities of the Jews, Flavius Josephus described Jerusalem in the Gospel era, stating that the Herodian Temple was "incredible". Set within a complex of over 35 acres, where the El-Aqsa Mosque and the Dome of the Rock now stand, it was the most magnificent construction of the era - far bigger than the Acropolis in Athens. However, the mighty edifice was demolished by the Roman legions of General Titus in AD 70. However, though the Roman's destroyed the Temple with their typical thoroughness, there was no mention of them finding the Treasure of the Temple.

Beneath King Solomon's Temple

Archaeologists, working from the middle 1800s, established the foundations of the Second and Third Temples (those of Zerubbabel and Herod), but it was not until 1973 that a concerted attempt was made to reveal the first House of the Lord - the Temple of King Solomon. The archaeological project was led by Prof. Benjamin Mazar of the Hebrew University, with field architect Dr. Leen Ritmeyer, who wrote up the account for the Biblical Archaeology Society.

With the aid of records from the Greek historian, Strabo (64 BC - AD 21), the team worked on site for five years, making many new discoveries, among which (at the lowest course level) were the original footings of King Solomon's Temple, with masonry quite different to that of the later periods. Also, to their astonishment, in the floor of the Holy of Holies above was the carved rectangular depression (48 inches by 31 inches), where the Ark of the Covenant once stood (1-Kings 8:6).

It transpired that the Solomonid footings had actually been logged some time previously by the Palestine Exploration Fund, but the information had not become widely known. It was known however that, in the tunnels beneath, a British military expedition had made a significant discovery in 1894. There, in the labyrinthine complex of arched corridors and cisterns, they discovered a 12th-century Templar cross, a broken Templar sword and other related artifacts. These were remnants from the early 1100s, when the Knights Templars excavated for the Ark and the Secreted Treasures of Jerusalem.

The Copper Scroll

Did the treasure of the Temple of Jerusalem exist or was it simply a nice legend? Well evidence would tend to point to the actual existence of a vast treasure that was hidden to keep it safe from invaders. The parchment known as the Copper Scroll was found in 1952 as part of the Dead Sea Scroll discovery. This scroll, which was unrolled and deciphered at Manchester University under the guidance of John Allegro, was a list of all the burial sites used to hide the various items both sacred and profane described as the treasure of the Temple of Jerusalem. Many of these sites have been re-excavated since the discovery of the Copper Scroll, and several of them have disclosed not Temple treasure but evidence of Templar excavation made in the twelfth century. So it would appear that the Templars may well have had access to a copy of this scroll.

The wording in this scroll reads a good bit like a treasure map. For example, one section reads as follows: "*In the fortress which is in the Vale of Achor, forty cubits under the steps entering to the east: a money chest and it [sic] contents, of a weight of seventeen talents.*"

It was found in 1952 in Cave 3 at Khirbet Qumran on the shores of the Dead Sea, one of the few scrolls to be discovered in the place where it had lain for nearly 2,000 years. Most of what are called the "Dead Sea Scrolls" were found by Bedouin and sold through antiquities dealers, but this one was actually discovered by archaeologists--a rare occasion during those years. In ancient times the text of the document had been incised on thin sheets of copper which were then joined together. At the time it was found, however, the document was rolled into two separate scrolls of heavily oxidized copper which was far too brittle to unroll. For five years scholars and experts discussed ways of opening the scroll. Finally, they decided to cut the scroll into sections from the outside using a small saw. Working very carefully they cut the scroll into 23 strips, each one curved into a half-cylinder. Before it was cut, one scholar thought he saw words for silver and gold and suggested that the scroll was a list of buried treasure. Sure enough, when it was deciphered that scholar turned out to be right! What about all that treasure? What is it? Has anyone found it? The answer to the last question is, no, at least that they are telling.

The treasure described in the Copper Scroll consists of vast quantities of gold and silver, as well as many coins and vessels. It is difficult to assess the value of what is described, since we are not sure what the weights in the scroll are actually equivalent to, but it was estimated in 1960 that the total would top $1,000,000 U.S.

So with such a valuable list, why has all of the treasure not been found?

With this great treasure list, you may ask, why isn't everyone out looking for the treasure? Well, the truth is, some people are looking for it, but it is not all that easy. To begin with, we do not know what all the words in the text mean. The text is in Hebrew, which is certainly a known language, but most ancient Hebrew texts that we have are religious in nature, and the Copper Scroll is anything but religious. Most of its vocabulary is simply not found in the Bible or anything else we have from ancient times. Not only is the vocabulary of the scroll very technical, some of the geographical locations are unknown after so many years, many are too specific and some refer to places that no longer exist. Take some of the following examples:

> *"In the gutter which is in the bottom of the (rain-water) tank..."*
>
> *"In the Second Enclosure, in the underground passage that looks east..."*
>
> *"In the water conduit of [...] the north[ern] reservoir..."*

There are those who have suggested that the treasure never actually existed, that the Copper Scroll is simply a work of fiction. Even if the treasure did exist, we do not know where it came from or who it belonged to. Some believe the scrolls refer to Temple treasure, hidden for safekeeping before the destruction of the Jerusalem Temple in 70 C.E. Others believe the treasure belonged to the sect that lived at Qumran, a sect usually identified with the Essenes, a Jewish group mentioned in the work of the Jewish historian Josephus, who wrote in the 1st century C.E. However, these are just educated guesses. Who the treasure belonged to, and what happened to it, we may never know.

The Templar Search for the Treasure of the Temple Jerusalem

There is certainly a great deal of evidnce that the Templar's knew exactly where to dig and what they were digging for. History tells us that at about the time the Templar excavations were near completion, Count Fulk of Anjou sped with all haste to Jerusalem where he took the oath of allegiance to the new order. He immediately granted the order an annuity of thirty Angevin livres before returning to Anjou. When one considers that the vast majority of knights joining the order stayed within its ranks for their lifetime, this action by Fulk of Anjou is a trifle strange. His apparent freedom of maneuver, despite his oath of allegiance to the Order of the Knights Templar can be explained by the fact that Fulk was not only the Count of Anjou and a member of the Templar Order but was married to the sister of the King of Jerusalem who died childless, thus Fulk himself later became the King of Jerusalem. Did Fulk know about the relics unearthed by the Templars?

The next notable figure to arrive in Jerusalem was the Count of Champagne who, as we have mentioned earlier, took the oath of membership as a member of the Order in 1124. Behind the scenes in Europe Bernard of Clairvaux, who had become a senior advisor to the pope, consolidated his position within the Church. Bernard began to persuade the pope that the new military order which was already active in the Holy Land should be given papal backing and a formal position within the Church. For this they would need a rule, a formal charter stating the aims and objectives of the order, the obligations of its members to it and the rules of membership as well as the establishment of a formal command structure.

The main excavations in Jerusalem were completed in late December of 1127. Whatever they sought was apparently found during this time period, since Hugh de Payen with all the knights of the new order returned to France. Since the entire Order left the Holy Land, it is clear that protecting the roads form Saracen raiders was not a major priority to the Templars. The Grand Master Hugh de Payen and his principal co-founder of the order, Andre de Montbard, traveled to England to see the King and, having obtained safe-conduct from him, went directly north across the border to Scotland, where the two knights stayed at Roslin with the St Clairs[26], who were Hugh's relatives by marriage. The lord of Roslin made an immediate grant of land to the new order which became their headquarters in Scotland. The oldest Templar site in Scotland, once known as Ballontrodoch, is now called Temple after the order. Was the newly unearthed treasure hidden at Ballontrodoch for a time?

The Granting of the Rule

It was not until after the conclusion of the excavations in the Stables of Solomon that the Templars began their climb to the heights of power and glory. The Templars gained official recognition and were granted their rule in 1128 at the Council of Troyes, which was dominated by the thinking of Bernard of Clairvaux, the man that many believe had been the guiding genius to the Templars. The new order soon gained an exceptional degree of legal autonomy, which placed its activities completely beyond the reach of bishops, Kings or emperors, making it responsible through its grand master to the pope alone.

Before his election the current pope had been a member of the Cistercian Order, and was a close friend of St Bernard, who was his principal advisor. This was not the only example of either nepotism or the 'old pals act' that can be found in the early years of the Templar Order. The grant of land at Ballontrodoch by the St Clairs of Roslin was followed by many similar gifts from other pious members of the aristocracy who also made generous donations of land and finance to the rapidly growing order. Membership grew with incredible speed and the order soon numbered among its ranks representatives from all the leading families in Western Europe. France, Provence, and the Languedoc-Roussillon areas became its major power base.

From the time of their founding until the fall of Acre, the Templars exerted influence and then great power in the Holy Land. Guarding the pilgrim routes, transporting men, materials and pilgrims from ports in Europe, important though it was, played only a small part in their activities. They built castles in important defensive positions and played a significant role in military and established important bases throughout the Holy Land, to the extent that the

---

[26] The St. Clair Family, or, as many call it today, the Sinclairs have long been powerful members of various Orders.

Knights Templar became one of the most significant forces within the Kingdom of Jerusalem. The Templars soon acquired a well-earned reputation for bravery in battle and never willingly surrendered to the enemy. However, their reputation for generalship and strategic thinking is not rated so highly. Their extensive and costly military activities in Outremer, as Palestine became known, were sustained by the profits from their estates and activities in Western Europe rather than their military successes in this area.

The Templar Fleet

Material wealth in the early twelfth century was almost invariably based on land and feudal dues. The Knights Templar owned estates of varying size scattered throughout every climatic zone in Europe from Denmark, Scotland and the Orkney Islands in the north, to France, Italy and Spain in the south. Their commercial interests were impressive and varied and their activities included the operation of farms, vineyards, stone quarries and mines. As a result of their two-fold interest in protecting pilgrims on the one hand and maintaining communications with their operative bases in the Holy Land on the other, the Templars operated a well-organized fleet which exceeded that of any state at the time. For military purposes, this included a number of highly maneuverable war galleys fitted with rams and for the purpose of carrying pilgrims, troops, horses and commercial cargoes, they owned a large number of ships which plied the Mediterranean between bases in Italy, France, Spain and the Holy Land. Their main seat of naval power in the Mediterranean was on the Island of Majorca, while their principal port on the Atlantic coast was the highly fortified harbor of La Rochelle from where, it is alleged, they conducted trade with Greenland, the British Isles, the North American mainland and Mexico. Within fifty years of their foundation, the Knights Templar had become a commercial force equal in power to many states; within a hundred years they had developed into the medieval pre-cursors of multi-national conglomerates with interests in every form of commercial activity of that time and were far richer than any kingdom in Europe.

Templar Commercial Activities in Europe

The transformative effect of Templar activity upon European culture and commerce was remarkable and yet many modern Church historians still accuse the order of being formed of illiterate knights. The so-called 'illiterates' developed sophisticated and coded means of communication which transcended the linguistic barriers which otherwise would have fragmented and diffused the commercial impact of their activities. Among the principal items of their trading activities were those which we would describe in modern terms as 'technology and ideas'. The Templar communication network was the principal route by which knowledge of astronomy, mathematics, herbal medicine and healing skills made their way from the Holy Land to Europe. Among the technological advances brought back by the warrior knights were mouth-to-mouth resuscitation, the telescope and a financial instrument which they acquired from the Sufis of Islam, known as 'the note of hand'.

The Templars were great builders. On their own estates they built and maintained fortified castles and farms, barns, outbuildings and mills as well as dormitory blocks, stables and workshops. Some Templar castles, particularly in southern Europe and the Holy Land, were built on defensive sites which posed incredible difficulties of construction. They were particularly renowned for building strategically situated castles with water gates on coasts and rivers. The classic round Templar church, founded on octagonal geometry and supposedly based on the design of the Church of the Holy Sepulchre in Jerusalem, became such a distinctive feature of Templar construction that it became almost diagnostic of their activity or involvement. This type of building formed only a small part of their church construction program, albeit of very special and cabalistic significance. The vast majority of Templar churches, especially those in the southern regions of Europe, are small, undecorated, rectangular structures often with apsidal ends.

According to many scholars, the Templars were openly involved in the financing and construction of the Gothic cathedrals. The sudden flowering of the Gothic style of architecture, which enabled cathedrals to be built of far greater height with more windows, brought about a new era in church design and art that allowed larger naves and greater spaces, uncluttered by pillars, to be created within church buildings. It is no coincidence that this architectural form, which cannot be explained as an evolutionary development from the Romanesque style that preceded it, arose after the knights returned from their excavations in Jerusalem.

While many of the great cathedrals were heavily influenced by Templar thinking, geometry and design, one above all others is a hymn to their direct involvement and belief, the Cathedral of Chartres. Constructed with almost unbelievable speed, Chartres Cathedral is portrayed by the Church as the product of co-operative effort by the townspeople, financed by the pilgrim trade. This totally fails to explain the massive and immediate input of financial resources that must have been necessary in order to pay for the quarrying and transport of the stone and the enormous expenditure on the vast numbers of stonemasons, sculptors and other craftsmen who would have been employed to complete such a vast and complex edifice at such speed. It is highly doubtful if the proceeds of the pilgrimage to Chartres over the period of its construction would have paid for the creation and installation of the stained-glass windows, much less for the construction and decoration of the entire building. The only source of finance in Europe at that time which could have produced the resources necessary to build such a massive project was the Order of the Knights Templar.

In England, craftsmen who work in stone are known as stonemasons. In France they are known collectively as members of the Compannonage who, in the twelfth century, were broadly divided into three groups. These fulfilled separate functions under the umbrella of the same craft: the Children of Father

Soubise were responsible for the construction of ecclesiastical buildings in the Romanesque style; the Children of Maitre Jacques were also known as Les Compagnons Passant and one of their primary functions was the art of bridge building. The craft masons who built the Gothic cathedrals were known as the Children of Solomon, named after King Solomon who, according to the scriptures, commissioned the first temple in Jerusalem. This branch of the Compannonage were instructed in the art of sacred geometry by Cistercian monks and it was the Knights Templar who, acting with the agreement of Bernard of Clairvaux, gave a 'rule' to the Children of Solomon in March 1145, which laid down the conditions required for living and working. The preface to his rule contains words which have been intimately associated with the Knights Templar ever since:

We the Knights of Christ and of the Temple follow the destiny that prepares us to die for Christ. We have the wish to give this rule of living, of work and of honour to the constructors of churches so that Christianity can spread throughout the earth not so that our name should be remembered, Oh Lord, but that Your Name should live.

Templar and Cistercians Holdings Compared

It was not only the Order of the Knights Templar who attained immense wealth, property, power and prestige in the years that followed the completion of their excavations in Jerusalem. Under the guiding hand of Bernard of Clairvaux the once struggling order of Cistercian monks expanded at a similar rate. Within Bernard's lifetime the Cistercians established over 300 abbeys throughout Europe, a truly outstanding era of growth that was never even approached, much less exceeded, by any monastic order other than the Templars. The Cistercians became known as the 'apostles of the frontier' due to their habit of refusing donations of land near major centres of population and opting instead to site their new establishments in marginal lands in the mountains and barren reaches of Christian Europe.

The Templars on the other hand, sited their possessions within cities, at centres of pilgrimage and sea ports as well as in the countryside, with a special emphasis on estates strategically situated near major trade and pilgrimage routes. In England and Wales they had over 5000 properties and they also owned a considerable number in Scotland, Ireland the Low Countries and the German states; they even had estates in Hungary guarding the overland routes to the Holy Land. Spain, long a centre of devout pilgrimage to the shrine of St James of Compostela, was liberally adorned with Templar strongholds and the order played its part in defending Christian Spain against Moorish incursions.

Similar Knightly Orders

Imitation is the sincerest form of flattery and similar orders arose and achieved some degree of renown by modeling themselves on the Templars. Two such orders in Spain were the Knights of Calatrava and the Knights of Alcantara.

Both orders were founded shortly after the Templars and St. Bernard of Clairvaux is known to have played a part in this. There were many Templar establishments in Italy, which was one of the major embarkation points on the sea routes to the kingdom of Jerusalem, but the most important power base for the Knights Templar in Europe was the present country of France. In the south are the regions of Provence and the Languedoc-Roussillon which, in the Templar era, were separate entities from the kingdom of France. Throughout these southern regions Templar holdings were plentiful, with over thirty per cent of the total estates owned by the Templars throughout Europe situated in the Languedoc-Roussillon alone.

Communication Routes

With Templar holdings strategically placed on hilltop positions that commanded panoramic views over the trade routes of Europe, important and transformative change soon took place. Prior to the Templars, Europe was a hegemony of squabbling feudal fiefdoms, counties and kingdoms. Long-distance trade was largely non-existent, except by sea, and all travelers were vulnerable to attack by brigands and extortion by feudal lords who charged a toll for safe passage through their lands. Towns were small and relatively powerless, being subject to the all-pervading will of the Church/State establishment or the arbitrary rule of the seigneur, or lord, of the district. With the advent of the Knights Templar all this was about to dramatically change.

The Templars declared objective of protecting the pilgrimage routes was not restricted to travel within the Holy Land. Not only did they control the routes spreading like a fan northwards from the Mediterranean coast, which were used by the devout in their attempts to reach the birth place of the Saviour, but they also policed all the other pilgrim routes as well. A complex series of communication networks linked every part of Europe to the major international sites of pilgrimage in Jerusalem, Rome and, most important of all in the twelfth to fourteenth centuries, St James of Compostela in Spain. These routes alone linked all the major population centres in Europe. In addition to these were all the national sites of pilgrimage, such as Canterbury in England; Chartres, Mont-St-Michel, Rocamadour and the many other sites of veneration of the Black Madonna in France. With Templar protection, travel by pilgrim or trader alike along the major routes of Europe was now possible in comparative safety and freedom from extortion or assault. One other innovation made by the Templars further enhanced the safety of trade and accelerated the change in the balance of power between the feudal lords and the towns. This was the creation of an efficient and sophisticated banking system.

The Templar Bankers

The Templars used their immense wealth with skill and wisdom. Not only did they make substantial strategic investments in land and agricultural pursuits, but they also invested in basic industries which provided the essential ingredients for the massive expansion in building, both lay and ecclesiastical, which began to change the face of Europe. Using their own commercial insights as well as techniques which they adopted from their Muslim opponents in the east, they developed the concept of financial transfer by 'note of hand' into something like its modern equivalent, developed the bankers cheque and the precursor of the credit card. This latter development arose from the financial needs created by the medieval equivalent of the 'package tour industry' - the pilgrimage trade. Whether to Rome, Jerusalem or Compostela, pilgrimage was a long, arduous and expensive enterprise for the pilgrim and a source of immense profit for the Church and innkeepers, ferrymen and others en route. The pilgrim would be wary of carrying large sums of money as he traveled, for fear of robbery, extortion or unforeseen accident. The answer was simple; seek out the master of the local Templar commandarie and deposit sufficient funds with him to cover the estimated cost of the return journey, including travel, accommodation and ancillary costs such as alms and gift-giving to the important ecclesiastical sites en route and at the final destination. In return for the financial deposit, the Templar treasurer would give the traveler a coded chit as a form of receipt and as a means of exchange.

At each overnight stop, or where alms or offerings had to be given, the pilgrim would hand his chit to the local Templar representative who would pay any dues outstanding, re-code the chit accordingly and return it to its owner. When the pilgrimage was over and the weary traveller had returned home, he would present the chit to the Templar treasurer who had first issued it. Any balance of credit would be returned in cash, or if the pilgrim had overspent he would be presented with the appropriate bill. The entire pilgrimage trade policed by the Templars, who also acted as the bankers for this form of travel, bears a startling resemblance to the modern package tour industry. The modern equivalent of the Templar chit is, of course, the credit card.

Templar banking practice was not restricted to the pilgrimage trade; they also arranged safe transfer of funds for international and local trade, the Church and the State. In the medieval era it was forbidden for Christians to charge interest on loans and therefore money lending as a profession had been traditionally restricted to the Jews. This did little to enhance the reputation of the Jews as a racial group, which was already jeopardized by the persistent allegation that they were 'Christ killers'. The Knights Templar found a way around this restriction which allowed them to lend considerable sums of money at interest without being subjected to the charge of usury. It was quite permissible to charge rent for the leasing of a house or land, so the Templars used this principle in their money lending and charged 'rent' rather than interest for their services rendered. The rent was payable at the time the loan was granted and was added to the capital sum borrowed. By this euphemism the Templars avoided being brought before the courts on the un-Christian charge of usury.

Templar wealth was such that their financial services were not only sought by the merchants and landowners of feudal Europe, but by the princes of the Church and State. They lent to bishops to finance church building programs; to princes, kings and emperors to finance state works, building programs, wars and crusades. Within the twin embrace of financial security and safe travel, Europe began to transform itself. Safe and effective trade over longer distances led to the accumulation of capital and the emergence of a newly prosperous merchant class, the urban bourgeoisie. The new-found wealth of the city merchants changed the balance of power still further in favor of the towns and cities. With the peace and tranquility of the countryside now ensured by the activities of the Knights Templar the feudal lords began to lose the raison d'etre on which their power was based.

The Order of the Knights Templar, despite its relatively short life span, was the major instrument of transformative change in medieval Europe. The Templars brought many blessings of knowledge and technology from their Arab opponents in the Holy Land that conferred immense benefits on the European population. The Gothic cathedrals that arose from their knowledge of sacred geometry still adorn the European landscape and form a permanent series of 'prayers in stone' that raise their spires skyward in silent supplication. When taken as a whole, rather than studied in isolation, the various activities of the Knights Templar are like a huge mosaic of individual pieces which together form a picture which accurately predicted the future. The order was not merely the medieval pre-cursor of the modern multi-national conglomerate but was in many respects an early embryonic form of the European Union. However, success, wealth and power stimulated jealousy and resentment, especially from those who were heavily in debt to the order.

The Suppression of the Order

Philip le Bel[27] (1268-1314), the King of France, was one monarch among many who was heavily in debt to the Order. He also had a further cause for resentment, for when a young man, his application to join it had been refused. During one period of civil unrest in his nearly bankrupt kingdom he sought refuge in the Paris Temple.29 Bedazzled by the vast store of bullion he saw there, he resolved to find a way to make it his own and cancel his enormous debt to the knightly bankers. He soon found an opportunity to destroy the Order.

Plausible reasons for an investigation of any suspect individual or organization were not hard to find in that age of repression and injustice. The perfect means for dubious enterprise had long been perfected. The dreaded Inquisition had honed its evil arts of torture, secret trial and condemnation during its sixty year novitiate in the campaign against the Cathars. Philip knew that there had been contact between the Templars and Islam and links had also been proved between the Knights and the Cathars. Certain knights who had been expelled from the Order were bribed or blackmailed into making accusations of heresy against their former brothers.

---

[27] Also translated as Philip the Fair.

The French King prepared his case with secrecy and skill. The death of the pope gave him the opportunity to suborn his successor. On Friday the thirteenth of October 1307, Jacques de Molay Grand Master of the Templars, and sixty of his senior knights were arrested in Paris: simultaneously many thousands of other Templars were arrested throughout the realm of France. A few escaped arrest and once the word got out the remainder simply fled; an episode commemorated by the saying Friday the thirteenth, unlucky for some.

Under the King's orders the members of the Templar high command that had been captured were tortured for several years. The financially astute monarch had the gall to charge the Order for their upkeep for the entire period of their imprisonment. The final barbaric act of this dreadful charade took place on the Ile des Juifs, on the 14th March 1314. The elderly Grand Master, Jacques de Molay and the Preceptor of Normandy, Geoffroi de Charney, were publicly burnt on a slow fire. Before his death de Molay is on record as prophesying the imminent demise of the king and the pope. Both died within the year.

When the King's agents visited the Templar treasury immediately after the first arrests, their great treasure, the very cause and objective of this brutal enterprise, had vanished without trace, as had almost the entire Templar fleet The king had been foiled. French Masonic ritual indicates that Scotland was designated as the place of refuge or safe keeping for the Templar treasures

Charges Against the Templars

One of the charges against the Templars was that of idolatry; the veneration or worship of an idol called Baphomet. Various translations have been offered for the name Baphomet; Idries Shah, author of *The Sufis*, claims that it is a corruption of the Arabic abufihamet (pronounced bufhimat) which translates as 'Father of Understanding'. Magnus Eliphas Levi the mystical writer of the last century proposed that it should be spelled in reverse as TEM. OHP. AB. This he then construed as Templi Hominum Pacis Omnium Abbas or 'Father of the Temple of Universal Peace Among Men'.

Another legend equates Baphomet with the severed head of St. John the Baptist who was venerated by the Knights Templar. The Atbash cipher, an esoteric code used by the Essenes to disguise the meaning of their scriptures, was applied to the name Baphomet by the Dead Sea Scroll scholar Hugh Schonfield. The cipher produced the word Sophia, the spiritual principle of Wisdom which is usually associated with the ancient Greek or early Mesopotamian goddesses. The Templar Cult of the Black Madonna, black carvings or icons of the Madonna and Child, supports this concept.

At first glance this cult looks like a variation upon normal Catholic practice of the time. The reality is very different however, especially when we take into account the influence of ancient Egyptian ideas on the Templars In ancient Egyptian symbolism, the colour black indicates wisdom. In the Cult of the Black Madonna the Templars were venerating the Mother of Wisdom, the ancient goddess Sophia embodied in the form of the goddess Isis with the Horus child. This pagan concept was disguised as the Christian Madonna and Child.

Reactions to the suppression of the Templars varied from country to country. German knights of the Order either joined the Hospitallers or the Teutonic Knights. One leading Scottish Templar, William St. Clair of Roslin, who was the great-great-grandfather of the founder of Rosslyn Chapel, was killed in Lithuania fighting for the Teutonic Knights. In Portugal the Templars were not suppressed at all, they simply changed their name to the Knights of Christ and carried on under royal patronage.38 Many years later Vasco de Gama the explorer, became a member and the famous Prince Henry the Navigator[28] was a Grand Master of the re-named Order. The Archbishop of Compostela made a vain plea for clemency for the brave knights by writing to the pope begging that the Templars be spared as they were needed for the Reconquista the fight against the Moors to recapture Spain for the Catholic monarchy.

This pressing need for military skills, discipline and dedication to the Christian re-conquest of Spain was fulfilled in a simple way. Ex-Templars were encouraged to join similar military Orders which differed only in that they owed their allegiance to the Spanish crown rather than the pope. One Order, that of St. James of the Sword or the Knights of Santiago, was actually affiliated to the Knights Hospitaller to ensure its survival. They too became immensely powerful and controlled more than 200 commandaries throughout Spain by the end of the fifteenth century. Thus Templar influence continued in mainland Europe. In France and England some Templars joined the Knights Hospitallers, but most simply seemed to vanish.

People condemned for heresy in medieval Europe shared a similar fate to the alleged dissidents condemned in Soviet Russia during the Stalinist era. The victims became 'non-persons', their records were destroyed and all traces of them and their beliefs were completely erased. The only records remaining intact are those of the persecutor, Holy Mother the Church, hardly the most even-handed or dispassionate of sources. Thus getting to grips with the reality that lies behind the romantic myths and legends surrounding the warrior knights is extremely difficult. The French local archives disclose many details of their land dealings while other documents disclosing some of their history do surface from time to time.

The Mysterious St. Bernard

Very important to the founding of the Templars and their elevation to an organization answerable only to the Pope was the man that history knows as St.

---

[28] The man known as Prince Henry the navigator was actually Henry Sinclair, an agent of the Knights Templar and hereditary Grand Master of the Freemasons. As we shall see the Sinclair family was one of the most famous and powerful of the Templar families. The prince's background in esoteric teachings, military strategy, geometry, astronomy, etc., provides an understanding of how a 14th century Earl could transport and hide the Holy Grail across the Atlantic and create a labyrinth of clues not uncovered until 1993.

Bernard, a holy man who seemed to command an enormous amount of influence with the early church leaders. There is not a lot of information available about this venerable holy man, but there are two accounts of his life.

From the work *Life of St. Bernard* by William of St. Thierry, we find that *Saint Bernard was born at Fontaines in Burgundy [near Dijon], at the castle of his father. His parents, among the privileged elite, were famed among the famous of that age, most of all because of their piety. His father, Tescelin, was a member of an ancient and knightly family, fearing God and scrupulously just. Even when engaged in holy war he plundered and destroyed no one; he contented himself with his worldly possessions, of which he had an abundance, and used them in all manner of good works. With both his counsel and his arms he served temporal lords, but so as never to neglect to render to the sovereign Lord that which was due him. Bernard's mother, Alith, of the castle Montbar, mindful of holy law, was submissive to her husband and, with him, governed the household in the fear of God, devoting herself to deeds of mercy and rearing her children in strict discipline. She bore seven children, six boys and one girl, not so much for the glory of her husband as for that of God; for all the sons became monks and the daughter a nun.*

As soon as Bernard was of sufficient age his mother entrusted his education to the teachers in the church at Châtillon and did everything in her power to enable him to make rapid progress. The young boy, abounding in pleasing qualities and endowed with natural genius, fulfilled his mother's every expectation; for he advanced in his study of letters at a speed beyond his age and that of other children of the same age. But in secular matters he began already, and very naturally, to humble himself in the interest of his future perfection, for he exhibited the greatest simplicity, loved to be in solitude, fled from people, was extraordinarily thoughtful, submitted himself implicitly to his parents, had little desire to converse, was devoted to God, and applied himself to his studies as the means by which he should be able to learn of God through the Scriptures....

Determined that it would be best for him to abandon the world, he began to inquire where his soul, under the yoke of Christ, would be able to find the most complete and sure repose. The recent establishment of the order of Cîteaux [in 1098] suggested itself to his thought. The harvest was abundant, but the laborers were few, for hardly any one had sought happiness by taking up residence there, because of the excessive austerity of life and the poverty which there prevailed, but which had no terrors for the soul truly seeking God. Without hesitation or misgivings, he turned his steps to that place, thinking that there he would be able to find seclusion and, in the secret of the presence of God, escape the importunities of men; wishing particularly there to gain a refuge from the vainglory of the noble's life, and to win purity of soul, and perhaps the name of saint.

When his brothers, who loved him according to the flesh, discovered that he intended to become a monk, they employed every means to turn him to the pursuit of letters and to attach him to the secular life by the love of worldly knowledge. Without doubt, as he has himself declared, he was not a little moved by their arguments. But the memory of his devout mother urged him importunately to take the step. It often seemed to him that she appeared before him, reproaching him and reminding him that she had not reared him for frivolous things of that sort, and that she had brought him up in quite another hope. Finally, one day when he was returning from the siege of a château called Grancey, and was coming to his brothers, who were with the duke of Burgundy, he began to be violently tormented by these thoughts. Finding by the roadside a church, he went in and there prayed, with flooded eyes, lifting his hands toward Heaven and pouring out his heart like water before the Lord. That day fixed his resolution irrevocably. From that hour, even as the fire consumes the forests and the flame ravages the mountains, seizing everything, devouring first that which is nearest but advancing to objects farther removed, so did the fire which God had kindled in the heart of his servant, desiring that it should consume it, lay hold first of his brothers (of whom only the youngest, incapable yet of becoming a monk, was left to console his old father), then his parents, his companions, and his friends, from whom no one had ever expected such a step.....

The number of those who decided to take upon themselves monastic vows increased and, as one reads of the earliest sons of the Church, "all the multitude of those who believed were of one mind and one heart" [Acts 32]. They lived together and no one else dared mingle with them. They had at Châtillon a house which they possessed in common and in which they held meetings, dwelt together, and held converse with one another. No one was so bold as to enter it, unless he were a member of the congregation. If anyone entered there, seeing and hearing what was done and said (as the Apostle declared of the Christians of Corinth), he was convinced by their prophecies and, adoring the Lord and perceiving that God was truly among them, he either joined himself to the brotherhood or, going away, wept at his own plight and their happy state....

At that time, the young and feeble establishment at Cîteaux, under the venerable abbot Stephen, began to be seriously weakened by its paucity of numbers and to lose all hope of having successors to perpetuate the heritage of holy poverty, for everybody revered the life of these monks for its sanctity but held aloof from it because of its austerity. But the monastery was suddenly visited and made glad by the Lord in a happy and unhoped-for manner. In 1113, fifteen years after the foundation of the monastery, the servant of God, Bernard, then about twenty-three years of age, entered the establishment under the abbot Stephen, with his companions to the number of more than thirty, and submitted himself to the blessed yoke of Christ. From that day God prospered the house, and that vine of the Lord bore fruit, putting forth its branches from sea to sea.

Such were the holy beginnings of the monastic life of that man of God. It is impossible to any one who has not been imbued as he with the spirit of God to recount the illustrious deeds of his career, and his angelic conduct, during his life on earth. He entered the monastery poor in spirit, still obscure and of no fame, with the intention of there perishing in the heart and memory of men, and hoping to be forgotten and ignored like a lost vessel. But God ordered it otherwise, and prepared him as a chosen vessel, not only to strengthen and extend the monastic order, but also to bear His name before kings and peoples to the ends of the earth....

At the time of harvest the brothers were occupied, with the fervor and joy of the Holy Spirit, in reaping the grain. Since he [Bernard] was not able to have part in the labor, they bade him sit by them and take his ease. Greatly troubled, he had recourse to prayer and, with much weeping, implored the Lord to grant him the strength to become a reaper. The simplicity of his faith did not deceive him, for that which he asked he obtained. Indeed from that day he prided himself in being more skillful than the others at that task; and he was the more given over to devotion during that labor because he realized that the ability to perform it was a direct gift from God. Refreshed by his employments of this kind, he prayed, read, or meditated continuously. If an opportunity for prayer in solitude offered itself, he seized it; but in any case, whether by himself or with companions, he preserved a solitude in his heart, and thus was everywhere alone. He read gladly, and always with faith and thoughtfulness, the Holy Scriptures, saying that they never seemed to him so clear as when read in the text alone, and he declared his ability to discern their truth and divine virtue much more readily in the source itself than in the commentaries which were derived from it. Nevertheless, he read humbly the saints and orthodox commentators and made no pretense of rivaling their knowledge; but, submitting his to theirs, and tracing it faithfully to its sources, he drank often at the fountain whence they had drawn. It is thus that, full of the spirit which has divinely inspired all Holy Scripture, he has served God to this day, as the Apostle says, with so great confidence, and such ability to instruct, convert, and sway. And when he preaches the word of God, he renders so clear and agreeable that which he takes from Scripture to insert in his discourse, and he has such power to move men, that everybody, both those clever in worldly matters and those who possess spiritual knowledge, marvel at the eloquent words which fall from his lips.

Then from *The Acta Sanctorum of Arnold of Bonneval & Geoffrey of Clairvaux*, c. 1153

Twelve monks and their abbot, representing our Lord and His apostles, were assembled in the church. Stephen placed a cross in Bernard's hands, who solemnly, at the head of his small band, walked forth from Cîteaux....Bernard struck away to the northward. For a distance of nearly ninety miles he kept this course, passing up by the source of the Seine, by Châtillon, of school-day memories, until he arrived at La Ferté, about equally distant between Troyes and Chaumont, in the diocese of Langres, and situated on the river Aube. About four miles beyond La Ferté was a deep valley opening to the east. Thick umbrageous forests gave it a character of gloom and wildness; but a gushing stream of limpid water which ran through it was sufficient to redeem every disadvantage.

In June, 1115, Bernard took up his abode in the "Valley of Wormwood," as it was called, and began to look for means of shelter and sustenance against the approaching winter. The rude fabric which he and his monks raised with their own hands was long preserved by the pious veneration of the Cistercians. It consisted of a building covered by a single roof, under which chapel, dormitory, and refectory were all included. Neither stone nor wood hid the bare earth, which served for a floor. Windows scarcely wider than a man's head admitted a feeble light. In this room the monks took their frugal meals of herbs and water. Immediately above the refectory was the sleeping apartment. It was reached by a ladder, and was, in truth, a sort of loft. Here were the monks' beds, which were peculiar. They were made in the form of boxes, or bins, of wooden planks, long and wide enough for a man to lie down in. A small space, hewn out with an axe, allowed room for the sleeper to get in or out. The inside was strewn with chaff, or dried leaves, which, with the woodwork, seem to have been the only covering permitted.

The monks had thus got a house over their heads; but they had very little else. They had left Cîteaux in June. Their journey had probably occupied them a fortnight; their clearing, preparations, and building, perhaps two months; and thus they were near September when this portion of their labor was accomplished. Autumn and winter were approaching, and they had no store laid by. Their food during the summer had been a compound of leaves intermixed with coarse grain. Beech nuts and roots were to be their main support during the winter. And now to the privations of insufficient food was added the wearing out of their shoes and clothes. Their necessities grew with the severity of the season, until at last even salt failed them; and presently Bernard heard murmurs. He argued and exhorted; he spoke to them of the fear and love of God, and strove to rouse their drooping spirits by dwelling on the hopes of eternal life and Divine recompense. Their sufferings made them deaf and indifferent to their abbot's words. They would not remain in this valley of bitterness; they would return to Cîteaux. Bernard, seeing they had lost their trust in God, reproved them no more; but himself sought in earnest prayer for release from their difficulties. Presently a voice from heaven said, "Arise, Bernard, your prayer is granted you." Upon which the monks said, "What did you ask of the Lord?" "Wait, and you shall see, ye of little faith," was the reply; and presently came a stranger who gave the abbot ten livres.

I think that it is interesting that this individual, though from a noble family, who professed to be a simple man who wanted to dedicate himself to his Lord, could rise to such heights that he was advising the Pope and was able through his own personal influence, to raise the Knights Templar to such unbelievable heights. Did he control, through his power over the Knights Templar, a secret so earth shattering that it gave him such power even over the Pope? It would appear that this was the case.

CHAPTER EIGHT
THE TEMPLAR RESPONSE TO THE SUPPRESSION

The formation of the Illuminati and Freemasons – and the instigation of the French Revolution and anti-papacy movements in the eighteen century – have been seen as a ulfillment of Templar revenge. General Albert Pike, Morals and Dogma

There is no question that Philip the Fair wanted the Templar treasure that he had seen in the Templar French Headquarters, but more importantly, he may have wanted possession of the great secret that allowed the Templars to flaunt the laws of the various countries. This powerful, wealthy Order answered only to the Pope, no sitting King could raise a hand against them. For this reason, Philip sat out to replace the Pope with a man he could control. Once this was accomplished, the Pope would remove the protection so long enjoyed by the order and then Philip could move in and grab the treasure. However, on that fateful day when he breached the walls of the Templar's headquarters in Paris, the treasure was gone.

The Templars had dedicated themselves to the defending Catholic Church and the institutions of Europe. However, at the urging of the King of France, the organizations that the Templars had defended with their very lives had turned against them, killing many of their members. Being some of the best warriors in the world, there was only one avenue open to them if they wanted to avenge the deaths of their comrades and the destruction of their order. The Knights Templar became a secret society, able to operate only in the shadows.

Historically, it is said that the Templars did not come into being until 1118, and yet they were already organized and operated quickly and efficiently to accomplish their goal of finding the treasures they sought in the Holy Land. Many believe that once their order was suppressed, the Templars simply vanished, and yet there is a substantial body of evidence that the Knights Templar simply went underground and continued to conduct its daily business through such acceptable organization as the Knights of Christ, the Teutonic Knights, the Swiss Guard and the Scots Guard. Certainly, after the public destruction of the order, the members of Knights Templar were directly responsible for the victory of the army of Robert Bruce of Scotland over the English King. A body of Templar cavalry, riding under their own flag for one of the last times in history, charged onto the battlefield at just the right time to completely rout the larger English army that was on the verge of destroying the Scottish forces. According to legend, the mere sight of the Templar force sent the English fleeing in unreasoned fear.

The members of Knights Templar were the force behind the scenes in the creation of the modern banking system as well as the resurgence of the Masonic Orders and a number of other organizations. Using learning taken from Templar archives, a number of well known historical figures changed the world as they knew it. Among those who used maps compiled by the Templars were such notables as Prince Henry, known to history as Henry the Navigator. What is not as well known was that he was also the grand master of the Knights of Christ, one of the reincarnations of the Templars after the banishing of the organization by the Pope.

When the Templar organization was forced to go underground, the Templar fleet and the massive Templar treasure both vanished from the face of the earth. However, the question at this point would be is it logical to assume that a world wide organization, such as the Templars, with one of the most feared military forces in the world, a powerful fleet and wealth greater than most countries, allow itself to be stamped ot? I don't think so. I think I will be able to show that the Templar set out to avenge the crushing of their order by the French King and set in motion a series of events that continue to have a major impact on the world even in the year 2005.

CHAPTER NINE
THE FOUNDING FATHERS

The American Revolution, viewed from its results, was one of the greatest movements in human history. The expenditure of life and treasure has often been exceeded in more recent conflicts, but the effect on the political life of the world is not easy to parallel. The chief result of this war was the birth of the first successful federal government in history, a government that was destined to expand from the few colonies on the eastern seaboard to the western ocean within a century and to grow into a nation of vast wealth and power and of still greater possibilities.

It is believed by many that the mild bond of union which held the American colonies to the mother country might have remained unbroken for an indefinite period, but for the unwise economic policies and open greed of those placed in high office, both in England as well as in the colonies. Be that as it may, it is certain that for more than fifty years before the Seven Years' War there was a strong attachment between the two peoples and the thought of severing their bond of union was nowhere entertained. It is true that the royal governors were forever complaining to the Lords of Trade about the unruly spirit of the colonial assemblies; it is also true that the colonists were constantly annoyed by the Navigation Acts, and that they thought it not robbery to evade them when they could; but these were only ripples on a smooth sea. And America was happy; the people continued to hew away the timbers and to build cities and churches and schools, to delve the soil, to raise grain and tobacco and cattle; they had grown strong in battling with the forest, the Indians, and the wolves: but with all their growing strength, of which they could not have been unconscious, they did not long to escape the mother wings; their proudest boast was still that they were Englishmen.

Mainstream historians have long said that a separation of the American Colonies form the motherland was inevitable, but there was no plot or conspiracy pushing America toward independence. In this I would have to differ, as there are simply too many coincidences for the American Revolution not to have been a plot. In fact, there is evidence that a number of European secret orders have been involved in almost every facet of the formation of what has become known as the

United States. However, it is true that the actions of these secret societies toward an independent country would have probably failed had there not been an ever widening rift[29] between the colonies and England.

It must be remembered that, while America was the child of England, it was not the child of the England of 1760, but rather of the England of 1600. The great Puritan immigration ceased with 1640, the Cavalier immigration ceased a few decades later, and in all the century that had passed since then the migration from England had been small. The English institutions, transplanted to America early in the seventeenth century, had developed on purely American lines, had been shaped by the social, political, and economic conditions peculiar to America. The result was that the two peoples unconsciously grew so far apart that they were no longer able to understand each other; and when England now attempted to play the part of parent the fact was brought out that the relations of parent and child existed no longer between the two countries. The colonies had reached a point in their development where they could govern themselves better than they could be governed by a power beyond the sea. Writers who find in the Stamp Act, the tax on tea, and the like, the sole cause of the Revolution, fail to look beneath the surface. These were but the occasion; they hastened its coming, but the true causes of the separation had their roots in the far past.

Again, the conquest of Canada changed the relations between England and the colonies. So long as this old enemy hung on the north, both England and her colonies were held in check: the colonies felt a certain need of protection; England felt that a contest with the colonies might drive them to a coalition with the French. But now as this obstacle was removed both could be natural in their relations with one another; and this normal relationship soon revealed how far apart they stood. England then failed to recognize this divergence; she attempted to deal with America, not as a part of the empire, which it was, but as a part of the British realm, which it was not. But for this false assumption by the British government and an attempt to act in accordance with it, the old relations might have continued for years to come.

But an evil day came. The sky had been specked with a little cloud here and there for many years. Why should so many criminals from the British prisons be forced upon the colonists? This was irritating, and had been so from the earliest period of their colonization. Why was the attempt of various colonies to preserve society by checking the African slave trade summarily crushed by the Crown, in order simply to enrich the English trader? This did not indicate a mother's affection for a child. Again, the overbearing hauteur of many of the royal governors, who were supposed to represent the king, was distasteful to a people who believed themselves as good as any other Englishmen. Still again, during the late war with the French, the British officers were ever ready to show their contempt for the provincial troops, and colonial officers were often replaced

---

[29] Of course it is also true that the Secret Societies helped widen the rift every change that came their way.

by British officers. All these things were at least unpleasant for the American-Englishman to contemplate; but they were not serious, and their effects would have passed away like a morning mist but for the greater events that were to follow.

CHAPTER TEN
BACON'S REBELLION

The greed and pettiness that had long plagued the old world was not long in coming to the new. Jamestown, founded in 1609, was one of the earliest settlements in what became known as Virginia, though it was not the first English settlement in the New World. It also became a dumping ground for second sons of wealthy fathers who wanted to make their own fortunes in the new world. This driving desire for wealth, unfortunately, led to the commission of many deeds that soured the relations between the Native Americans and the colonists.

Bacon's Rebellion, for example, was probably one of the most confusing yet intriguing chapters in Jamestown's history. For many years, historians considered the Virginia Rebellion of 1676 to be the first stirring of revolutionary sentiment in America, which culminated in the American Revolution almost exactly one hundred years later. However, in the past few decades, based on findings from a more distant viewpoint, historians have come to understand Bacon's Rebellion as a power struggle between two stubborn, selfish leaders rather than a glorious fight against tyranny[30].

The central figures in Bacon's Rebellion were opposites. Governor Sir William Berkeley[31], seventy when the crisis began, was a veteran of the English Civil Wars, a frontier Indian fighter, a King's favorite in his first term as Governor in the 1640's, and a playwright and scholar. His name and reputation as Governor of Virginia were well respected. Berkeley's antagonist, young Nathaniel Bacon, Jr., was actually Berkeley's cousin by marriage. Lady Berkeley, Frances Culpeper was Bacon's cousin. Bacon was a troublemaker and schemer whose father sent him to Virginia in the hope that he would mature. Although disdainful of labor, Bacon was intelligent and eloquent. Upon Bacon's arrival,

---

[30] http://www.nps.gov/colo/Jthanout/BacRebel.html
[31] There have been a number of stories linking Sir William Berkeley with one of the Masonic Orders.

Berkeley treated his young cousin with respect and friendship, giving him both a substantial land grant and a seat on the council in 1675.

Bacon's Rebellion can be attributed to a myriad of causes, all of which led to dissent in the Virginia colony. Economic problems, such as declining tobacco prices, growing commercial competition from Maryland and the Carolinas, an increasingly restricted English market[32], and the rising prices from English manufactured goods (mercantilism) caused problems for the Virginians. There were heavy English losses in the latest series of naval wars with the Dutch and, closer to home, there were many problems caused by weather. Hailstorms, floods, dry spells, and hurricanes rocked the colony all in the course of a year and had a damaging effect on the colonists. These difficulties encouraged the colonists to find a scapegoat against whom they could vent their frustrations and place the blame for their misfortunes.

The colonists found their scapegoat in the form of the local Indians. The trouble began in July 1675 with a raid by the Doeg Indians on the plantation of Thomas Mathews, located in the Northern Neck section of Virginia near the Potomac River. Several of the Doegs were killed in the raid, which began in a dispute over the nonpayment for some items Mathews had apparently obtained from the tribe. The situation became critical when, in a retaliatory strike by the colonists, they attacked the wrong Indians, the Susquehanaugs, which caused large scale Indian raids to begin. History shows that Mathews encouraged the colonists in their desire for revenge in order to insure that he never had to pay his debt to the Doegs.

To stave off future attacks and to bring the situation under control, Governor Berkeley ordered an investigation into the matter. He set up what was to be a disastrous meeting between the parties, which resulted in the murders of several tribal chiefs. Throughout the crisis, Berkeley continually pleaded for restraint from the colonists. Some, including Bacon, refused to listen. Nathaniel Bacon disregarded the Governor's direct orders by seizing some friendly Appomattox Indians for "allegedly" stealing corn. Berkeley reprimanded him, which caused the disgruntled Virginians to wonder which man had taken the right action. It was here the battle lines were about to be drawn.

A further problem was Berkeley's attempt to find a compromise. Berkeley's policy was to preserve the friendship and loyalty of the subject Indians while assuring the settlers that they were not hostile. To meet his first objective, the Governor relieved the local Indians of their powder and ammunition. To deal with the second objective, Berkeley called the "Long Assembly" in March 1676. Despite being judged corrupt, the assembly declared war on all "bad" Indians and set up a strong defensive zone around Virginia with a definite chain of command. The Indian wars which resulted from this directive led to the high taxes to pay the army and to the general discontent in the colony for having to shoulder that burden.

---

[32] Caused in large part by the urging of the Bank of England.

The Long Assembly was accused of corruption because of its ruling regarding trade with the Indians. Not coincidentally, most of the favored traders were friends of Berkeley. Regular traders, some of whom had been trading independently with the local Indians for generations, were no longer allowed to trade individually. A government commission was established to monitor trading among those specially chosen and to make sure the Indians were not receiving any arms and ammunition. Bacon, one of the traders adversely affected by the Governor's order, accused Berkeley publicly of playing favorites. Bacon was also resentful because Berkeley had denied him a commission as a leader in the local militia. Bacon became the elected "General" of a group of local volunteer Indian fighters, because he promised to bear the cost of the campaigns.

After Bacon drove the Pamunkeys from their nearby lands in his first action, Berkeley exercised one of the few instances of control over the situation that he was to have, by riding to Bacon's headquarters at Henrico with 300 "well armed" gentlemen. Upon Berkeley's arrival, Bacon fled into the forest with 200 men in search of a place more to his liking for a meeting. Berkeley then issued two petitions declaring Bacon a rebel and pardoning Bacon's men if they went home peacefully. Bacon would then be relieved of the council seat that he had won for his actions that year, but he was to be given a fair trial for his disobedience.

Bacon did not, at this time, comply with the Governor's orders. Instead he next attacked the camp of the friendly Occaneecheee Indians on the Roanoke River (the border between Virginia and North Carolina), and took their store of beaver pelts.

In the face of a brewing catastrophe, Berkeley, to keep the peace, was willing to forget that Bacon was not authorized to take the law into his own hands. Berkeley agreed to pardon Bacon if he turned himself in, so he could be sent to England and tried before King Charles II. It was the House of Burgesses, however, who refused this alternative, insisting that Bacon must acknowledge his errors and beg the Governor's forgiveness. Ironically, at the same time, Bacon was then elected to the Burgesses by supportive local land owners sympathetic to his Indian campaigns.

Bacon, by virtue of this election, attended the landmark Assembly of June 1676. It was during this session that he was mistakenly credited with the political reforms that came from this meeting[33]. The reforms were prompted by the population, cutting through all class lines. Most of the reform laws dealt with reconstructing the colony's voting regulations, enabling freemen to vote, and limiting the number of years a person could hold certain offices in the colony. Most of these laws were already on the books for consideration well before Bacon was elected to the Burgesses. Bacon's only cause was his campaign against the Indians.

---

[33] History does not show that he was quick to correct the error in perception.

Upon his arrival for the June Assembly, Bacon was captured, taken before Berkeley and council and was made to apologize for his previous actions. Berkeley immediately pardoned Bacon and allowed him to take his seat in the assembly. At this time, the council still had no idea how much support was growing in defense of Bacon. The full awareness of that support hit home when Bacon suddenly left the Burgesses in the midst of heated debate over Indian problems. He returned with his forces to surround the statehouse. Once again Bacon demanded his commission, but Berkeley called his bluff and demanded that Bacon shoot him.

"Here shoot me before God, fair mark shoot."

Bacon refused. Berkeley granted Bacon's previous volunteer commission but Bacon refused it and demanded that he be made General of all forces against the Indians, which Berkeley emphatically refused and walked away. Tensions ran high as the screaming Bacon and his men surrounded the statehouse, threatening to shoot several on looking Burgesses if Bacon was not given his commission. Finally after several agonizing moments, Berkeley gave in to Bacon's demands for campaigns against the Indians without government interference. With Berkeley's authority in shambles, Bacon's brief tenure as leader of the rebellion began.

Even in the midst of these unprecedented triumphs, however, Bacon was not without his mistakes. He allowed Berkeley to leave Jamestown in the aftermath of a surprise Indian attack on a nearby settlement. He also confiscated supplies from Gloucester and left them vulnerable to possible Indian attacks. Shortly after the immediate crisis subsided, Berkeley briefly retired to his home at Green Springs and washed his hands of the entire mess. Nathaniel Bacon dominated Jamestown from July through September 1676. During this time, Berkeley did come out of his lethargy and attempt a coup, but support for Bacon was still too strong and Berkeley was forced to flee to Accomack County on the Eastern Shore.

Feeling that it would make his triumph complete, Bacon issued his "Declaration of the People" on July 30, 1676 which stated that Berkeley was corrupt, played favorites and protected the Indians for his own selfish purposes. Bacon also issued his oath which required the swearer to promise his loyalty to Bacon in any manner necessary (i.e., armed service, supplies, verbal support). Even this tight reign could not keep the tide from changing again. Bacon's fleet was first and finally secretly infiltrated by Berkeley's men and finally captured. This was to be the turning point in the conflict, because Berkeley was once again strong enough to retake Jamestown. Bacon then followed his sinking fortunes to Jamestown and saw it heavily fortified. He made several attempts at a siege, during which he kidnapped the wives of several of Berkeley's biggest supporters, including Mrs. Nathaniel Bacon Sr., and placed them upon the ramparts of his siege fortifications while he dug his position. Infuriated, Bacon burned

Jamestown to the ground on September 19, 1676. (He did save many valuable records in the statehouse.) By now his luck had clearly run out with this extreme measure and he began to have trouble controlling his men's conduct as well as keeping his popular support. Few people responded to Bacon's appeal to capture Berkeley who had since returned to the Eastern Shore for safety reasons.

On October 26th, 1676, Bacon abruptly died of the "Bloodie Flux" and "Lousey Disease" (body lice). It is possible his soldiers burned his contaminated body because it was never found. (His death inspired this little ditty; *Bacon is Dead I am sorry at my hart that lice and flux should take the hangman's part*".)

Shortly after Bacon's death, Berkeley regained complete control and hanged the major leaders of the rebellion. He also seized rebel property without the benefit of a trial. All in all, twenty-three persons were hanged for their part in the rebellion. Later after an investigating committee from England issued its report to King Charles II, Berkeley was relieved of the Governorship and returned to England where he died in July 1677.

Thus ended one of the most unusual and complicated chapters in Jamestown's history. Could it have been prevented or was it time for inevitable changes to take place in the colonial governmental structure? Obviously, the laws were no longer effective as far as establishing clear policies to deal with problems or to instill new lifeblood into the colony's economy. The numerous problems that hit the colony before the Rebellion gave rise to the character of Nathaniel Bacon. Due to the nature of the uprising, Bacon's Rebellion does seem at first glance to be the beginnings of America's quest for Independence. However, closer examination of the facts reveals what it really was: an unfortunate combination of a man attempting to start a war to get out of paying a just debt as well as a power struggle between two very strong personalities. Between them they almost destroyed Jamestown.

Also notice that as outlined in Operation Northwoods, the events leading up to Bacon's rebelling included rumors started by Mathews that the Doegs were on the warpath after the attack on his plantation which led to the colonists attack on the friendly Susquehanaugs. After this raid, events quickly escalated to the point that there was a major war in the making. These disturbances suited the purposes of those in power since it took the citizens minds off of the many economic problems in the Colony, such as declining tobacco prices, growing commercial competition from Maryland and the Carolinas. An increasingly restricted English market and the rising prices from English manufactured goods (mercantilism) caused problems for the Virginians. There were also heavy English military losses in the latest series of naval wars with the Dutch and, closer to home there were many problems caused by weather. Hailstorms, floods, dry spells, and hurricanes rocked the colony all in the course of a year and had a damaging effect on the colonists. These difficulties encouraged the colonists to find a scapegoat against whom they could vent their frustrations and place the blame for their misfortunes.

Bacon continued to stir the pot, so to speak to justify his being appointed to a high military post. Had the situation not gotten out of control, he would never have been more than a very small footnote in history. However, what took place before and during the event known as Bacon's Rebellion are in keeping with the philosophy of Operation Northwoods. However, history records Bacon's Rebellion as being the first step to the forming of the United States as a free nation, rather than what it was, an attempt to grab power by someone who needed a war to propel himself into the limelight. Once again, this was a conflict brought about by the actions of the colonists, not an unprovoked attack by bloodthirsty Indians.

CHAPTER ELEVEN
THE AMERICAN REVOLUTION

The Causes

History has painted the American Revolution as an uprising of a people that wanted to be free. This is actually not the case. The Revolution, in large part, was caused by the English Parliament wanting to tax the Colonists to pay for the war with the French in the New World. The long war between England and Ffrance was nearing its close; Quebec had fallen and British arms were triumphant in all parts of the earth, but the British debt had risen to alarming proportions. The colonies also had incurred heavy debts by the war, and a small portion of them had been paid from the English treasury. There was now a general feeling among British statesmen that the colonies should, in some regular and systematic way, be made to bear a portion of the burdens of the empire.

George Grenville now became head of the English government; and, no doubt with good intentions, he decided on a threefold policy in relation to the colonies. First, the Navigation Acts must be enforced. The high duties of the Molasses Act of 1733, which had always been evaded, were lowered in the Sugar Act of April, 1764, after which it was determined to enforce them. Second, it was decided that a standing army must be maintained in America; and third, the colonies should be taxed in order to help defray some of this cost.

In order to enforce the navigation laws custom officers were to be armed with "Writs of Assistance," or general search warrants, which authorized them to enter any store, warehouse, or private dwelling to search for smuggled goods. This system of spying was very distasteful to the people, and their resentment was intensified by the genius of James Otis[34], (1725-1783) a brilliant young Boston lawyer, who must be considered the pioneer of the Revolution. Otis was an advocate of the king, but he resigned the office and took up the cause of the

---

[34] A member of the Brotherhood of Free and Accepted Masons. James Otis The Pre-Revolutionist by J.C. Ridpath Hypertext Meanings and Commentaries from the Encyclopedia of the Self by Mark Zimmerman

people. In a fiery, passionate address before the Superior Court he sounded a clarion note, declaring that the power used in issuing the writs was the kind of power, the exercise of which had "cost one king of England his head and another his throne," and calling upon the people to resist.

The people took up the cry, and it spread from the New England hills to the valleys of the Hudson, the Delaware, and the James. In a short time the whole country was roused to resistance against the infringement of their liberties. Otis based his argument on the broad ground of the rights of the colonists as Englishmen. The speech of Otis was an epoch-making one; it sounded the first note of resistance to British authority heard in colonial British America, and has been called the opening scene of the Revolution. John Adams[35], then a young law student, listened to the passionate eloquence of Otis, and wrote, fifty-six years later, "Then and there the child Independence was born."

No crisis had yet been reached. Otis and Patrick Henry[36] had each made more than a local reputation at the expense of British authority, and they had both won. The writs of assistance had fallen stillborn, and the king had yielded in the Parson's Cause. A shadow was thus cast over the royal prerogative, but it was not threatening; American loyalty was too deep-seated to be seriously shaken by such trifles. But greater events were soon to follow.

Every source of English revenue was drained on account of the great war debt, and it was proposed to lay a tax on the colonies, not to pay the interest on the national debt, nor to be expended in England in any way, but solely for the protection and defense of the colonies. It was thought necessary to maintain a standing army in the colonies to preserve order and to prevent Indian outbreaks, and this belief was confirmed by the great conspiracy of Pontiac[37].

The colonists, however, strenuously denied the need of British troops on American soil in time of peace. They believed that the true reason was to hold them in awe. Franklin[38], who was then in London, stated to a committee of Parliament that there was no occasion whatever to inaugurate such a movement, that the colonists when but a handful had defended themselves against the Indians, and that they were more competent to do so now. But all protest was unavailing, and the government decided to quarter an army of ten thousand men among the Americans, and to tax the latter for its partial support. Lord Grenville

---

[35] John Adams is not known to have actually been a member of a Masonic order, but he spoke very sympathetically about their goals and helped achieve them whenever he could.

[36] A written copy of his famous "Give Me Liberty or Give Me Death" speech given March 23d, 1775, was signed Patrick Henry, Christian Freemason.

[37] See next chapter

[38] Franklin, Benjamin was an American printer, author, diplomat, philosopher, and scientist, whose contributions to the American Revolution (1775-1783), and the newly formed federal government that followed, rank him among the country's greatest statesmen. He held the Masonic title of Grand Master of Pennsylvania and was one of the 13 Masonic signers of the Constitution of the United States.

sought how to raise the revenue by the easiest method without offending the colonists. There is little doubt that he was sincere and that he did not mean to offend them. A stamp tax suggested itself; but the idea was not original with Grenville. As early as 1728 Governor Keith of Pennsylvania had proposed a stamp tax for America. Governors Shirley and Dinwiddie had again proposed it about 1755, but the oncoming war had deferred the matter.

Grenville proposed the stamp duties in the spring of 1764, a year before the act was to be passed. His object, as he said, was to consult the colonial agents and even the colonial assemblies, requesting them to propose some better method, if possible, for raising the necessary revenue. No doubt Grenville, like most British statesmen, felt piqued at the evasion of the navigation laws in America and at the failure of the writs of assistance; but there is no proof that he desired to humble the colonists with an army and with stamps. He doubtless meant it all for the best, but with all his sincerity, he was narrow-minded, and never perhaps dreamed of the storm he was about to raise.

The year passed, and a majority of the colonial assemblies spoke against the proposed law, none offering an alternative; the universal voice from America was against it. But this warning was not heeded; and in March, 1765, the Stamp Act became a law and was to go into operation on the first of the following November. The colonies were not without friends in the Commons during the debate that preceded the passage of the law, the foremost of whom was Colonel Barre, who had fought by the side of Wolfe at Louisburg and Quebec. In a sudden burst of eloquence, in answer to the statement that the colonies were "children planted by our care, nourished by our indulgence, and protected by our arms," Barre made his famous reply: "They planted by your care! No; your oppression planted them in America. Nourished by your indulgence! They grew up by your neglect of them. They protected by your arms! Those sons of liberty have nobly taken up arms in your defense."

The stamps, ranging in value from a few pence to several pounds, were to be placed on newspapers, marriage licenses, deeds, shipping bills, and many kinds of legal papers -- fifty-four kinds of documents in all.

The promoters of this law in Parliament doubtless expected some protest from America, but they were not prepared for the violence of the opposition that was awakened. A few weeks after the news of the act reached the colonies the storm broke forth in all its fury. The Virginia legislature was then in session, and Patrick Henry, who was now a member, offered a series of resolutions in which he declared that the people of that colony were entitled to all the privileges of natural-born subjects of England; that they, through their assembly, had the exclusive right to tax the colony; that they were not bound to yield obedience to any law, except of their own making, designed to impose any taxation whatsoever upon them; and that any person or persons who assert or maintain such right "shall he deemed an enemy to his Majesty's colony." In supporting his resolutions Henry made one of his great speeches, in which the well-known passage occurs, "Caesar had his Brutus, Charles I his Cromwell, and George III"

-- "Treason," shouted the speaker, and the cry was echoed from the chamber. "George III," continued Henry firmly, "may profit by their example. If that be treason, make the most of it." The old conservative members opposed the resolutions, but Henry's impetuous eloquence carried them through by a narrow margin. These ringing resolutions were sent over the land to the North and to the South, and by midsummer they had been published in all the leading newspapers in America.

Massachusetts again joined hands with Virginia in upholding colonial liberty. The legislature, led by Otis, issued a circular letter to all the colonies, calling for a general congress to meet the following autumn. The Stamp Act Congress, in response to this call, met in the city of New York. Nine of the colonies were represented, while the remaining four sent their expressions of good will. This congress sat but three weeks. Otis was its leading spirit, ably seconded by Christopher Gadsden[39] of South Carolina. It framed a Declaration of Rights, and respectfully petitioned the king and both houses of Parliament. Gadsden, in a notable speech used the significant words, "There ought to be no New England men, no New Yorkers, known on the continent, but all of us Americans." This congress was important in that it fostered concerted action and established a precedent for union.

Meantime, during the summer, the opposition to the Stamp Law grew in intensity. The Sons of Liberty[40] organized in every colony, determined to prevent the operation of the law. Most of the colonial legislatures took action against it, and as the time drew near, riots occurred in various sections, and mass meetings were held to denounce the odious law. As the first installments of stamps began to arrive and the names of the distributors were made known, the rioting increased and reached its culmination in Boston, where the usual meeting place, Faneuil Hall, became known as the Cradle of Liberty. Boxes of stamps were seized and destroyed by the mob; distributors were burned in effigy. The fine residence of Chief Justice Hutchinson of Massachusetts was sacked and his valuable library destroyed. In New York Lieutenant Governor Colden attempted to enforce the act, but the people were furious. He threatened to fire on the crowd, and was informed that if he did so he would speedily be hanged to a lamp-post. Colden's best chariot was seized, dragged through the streets with the images of himself and of the devil sitting side by side in it, and burned in the open square in view of his own house. Merchants and business men banded

---

[39] He became a General in the Continental Army under Washington, but is not known to have been a member of any of the Masonic orders.

[40] Sons of Liberty grew out of The Loyal Nine: A group of middle class workers joined this association in the summer of 1765 in order to resist the Stamp Act. They realized that if they could intimidate stamp distributors with house-wrecking and tar-and-feathers, they could bully them into resigning before the act could be put into effect, making it impracticable.

together and agreed not to import goods from England until the law was repealed; newspapers came out with a death's-head and crossbones where the stamps were required to be. In short, the opposition was so determined and widespread that it was evident that the law could not be enforced except at the point of the bayonet.

Viewing the matter calmly from this distance, it must be confessed that no better or more equitable method of taxing the colonies could have been found than by means of stamps, if it be conceded that England had the right to tax them at all. But this was exactly what the colonists denied. "*Taxation without representation is tyranny*," became their battle cry. Lord Mansfield and others explained that the colonies were represented in Parliament, as every member of the Commons represents in a broad sense the whole British Empire, and that the colonists were as truly represented as were eight ninths of the inhabitants of England, who had no vote for members of Parliament and yet were taxed by them. The Americans answered that there was a great difference between the Englishman who had no vote and the colonist; as the former was a part of the British public to which the member of Parliament was responsible, while the latter, three thousand miles away, could not appeal to his interests or his fears. If we agree that America was not represented in Parliament, it cannot be denied that the colonists were clearly in the right. It is a badge of slavery to be taxed by a foreign power. The men that lay a tax should be a part of the people that pay the tax. Thus they are taxing themselves as well as their fellows, and the danger of abuse is reduced to a minimum.

The British Parliament heard the wild clamor from the American wilderness. Under a new ministry, with the Marquis of Rockingham at its head, the subject of repealing the Stamp Act became the principal business. William Pitt, now Earl of Chatham, rose from a sick bed to make one of his great speeches in favor of the colonists, rejoicing, as he said, that America had resisted. Pitt took the moderate ground that while Parliament had a right to lay external taxes, as in the navigation laws, she had no right to lay internal taxes. The other side was presented by Grenville with candor and ability, but Pitt carried the day, and the law was repealed in February, 1766. With the repeal was passed the "Declaratory Act," a declaration that Parliament had the right to tax the colonies "in all cases whatsoever."

The Americans gave little heed to the Declaratory Act. They rejoiced in the repeal of the Stamp Act, and were ready to return to their former allegiance. But the very next year Parliament, with a foolhardy rashness that admits of no explanation, wantonly probed into the half-healed wound. The Rockingham ministry soon fell, and the Great Commoner was called again to take the helm. He became nominal premier, but his health was broken and he retired to the country. The ministry was composed of men of various shades of political doctrine, and each became practically the master of his own department. Against the wishes of Pitt, Charles Townshend became the Chancellor of the Exchequer, and held in his hands the matter of taxing the colonies. He was a man of brilliant talents, but without the conservatism and foresight necessary to statesmanship. He was a firm believer in the right of Parliament to tax the colonies, nor was he willing that the Declaratory Act be left on the statutes a dead letter. He would tax the colonists again without delay and show them who their master was.

It was Townshend, above all men except his sovereign, who was responsible for the Revolution. Through his guidance Parliament laid an import duty on tea, glass, paper, lead, and a few other articles imported into the colonies. The revenue thus raised was to be used in paying the royal governors and the other officials appointed by the Crown. This form of taxation, known as "external," as contrasted with the "internal" taxation of the Stamp Act, had been acknowledged to be legal by the colonists. But they could not escape the belief that the act was meant to annoy and humble them. The same Parliament had pronounced the writs of assistance legal, and had suspended the functions of the New York legislature for refusing to make certain required appropriations. This was a blow at the independence of colonial assemblies. Moreover, the colonists had always insisted on paying the salaries of their own governors, and thus making them feel responsible to the respective assemblies; and to have this privilege taken out of their hands without their consent was not conducive to harmony. All this was irritating in the extreme, and the colonists, who had discovered their strength in opposing the Stamp Act, were in no condition to be thus dealt with. Their fury rose again, and for the third time within six years colonial America, from the mountains to the sea, was aflame with indignation against the mother country.

A new light now arose in the Massachusetts assembly in the person of Samuel Adams[41], who became the most powerful political leader during the early years of the Revolution. John Dickinson[42], of the Pennsylvania assembly, in a series of able "Letters from a Farmer," attacked the British position with great force, while George Washington[43] led the planters of Virginia to resistance. Led by such men, the colonists determined to purchase no English goods on which the import duties had been laid.

Important events now followed rapidly upon one another. The Mssachusetts assembly sent a circular letter to the other colonies, setting forth the rights of the colonists as Englishmen and urging a united petition to the king. The English government demanded that the letter be withdrawn, though it had expressly disavowed a desire for independence; the assembly refused, and was dissolved by Governor Bernard. The Virginia House of Burgesses issued a still bolder circular, calling for union. This circular, the "Virginia Resolutions," 1769, condemned the Townshend Acts, and declared that the people of Virginia could

---

[41] Samuel Adams was a close and principle associate of Hancock, Revere & other Masons

[42] Member of a Lodge in Dover, Delaware.

[43] George Washington was a Mason in the Lodge at Fredericksburgh (now Fredericksburg Lodge #4), Virginia, later appointed but did not actually serve as 1st Master of Alexandria Lodge #22 under its Virginia Charter, 1788-1789

be taxed only by their own representatives. The governor then dissolved the assembly; but the members met again, in the Raleigh tavern, and pledged themselves to the non-importation policy.

Regiments of British troops had been sent to Boston to enforce the Townshend Acts, and a few of their number, in answer to the taunts and jeers of the people, fired on the latter, several of whom were killed. This became known as the "Boston Massacre." The people were maddened by the massacre; a great meeting was held in Old South Church, and through Samuel Adams they demanded that the troops be instantly removed from the town. The lieutenant governor, acting for the absent governor, saw that the temper of the people was such that he dare not refuse, and the soldiers were removed to Castle William, on a little island in the harbor. In 1771 Governor Tryon of North Carolina, with fifteen hundred troops, fired upon the people who had organized as "regulators" to maintain public order.

The coast of Rhode Island had been menaced by an armed British schooner, the Gaspee, whose captain, in pretense of enforcing the revenue laws, committed many outrages upon the people, until, in June of 1772, it was burned to the water's edge by a band of infuriated citizens. The ministry then ordered that the offenders be sent to England for trial, but the Rhode Island authorities declined to obey the order.

This rapid succession of events showed plainly that the breach was widening, and that the signs of the times pointed to still more serious differences between England and America. Meanwhile Parliament had receded a little; it had repealed the Townshend duties, but one, the duty on tea, and that was retained in order to maintain the principle at stake -- the right to tax the colonies. This duty was retained at the instance of one man, the man who had now become the real as well as the nominal master of the British realm.

Unsteady is the Head That Wears The Crown

It was a sad day for the British Empire when King George became its political master. He was a man of narrow intellect, and lacked every element of the greatness of statesmanship. "He had a smaller mind," says the British historian, Green, "than any English king before him save James II." He showered favors on his obsequious followers, while men of independent character whom he could not bend to his will became the objects of his hatred. Pitt he pronounced a "trumpeter of sedition"; Burke and Camden were the objects of his wrath. He had not the capacity to shield his natural littleness by surrounding himself with great men, as many a mediocre sovereign has done.

He despised Grenville for his independence and got rid of him as soon as he could. He recalled Chatham to the premiership because he could not help doing so, but he rejoiced that the old Commoner was broken with age and infirmity, and even expressed a wish that he would die. At length, in 1770, the king, having become supreme in the government, chose as his chief minister a man that he could mold as the potter molds his clay, a man of many noble impulses, but of the class who believed that the king could do no wrong.1 This man, whose "lazy good nature and Tory principles" led him to defer to the king's judgment rather than to his own, was kept at the head of the government, even against his own will, for twelve years -- until the Revolution had been accomplished and America was free. Yet withal, King George has his redeeming traits: he was a man of prodigious industry, he was devoid of hypocrisy, and he led a moral life in the midst of a corrupt court.

Many would law the fault for the American Revolution at the door of George III. However, there is no question that there as an organized movement to inspire a revolution to break free of England. The Templars had worked long and hard to avenge themselves against those that had turned on them and England was on country that had acted to suppess the Order. What the future might have unfolded had not this union been broken when it was must be relegated to the field of conjecture; but that this union was severed between the "beautiful mother and the more beautiful daughter" in the last half of the eighteenth century was chiefly the work of conspiractors.

King George III had little to do, perhaps, with the beginnings -- with the enforcement of the navigation laws and the writs of assistance of 1761. But after the colonies had once offended him by defying British authority, he did pursue them with the same vindictive spirit which he exhibited toward Pitt and other statesmen that he could not control -- he determined to humble them at all hazards. He opposed the repeal of the Stamp Act, but his power was not yet great enough to prevent it. When the English merchants made an outcry against the Townshend duties, on account of their loss of trade, it was the king, as stated above, who retained the duty on tea and thus kept alive the embers until they burst forth into the flame of war.

The Americans now refused to purchase tea from England; they smuggled it from Holland. The English then, by an ingenious trick, made their tea cheaper in America than it was in England, or than that smuggled from Holland. They did this by removing the duty always paid at an English port by the tea merchant on his way from the Orient to America. But the colonists still refused to buy the tea. The principle was at stake, -- the right of Parliament to tax them at all, -- and they were as determined as the English king. Tea-laden ships reached Charleston, Philadelphia, New York, and Boston late in the autumn of 1773. Excited meetings of citizens were held in all these cities. In Charleston the tea was landed, only to rot in storage; the Philadelphians refused to permit the ships to land.

Three ships lay in the harbor at Boston, but the people kept watch day and night to prevent the landing of the tea. The owner of the vessels was informed by the excited people that he must take back his tea to London; but this he could not do, as the governor refused him permission to sail and two of the king's ships guarded the harbor. Meetings were held nightly in Faneuil Hall, or Old South Church, and at length, on December 16, after every legal method for returning the tea had been exhausted, a body of seven thousand men resolved that it should not he landed; and half a hundred men, in the disguise of Mohawk Indians[44], after giving a war whoop, ran silently to the harbor, boarded the ships, broke open the tea chests, about three hundred and forty in number, and threw the contents into the sea. The people looked on from the shore, taking the proceedings as a matter of course. Boston slept that night as if nothing had happened. Who these fifty Indian-garbed king-defiers were is not known; but it is known who instigated the mob, who was the mouthpiece of Boston at this moment, and of Massachusetts, of New England, of America -- it was Samuel Adams[45], the "Palinurus of the Revolution."

England stood aghast at the temerity of her sometime docile colonists. The irate king, with monumental obstinacy and inability to discern the signs of the times, resolved to humble the Americans once for all; nor did his short-sighted Majesty seem to doubt for a moment his ability to do so. Of the colonists he writes, "They will be lions while we are lambs: but if we take the resolute part, they will undoubtedly prove very meek."

King George now led his Parliament to pass in quick succession four drastic measures against the people of Massachusetts. First, the Boston Port Bill, which removed the capital from that city to Salem and closed the port of Boston to the commerce of the world; second, the Regulating Act, which annulled the Massachusetts charter and transformed the colony to an absolute despotism; third, an act providing that persons accused of certain crimes in connection with riots be transported to England, or to some place outside of the colony for trial; while the fourth made it legal to quarter troops in any town in Massachusetts. These were soon followed by the Quebec Act, which extended the province of Quebec to include all the territory west of the Alleghanies and north of the Ohio River to the Mississippi -- except what had been granted by royal charter. It is supposed that the act was intended to prevent pioneers from settling in the Ohio country, and to win the favor of the French Catholics.

---

[44] See the Order of the Red Men in Appendix A.
[45] A mason

CHAPTER TWELVE
PREPARATION FOR WAR

Two years before these acts were passed (1772), Massachusetts, led by Samuel Adams, had made an important move toward concerted action. "Committees of Correspondence" had been appointed in every town in the colony for the purpose of guarding the interests of liberty. The next year Virginia suggested the forming of a permanent Committee of Correspondence to extend to all the colonies. This was gradually done, and the system was very effective in spreading the doctrine of resistance.

Against the drastic British measures Massachusetts now made an appeal for aid, and through these committees the people were prepared for an immediate response. From Maine to Georgia they made common cause with their brethren of the Bay colony, and South Carolina sounded the keynote in these ringing words, "The whole country must be animated with one great soul, and all Americans must stand by one another, even unto death."

Washington offered to arm and equip a thousand men at his own expense and to lead them to the relief of Boston. Thomas Jefferson[46] set forth the view in a pamphlet, the "Summary View," that Parliament had no right to any authority whatever in the colonies. Nearly all the colonies joined in an agreement of non-intercourse with England. As the day approached for the Port Bill to take effect, cattle, grain, and produce from the other colonies began to pour into Boston. The day came, and throughout the country it was generally kept as a day of fasting and prayer; the church bells were tolled, and flags were put at half-mast on the ships in the harbors. Had the English king been able to glance over America on that day, he must have abandoned every thought of punishing a single colony without having to deal with them all; he must have seen that but two courses lay before him -- to recede from his position, or to make war upon a continent.

---

[46] He was a member of the Lodge of the Nine Muses in Paris and the Beenan Order (Order of the Bees) known outside Bavaria as the Illuminati. He was also known to be a Deist with some Masonic connections.

The events above noted gave unmistakable evidence of the unity of American sentiment against British oppression; but something more must be done to bring about united action. There must be some central authority to which all the colonies could turn for guidance. This political union came about in the formation of a Continental Congress. This Congress was the result of a spontaneous and almost simultaneous movement throughout the country. From New York came the first call. Paul Revere[47] had been sent from Boston on a fleet horse to rouse the people of New York and Philadelphia, but ere he reached the former the Sons of Liberty had taken action for a congress. The Massachusetts legislature added its voice in June. Delegates were chosen in all the colonies except Georgia, and they met in Carpenter's Hall, Philadelphia. Among them we find such leaders as Washington, Lee[48], and Henry of Virginia, Dickinson of Pennsylvania, Samuel and John Adams of Massachusetts, Roger Sherman[49] of Connecticut.

The Congress at this time was not a constitutional body; many of its members had been chosen irregularly, though most were of the wealthy class. Its authority was limited to the willingness of the people to respect and obey its suggestions and mandates. It was less a congress than a national committee, an advisory council of continental magnitude. It attempted no national legislation. It was controlled by wealthy conservative men who counseled moderation. They made a declaration of rights, mild but deeply sincere; they prepared an address to the king, *disavowing a desire for independence*, another to the people of England, and still another to the people of Canada. They also approved the policy of non-intercourse with Great Britain, and formed an association to carry it out.

The forming of this association, which at first constituted the revolutionary machinery, was an act of great importance. Its object was to secure a redress of grievances by peaceful methods, by enforcing the non-importation and non-consumption agreement. To carry out this purpose committees were to be formed in every county or township in the colonies. These worked under the guidance of the Committees of Correspondence. The local committees marked out for persecution every loyalist who refused to comply with the recommendations of the Congress. The loyalists made a feeble effort at counter organization; but the patriots were so furious in their opposition that little came of it. Not until the next year, 1775, did the patriots begin to form associations pledged to oppose the aggressions of the king by force of arms.

Among other things this Congress indorsed a set of resolutions from Suffolk County, Massachusetts, drawn up by Joseph Warren[50]. By these it was declared that the king who violates the chartered rights of the people forfeits their allegiance, that the Regulating Act was null and void, and so on. After Congress

---

[47] He was a well known Mason.
[48] A suspected Mason.
[49] There is a body of evidence that he was a member of a Masonic order.
[50] Joseph Warren, the Grand Master of Massachusetts, was killed at Bunker Hill.

had adopted them, Massachusetts, in accordance with their spirit, proceeded to set up a provisional government.

In Massachusetts the summer had been one of unusual excitement. The people set the Regulation Act at defiance and banded together in thousands to prevent its operation. They surrounded the courthouses and forced the king's officers to resign; they refused to serve as jurymen; they met for military drill on the village green of every town. The leaders of the people, in the absence of Samuel Adams, were John Hancock[51], a man of refinement and culture and the richest merchant in New England, and Joseph Warren, a prominent physician, a man of unsullied patriotism, and the bosom friend of Adams.

General Gage had returned to Massachusetts with an army with which to awe the people, and he was made civil as well as military governor. The people answered these proceedings by organizing into bands of "minutemen," ready to move on a minute's notice. On one occasion Gage sent a party of soldiers to seize some powder at Charlestown; the rumor spread that they had fired on the citizens, and in less than two days twenty thousand farmers were under arms, marching toward Boston. But the rumor proved false, and they returned to their homes.

Late in October a provincial congress met at Concord, with Hancock as president and Warren the chairman of a committee appointed to collect military stores. This congress dissolved in December, and another met at Cambridge in February and proceeded to organize the militia and to appoint officers.

During the winter and spring of 1775 the estrangement continued to increase, and every index pointed to a conflict of arms. The king and Parliament and Gage had miscalculated when they believed that the presence of an army would awe the colonists and change them from roaring lions into fawning lambs. Nor were the colonists making a leap in the dark; they were strong, and they knew that they were strong. Their bodies had been developed in clearing away the forest, in tilling the soil, in fishing and shipbuilding; they had become expert marksmen in fighting Indians and wild animals, and many of them had gained an excellent military training in the late war with France.

Warren and his associates were determined to foment a revolution so he set about using his Masonic contacts to create a spy web in the colonies. The wife of the British general was rumored to be a spy for Warren. But the Colonies had not risen up in revolt against the British rule, only a few rag-tag militias had begun to train. Warren needed to manufacture a bold stroke to capture the attention of the Colonies and the world.

In May of 1775, Warren learned from his spies that General Gage, the ranking British officer in the Colonies, was soon to be replaced. Speculating that the General would try to go out a winner, Warren and others conspired to set him

---

[51] One of nine Masons - and the first signer of the Declaration of Independence, he was President of the Continental Congress and served nine terms as Governor of Massachusetts.

up. Warren let it leak through his network that Brother Sam Adams and Brother John Hancock, who had outstanding arrest warrants issued for them, were stockpiling munitions in Lexington and Concord. Gage was tricked into thinking he could capture the two and defuse the troubles with one stunning military victory, saving his damaged career. On the night of the 18th of April, Gage sent a body of eight hundred regulars to make the arrest and, at the same time, to move on a few miles farther and destroy the military stores at Concord. Silently in the darkness the troops were rowed across the Charles River, and by midnight they were well on the way to Lexington. Every precaution for secrecy had been taken, but the vigilance of the patriots was too keen to be eluded.

As his troops approached, they encountered armed Colonial troops. Then, "The Shot Heard Round The World" rang out. But who fired it? A British Officer stated that the shot was fired from the Buckman Tavern, which, coincidentally, was where Brother Revere was located. Brother Revere stated later that he "saw and heard a gun fired, which appeared to be a pistol." He carefully avoided saying who fired it[52].

Eight Colonists died and ten more were wounded. Warren and Revere got the propaganda machine lubed up and created a press release that stated that the British had mowed down a bunch of innocent bystanders. His incendiary rhetoric was sure to inflame the passions of the Colonies. He made sure the second Continental Congress, which had just begun to meet in Philadelphia, got an advance copy.

His carefully planned script continued to play out. As the British left the town, snipers took them out at the bridge. The retreat became a rout in a fine example of the virtues of guerrilla warfare. But the Continental Congress dragged its heels about declaring war.

In July of 1776, a group comprised largely of Masons validated what had been done earlier by Warren et.al.: the Declaration of Independence was signed. General (and Mason) George Washington raised an army, with the upper ranks being nearly all Masons. Among Washington's Masonic generals were: Horatio Gates, Henry Knox, Israel Putnam, Baron von Stuben and the Marquise de Lafayette. John Paul Jones, of course, was also a mason.

After the war had ended, the Masons got together one more time to seal the deal. In 1787, they signed the Constitution, and made a government designed per their view of the world: a Masonic view. Since that time, the Masonic Conspiracy has continued. Mason George Washington was elected as the first President, and the office has continued to be comprised of Masons ever since.

Now the important question must be asked. Was the American Revolution forced on the British by the Colonial Secret Society members or were their actions just the natural result of the British actions. One of the most influential members of the House of Commons was 1765-1795 Edmund Burke,

---

[52] There is much speculation that the Colonists began the hostilies as the British had strick orders not to fire unless as a last resort.

was born Dublin Ireland and was known to be a life long Mason. Entered the House of Commons in 1765 abd served until 1795. As a member of Parliament he became known as a Political thinker and important in the history of political theory. He was instrumental in organizing quiet support fot the independence movement in the colonies.

History would show that had there not been the militant acts of the Minutemen and other groups that the British troops would not have been willing to respond with force. General Gage was certainly not someone who desired to kill innocent men and women. However, after Concord and Lexington, the British had no choice but to fight.

Every indication now pointed to a long and bloody war. Franklin, just returned from England, declared that the colonies were lost forever to the British Crown. Yet the thought of independence had scarcely at that date entered the colonial heart; reconciliation was still possible, but only on the ground that England would yield every point at issue. This the proud, obstinate monarch could not do, and events moved rapidly on till the opportunity was lost[53].

---

[53] http://www.usahistory.info/American-Revolution/Lexington.html

CHAPTER THIRTEEN
HOW TO THROW A FIGHT

"Give me a grain of truth and I will mix it up with a great mass of falsehood, so that no chemist shall ever be able to separate them." - John Wilkes

The British Army of the 1700s was the most formidable fighting force in the world. It had beaten the powerful French both on the Continent and in Canada and had defeated most of the armies of Europe at one time or another. The commanders of the British forces in America were some of the most brilliant commanders in the Empire. However, for some reason, this unbeatable fighting force and its seasoned commanders were completely outclassed by a ragtag collection of militias banded together into a makeshift army commanded by a General who had never commanded any force remotely as large. History would have us believe that the victory of the American Colonies over the British was nothing short of a Miracle. Well, behind every miracle are some little known facts and, so too, are there little known facts about the American Revolution.

Introduction
From early 1774 to 1783, the British government and its upstart American colony became locked in an increasingly bitter struggle as the Americans moved from violent protest over British colonial policies to a burning desire for independence. As this scenario developed, intelligence and counterintelligence played important roles in America's fight for freedom and British efforts to save its empire.

Most histories of General Gage simply report that he was Thomas Gage, b. 1719 or 1720, d. Apr. 2, 1787. He was a British general and colonial governor in America. His aggressive actions against the colonists contributed to the American Revolution. In 1774 he became governor of Massachusetts, where he attempted to quell agitation and enforce the Intolerable Acts. It was Gage who ordered the troops to Lexington and Concord in April 1775. After the Battle of Bunker Hill, he was recalled to England.

What is not normally mentioned in that he was actually Thomas Gage and he was a younger son of the first Viscount Gage. He was born in Firle, England and entered the British army in 1740 as a lieutenant and as an aide de camp to Lord Albemarle. In 1751 became lieutenant colonel of the 44th Regiment, one of two regiments of regulars sent to America under General Braddock in the French and Indian War late in 1754. Gage led the advanced detachment on Braddock's march toward Fort Duquesne and was wounded in the rout of that expedition. Subsequently he was employed at Oswego. In 1758 he raised a regiment of light infantry, designated the 80th. He was married the same year to Margaret Kemble, daughter of a member of the New Jersey Council.

He served under Abercromby in the attack on Fort Ticonderoga and later was stationed at Crown Point as a brigadier general. After the capture of Fort Niagara in 1759, Gage succeeded Sir William Johnson as commander in that region and led the rear guard of the army under Amherst which moved on Montreal and forced the capitulation of Canada in 1760. In 1761 he was appointed a major general and military governor of Montréal, where his unyielding character and stern efficiency brought him to the attention of the colonial authorities.

In 1763 Gage was appointed commander in chief of all British forces in North America--the most important and influential post in the colonies. Headquartered in New York, he ran a vast military machine of more than 50 garrisons and stations stretching from Newfoundland to Florida and from Bermuda to the Mississippi.

He exhibited both patience and tact in handling matters of diplomacy, trade, communication, Indian relations, and western boundaries. His great failure, it would appear, was in his assessment of the burgeoning independence movement. As the main permanent adviser to the mother country in that period, he sent critical and unsympathetic reports that did much to harden the attitude of successive ministries toward the colonies

When resistance turned violent at the Boston Tea Party (1773), Gage was instrumental in shaping Parliament's retaliatory Intolerable (Coercive) Acts (1774), by which the port of Boston (Boston Port Act) was closed until the destroyed tea should be paid for. He was largely responsible for inclusion of the inflammatory provision for quartering of soldiers in private homes and of the Massachusetts Government Act, by which colonial democratic institutions were superseded by a British military government. Thus Gage is chiefly remembered in the U.S. as the protagonist of the British cause while he served as military governor in Massachusetts from 1774 to 1775. In 1774 he returned to America to become governor and military commander of the Massachusetts colony.

Not An Intelligence Failure

Most people in General Gage's position would claim that his intelligence people let him down. However, it is apparent that British General Thomas Gage, commander of the British forces in North America since 1763, had good intelligence on the growing rebel movement in the Massachusetts colony prior to the Battles of Lexington and Concord. His highest paid spy was Dr. Benjamin Church[54], a member of both the Provincial Congress of Massachusetts and a member of the Sons of Liberty[55] rebel organization along with other patriot leaders such as John and Samuel Adams, Paul Revere and John Hancock. He was a man who sat in the inner circle of the small group of men plotting against the British. However, even with this tremendous advantage, Gage failed miserably in the covert action and counterintelligence fields. Gage's successor, General Howe, absolutely shunned the use of intelligence assets, which impacted significantly on the British efforts. General Clinton, who replaced Howe, built an admirable espionage network but by then it was too late to prevent the American colonies from achieving their independence.

On the other hand, George Washington was a first class intelligence officer who placed great reliance on intelligence and kept a very personal hand on his intelligence operations. Washington also made excellent use of offensive counterintelligence operations and seemed to have excellent sources of information, but he never created a unit or organization to conduct defensive counterintelligence or to coordinate its activity. This he left to his commanders and to committees established in the colonies.

Compare the Commanders

The very unusual characteristics of the two very different military commanders, Gage and Washington raises some interesting questions that history has never discussed. George Washington has been hailed as a miracle worker in taking the colonial army to victory over the thoroughly professional British Army. Although he never received more than an elementary school education[56], Washington was a genius when it came to getting the assistance of the influential. He was befriended by Lord Fairfax and through this influence Washington became a surveyor and received a commission in the British Army. During the French and Indian War, Washington led a poorly trained and equipped force of

---

[54] Benjamin Church was a member of both the Provincial Congress of Massachusetts and a member of the Sons of Liberty rebel organization along with other patriot leaders such as John and Samuel Adams, Paul Revere and John Hancock. However Benjamin Church was really a paid spy for the British general, Sir Thomas Gage. Six weeks before the battle of Lexington, Church sent Gage letters detailing hidden military and political secrets of the American rebel forces (these letters can also be found at the William L. Clements Library in the Sir Thomas Gage Collection). In October of 1775, one of Church's spy letters to Gage was captured and delivered to General Washington. Church was arrested, stood trial for treason and imprisoned until 1777. After his release, Church sailed to West Indies in a schooner that disappeared at sea.

[55] History shows that, to a man, the members of the Sons of Liberty were members of one or more of the Masonic Orders in the colonies. Thus, there is strong evidence that Dr. Benjamin Church was also a Mason.

[56] http://www.americanpresident.org/history/GeorgeWashington/

150 men to build a fort on the banks of the Ohio River. On the way, he encountered and attacked a small French force, killing a French minister in the process. The incident touched off open fighting between the British and the French, and in one fateful engagement, the British were routed by the superior tactics of the French.

Although hailed as a hero in the colonies when word spread of his heroic valor and leadership against the French, the Royal Government in England blamed the colonials for the defeat. Angry at the lack of respect and appreciation shown to him, Washington resigned from the army and returned to farming in Virginia. In 1759, he married Martha Custis, a wealthy widow, and thereafter devoted his time to running the family plantation. By 1770, Washington had emerged as an experienced political leader—a justice of the peace in Fairfax County, a member of the Virginia House of Burgesses, and a respected vestryman (a lay leader in his church). He also was among the first prominent Americans to openly support resistance to England's new policies of taxation and strict regulation of the colonial economy (the Navigation Acts) beginning in the early 1770s.

The Second Continental Congress, comprised almost entirely of members of the various Masonic Orders, appointed Washington commander of all the colonial forces. Showing the modesty that was central to his character, and would later serve the young Republic so well, Washington proclaimed, "I do not think myself equal to the command I am honored with."

After routing the British from Boston in the spring of 1776, Washington fought a series of humiliating battles in a losing effort to defend New York. But on Christmas Day that same year, he led his army through a ferocious blizzard, crossed the Delaware into New Jersey, and defeated the Hessian forces at Trenton. In May 1778, the French agreed to an alliance with the Americans, marking the turning point of the Revolution. Washington knew that one great victory by his army would collapse the British Parliament's support for its war against the colonies. In October 1781, Washington's troops, assisted by the French Navy, defeated British General Cornwallis at Yorktown. By the following spring the British government was ready to end hostilities. Following the war, Washington quelled a potentially disastrous bid by some of his officers to declare him king.

As outlined above, General Thomas Gage was a very experienced competent military leader. So how did Gage with all of the advantages, to include knowing the plans of the plotters of the Revolution, get beaten by Washington, who was less than a military genius? History is silent on that point.

Collusion?

Even though Gage and Washington had served together in General Braddocks disastrous campaign during the French and Indian War, history does not show that they knew each other well. However, they did have one thing in common; both appear to have been associated with Masonic Orders. History has spoken much of Washington's affiliations with the Masons; however, there is also evidence that General Gage was also involved.

Proof of this affiliation on the part of General Gage can be found in the history of Prince Hall Lodge. We can trace the origin of Prince Hall back to Boston, Mass. Prince Hall and 14 other Negro Freemen were made Masons in a *Military Lodge associated with the Army of General Gage* during the Revolutionary War in 1775-1776. This action by the Military Lodge was only taken after their prayer with proper avouchment would not be heard by no less a Masonic Body than the Lodge of St. Andrew in Boston.

History would show that a military lodge would not be so benevolent without the full support of the commander of the forces in which it operated. Thus, even if he was not a member, General Gage was a supporter of the the Masonic Orders.

The Franklin Connection

History has spoken a great deal about the support that Benjamin Franklin was able to garner in England in support of the Colonies. What history does not speak about much is that a great deal of this support was gained through connections that Franklin gained as a member of the notorious HellFire Club.

The history of this unusual gathering of some of the most powerful members of the government of England's King George III has never been thoroughly examined for the affiliations of some of the members. Suffice it to say that immensely powerful members of His Majesty's Government, important intellectuals, and influential artists could sometimes be seen travelling up the Thames River by gondola to a ruined abbey near West Wycombe. There, to the sonorous tolling of the deconsecrated cloister's bell, they dressed in monkish robes and indulged in every manner of depravity, culminating in a Black Mass celebrated on the naked body of a debauched noblewoman and presided over by that notorious rake Sir Francis Dashwood[57]. Their diabolical devotions concluded, the inner circle would adjourn to plot the course of the British Empire.

This "unholy sodalily," as it has been called, styled themselves, with suitably Gothic flair, "The Friars of St. Francis of Medmenham," though they have been immortalized by their popular epithet "The Hell-Fire Club." In that gossipy age there was much speculation about the infernal activities of the society, and in 1765, Charles Johnstone published a roman a clef entitled Chrysal, or the Adventures of a Guinea, which was popularly believed to reveal the secrets of the "Medmenham Monks."

---

[57] Frances Dashwood was the 7th Baron of Ashby having assumed the title from his father in 1779. He died at the rather young age of 58 due to heart failure brought on by his many excesses.

The Club's Precursors

Although the Medmenham Monks are the most famous band to be dignified with the appellation, they were certainly not the original Hell-Fire Club. The first half of the century saw the establishment of many circles of rakehells throughout the British Isles, and tales of their activities have often been transferred to Dashwood's group. (2)

The Monks' most important precursor is the Hell-Fire Club founded around 1719 in London by Philip, Duke of Wharton[58] (1698-1731). Wharton was a prominent Whig politician, Freemason, and atheist who sought to ridicule religion by publicly presiding over festive gatherings with "Satanic" trappings. These meetings were often held in a tavern near St. James's Square, although a nearby riding academy was sometimes pressed into service to permit the attendance of ladies of good reputation who could not be decently expected to be seen in a public house.

Of the female members, one in particular stands out: Lady Mary Wortley Montagu[59], Wharton's mistress and a notable figure in her own right. Lady Mary was a strong-willed individualist who was not content with the polite life of a married lady. She travelled extensively on the Continent without an escort and was rumoured to have infiltrated the Sultan's harem in Constantinople, where she discovered the secret of the smallpox vaccine.

The eventual fate of Wharton's group is of interest. In 1720 Parliament passed the South Sea Bill, a dubious piece of legislation which permitted the South Sea Company to assume the entire national debt in order to pay it off out of its profits. This bizarre attempt at privatization resulted in a short-term stock market boom followed by a disastrous crash. Thousands lost their fortunes, including Wharton. A modern reader cannot help comparing the situation to the recent savings and loan scandal.

Wharton, who had opposed the scheme from the beginning, soon found himself at the head of a shaky coalition of opposition Whigs and Tories who were unified only by their outrage against the government headed by Lord Sunderland. With this sort of backing, Wharton and his "Grumbletonian" Whigs were a political force to be reckoned with. (5)

The majority Whigs unleashed a brilliant counterattack. To divert public attention from the South Sea Bubble and undermine Wharton's political credibility, Sunderland and Sir Robert Walpole denounced Wharton's Hell-Fire activities before Parliament. These charges of immorality alienated the conservative Tories and moderate Whigs, and Wharton's power was broken.

As a result of this political crusification, the Hell-Fire Club was disbanded, and Wharton went on to become Grand Master Mason of the London

---

[58] He was elected the sixth Grand Master of the Lodge at the King's Arms, near St. Paul's on June 24, 1722.

[59] Daughter of the 1st Duke of Kensington and wife of a prominent member of Parliament. Her daughter was the wife of Lord Bute, George III's right hand man.

Grand Lodge in 1722. During the instalment ceremony, the orchestra played "Let the King Enjoy His Own Again," a Jacobite anthem. This amounted to a dangerous declaration of political allegiance against the Honoverian overlords..

The Jacobites favoured the Catholic House of Stuart's claim to the British throne over that of the Protestant, but very German, House of Hanover's. There were many reasons why one might support the Jacobite cause, from Catholic sympathies and a mystical sense of sovereignty to xenophobia and a dislike for the character of the Hanoverian King George I (who reigned from 1714 to 1727), an arrogant "foreigner" who never bothered to learn English.

Consequently, the moment attracted a wide variety of adherents with differing political philosophics, and the term soon came to be applied to anyone who held subversive ideas, much like the word "commie" in our own time. Whatever Wharton's motivations, he threw himself into the Jacobite cause, was awarded the Star and Garter by the Old Pretender, James Stuart, and died destitute at the age of thirty-two. This also shows a distinct basis for those affiliated with this group of prominent men to perhaps entertain very unpatriotic ideas when it came to the English King.

The Fledgling Rake

Francis Dashwood was born in 1708 into an illustrious line of Turkey merchants who had raised themselves into the ranks of the aristocracy by a combination of hard work, political prowess, and strategic marriage. In fact the first Baron of Ashby was a privateer knighted for his services to the throne. Dashwood's mother died when he was two years of age and he was soon packed off to Eton for his education. Upon hearing of his father's death in 1724, he locked himself in a cellar for a week to get drunk.

In 1726, the fledging rake left England for his grand tour of the Continent. To Dashwood's credit, it must be said that this trip did inspire him with admiration for more than fine wine and courtesans. While in Florence, he made the acquaintance of the Catholic Jacobite Freemason Abbe Nicolini and was entered in the English Lodge there. When the Earl of Middlesex became master of this lodge some years later, a medal was struck to commemorate the event. It bore a likeness of the Egyptian god Harpocrates, the symbol of the newly born aeon, a child whose finger is raised to his lips as an exhortation to silence.

The Hell-Fire Club

Tradition asserts that Dashwood's Hell-Fire Club originally met in London at the George and Vulture Inn. It is possible that Dashwood and his friends gathered in a public house to revel in the freedom now implicitly granted to witches, resurrecting Wharton's Hell-Fire Club in a spirit of mockery. On the other hand, in the early eighteenth century taverns were frequently the meeting places for Masonic lodges, so it is also quite possible that the nascent Hell-Fire

Club was a cabal of Jacobite Freemason s. Indeed it might very well have been both.

In 1750, Dashwood rented Medmenham Abbey and began its restoration the following year. "Restoration," however, is perhaps a misleading choice of words. The original abbey dated from the thirteenth century, and had been added to extensively during the Tudor period. Dashwood added a ruined tower and cloister to enhance the building's Gothic atmosphere. Above the (deliberately) crumbling entrance were emblazoned the words of the sixteenth-century philosopher-satirist Francois Rabelais: "Fay ce que voudras" ("Do what thou wilt"). This folly became the new seat of Dashwood's club, which might very well have been known to its erudite familiars as the "Abbey of Theleme."

The abbey's library was said to contain an enviable collection of erotica, although the only volumes it is specifically known to have contained are a Latin Bible published in 1714, a hagiography, and a copy of Conjecture Cabalistica. The walls in one room were decorated with portraits of English kings; Henry VIII's eyes were pasted over with paper. The god Harpocrates, finger to lips, presided over the refectory.

The "chapter-room" is the key to understanding the Monks' activities. Its furnishings remain unknown, and consequently the use to which it was put remains a mystery. Sensationalist authors assume it was a Satanic sanctuary, although it seems more reasonable to conclude that it was used for Masonic ceremonies. John Wilkes, an important member of the Medmenham circle who did not become a Freemason until after his parting of the ways with the group, whines in an article defaming his former friend: "No profa ne eye has dared to penetrate into the English Eleusinian mysteries of the chapter-room, where the monks assembled on all solemn occasions, the more secret rites were performed and libations poured forth in much pomp to the BONA DEA." Author Michael Howard has interpreted this mention of the bona dea, or "good goddess," to mean that Dashwood practised druidic rites, for which he was expelled from the eighteenth-century druidic revival gr oup An Ulieach Druidh Braithreachas in 1743.

Sir Robert Walpole's son Horace, one of Dashwood's political enemies and certainly a stranger to the abbey, mocked: "Whatever their doctrines were, their practice was rigorously pagan: Bacchus and Venus were the deities to whom they almost publicly sacrificed; and the nymphs and the hogsheads that were laid in against the festivals of this new church, sufficiently informed the neighbourhood of the complexion of those hermits."

On the other hand, the only activity that outsiders ever actually observed the brethren engaged in was the occasional boating trip on the Thames. The membership roll of the Medmenham Monks no longer exists, if it ever did, but the names most reliably associated with the group include Dashwood's brother, John Dashwood-King; John Montagu, Earl of Sandwich[60]; John Wilkes; George

---

[60] John Montagu was the 4th Earl of Sandwich and became 1st Lord of the Admiralty.

Bubb Dodington, Baron Melcombe; Paul Whitehead; and a collection of the local lesser gentry and professional men. This was hardly the "Hell-Fire Cabinet" of popular legend, but a group of men sufficiently in t he public eye to create scandal.

Sex and Politics

Dashwood married Sarah Gould in 1745, but in an era when prostitution was the surest means for a woman to advance in society and the fate of nations might be determined by syphilis-spawned madness, it would have been unnatural for the Medmenham Monks not to have had some sexual aura about them. Legend portrays the Monks as indulging in sadomasochistic orgies, but given the rumours about Lady Mary Wortley Montagu and the Divan Club, one might well wonder if there is not a hint of Oriental sex magic in all this.

Certainly the monks engaged in ribald jesting. One of their members, probably the satirist George Selwyn, praised the Earl of Sandwich's sexual prowess in an Anglo-Saxon-laced lampoon of Popes Essay on Man. John Wilkes printed a private edition of twelve copies of this "Essay on Woman" for distribution to his Medmenham cronies.

The Hell-Fire Club does not seem to have had a unified political agenda. Although most of is members were Whigs, the Earl of Sandwich, who became First Lord of the Admiralty, had distinctly Tory inclinations, and John Wilkes eventually became the most notable populist radical since Wat Tyler. Given the club's Rabelaisian motto, however, it is likely that they all shared a common view of humanity's ability to govern itself without an imposed body of law[61].

Dashwood himself was politically an independent, believing that it was more important to vote in accord with his conscience on each issue than to follow a party line. During his long and controversial career, he sat in both houses of Parliament and served as Chancellor of the Exchequer and postmaster general. He devoted much energy to public works projects and to a Poor Relief Bill, and continually advocated the formation of a national militia. This would abolish the need for a standing army and German mercenary troops, implicitly undermining royal power.

Dashwood was drawn into the orbit of Prince Frederick[62], the heir apparent to George II, a Freemason who attracted many Jacobites into his train. Dashwood evidently became a confidant of "Prince Fritz," resulting in a political setback for Dashwood upon the prince's death in 1751.

When "Bonnie Prince Charlie" embarked on his ill-fated attempt to invade England and regain the throne with Franco-Scottish support in 1744, the House of Commons was whipped into a patriotic frenzy. An "Address of Loyalty" to George II was made mandatory; Dashwood proposed an amendment

---

[61] They certainly had no driving need to support the Monarchy's hold over the colonies.
[62] Even the Royal Family was involved in the Masonic world.

which warned the sovereign not to infringe on the liberty of his subjects. He was branded a Jacobite for his efforts.

In 1770, Dashwood and his fellow Mason Benjamin Franklin produced a plan of reconciliation for Britain and her increasingly rebellious colonies in North America. The plan was ignored, with well-known consequences.

Religion

In 1773 Dashwood and Benjamin Franklin revised the Book of Common Prayer - an odd activity for a supposed Satanist. Possibly the two Freemasons were trying to bring the Anglican Church in line with Masonic Deism. In his introduction to this work, Dashwood stressed the usefulness of the church to the community and affirms the teachings of Jesus Christ in such a way that his allegiance to the Church of England is equivocal at best. Most of their changes involve removing all references to the Old Testament and eliminating repetitions wherever possible. This liturgy is still used by some Protestant sects in America.

The whole question of religion is central to the fascination that Dashwood continues to exercise. One could simply accept the popular belief that he was a Satanist and leave it at that. A more sophisticated interpretation might seize upon the rumours of sexual magic, the abbey's kabbalistic book, the recurring image of Harpocrates, Dashwood's tenuous connection with the Masonic Order of the Temple, and of course the Thelemic motto on Medmenham Abbey to conclude that the Hell-Fire Club was an early manifestation of "Crowleyanity." A more sober-minded approach would pick out Dashwood's Masonic contacts and conclude, probably correctly, that the "chapter-room" was a Masonic temple.

It may also be significant that most of Dashwood's Masonic associates were Catholic Jacobites[63]. As a newly arrived peer, Dashwood would have been very conscious of his lack of lineage and might have been attracted to the chivalrous glamour of the Jacobite "Templar[64]" orders. Bearing this in mind, we might pause to reconsider Dashwood's "conversion" in Rome. Wilkes mentions "mock celebrations of the more ridiculous rites ... of the Church of Rome."

Is it possible that Wilkes got it all wrong? Catholics were not allowed to hold public office in England until the end of the eighteenth century. Might what Wilkes took to be a parody of the sacraments, a "Black Mass," have actually been a Roman Mass? Ever since Henry VIII had usurped Rome's spiritual authority over his subjects, Catholicism had been "demonized" in England. The Satanic monk was becoming a stock figure in the increasingly popular "Gothick Romances" of the time. To English eyes, anything "Papist" might seem Satanic.

---

[63] All of whom were opposed to King George and his line retaining the English throne. This would support the notion that they worked for the benefit of the Colonials in their fight for freedom.
[64] The Templar philosophy was very strong in the Jacobite controlled areas.

The Latin Bible, the hagiography, the defaced portrait of Henry VIII, the equivocation in the Book of Common Prayer - is it possible that Sir Francis Dashwood, the notorious Satanist, was in fact a Jacobite Freemason and secret Roman Catholic who worked to undermine the existing order?

Ulterior Motives

So did the Colonists outfight the British, or were the British forces placed in a position to where they had to give up due to being undermined by the actions of their leaders. The loss of the colonies would be a serious blow to King George and might lead to a revolt that would bring back the Stuart Line to the throne. Many of the British political leaders were supporters of the Stuart Cause so this would surely be a justification for "throwing the fight", so to speak.

CHAPTER FOURTEEN
THE QUASI-WAR

There is little mention in the history books regarding the next war in which America found itself engaged. Called the Quasi-War, this period of altercations was actually an undeclared war fought entirely at sea between the United States and France from 1798 to 1800.

The pirates of the Mediterranean Sea caused the U.S. Congress in 1794 to begin building a navy for the protection of commerce. Shortly thereafter, depredations by the privateers of Revolutionary France required the US Navy to protect the expanding merchant shipping of the United States. Naval squadrons sought out and attacked enemy privateers until France agreed to an honorable settlement.

The Quasi-War started on July 7, 1798 when the United States Congress rescinded treaties with France. The Revolutionary leaders responded by urging its naval leaders to exact a vengeance from American shipping for the actions of the American Government. Some of the privateers sent out by the French leaders actually captained former men of war.

The Quasi-War began during the period of the French Revolution which is a very important time in both the history of France and the world. The French Revolution Period specifically covers the years between 1789 and 1799, in which democrats and republicans overthrew the absolute monarchy and the Roman Catholic Church was forced to undergo radical restructuring[65]. While France would oscillate among republic, empire, and monarchy for 75 years after the First Republic fell to a coup by Napoleon Bonaparte, the revolution nonetheless spelled a definitive end to the ancien régime[66], and eclipses both subsequent

---

[65] As outlined elsewhere, the revolution was actually funded by the House of Rothschild and orchestrated by several of the Masonic Orders. At the beheading of the King, a man dipped his finger in the King's blood and said *"Jacques DeMolay, thou art avenged!"*

[66] Ancien Régime means Old Rule or Old Order in French; in English, the term refers primarily to the social and political system established in France under the Valois and Bourbon dynasties. More generally it means any regime which shares the former's

revolutions in France in the popular imagination. It downplays the previous trend of absolutism and people as subjects and amplifies the power of the people, boosting them to the status of citizens.

Captain Thomas Truxtun and the frigate Constellation won two victories over French men-of-war during this war. The American sea power during this period consisted of eight cutters (one sloop, five schooners, and two brigs) that operated along the southern coast of the United States and among the islands of the West Indies. The two brigs and two of the schooners each carried 14 guns and 70 men. The sloop and the other schooners each had ten guns and 34 men.

Of the twenty-two prizes captured by the United States between 1798 and 1799, eighteen were taken by unaided cutters. Revenue cutters also assisted in capturing two others. The cutter Pickering made two cruises to the West Indies and captured ten prizes, one of which carried 44 guns and was manned by some 200 sailors, more than three times Pickering's strength.

History of the Quasi-War

France had been America's major ally in the War of Independence, and without its assistance the United States may not have won independence. But the new government of Revolutionary France viewed a 1794 commercial agreement between the United States and Great Britain, known as Jay's Treaty, as a violation of France's 1778 treaties with the United States. In response, the French increased their seizures of American ships trading with their British enemies and refused to receive a new United States minister when he arrived in Paris in December 1796.

In his annual message to Congress at the close of 1797, President John Adams[67] reported on France's refusal to negotiate and spoke of the need "to place our country in a suitable posture of de- fense."10 In April of 1798 President Adams informed Congress of the infamous "X Y Z Affair," in which French agents demanded a large bribe for the restoration of relations with the United States.

Outraged by this affront to national honor, on 27 April 1798 Congress authorized the President to acquire, arm, and man no more than twelve vessels, of up to twenty-two guns each. Under the terms of this act several vessels were purchased and converted into ships of war. One of these, the Ganges, a Philadelphia-built merchant ship, became "the first man-of- war to fit out and get to sea [24 May 1798] under the second organization of the Navy."

---

defining features: a feudal system under the control of a powerful absolute monarchy supported by the doctrine of the Divine Right of Kings and the explicit consent of the established Church, essentially how Europe had been organized since at least the 8th century. This form of government was the specific target of the Templar revenge.

[67] 1797-1801 John Adams was the second President of the United States. His personal Masonic status is not known, but his Vice President, Thomas Jefferson was a confirmed member of the Illuminati.

In March 1798, overworked Secretary of War James McHenry[68] brought before Congress the problem of his responsibility for naval affairs. Naval administration had become a significant portion of his department's work, as it had for the Department of the Treasury, which oversaw all the Navy's contracting and disbursing. The Department of War also had received congressional criticism for what was seen as the mismanagement and the excessive cost of the naval construction program. In addition, the growing trouble with the French induced Congress to authorize an increase in the size of the navy and raised the possibility that the navy would be called on to confront French privateers.

In response to the obvious need for an executive department responsible solely for, and staffed with persons competent in, naval affairs Congress passed a bill establishing the Department of the Navy. President John Adams signed the historic act on 30 April 1798. Benjamin Stoddert, a Maryland merchant who had served as secretary to the Continental Board of War during the American Revolution, became the first secretary of the navy. One historian writes that Stoddert "was a classic Navalist" who "desired an American navy which could, not only protect commerce, but which would increase American prestige."

On 28 May Congress authorized the public vessels of the United States to capture armed French vessels hovering off the coast of the United States, initiating an undeclared Quasi-War with France. That conflict led to the rapid passage of several pieces of naval legislation. An act of 30 June gave the President authority to accept ships on loan from private citizens, who would be paid in interest-bearing government bonds. On 9 July Congress authorized U.S. naval vessels to capture armed French vessels anywhere on the high seas, not just off the coast of the United States. This act also sanctioned the issuance of privateering commissions. Two days later, the president signed the act that established the United States Marine Corps. On 16 July Congress appropriated funds to build and equip the three remain- ing frigates begun under the Act of 1794: Congress, launched at Portsmouth, N.H., on 15 August 1799; Chesapeake, at Gosport, Va., on 2 December 1799; and President, at New York, N.Y., on 10 April 1800.

Quasi-War with France

Secretary of the Navy Benjamin Stoddert realized that the navy possessed too few warships to protect a far-flung merchant marine by using convoys or by patrolling the North American coast. Rather, he concluded that the best way to defeat the French campaign against American shipping was by offensive operations in the Carribean, where most of the French cruisers were based. Thus at the very outset of the conflict, the Department of the Navy adopted a policy of going to the source of the enemy's strength. Nevertheless, by 1799, in response to the merchant's insistent demands for protection, naval

---

[68] Member of Spiritual Lodge No. 23, Maryland.

vessels were convoying merchant ships in the Caribbean in addition to cruising against the enemy.

When Stoddert became secretary in June 1798, only one American naval vessel was deployed. By the end of the year a force of twenty ships was planned for the Caribbean. Before the war ended, the force available to the navy approached thirty vessels, with some 700 officers and 5,000 seamen.

The highlight of the first year of the undeclared war was the capture by Thomas Truxtun's *Constellation* of the French frigate *l'Insurgente* in February 1799. In addition, American naval vessels seized nineteen French privateers during the winter of 1798-99. The French challenge to American naval forces increased late in 1799 as six French warships arrived in the Antilles with instructions to intensify the commercial war. The American squadrons responded aggressively. Constellation fought to a draw the more powerful *la Vengeance* on 1 February 1800. Silas Talbot engineered an expedition in the Puerto Plata harbor in St. Domingo, a possession of France's ally Spain, on 11 May 1800 in which a naval force under Lieutenant Isaac Hull cut out the French privateer Sandwich from the harbor and spiked the guns in the Spanish fort. By the end of the war American ships had made prizes of approximately eighty-five French vessels. American successes resulted from a combination of Stoddert's administrative skill in deploying effectively his limited forces and the initiative of his seagoing officers.

Although they were fighting the same enemy, the Royal Navy and the United States Navy did not cooperate operationally, nor did they share operational plans or come to mutual understandings about deployment of their forces. The British did sell the American government naval stores and munitions. And the two navies shared a system of signals by which to recognize each other's warships at sea and allowed merchantmen of their respective nations to join their convoys.13

By October 1800, aggressiveness of the cruisers of the United States Navy, as well as those of the Royal Navy, combined with a more conciliatory diplomatic stance by the French toward America, produced a reduction in the activity of the French privateers and warships. In mid-December 1800 news reached Washington that a peace treaty with France (Convention of Mortefontaine, 30 September 1800) ended the Quasi-War.

The war highlighted several weaknesses in the fledgling navy, both in the shore establishment and in the operational forces. Problems arose in procurement, provisioning, manning of ships, delegation of authority, and planning for an extensive campaign. Squadron commanders learned that they required smaller ships to pursue enemy privateerws in shallow waters. Many of the merchantmen converted into men-of-war proved to be poor sailers. During the first year of the war, Stoddert did not fully coordi- nate the rotation of vessels refitting in port with those on stations requiring relief. By restricting the enlistments in the navy to one year, Congress effectively limited the time that ships could remain deployed. The leadership qualities among Stoddert's senior officers varied widely and politics and personal jealousies often stymied his attempts to assign them the the navy's best advantage. One of the navy's senior officers, Captain Isaac Phillips, was dismissed for permitting a British officer to board his ship, USS Baltimore, and press several seamen.

Despite these problems, the newly reestablished United States Navy acquitted itself well during the Quasi-War and succeeded in achieving its limited goal of stopping the depredations of the French corsairs against American commerce. In the war, the navy proved itself an effective instrument of national policy. The United States now had a powerful weapon with which to begin its long journey toward being a world power. Of course, at the time, without the threat to commerce, the American people would never have agreed to the building of a strong navy, believing, as did Washington that such a weapon would eventually be used to embroil American in the wars of Eueope.

The Rise of Bonaparte

One result of the French defeat in the Quasi-War may well have been the rise of Napoleon Bonaparte[69] which set the world stage for America's next war. Bonaparte came to power through what is called the coup of 18 Brumaire or sometimes simply Brumaire. This refers to the coup d'état by which General Napoleon Bonaparte overthrew the government of the Directory to replace it by the Consulate. This occurred on November 9, 1799, which was 18 Brumaire in the year VIII under the French Republican Calendar.

The name, already well established in common use, was reinforced by the title of Karl Marx's The Eighteenth Brumaire of Louis Bonaparte, an account of December 2, 1851 coup by Napoleon's nephew which begins with the much-quoted "*Hegel remarks somewhere that all great world-historic facts and personages appear, so to speak, twice. He forgot to add: the first time as tragedy, the second time as farce.*"

Ironically, the ground for Bonaparte's coup may have been laid more by his few defeats than by his many victories. In November 1799, France was suffering the effects of military reverses brought on by Bonaparte's adventurism in the Middle East. The looming threat of opportunistic invasion by the Second Coalition had provoked internal unrest, with Bonaparte stuck in Egypt.

The coup was first prepared not by Bonaparte, but by the Abbé Sieyès[70], then one of the five Directors, attempting to head off a return to Jacobinism. Dazzled by Bonaparte's victories in the East, the public ignored the impending calamitous ending of the Egyptian expedition, and received Bonaparte with an

---

[69] Napoleon Bonaparte (1769-1821) was initiated into Army Philadelphia Lodge in 1798. His brothers, Joseph, Lucian, Louis and Jerome, were also Freemasons. Five of the six members of Napoleon's Grand Council of the Empire were Freemasons, as were six of the nine Imperial Officers and 22 of the 30 Marshals of France.

[70] A member of the Jesuit Order.

ardor which convinced Sieyès that he had found the general indispensable to his coup.

However, beginning with his return from Egypt in September 1799, Bonaparte began a coup within the coup. Ultimately, the coup brought Bonaparte to power, not Sieyès. Perhaps the gravest potential obstacles to a coup came from the army. Some generals like Jean-Baptiste Jourdan, honestly believed in republicanism; others, like Bernadotte, believed themselves capable of governing France. With perfect subtlety, Bonaparte worked on the feelings of all and kept his own intentions secret.

An army contractor named Collot advanced two million francs to finance the coup. The plan was, through the use of troops conveniently arrayed around Paris, first to persuade the Directors (see French Directory) to resign, then to persuade the two Councils to appoint a pliant commission to draw up a new constitution.

The events of 18 Brumaire in the year VIII

On the morning of 18 Brumaire, members of the Council of Elders sympathetic to the coup warned their colleagues of a Jacobin conspiracy and persuaded them to remove to Saint-Cloud, west of Paris. Bonaparte was charged with the safety of the two Councils. Later that morning Sieyès and Roger-Duclos resigned as Directors; Talleyrand persuaded Barras to do the same. (The presence of troops in the garden outside was no doubt, rather persuasive.)

The resignation of three Directors was sufficient to destroy the quorum, but the two Jacobin Directors, Gohier and Moulin, refused to resign. Moulin escaped; Gohier was taken prisoner. However, the two Councils were not immediately intimidated and continued to meet.

The events of 19 Brumaire

By the following day, the deputies had, for the most part, worked out that they were facing an attempted coup rather than being protected from a Jacobin rebellion. Faced with their recalcitrance, Bonaparte stormed into the chambers accompanied by a small escort of grenadiers. While perhaps unplanned, this proved to be the coup within the coup: from this point, this was a military affair.

Accounts of Bonaparte's confrontation with the councils differ; the following two paragraphs might be improved by resort to more sources. Bonaparte met with heckling as he addressed the Council of Ancients with such "home truths" as, "the Republic has no government" and, most likely, "the Revolution is over." One deputy called out, "And the Constitution?" Bonaparte replied, referring to earlier parliamentary coups, "The Constitution! You yourselves have destroyed it. You violated it on 18 Fructidor; you violated it on 22 Floreal; you violated it on 30 Prairial. It no longer has the respect of anyone."

Bonaparte withdrew to the Orangerie, where the Council of Five Hundred was meeting. His reception here was even more hostile: Napoleon and the grenadiers entered just as the legality of Barras' resignation was being challenged by the Jacobins in the chamber. Upon entering, Napoleon was first jostled and then outright assaulted. Depending on whose account is accepted, he may or may not have come close to fainting. Not Napoleon himself, but his brother Lucien, President of the Council, called upon the grenadiers to defend their leader. Napoleon escaped, but only through the use of military force.

A motion was raised in the Council of Five Hundred to declare Napoleon Bonaparte an outlaw. At this point, Lucien Bonaparte[71] apparently slipped out of the chamber and told the soldiers guarding the parliament that the majority of the Five Hundred were being terrorised by a group of deputies brandishing daggers. Then, according to Michael Rapport, "He pointed to Napoleon's bloody, pallid face as proof. Then, in a theatrical gesture, he seized a sword and promised to plunge it through his own brother's heart if he were a traitor."

Lucien ordered the troops to expel the violent deputies from the chamber. Grenadiers under the command of General Murat[72] marched into the Orangerie and dispersed the Council. This was, effectively the end of the Directory.

The Ancients passed a decree which adjourned the Councils for three months, appointed Bonaparte, Sieyès, and Ducos provisional consuls, and named the Legislative Commission. Some tractable members of the Five Hundred, swept up afterwards, served to give these measures the confirmation of their House. Thus the Directory and the Councils came to an end.

Aftermath

The Directory was crushed, but the coup within the coup was not yet complete. The necessity to use military force had certainly strengthened Bonaparte's hand vis a vis Sieyès and the other plotters. With the Council routed, the plotters convened two commissions, each consisting of twenty-five deputies from the two Councils and essentially intimidated them into declaring a provisional government, the first form of the consulate with Bonaparte, Sieyès, and Roger-Duclos as consuls, and then into drawing up what Malcolm Crook refers to as the "short and obscure Constitution of the Year VIII", the first of the constitutions since the Revolution without a Declaration of Rights.

The lack of reaction from the streets proved that the revolution was, indeed, over. In the words of the 1911 Encyclopædia Britannica, "A shabby compound of brute force and imposture, the 18th Brumaire was nevertheless condoned, nay applauded, by the French nation. Weary of revolution, men sought no more than to be wisely and firmly governed." Resistance by Jacobin officeholders in the provinces was quickly crushed, twenty Jacobin legislators were exiled, and others were arrested.

---

[71] A Mason.
[72] MURAT, JOACHIM (1767-1815): French General and Prince, King of Naples; Senior Grand Warden of Grand Orient of France; subsequently assumed supreme command of both Grand Orient and Supreme Council of Naples. When Napoleon's armies were in Egypt between 1798 and 1800, the general in charge was Marshal Murat.

Bonaparte completed his coup within a coup by the adoption of a constitution under which the First Consul, a position he was sure to hold, had greater power than the other two. In particular, he appointed the Senate and the Senate interpreted the constitution. The Bonapartist Senate allowed him to rule by decree, so the more independent State Council and Tribunate degenerated into the status of window dressing.

Napoléon Bonaparte played many parts in the saga that is the history of France. He was first a general of the French Revolution and then he became the effective ruler of France in 1799. He was then the First Consul (Premier Consul) of the French Republic from November 11, 1799 until May 18. 1804. Finally, he became the Emperor of the French (Empereur des Français) under the name Napoléon I, ruling from May 18, 1804 until April 6, 1814, and again briefly from March 20 to June 22, 1815.

CHAPTER FIFTEEN
THE WAR OF 1812

The next war in which the United States became involved in was the War of 1812. Will the pattern found in Operation Northwoods hold true for this war as well? History says that the War of 1812 was fought because England impressed US sailors off of US ships. However, this is only part of the story.

The War of 1812 is one of the forgotten wars of the United States. The war lasted for over two years, and while it ended much like it started; in stalemate; it was in fact a war that once and for all confirmed American Independence and began what are called wars of expansion. The offensive actions of the United States failed in every attempt to capture Canada, which had long been a prize lusted after by the expansionists. On the other hand, the British army was successfully stopped when it attempted to capture Baltimore and New Orleans. There were a number of American naval victories in which American vessels proved themselves superior to similarly sized British vessels. These victories coming after victories in the Quasi War (an even more forgotten war) launched American naval traditions and began the US's control of the sea.

Banking and the War of 1812

As with all wars, there was a great deal of behind the scenes activity. One of the principle players in the War was the House of Rothschild, the largest, most powerful merchant bank in the world. Rothschild had put into motion the concept of each country creating a central bank, which in turn he could control. The United States had originally created one after the forming of the Federal government, but in 1811, Congress refused to renew the charter of the first Bank of the United States, so the nation was once again free of a central bank. This greatly displeased the international bankers in London and lead directly to a British attempt to recapture her former American colonies.

When Jefferson (1801-09) became President, he opposed the bank as being unconstitutional, and when the 20 year charter came up for renewal in 1811, it was denied. Nathan Rothschild, head of the family bank in England, had recognized America's potential, and made loans to a few states, and in fact became the official European banker for the U.S. Government. Because he supported the Bank of the United States, he threatened: *"Either the application for renewal of the Charter is granted, or the United States will find itself in a most disastrous war."*

When the United States refused to renew the charter, it is said that Rothschild then ordered British troops to "teach these impudent Americans a lesson. Bring them back to Colonial status." This brought on the War of 1812, our second war with England, which facilitated the rechartering of the Bank of the United States. The war raised our national debt from $45 million to $127 million.

Jefferson wrote to James Monroe (who later served as our 5th President, 1817-25) in January, 1815: "The dominion which the banking institutions have obtained over the minds of our citizens ... must be broken, or it will break us." In 1816, Jefferson wrote to John Tyler (who became our 10th President, 1841-45): "If the American people ever allow private banks to control the issuance of their currency, first by inflation, and then by deflation, the banks and the corporations that will grow up around them will deprive the people of all property until their children wake up homeless on the continent their father's conquered ... I believe that banking institutions are more dangerous to our liberties than standing armies ... The issuing power should be taken from the banks and restored to the Government, to whom it properly belongs."

In America, the Federalists continued to press for a central bank. In 1816, the Second Bank of the United States was chartered for twenty years. Thus we had our third central bank

Other Factors

At the same time that the Banking War was playing out in the Boardrooms of the world, the War of 1812 began on June 18, 1812. In this same year, Napoleon invaded Russia and was ultimately forced to retreat. The war continued until December 24, 1814, concluding with the Treaty of Ghent. The United States survived its first major challenge.

The United States declared War on Great Britain on June 12, 1812. The war was declared as a result of long simmering disputes with Great Britian. The central dispute surrounded the impressment of American soldiers by the British. The British had previously attacked the USS Chesapeake and nearly caused a war two year earlier. In addition, disputes continued with Great Britain over the Northwest Territories and the border with Canada. This was a golden opportunity for the Hawks who felt that the United States should annex Canada and the Northwest Territories. The attempts of Great Britain to impose a blockade on France during the Napoleonic Wars were a constant source of conflict with the United States.

The War of 1812 has frequently been mythically portrayed as a stout contest in which outnumbered United States forces fought valiantly against British regulars and their Indian allies, suffered early setbacks, and finally won a gallant victory that validated national institutions and presaged the growth and expansion of the young Republic. This assessment, preached to students over many generations, has taught some of the wrong lessons[73].

In 1812, Congress declared a war that the nation was unprepared to fight, and, in many actions, U.S. forces outnumbered the British enemy but still failed to win decisively. The final outcome was a stalemate that resulted in a negotiated peace for the nearly bankrupt and divided nation. The results of the war also demonstrated that the nation's founders and their successors had seriously miscalculated the efficacy of American military institutions as they had evolved in the years 1783-1812.

The United States went to war in June 1812 because Great Britain had violated U.S. sovereignty in ways that suggested that the new nation was still a colonial entity, subject to imperial whim. By May 1812 a consensus had developed in Congress that suggested there was no alternative to war if national honor were to be maintained. When the Jeffersonian Republicans came to power in 1801, tensions between Great Britain and the United States had gradually increased while diplomatic relations worsened, despite the strenuous efforts of U.S. statesmen to seek a resolution of the differences that separated the two countries.

The issues that divided the United States and Great Britain came into sharper focus after 1805. The Napoleonic wars in Europe had created great opportunities as well as great dangers for the U.S. Republic. Beginning with the Treaty of Paris of 1783, which ended the American Revolution, the overseas trade of U.S. merchants had grown steadily, taking over markets formerly serviced by Great Britain.

After the outbreak of the War of the First Coalition, pitting France against Austria, Prussia, and Sardinia in 1792 and England, Holland, and Spain in 1793, the United States remained neutral and its citizens endeavored to trade with both sides. Exports from the United States had averaged $20 million annually from 1790 to 1792. Thereafter, the trend was sharply upward, reaching $94 million in 1801 and a high of $108 million in 1807. Imports followed the same trend, rising from $23 million in 1790 to $110 million in 1801. After a brief contraction, they surged again to a new high of $138.5 million in 1807.

This situation became increasingly difficult, as both France and England objected to this trade as not being "neutral." U.S. merchant ships were in danger of being halted on the high seas, boarded, inspected, and, if their papers revealed trade with the opposing power, seized and confiscated. From 1803 until the issuance of the British Orders in Council of 1807, the British seized 528 American ships, while France seized 206 from 1803 until France issued the

---

[73] Federalist Opposition To The War Of 1812 Engaged in a War That Was To End In A Stalemate, Did America's Founders Miscalculate Its Military Institutions? By John B. Hoey

Berlin Decree in 1806. In England influential essayists pointed out the folly of allowing the United States to supersede the former mother country in trade with the West Indies and Canada.

At the same time, commanders of British warships patrolling the Atlantic, short of seamen in their own ships, pressed American merchant seamen into service. When boarding a U.S. ship for inspection, British officers frequently demanded a muster of the ship's crew in order to search for deserters. Without doubt, some American merchantmen had signed on British deserters, but the majority of men taken were naturalized U.S. citizens who had been born in the British Isles or colonies. The British, however, did not recognize changes in citizenship. A man born a British subject always owed service and allegiance to the Crown. Thus, a seaman on board an American vessel who could not prove his U.S. origins risked being seized and virtually enslaved on board a British warship for years. Similarly, the British press gangs in English ports were infamous for carrying away to sea any able-bodied men found in their way. This practice, called impressment in the American p opular press, grew to be a detested evil.

In December 1806, with tensions increasing between Great Britain and the United States, President Thomas Jefferson sought grounds for amicable settlement of grievances through a new treaty, negotiated by James Monroe[74] and William Pinkney[75]. Its principal aims were to obtain the end of impressment of U.S. seamen; the restoration of the West Indian trade, which Great Britain had forbidden; and to obtain payments of indemnities for ship seizures made after 1805. When the two diplomats faced British intransigence, however, they yielded on some points and failed to follow their instructions on the issue of

---

[74] James Monroe was initiated on November 9, 1775, in the St. John's Regimental Lodge in the Continental Army. Monroe was not yet eighteen, but "lawful age" had not yet been universally fixed at twenty-one. Later, Brother Monroe took Membership in Williamsburg Lodge No. 6, Williamsburg, Virginia. He was also a member of the Knights Of The Garter. Order of the Garter is the core leader of the Committee of 300.

[75] William Pinkney (March 17, 1764–February 25, 1822) a statemans and the 7th Attorhey General of the United States. He was born in Maryland where he studied medicine (which he did not practice) and law, becoming a lawyer after his admission to the bar in 1786. After some time practicing law in Harford County, Maryland Pinkney served in the Maryland House of Delegates from 1788 to 1792 and then again in 1795, and then served as a U.S. Congressman from Maryland in 1791 and also from 1815 until 1816. He was mayor of Annapolis from 1795 to 1800, as Maryland's state attorney general from 1805 to 1806, and then as co-U.S. Minister to Great Britain with James Monroe from 1806 to 1807 and Minister Plenipotentiary from 1808 until 1811, then returned to the Maryland state legislature, serving in the Maryland Senate in 1811, became the U.S. Minister Plenipotentiary to Russia, along with a special mission to Naples from 1816 until 1818. In 1811 he joined James Madison's cabinet as Attorney General.

He was a major in the U.S. Army during the War of 1812 and was wounded at the Battle of Bladensburg, Maryland in August 1814. He was a U.S. Senator from Maryland from 1819 until his death in 1822. He is buried at the Congressional Cemetery in Washington, D.C..

impressment. When they returned with the treaty in early 1807, Jefferson refused to submit it to the Senate for ratification.

Following this diplomatic fiasco, Jefferson had to cope with the most serious threat to peace since his assumption of the presidency. In 1807, Captain Salusbury Humphreys, commander of the British frigate Leopard, who knew in advance that Commodore James Barron[76]'s flagship Chesapeake carried British deserters among its crew, followed the Chesapeake to sea from Hampton Roads, Virginia, on June 21. The following day, several miles out, Humphreys signaled the Chesapeake to heave to. The British boarding officer demanded that Barron have the crew mustered, which the commodore refused to do, and minutes later the Leopard opened fire on the unprepared U.S. frigate. Barron ordered the colors struck and submitted to the British, who mustered the crew of the Chesapeake and took off four men, claiming them to be British subjects and deserters. Humphreys refused to accept Barron's sword and allowed him to precede back into port, a disgraced man in a wounded and disgraced ship.

This outrageous act incensed the American populace and President Jefferson could have gone to war immediately, but he was content merely to proclaim the British warships unwelcome visitors in U.S. ports. He did not believe the time had come for hostilities and was wedded to the concept of economic warfare.

Jefferson's method of extracting concessions from the British would henceforth be that of withholding trading privileges[77]. Thus, the Embargo Act of 1807 and various nonimportation acts were intended to damage the British economy in the midst of its war against France. The effects, Jefferson hoped, would persuade England that it needed U.S. trade more than it needed impressed seamen or confiscated cargoes, but Jefferson's efforts failed. British officials viewed his attempts at economic coercion as the efforts of a weak nation that did

---

[76] Barron was later court martialed and suspended for five years. Upon his return, he became involved in a duel with Commodore Stephen Decatur and killed Decatur in a duel in 1820. During the Nineteenth Century, Lafayette Square, the location was the duel, picked up the name "Tragedy Square," mainly because strange and often violent deaths occurred there. For example, at 748 Jackson Place N.W. stands the Decatur House. Stephen Decatur, then the youngest captain in the U.S. Navy and a hero of the war with the Barbary pirates, commissioned the famous Masonic architect, Benjamin Henry Latrobe, to design and build the townhouse. The three-story red-brick mansion with its tall windows and distinctive chimneys was completed in 1819. A year later, Commodore Decatur was killed in a duel with another officer, Commodore James Barron. Ever since then, the mansion has been haunted. Just a few doors away, on Lafayette Square, is another of Latrobe's works--St. John's Church, with its Greek portico and (minus the steeple, which was added later--J.T.) its eerie resemblance to the temple of Athena Nike in Greece.

[77] Similar to President Jimmy (Mr. Peanut) Carter withholding our Olympic Team to punish the Russians. Can you just imagine the terrible consequences that the Russian people suffered after we withheld out Olympic Team?

not have the will or the resources to commit to war. In effect, the president had failed to understand the nature of the balance of the power in Europe and the degree to which British policy reacted to French actions, not those of the United States.

The government of Napoleon Bonaparte took advantage of the U.S. situation. The U.S. embargo of British goods placed the United States in the position of being a French ally while not having any of the advantages of such a position. Indeed, Napoleon's restrictive decrees increased the danger of U.S. ships being taken by the French navy and others. Such was his Berlin Decree of November 21, 1806, which placed the British Isles under blockade, forbidding commerce with them and authorizing the confiscation of ships suspected of trading with the British.

Retaliation came in the form of the British Orders in Council of November 1807, forbidding trade with France and its allies. Responding with his Milan Decree on December 17, Napoleon declared that even vessels that were searched by the British or that obeyed the Orders in Council were subject to seizure.

On April 17, 1808, with the Bayonne Decree, Napoleon authorized confiscation of any U.S. ship in European harbors, arguing that he was helping enforce the U.S. embargo act. Despite these offensive measures, President Jefferson took no effective action to oppose the French. He had hoped that France would force Spain to cede the Floridas to the United States in gratitude for his anti-British posture. Fearing Great Britain more than France, Jefferson played the French card but was ultimately to be disappointed.

President James Madison[78] also felt the sting of French duplicity. On May 1, 1810, Congress enacted Macon's Bill No. 2, a law that ended commercial restrictions against the belligerents but also provided a lure. If either France or Britain removed their restrictions on U.S. trade and the other did not, the U.S. government would reimpose its nonimportation policy against the recalcitrant nation.

On hearing that Congress had passed Macon's Bill No. 2, Napoleon ordered his foreign Minister, the Duc de Cadore, to inform U.S. Ambassador John A. Armstrong[79] that France would revoke the Berlin and Milan decrees if the United States would renew nonintercourse against Great Britain. Contrarily, Napoleon also ordered the sequestration of U.S. vessels that had called at France ports in 1809-1810. The Duc de Cadore, however, wrote Madison that the decrees had already been revoked, and the United States halted commerce with Great Britain and opened trade with France. The letter of the Duc de Cadore became well-known as the document that duped Madison and his foreign policy

---

[78] Madison is said to have been a Member of Hiram Lodge No. 59, Westmoreland County, Virginia a Lodge which had only a short existence, and whose records are lost.
[79] A member of the Masonic Order who would shortly become Secretary of War under President Madison.

officials, the second Republican administration to fail in an attempt to play the French against the British.

During almost ten years of attempted economic coercion and failed diplomatic efforts, two U.S. presidents experienced the frustrations and embarrassments that prepared the way for war as the ultimate remedy for the loss of U.S. ships, cargoes, seamen, and wounded national honor. Following the passage of Macon's Bill No. 2 and the Cadore letter episode, an increasing number of Americans felt that war was the only remaining path by which U.S. interests and national honor could be protected. In 1811, Congress finally contemplated preparation for war, while the mood of the American people and their government vacillated between fear and boastful posturing.

The second war with England, which began in June, 1812 and lasted into 1815, was the most unpopular war that the United States ever waged, not even excepting the Vietnam conflict. The war declaration on June 18 passed by a vote of seventy-nine to forty-nine in the House, and nineteen to thirteen in the Senate. Eight out of ten New England senators and eleven out of fourteen New York representatives voted against it, and twenty-five percent of the Republicans in Congress abstained, for there was a strong anti-war faction within President James Madison's own party, led by John Randolph[80] of Roanoke.

Although the South and the West were keen for the war when it began, their enthusiasm soon evaporated, judging from recruitment statistics. The War Department could never build up the regular army to half its authorized strength, and obtained only ten thousand one-year volunteers out of fifty thousand authorized by Congress. Even Henry Clay[81]'s Kentucky furnished only four hundred recruits in 1812. Interestingly enough, the loyal minority in the New England states more than compensated for the discouraging stand of the Federalist state governments; those five states provided the regular army with nineteen regiments as compared to fifteen from the middle states and ten from the southern states. The truth seems to be that Hull's surrender to the British at Detroit had shown that the war would be no walkover. Support for it waned throughout the country, popularity returning after the war had ended.

The Federalists opposed the war for several specific reasons. For one thing, they saw it as a party war designed to further the interests of Republicans and to silence the opposition – a view that was reinforced by the Baltimore Riots

---

[80] John Randolph of Roanoke, (1773-1833): U.S. Senator, Congressman and a Mason. Confirmed by Denlow's 10,000 Famous Freemasons.
[81] Henry Clay ran for President in 1824, but lost. He was a confirmed Mason, being the Grand Master of the Grand Lodge of Kentucky and Grand Orator for the G.L. 1806-09. He was also very good friends to the Illuminati Dupont's. The Dupont's were already one of the primary top families and it was rumored that Clay was coming to them for guidance on how to steer the nation. The Dupont's played a role in the building of the American capital, which was laid out and constructed with numerous occult patterns. Clay also became the leader of the Whig Party.

in 1812 and the refusal of the administration to accept Federalists into the Cabinet in1814. "I regard this war, as a war of party, and not of the country," said Rufus King in 1812. "The people are no more obliged ... to approve and applaud the measure," added the United States' Gazette, "than ... any other party project."

The Federalists also feared that the war would throw the nation into the arms of Napoleon, who was variously described as "the great destroyer," "the little tyrant," the "monster of human depravity," and "the arch-fiend who has long been the curse and scourge of the European World." The initial protests against the war, particularly in New England, often expressed greater fear of a French alliance than of the war itself. "The horrors of war, compared with it, are mere amusement," said Timothy Dwight. "The touch of France is pollution. Her embrace is death." French Dominion, added William Ellery Channing, threatened not just the wealth, but "the minds, character, morals, and the religion of our entire nation."

Even after the danger of a French alliance had receded, Federalists continued to oppose the war because they considered it an "offensive" war aimed at Canada. Although willing to support a war to protect American commerce or to defend the nation's frontiers, they refused to sanction the conquest of Canada. "Let it not be said," Congressman Morris Miller of New York told the Republicans in 1813, "that we refuse you the means of defense. For that we have always been – we still are ready to pen the treasure of the nation. We will give you millions for defense; but not a cent for the conquest of Canada – not the ninety-ninth part of a cent for the extermination of its inhabitants."

Even if the invasion of Canada had succeeded, Federalists were convinced that the war would do more harm than good. "Whether we consider our agriculture, our commerce, our moneyed systems, or our internal safety," declared the Alexandria Gazette, "nothing but disaster can result from it." Nor did the Federalists expect the nation to win any concessions from the enemy, certainly not on an issue as vital as impressment. They believed it to be of a temporary nature that would be terminated when the tyrant Napoleon was defeated. "No war of any duration," said James A. Bayard of Delaware, the Federalist minority leader in Congress, "will ever extort this concession."

An important but sometimes overlooked aspect of Federalist opposition to the war is that the party did have a legitimate fear for the future of the nation, at least in the social context. The Federalist antiwar clergy stressed that the war was an outward expression of God's displeasure and a corrupting influence on the citizenry that made them less virtuous and posed a serious danger to the constitutional balance of the republic. Armies were irreligious repositories of depravity that transformed law-abiding citizens into savages who corrupted communities with disruptive, sinful practices. War disrupted commerce and farming, forced burdensome taxation, created idleness and unemployment, extended bureaucracy, and encouraged smuggling. Federalist politicians argued for limited, peaceful dissent tempered with prudence and channeled through committees of correspondence and public meetings. Federalist war opposition was grounded in a reverence for the Constitution and an adherence to traditional Republican values.

In sum, Federalists saw the war as a costly, futile, and partisan venture that was likely to produce little good and much evil. The best way to bring the conflict to an end, most Federalists agreed, was to oppose it. Hence they wrote, spoke, and preached against the war; they discouraged enlistments in the army and subscriptions to the war loans. The Federalists vigorously condemned all who supported the war and worked for their defeat at the polls.

Traditionally, Americans had dealt with crises by calling a convention. The Albany Congress (1754), the Stamp Act Congress (1765), the First Continental Congress (1774), and the Constitutional Convention (1787) were all convened to deal with crises. In New England there was recurring talk of calling a convention: First in 1808-1809, when the long embargo brought trade to a halt; then in the summer of 1812, when the declaration of war threatened to drive America into an alliance with France; and finally in 1814, after a new embargo had been imposed.

Fear and frustration showed plainly in the results of the elections of 1814. The Federalists gained large majorities in both state and national offices, and the party leadership interpreted its success as a mandate for action against "Mr. Madison's War." The activities of Governor Caleb Strong of Massachusetts demonstrated how extreme such action might become. In November, 1814, Strong offered thinly veiled hints of a separate peace and an alliance to General Sir John Sherbrooke, the British Governor of Nova Scotia. Strong's overtures to the enemy came to nothing, but they served as an index of the desperation which infected Strong's section and his party.

This same mood of desperation moved Strong to call the Massachusetts General Court, or legislature, into special session in October, 1814. It responded to the crisis by calling for a convention of delegates from the New England states to meet at Hartford, Connecticut, on December 15. According to Harrison Gray Otis, the acknowledged author of the convention plan, the delegates were to discuss ways and means of sectional defense and to take steps to revise the United States Constitution to accord with sectional interests.

Three of the five New England States heeded Massachusetts' call. The legislatures of Connecticut and Rhode Island joined the Bay state in selecting delegations. Vermont and New Hampshire took no official action, but delegates chosen by local and county conventions in those states attended the Hartford sessions. Twenty-six men took part in the convention, and for the most part they were of a moderate temper. Extremists, such as Jack Lowell and Timothy Pickering, took no part in the proceedings and privately bewailed the convention's lack of "bold and ardent men." Well aware that a firm but fine line separated political opposition from treason in wartime, the Hartford delegates sought to play a positive, not negative, role.

The Hartford Convention, when assembled and organized, conducted most of its business in committees. George Cabot, the leader of the

Massachusetts delegation who had explained that one of his objectives was to prevent "hot-heads from getting into mischief," was probably instrumental in stacking the committees with moderate men. Otis was apparently the guiding spirit of the committees and the author of the report adopted by the convention on January 3, 1815.

Otis' report, the product of the Hartford Convention, began by stating the mission of the convention, which was to provide for concerted sectional defense and to propose repairs to the Constitution. The report then discussed at length the circumstances which gave rise to the convention. It focused upon the disaffection of extremists, and although it opposed radical solutions, such as dissolving the Union, it plainly implied that the Union was in peril. In effect it contained a mild ultimatum to the Madison administration to listen to the convention and its moderate solutions or be prepared to face the radicals and disunion. There followed a cataloging of the sins of Republican administrations past and present.

Finally, the convention offered its solution in the form of a series of seven amendments to the Constitution providing that: (1) the "three-fifths compromise," which allowed states to count a portion of their chattel population in determining proportionate representation in Congress and the Electoral College, be abolished; (2) a two-thirds vote of both houses of Congress be required to admit new states into the Union; (3) no embargo be imposed for more than sixty days; (4) a two-thirds vote of both Houses of Congress be required to adopt declarations of war; (5) a two-thirds vote of both Houses of Congress be required to adopt declarations of commercial nonintercourse acts; (6) naturalized citizens by ineligible for federal office, elective or appointive; (7) no President might succeed himself, nor should successive Presidents be from the same state.

The work of the convention reflected a mixture of sectional complaints and political rancor. Its enemies accused the assembly of treason; yet its temper was moderate. Although the convention addressed itself to some legitimate sectional grievances, it lapsed into the rhetoric of narrow partisanship. Perhaps no man came closer to the truth than John Adams, who described the Hartford delegates as "intelligent and honest men who had lost touch with reality."

The supreme irony was that even while the convention debated, American arms won a great victory at New Orleans, and the British and Americans made peace at Ghent. By the time representatives carrying the report of the Hartford Convention arrived in Washington, the country knew that peace had come. Such circumstances blunted New England sectionalism, and the Federalist Party seemed treasonous, ludicrous, or both. Its demise was imminent.

To be sure, the meeting at Hartford put an end to the already waning national fortunes of the Federalist Party while giving legitimacy to the notion of nullification which would haunt the nation later. Yet the Hartford Convention preserved the centrist course of New England Federalism. Indeed, as the most notable instance since the Second Continental Congress of men organizing to satisfy, direct, and control an aroused populace, it was a monument to the growth of electoral democracy.

But more than this, the Hartford Convention was another of the continuing attempts to define the meaning of the American experiment in a hostile and unstable world and to hold the nation to the standards under which it began. Men may debate how these standards are to be met, and the Convention may not have represented all that was best in the New England tradition. Yet the Federalists of New England were trying to raise, sincerely and anxiously, some enduring questions – some of them for the first time in the young republic's history – about the conduct of government and the quality of society, both in and out of war. As such their concerns have never lost their timeliness. The Federalists of the Hartford Convention were, if nothing else, steadfast in their republican faith.

That faith, however, could have many consequences and take many forms. It was the dark legacy of the Hartford Convention not only to taint ineradicably the Federalist Party with disloyalty and irrelevance, from which it died in 1820, but also to provide precedent and philosophy for future acts of defiance toward policies of the national government. South Carolina's efforts to nullify the collection of federal tariff duties in 1832 echoed the themes of regional interest and reserved constitutional rights laid down in 1814. More fatefully, those same principles of nullification remained alive in the South throughout the 1840s and 1850s, finally gaining enough acceptance by 1860 to justify the South's secession because of Abraham Lincoln's determination to prevent the further extension of black slavery in the United States. Thus it was that, in a small Connecticut town forty-six years before, were planted some of the seeds of the resort to arms that ensued, of the bloodiest war in the nation's history, of the emancipation of the slaves, and of the survival of the American union.

So between the desire to expand national borders and the machinations to create a central bank funded by the Rothschild interests, a number of influential people saw a chance to make a lot of money I the event of a war. I think that there is no question that in the War of 1812, the United States was not an innocent bystander.

It is also interesting to note that Napoleon, a Mason, took control of France from the Revolutionary Party, many members of which were also Masons, and those who aided him in ascending the throne were all members of the Masonic Order. The Napoleonic Wars saw the beginning of the end for the British Empire, a further oppression of certain parties in France and the rising of the star of the United States. These were all goals that would have fit in nicely with the desires of the Templars.

Once again, the American people did not want to get involved in the wars of Europe, but the actions of the English, brought about in response to actions of Napoleon left the United States no choice by to go to war.

CHAPTER SIXTEEN
THE MEXICAN WAR

The war between Mexico and the United States grew out of unresolved conflicts between Mexico and Texas. After having won its independence from Mexico in 1836, the Republic of Texas was annexed by the United States in 1845; however, the southern and western borders of Texas remained disputed during the Republic's lifetime. That same year tensions between the two countries over territory were raised when the United States government offered to pay off the Mexican debt to American settlers if Mexico allowed the U.S. to purchase the territories of Alta California and Nuevo México from Mexico.

Declaration of war

The U.S. government claimed that the southern border of Texas was the Rio Grande; Mexico maintained it to be the Nueces River. President James K. Polk[82] ordered General Zachary Taylor[83] to place troops in the contested region between the two rivers. Taylor crossed the Nueces, ignoring Mexican demands that he withdraw, and marched south to the Rio Grande where he began to build Fort Brown. Fighting began on April 24, 1846 when Mexican cavalry captured one of the American detachments near the Rio Grande.

After the border clash and battles at Palo Alto and Resaca de la Palma, Polk requested a declaration of war, announcing to Congress that the Mexicans had "invaded our territory and shed American blood upon American soil". The U.S. Congress declared war on May 13, 1846. Northerners and Whigs generally

---

[82] 1845-1849 James K. Polk, 11th. President of the United States was a confirmed Mason. (The New Age Magazine, January 1953, pg. 44) H was Initiated on June 5, 1820, Columbia Lodge No. 31, Columbia, Tennessee. Brother Polk assisted in the Cornerstone Laying of the Smithsonian Institution, Washington, D.C., May 1, 1847. Governor of Tennessee 1839-1841.

[83] 1849-1850 Zachary Taylor, 12th. President of the United States (Whig) was a confirmed Mason. Also a member of the Knights Of The Garter. Order of the Garter is the core leader of the Committee Of 300.

opposed the war while Southerners and Democrats tended to support it. Mexico declared war on May 23. It is clear that Mexico declared war because it felt that it had been invaded.

Combatants

During the course of the war, around 13,000 American soldiers were killed. Of these deaths, only about 1.5% (~195) was from actual combat; the rest stemmed from disease and unsanitary conditions during the war. It is also estimated that, if post-war deaths from war-related causes are counted, the combined U.S. casualty rate for the war was very high, 30-40%. Mexican casualties remain somewhat of a mystery, and are estimated at 25,000.

A noteworthy, if controversially–remembered, group of fighters was Saint Patrick's Battalion (San Patricios), a group of several hundred immigrant soldiers (mostly from Ireland) who deserted the U.S. Army in favor of the Mexican side. According to one version of events, the Battalion deserted after having experienced harsh religious discrimination in the United States military, and found common cause with Mexico due to its status as a largely Catholic country. Most would die in the conflict. Some were captured and hanged, reputedly by generals instructed to make sure that the last thing they saw was the lowering of the Mexican flag and the raising of the U.S. flag. Some historians claim that these men were actually prisoners of war and forced to fight for Mexico. Others argue that they were simply traitors and deserters. There are, in any event, a number of monuments to these soldiers in present-day Mexico.

According to data from the United States Department of Veterans Affairs, the last surviving US veteran of the conflict, Owen Thomas Edgar, died on September 3, 1929 at the age of 98.

Political implications of the war

Mexico lost much of its territory in the war, leaving it with a lasting bitterness towards the United States. Santa Anna fled to exile in Venezuela. General Porfirio Díaz, President of Mexico from 1877–1911, would later lament: "¡Pobre México! Tan lejos de Dios, y tan cerca de los Estados Unidos." ("*Poor Mexico! So far from God, and so close to the United States.*")

In the United States, victory in the war brought a surge in patriotism as the acquisition of new western lands – the country had also acquired the southern half of the Oregon Country in 1846 – seemed to fulfill citizens' belief in their country's Manifest Destiny. While Ralph Waldo Emerson rejected war "as a means of achieving America's destiny," he accepted that "most of the great results of history are brought about by discreditable means." The war made a national hero of Zachary Taylor, a Southern Whig, who was elected president in the election of 1848.

However, this period of national euphoria would not last long. The war had been widely supported in the southern states but largely opposed in the northern states. This division largely developed from expectations of how the expansion of the United States would affect the issue of slavery. At the time, Texas recognized the institution of slavery, but Mexico did not. Many Northern abolitionists viewed the war as an attempt by the slave-owners to expand slavery and assure their continued influence in the federal government. Henry David Thoreau wrote his essay *Civil Disobedience* and refused to pay taxes because of this war.

The main issue which furthered sectionalism was the expansion of slavery into the national territories. The Missouri Compromise of 1820 banned slavery in national territories north of 36 degrees, 30 minutes (roughly the southern border of Missouri, although that state had been exempted). Also, the Senate was constructed to give equal balance to slave and free states. The Missouri Compromise, however, left room for more free states than slave states and, if continued, would upset the balance of power within the Senate. Thus, many Southerners supported the war to provide more room for slavery to expand (believing that if slavery were not allowed to continue to expand, it would ultimately die out). There were proposals during this time to split Texas (which was easily the largest state in the Union geographically) into multiple slave states, but this did not come to pass.

During the first year of the war, Congressman David Wilmot introduced a bill which would prohibit slavery in any new territory captured from Mexico. This bill, which became known as the Wilmot Proviso caused an immediate outcry from Southerners on both sides of the congressional aisle. To Southerners, it looked as if the north was willing to abandon parity within the senate, and the Wilmot Proviso sparked further hostility between the sections. The bill itself was passed by the House of Representatives but failed in the Senate, with both votes on sectional lines.

In 1848 Democrats proposed a new solution to the issue of whether territories should have slavery, known as popular sovereignty. This would allow for voters within a territory to determine for themselves whether or not they would allow slavery within their territory. The Kansas-Nebraska Act of 1854 would make popular sovereignty the law of the land, striking down the Missouri Compromise. In protest of this, the Republican Party was organized that year by opponents of the expansion of slavery.

Ulysses S. Grant, who served in the war under Taylor's command, would later consider the war with Mexico to be one of the causes of the American Civil War: "The occupation, separation and annexation of Texas were ... a conspiracy to acquire territory out of which slave states might be formed for the American Union." Many of the generals of the latter war had fought in the former, including Grant, Ambrose Burnside, Stonewall Jackson and Robert E. Lee.

CHAPTER SEVENTEEN
THE AMERICAN CIVIL WAR

History teaches us that the American Civil War was fought in order to free the slaves that worked the cotton fields of the South. Many people like to wax eloquently about the courge of Abraham Lincoln in freeing the slaves, but truthfully, the freeing of the slaves of simply a by product of the overall Civil War. The true causes of the American Civil War were many and varied. The South felt that it was not getting fair treatment from he industrialized North and many of the leadership in the South felt that it was time to dissolve the Union. Those in the North were totally opposed to allowing states to withdraw,

The ironic thing about this particular argument that member states could withdraw form the Union was that the basis for it was raised by the Northern States during the War of 1812. The Hartford Convention, established by George Cabot and other nothern leaders was the first step toward confirming the legality of dissolving the ties that bound the states together.

As outlined earlier, the Otis' Report, which was a product of the Hartford Convention, began by stating the mission of the convention, which was to provide for concerted sectional defense and to propose repairs to the Constitution. The report then discussed at length the circumstances which gave rise to the convention. It focused upon the disaffection of extremists, and although it opposed radical solutions, *such as dissolving the Union*, it plainly implied that the Union was in peril. In effect it contained a mild ultimatum to the Madison administration to listen to the convention and its moderate solutions or be prepared to face the radicals and disunion. There followed a cataloging of the sins of Republican administrations past and present.

Finally, the convention offered its solution in the form of a series of seven amendments to the Constitution providing that: (1) the "three-fifths compromise," which allowed states to count a portion of their chattel population in determining proportionate representation in Congress and the Electoral College, be abolished; (2) a two-thirds vote of both houses of Congress be required to admit new states into the Union; (3) no embargo be imposed for more than sixty days; (4) a two-thirds vote of both Houses of Congress be required to adopt declarations of war; (5) a two-thirds vote of both Houses of Congress be required to adopt declarations of commercial nonintercourse acts; (6) naturalized citizens by ineligible for federal office, elective or appointive; (7) no President might succeed himself, nor should successive Presidents be from the same state.

The work of the convention reflected a mixture of sectional complaints and political rancor. Its enemies accused the assembly of treason; yet its temper was moderate. Although the convention addressed itself to some legitimate sectional grievances, it lapsed into the rhetoric of narrow partisanship. Perhaps no man came closer to the truth than John Adams, who described the Hartford delegates as "intelligent and honest men who had lost touch with reality."

To be sure, the meeting at Hartford put an end to the already waning national fortunes of the Federalist Party while giving legitimacy to the notion of nullification which would haunt the nation later. Yet the Hartford Convention preserved the centrist course of New England Federalism. Indeed, as the most notable instance since the Second Continental Congress of men organizing to satisfy, direct, and control an aroused populace, it was a monument to the growth of electoral democracy.

But more than this, the Hartford Convention was another of the continuing attempts to define the meaning of the American experiment in a hostile and unstable world and to hold the nation to the standards under which it began. Men may debate how these standards are to be met, and the Convention may not have represented all that was best in the New England tradition. Yet the Federalists of New England were trying to raise, sincerely and anxiously, some enduring questions – some of them for the first time in the young republic's history – about the conduct of government and the quality of society, both in and out of war. As such their concerns have never lost their timeliness. The Federalists of the Hartford Convention were, if nothing else, steadfast in their republican faith.

To the Common Man

When the armies for the North and South were first formed, only a small minority of the soldiers on either side would have declared that the reason they joined the army was to fight either "for" or "against" slavery. Northern soliders generally came to defend the Union while the Southern soldiers were fighting to protect their freedom to choose their form of government.

It has long been said that "*Had there been no slavery, there would have been no war. Had there been no moral condemnation of slavery, there would have been no war*[84]." However, this attempts to simplify a complex situation and dress it up in the highest moral garments. Such is both improper and ignorant. While it is true that Lincoln made a point to free the slaves with the

---

[84] This statement was made by Sydney E. Ahlstrome, in his monumental study of religion in America *A Religious History of the American People*, Yale University Press, 1972, on p. 649.

Emancipation Proclamation, this was simply an attempt to strike a blow at an already teetering economy in the South. He had no driving moral imperative to free the slaves.

Background

The curious thing is that although slavery was the public moral issue of the nineteenth century that divided the political leaders of the land, the average American had very little interest in slaves or slavery. Most Southerners were small farmers that could not afford slaves. Most Northerners were small farmers or tradesmen that had never even seen a slave.

But political leaders on both sides were very interested in slaves and slavery. The South's economic system was based upon cotton--and the slaves that worked the fields. The political leaders of the South, such as Robert Barnwell Rhett of South Carolina, William Lowndes Yancey of Alabama, The Fire-Eatersand Robert Augustus Toombs of Georgia, recognized that if the South lost her slaves (i. e., had to pay slaves wages similar to what white laborers were paid), her entire socio-economic system would probably collapse. Hence any political action that took place that threatened the slavery system in use in the South received the undivided attention of the South's political leaders, many of whom were slave owners[85]. It was clear to everyone that the plight of the northern worker was little better than that of the slaves of the South, but at least the northern worker could brag that he was "free."

Political leaders in the North were much more divided about the slavery issue. Many of the powerful abolitionists, such as William L. Garrison of Massachusetts, were either religious leaders or newspaper editors. They were great at making thunderous speeches, but rather short on the follow through. A fewer number of abolitionsits, such as Senator Edwin Sumner of Massachusetts and Salmon P. Chase of Ohio, were politicians. The north had equally powerful political leaders such as democratic Senator Stephen A. Douglas who were either indifferent towards or supportive of slavery.

Today we recognize slavery as a moral issue. But in the early nineteenth century, it was seen as an economic issue first, moral issue second. A series of legislative actions, most notably the Missouri Compromise of 1820, had been enacted by Congress to put limits on the propagation of slavery, but compromise with northern and southern interests was always kept in mind. The South had an economic interest in the spread of slavery to the new territories so that new slave states could be created and the South's political influence would remain strong. The North had an interest in limiting the spread of slavery into the new territories for both purposes of controlling Southern political power AND support of the moral issue.

---

[85] Itshould be clearly noted that the leaders on both side were guilty of the severest form of conflict of interest.

Up until the middle 1800s, slavery was kept as a background issue that remained largely the concern of political leaders of the South, and abolitionists of the North. But in 1854, the Kansas-Nebraska Act, sponsored by Democrat Stephen A. Douglas, brought slavery to the forefront of national attention. Kansas-Nebraska eliminated the old Missouri Compromise (which in 1820 had designated areas of the new territories in which slavery could and could not be introduced) and made it possible for slavery to be introduced in virtually any new territory. Douglas called the concept of allowing residents of the territories to decide the slavery issue for themselves Popular Sovereignty. Kansas-Nebraska caused a firestorm to errupt in the North, awakening many people to the danger of the potential spread of slavery. Moderate politicians such as Abraham Lincoln became active in the cause of fighting both the Kansas-Nebraska Act and the spread of slavery.

Conclusion

Although the majority of the American people-- including many moderate politicians like Abraham Lincoln--wanted to avoid Civil War and were content to allow slavery to die a slow, inevitable death, the most influential political leaders of the day were not. On the southern side, "fire-eaters" like Rhett and Yancey were willing to make war to guarantee their "right" to own slaves. On the northern side, abolitionists like John Brown[86] and Henry Ward Beecher[87] of Connecticut were willing to make war in order to put an immediate end to the degrading institution of slavery.

These leaders, through either words or action, were able to convince the majority that it was necessary to go to war, and in order to convince them they

---

[86] It can be said of Brown that he was willing to put his money where his mouth war. He led a revolt to free the slaves that failed. Howsever, he was funded by many of the religious leaders of the day who felt that a rebellion was worthwhile in order to free the slaves.

[87] Henry Ward Beecher, the eighth son of the Rev. Lyman Beecher, was born in Litchfield, Connecticut, on 24th June, 1813. The brother of Harriet Beecher Stowe, he was educated at the Lane Theological Seminary before becoming a Presbyterian minister in Lawrenceburg (1837-39) and Indianapolis (1839-47). His pamphlet, Seven Lectures to Young Men, was published in 1844.

Beecher moved to Plymouth Church, Brooklyn in 1847. By this time he had developed a national reputation for his oratorical skills, and drew crowds of 2,500 regularly every Sunday. He strongly opposed slavery and favoured temperance and woman's suffrage.

Beecher condemned the passing of the Kansas-Nebraska bill from his pulpit and helped to raise funds to supply weapons to those willing to oppose slavery in these territories. These rifles became known as Beecher's Bibles. John Brown and five of his sons, were some of the volunteers who headed for Kansas.

He supported the Free Soil Party in 1852 but switched to the Republican Party in 1860. During the Civil War Beecher's church raised and equipped a volunteer regiment. However, after the war, he advocated reconciliation.

justified the war with arguments that only indirectly referred to the subject of slavery.

Southern politicians convinced their majority that the North was threatening their way of life and their culture. Northern politicians convinced their majority that the South, if allowed to secede, was really striking a serious blow at democratic government. In these arguments, both southern and northern politicians were speaking the truth--but not "the whole truth." They knew that to declare the war to be a fight over slavery would cause a lot of the potential soldiers of both sides to refuse to fight.

So-was the war about slavery? Only from the standpoint that the southern politicians would have been much less likely to seek "their right to secede" had the idea of freeing the slaves not been damaging to their pocketbooks. But was it only about slavery? No. It was also about the constitutional argument over whether or not a state had a right to leave the Union, and--of primary concern to most southern soldiers--the continuation of antebellum southern culture.

Other Influences

The division of the United States into two federations of equal force was decided long before the Civil War by the High Financial Power of Europe. These bankers were afraid that the United States, if they remained in one block and as one nation, would attain economical and financial independence, which would upset their financial domination over the world. The voice of the Rothschild family predominated. They foresaw tremendous booty if they could substitute two feeble democracies, indebted to the same group of financiers that had funded the French Revolution and the Russian Revolution, to the vigorous republic, confident and self-providing. Therefore, they started their emissaries in order to exploit the question of slavery and thus to dig an abyss between the two parts of the republic. Lincoln never suspected these underground machinations. He was anti-slavery, and he was elected on this platform. However, he was more concerned with preserving the Union that he was in freeing the slaves. But his character prevented him from being the man of one party. When he had the affairs of government firmly in his hands, he perceived that these sinister financiers of Europe, the Rothschilds, wished to make him the executor of their designs.

Through the maneuverings of their agents, such as Albert Pike, a Masonic Leader and a Confederate General, the Merchant Bankers of Europe made the rupture between the North and the South imminent and impossible to avoid! The masters of finance in Europe made this rupture definitive in order to exploit it to the utmost. However, Lincoln's personality surprised them: they thought to easily dupe the candidate woodcutter. But Lincoln read their plots and soon understood that the South was not the worst foe, but rather the banking powers were far more dangerous. He did not confide his apprehensions; he watched the gestures of the Hidden Hand; he did not wish to expose publicly the questions which disconcert the ignorant masses.

It had been expected that both Lincoln and Davis would borrow the money needed to conduct the war from the European Banking powers. Instead, Lincoln decided to eliminate the international bankers, by establishing a system of loans, allowing the states to borrow directly from the people without intermediary. He did not study financial questions, but his robust good sense revealed to him that the source of any wealth resides in the work and economy of the nation. He opposed emissions through the international financiers. He obtained from the Congress the right to borrow from the people by selling to it the bonds of the states. The local banks were only too glad to help such a system. And the government and the nation escaped the plots of foreign financiers.

However, no one opposes the banking powers and for their part, the Bankers understood at once that if Lincoln continued his programs, then the United States would escape their grip. The death of Lincoln was resolved upon. Nothing is easier than to find a fanatic to strike and there was one that was tailor made for them. It is interesting to note that there was actually some borrowing from Europe by both sides. Financing for Union and Confederacy came from the same European banking network. August Schonberg "Belmont" was the intermediary to the North, and Judah Benjamin represented the South. As far as the Bankers were concerned, the last straw was when Lincoln greatly upset the Eastern Establishment bankers by issuing non-interest-bearing "Greenback" currency, when the interest rates they demanded became prohibitive.

It should also be interesting to note that the French thought to profit by America's preoccupation with the Civil War by invading Mexico. There were rumors that French forces would reinforce the Southern Armies by coming into the US from Mexico. There was also the distinct possibility that the British Government would recognize the Southern Confederacy and, if requested, furnish military assistance. Either possibility would be more than the Union wold be able to handle. The Czar of Russia sent two fleets, each ferrying a full army, one to New York and one the San Ffrancisco. At that time, the Russian Army was a force to be feared. The Czar told both England and France that if either actually took part in the American Civil War, that Russia would invade[88].

So the stage was set for trouble as the election of 1860 approached. The South was facing economic ruin if Lincoln was elected. Though the Republican part was strong enough to elect Lincoln over his more moderate opponent Stephen Douglas, not even every Northern leader supported Lincoln. The Free City of Tri-Insula was a proposed independent republic that would be formed out of the islands of Manhattan, Staten Island, and Long Island immediately prior to

---

[88] It is also interesting to note that Lincoln had promised the Russians that he would reimburse them for any expenses. The cost was $64,000000.00. After Lincoln's death, Congress reneged on the promise to reimburse the Czar. So the United States purchased Alaska for the sum of $64,000,000.00.

the United States Civil War. The idea was raised in early 1861 by New York City Mayor Fernando Wood, who opposed the impending war between theUnited States and the Confederate States of AmericaConfederate States of America. According to him, war would adversely affect the New York economy because of the loss of cotton revenues. The idea was rejected by the City Council and popular opinion.

Before Abraham Lincoln was inaugurated, delegates from seven southern states met together and established themselves as the Confederate States of America. They thought that his election doomed slavery in the United States, that the new Congress elected with Lincoln would begin action to end slavery. The seven states took this step to preserve the southern way of life. They elected Jefferson Davis as their president. He had been active for years in efforts to create new slave states to swing the balance. His efforts focused on the west, to bring slavery to the west coast and south into New Mexico and into Mexico itself. Now all of that might be lost unless they formed this new nation.

When Lincoln took office, he found to his dismay that seven states had already withdrawn from the Union. This presented him with an immediate but expected challenge. Fort Sumter, occupied by a unit of the Union Army, was located in the harbor at Charleston, South Carolina. Many felt that the Union presence in Charleston Harbor represented a blight against the Confederacy that could not be endured. Shortly after the establishment of the Confederacy, Fort Sumpter was fired upon and eventually fell to Southern forces.

Immediately the nation was at war with itself, and the President began to take action. The United States Congress was not yet meeting, so there was no chance to debate the issue. Lincoln moved forward at war with the secessionists in order to preserve the Union, to keep them in the Union. He took action and made decisions which the Congress would have to act upon when they met in three months. His decisive actions were solely to preserve the Union and not to abolish slavery. The slavery question was one for the new Congress. Furthermore there were slave states that had not seceded. There was no need to offend them.

The Confederacy took steps to be recognized as a new nation fighting for its independence. Lincoln established a blockade to prevent the shipment of cotton and the importation of products which could be used in the Confederate war effort. The Union had few ships in its navy and the Confederacy had none, consequently the blockade was partially effective. Its effectiveness was enhanced by the fact that foreign governments and their merchant fleets were very afraid of the possibility of American privateers. Privateers (licensed pirates) were merchant ships which were armed and licensed by the government. Investors would then set out to seize and hold merchant ships attempting to trade with the South, taking their cargo as spoils. Privateers had been licensed by the United States during the War of 1812, and devastated the British merchant fleet, while greatly enriching the United States and those investors who armed merchant ships for war as privateers. The British chose not to face this threat again.

After several months of the War Between the States the economy of the South deteriorated extensively, but so did that of the British. No cotton imports from the southern states meant there would be nothing to run in Britain's fabric mills. The mills were going bankrupt. New England mills were similarly affected. As a consequence, the British Cabinet began to call for the recognition of the Confederate States of America. This would put the Union at war with the British, if they continued the blockade or began to license privateers. Europe was beginning to view the American Civil War as a clear bid for freedom by a new nation. There was growing support for this fledgling government. Abraham Lincoln well understood the dangers of British recognition. He needed another issue integrated into the war. He chose slavery and wrote up a document called "The Emancipation Proclamation". If he issued this, the British would then be in the position of supporting slavery, a stance they could not possibly hold.

Lincoln discussed his carefully wrought Proclamation with his former opponent and Secretary of State, William H. Seward. Seward had run against Lincoln in a bitter struggle. Lincoln appointed him Secretary of State because of the skills and abilities Seward possessed. Seward served well and loyally, and the two men became intimate friends. Seward examined the Proclamation with great care and agreed with its rightness and its desperately needed effect on England. However, he pointed out that since the Union had lost several battles, the Proclamation could be construed as a last desperate effort on the part of a government with a lost cause. He urged the President to sit on the document and wait for a significant Union victory. That event occurred on 17 September 1862 at the horribly bloody Battle of Antietam (just two months after the discovery of gold at Bannack). In this battle there was both a significant Union victory and the end of the invasion of Pennsylvania by General Robert E. Lee. But more important, this victory permitted the issuing of the Emancipation Proclamation. This effectively ended the possibility that Britain could recognize the Confederacy as a new nation struggling for its freedom. The British Cabinet could not possibly come out on the side of slavery. The slavery issue was therefore not a moral issue to be trumpeted from the rooftops, but rather a political cause that could be used to sway supporters to or from the issue. It is only since the War that the slavery issue has been cloaked in the finery of a moral imperative.

The War Between the States was now a completely different war. Internationally it was no longer the struggle of a new nation to gain its freedom from an oppressor but a war against slavery. The national impact of the Emancipation Proclamation was even stronger. Powerful disaffection had been brewing in the North over the seemingly unendurable cost of the war, Union Army losses and the difficulty of defining a cause (other than punishing the errant states for seceding) for the bloody and expensive war. This resulted in some attrition in Lincoln's congressional support in the elections of 1862. What the President now needed was the extensive energy and stamina that had been shown by the Abolitionists before the war broke out. The Emancipation

Proclamation stimulated those voices. The war now had a moral cause for the actions of the Union. Not surprisingly, the population was increasingly moved by this cause. Now the war which had been fought only to preserve the Union against secession became a war to end slavery.

To understand the political brilliance of Lincoln's actions it is important to realize that the Emancipation Proclamation freed **ONLY** the slaves of the Confederate States of America and specifically did not free the slaves in those slave states which remained with the Union. In wartime, Lincoln had such powers against the secessionist states, while he did not have such powers over the slave states which remained with the Union. Slavery would be decided by the Congress and not by presidential proclamation. In order to hold their affiliation with the Union, the slave states of Kentucky, Missouri, Maryland and the non-secessionist areas of Tennessee and Virginia were exempt from the Proclamation.

The British were critical, because, they thought, Lincoln had freed the slaves where he had no power and retained slavery where he had power, while in fact, he had no power to free any of the slaves in the United States, however, his wartime powers enabled him to establish the Emancipation Proclamation in the separated states. In spite of this blight on the moral issues, the Proclamation gave a new enthusiasm in the North for fighting the lagging war. Enlistments increased.

Virginia City: Strategic Thorn in the Flesh

Since history is always written by the winnders, much has been written and said about Abe Lincoln's actions to establish freedom for the oppressed, but little has been written about some of the underhanded methods that were used to do it. From President Lincoln's perspective as Commander in Chief, by the dawn of the year 1863 he had held off any British help for the Confederacy (in spite of their languishing fabric mills) and had integrated Union sentiments behind the Union cause in this bloody and inhuman struggle. Now his focus was on the Mississippi and its waterway and population. Beyond that were several states and territories which needed to be held within Union control, especially Idaho with its immense supply of gold, which, he was told, was already occupied by a population loyal to the Confederacy.

A territory, of course, was not in the Union, but rather it was a federally owned political unit. It could not secede since it was not part of the Union, but the population could cause problems. A few Confederate units aimlessly roamed west of the Mississippi, and others were located in the southwest. There were almost no armed forces of either side in the remote and valuable northern regions, with the exception of whatever Confederate interests secretly diverted Montana gold to the South and the contingents of fifty or so troops who escorted the Northern emigannts to the gold fields. However, the solid loyalty of the population to the South was a problem for the North because of the threat to the Union gold supply.

The secessionist population certainly was a problem for the Union administrators. The population was already personally secessionist and very rebellious about it, but they had little taste for the war "back in the States". But the war had definite a taste for them. That war and the entire Union cause depended to a very large extent upon the gold that flowed east from Virginia City. The Confederates had the same need.

Others, in the name of liberty of course, saw a chance to get rich and get revenge upon their enemies. One such opportunist, Captain James Liberty Fisk presented an opportunity for the Union to import emigrants to control the unruly Rebels. Fisk stimulated Union interest in the gold fields by bringing two beautiful gold nuggets from Alder Gulch to President Lincoln. He had been the leader of a troop of Union soldiers who protected a group of emigrants through Indian Territory to the gold fields, which were at that time mostly on the western (Idaho) slopes of the Rockies. They arrived in Fort Benton on the eastern slopes of Idaho Territory in September 1862 and then the party split between the western and eastern slopes. A major part of the wagon train consisted of Republican professionals and merchants who were exempt from conscription because they had employed substitute or otherwise bought themselves out of battle[89]. Their arrival in Idaho Territory began to make a notable difference in the management of the disruptive miners and rebellious secessionists.

The Congress acted to set aside a significant sum for the War Department specifically to protect emigrants who wished to go from St. Paul to Virginia City. Captain Fisk was now regarded as part of the war effort as he brought northern Republicans into Virginia City to assure that the immense flow of gold was for the Union and not the Confederacy. Through the efforts of these men the Territory of Idaho (later to become the Territories of Idaho and Montana) was subdued in its lawlessness and in its most rebellious expressions of its continued secessionist sentiments, although those secessionist sentiments were later expressed in the ballot boxes.

The Civil War that was fought in Montana was a vital part of the whole war effort, however, very little had ever been written about it. It is well known that a main reason for the defeat of the Confederacy was its lack of resources. It certainly had the finest of officers, especially generals. The blockade of the Confederate States by the Union was only partially effective, a trickly of imports still arrived in the South. If the truth be told, it was the soft slave-based agricultural economy of the South and the general lack of manufacturing capacity and skill contributed greatly to the defeat of the South. However, the most powerful force in the demise of the Confederate military capacity was the lack of liquid wealth. In reference to the Confederate currency, it was facetiously said that small purchases had to be made with bales of the stuff. Arms and war materiel were almost impossible to purchase without some form of recognized

---

[89] As in almost every war, those who did not serve were the most patriotic and war mongering.

fluid money. Factories could not be built without dependable cash, which meant gold. In the North the greenback had some value abroad, but for both sides the availability of silver and gold was universally essential for the war economies.

Attempts were made to ship precious metals from Virginia City, Nevada, to the Confederacy. They were usually thwarted through the efforts of greedy middlemen or Union spies. Evidently Union interference was also effective in preventing the movement of significant amounts of gold from Idaho and Montana to Confederate causes. This was a central war concern of Abraham Lincoln, his Cabinet and the United States Congress. It was because of the tremendous liquid wealth being mined in the Montana gold fields and because Montana was, in fact, a Confederate settlement within Union territory during the entire Civil War, that a plan to hold these resources for the Union cause was essential.

Consider the facts, as closely as they can be estimated. Using N.P. Langford's 1864 estimates, which are as reliable as any, Montana was eighty percent avowed, vociferous and active secessionists. They were mining over six hundred thousand dollars worth of gold each week in Virginia City alone. To understand the quantity of "liquid assets" that means, expressed in today's gold prices and conservatively defined, the miners were extracting eighteen million dollars in gold from the ground every week.

You can look at it from another point of view, to get a more accurate estimate of what Montaña meant to Lincoln's government while thousands of his troops were dying for the Union Cause. Three hundred dollars was a basic annual wage for a working man at the time, while, again conservatively, fifteen thousand is the equivalent today. That means that the miners were extracting in laborers' salary the equivalent of thirty million dollars from the ground each week. On an annual basis, that's over six billion dollars worth of gold or one billion dollars in cash (today's equivalent) for the year. That is why Montaña was a keystone in Old Abe's fortress and war machine. It was absolutely necessary to keep this huge source of liquid assets away from the Confederacy and available to the Union. This would be a bit of a trick, considering the overwhelming dominance of Confederate sympathizers. All effort would be made to assure that the flow of liquid assets would continue east to support Washington's war effort[90], with no leaks to assist the South. This also meant that, as far as the Northern leaders were concerned, no significant wealth would be left to enrich Montaña, a debilitating process which continues to this day.

Action in Montana

The Civil War was actively being fought in Montaña. It was being fought in several different ways, each leaving its own footprints behind. The geographical struggle was bloodless and complicated. Bannock, Montaña was founded as Bannock, Dakota Territory. The government of the Territory was too

---

[90] And line a few Republican pockets.

far away to be able to manage these rowdy intruders from the California gold rush who had been digging gold on the western slopes of the Rocky Mountains in the Territory of Washington until richer diggings were found on the Eastern slopes of the Rockies in Dakota Territory. A large population center began to grow on both sides of the Rockies, at first on the western slopes. In response to the new need for control of the wealth and the people in these areas, a large slice of eastern Washington Territory was united with a similar piece of western Dakota Territory to form Idaho Territory in the spring of 1863. Idaho Territory consisted of what is today the State of Idaho together with the states of Wyoming and Montaña.

The new Territory, created in 1863, was administered from what is now Lewiston, Idaho, near where most of the population could be found. Thus Bannock, which had been Bannock, Dakota Territory, now became Bannock, Idaho Territory. And that was a problem. Not three hundred miles away in Washington Territory there was another Bannock. That meant that there were two Bannocks in Idaho Territory. Consequently, to distinguish between the two cities, they were briefly known as "East Bannock" and "West Bannock". Then Bannock, Montaña changed its name to Bannack, Idaho Territory. Some time later, Bannock, Idaho Territory, changed its name too. Today Bannock is known as Idaho City, Idaho. For the citizens, these geographical shifts were confusing. In county records for Bannack, Montaña, properties located near each other are recorded on 4 April 1863 in Idaho Territory, and the next deed dated 5 April 1863 is recorded as located in Dakota Territory.

Wallace Street, Virginia City

Representatives to the new government of Idaho Territory found that the trip to the capitol in Lewiston was almost impossible. They had to push through deep snow in the mountain passes to get to the western slopes. At just about the same time that the new Territory of Idaho was created with its administration on the western slopes, the population started to move across the Rockies to the eastern slopes and thus further out of the control of the Union government whose possession it was. The governing organization could not possibly control the unruly Rebels on the other side of the mountains. On 21 January, after being satisfied that five bodies swung from a rafter on Wallace Street in Virginia City as part of the Union effort to control this Rebel area, Sidney Edgerton, whom Lincoln had appointed Chief Justice of Idaho Territory, hurried back to Washington carrying a large display of gold for the President and Congress which would dramatize the importance of Montaña to the war effort and to stimulate the creation of another new territory to consist of the eastern regions of Idaho Territory. Did I say "hurried"? In mid winter he mushed off on snow shoes, or perhaps on a horse, headed to the stagecoach in Salt Lake City four hundred miles away. On 26 May, 1864, the Territory of Montaña was signed into being. There was no opposition to the establishment of the new Territory or to appropriation of the money for Fisk to deliver the emigrants. After all, this was war.

The Commanding Officers in Montana

Sidney Edgerton, who was Abraham Lincoln's "commanding officer", arrived in Bannack in a small wagon train from Omaha on 17 September, 1863. Edgerton was one of the founding members of the Republican Party. He had been appointed Chief Justice of Idaho Territory, with the mission of staying on the richer gold bearing eastern side of the Rocky Mountains to control the necessary flow of precious metal for the Union. He was accompanied by his family and a nephew, Wilbur Fisk Sanders, a capable lawyer whom one might call Edgerton's "aide de camp". His most able field officer was Captain James Liberty Fisk, who commanded a unit of the Union Army whose mission was to transport emigrants from St. Paul to the gold fields. These emigrants were Northern sympathizers who would either mine the gold or subdue the overwhelming number of strong and vociferous secessionists in the area. Edgerton's "Unit Commander" in charge of identifying and hunting down the victims to be lynched was Sergeant James Williams.

In the spring of 1863, when Idaho was made a territory from Dakota and Washington Territories, Lincoln appointed W. W. Wallace (for whom Wallace Street in Virginia City, Idaho, was named) as governor of Idaho Territory, and Sidney Edgerton Chief Justice. The strategy was to have Edgerton govern the increasingly strategic eastern slopes of the Rockies (now Montana). In the few months after Edgerton's arrival he observed the rapid increase in population and productivity on the eastern slopes, especially in Virginia City. He experienced the dangerous hold the secessionists had on the area, and the impossibility of governing the area from Lewiston across the often impassable Rocky Mountains over on the western slopes. Consequently he set out almost immediately for Washington, D.C. (which the local secessionists insisted was now in Rebel hands) to create once again a new territory. He took with him on his long, cold ordeal, a considerable show of gold with which to dramatize the necessity of a new territory and the importance of his personal "command" for the war effort. As a result of his efforts the proposal was quickly acted upon and Montaña Territory was born with Sidney Edgerton appointed Governor by his friend, Abraham Lincoln.

That this strategy was clearly planned ahead by Edgerton and Lincoln as a vital part of the war effort is made clear by the opposition to the plan. There was none. Even the "luxury" of Captain Fisk's mission, to escort emigrants from the north to the gold fields at government expense while Congress was trying to find money to fight a very expensive war was not opposed. The money bill specifically for Fisk's mission appears in the records next to another money bill to fund troops for Kentucky to hold off Confederate threats. There is not one word of opposition to either of these appropriations because they were known to be part of the Union strategy for conduct of the Civil War raging around them.

Montaña Territory was born as part of Abraham Lincoln's strategy to win the War Between the States. But Edgerton soon discovered that this was just one of the beginnings of the battle. Another had begun as he left Montaña on snow shoes to set aside a new territory.

Lawlessness usually brings to mind images of rebellious people doing illegal, violent or hurtful things to other citizens. The very hard and frightening life on the frontier certainly commended violent actions on every quarter. The Civil War, raging "back in the States" nurtured cruelty as a way of life, as has already been described in the Sand Creek, Colorado, massacre of friendly Indians by Union forces. This was an action of inhuman proportions carried out by officers and men of the United States Army. The men of Bannock had their own little Sand Creek. On 19 January 1863 two men, Charley Moore and Charley Reeves, went up a hill just a few yards out of Bannock looking for an escaped squaw. They commenced firing their revolvers into the wikiups of a small band of friendly Bannock Indians who lived there. They killed a man and a boy and wounded another. They went away and reloaded and then returned and killed and wounded a few more. They were convicted and sentenced to permanent banishment, but Reeves was back within a month. Violence to cover fear was a characteristic of the time and place.

A Culture of Violence

Even the "good" side of life was violent. In Virginia City, school teachers were hired on the basis that they could beat up the large boy bullies in the classroom. Hangings became spectacles that "good" mothers took their children to, in order to show them what would happen if children were "bad". Indian chiefs were beheaded and their heads stuck on stakes. Bodies were dug up by Vigilantes and their skulls taken and used in various ways. Bullets were used for emphasis, killing whom they would. Strangling was used rather than hanging because the horror of watching someone die slowly, struggling to stop the pain, was more terrorizing than the broken neck of a quick hanging. It also pleased the emotions of vengeful or frightened hangmen such as X. Beidler. Violence was deeply ingrained in the life of the gold camp, and most citizens were not concerned about who might be the victim as long as it wasn't them.

This was the culture of Virginia City; into this setting, poured individuals who had other relationships with violence. There was a large number of wanted criminals (like Boone Helm), many of whom had been violent in a much less violent society, and who enjoyed the opportunity to express a level of violence which exceeded the "norm" in societies outside the gold camp. Along with them were a considerable number of deserters and recovering or invalid soldiers. They had often been involved in a level of violence which made violence in Virginia City look like a Sunday School picnic. They had watched their friends killed in the midst of a nightmare of violence and many had participated in battlefield rapes and plundering as they made their way through "enemy" territory as the Union forces did as they ravaged the Carolinas because (they believed) this is where the horrid war started. Killing and abuse of every kind was an incidental coincident to all aspects of life. In addition to this was the specter of the ongoing war back in the States, which everyone wanted to forget but everyone had strong feelings about.

In mid September 1862, less than two months after the quiet discovery of gold on Grasshopper Creek, which led to the establishment of Bannock, the bloodiest battle of the Civil War was taking place at Sharpsburg, Maryland on Antietam Creek. There, so many miles away, Confederate General Robert E. Lee met head on the Union Army of the Potomac. In a very short while twenty six thousand Americans lay dead, dying or wounded on the battlefield. Some who could move piled other corpses around them to protect them from further fire. Bodies were mutilated beyond recognition by the actions of war. Arms, legs, heads and exploded torsos were strewn in bloody messes. The moans and cries of the wounded filled the air. Bayonets, bullets and hammers were used to quiet the wounded so they would not be so annoying. Then, in another two months, a future governor of Montana, General Thomas Francis Meagher, led his Irish Brigade into devastating Confederate fire at Fredericksburg, Virginia. His soldiers marched over bodies of their comrades and approached within a few feet of their enemies' stone wall before the few Federal survivors were turned back.

Violence in the forms of killing and abuse were common to the day. The miners were used to it, while most of the early day carpet baggers and reconstructionists had been exempt from the violence. The secessionist majority would often let their anger out. They would hoist a Rebel flag and dare anyone to interfere. They were angered by the consistent Union side expressed publicly by newspapers, and they delighted in their stories (which everyone believed) of Union defeats, the sacking of Washington and the capture of President Lincoln. Feelings always ran high and erupted in violence. Then they were just as quickly avoided to permit the violence to subside.

The free hand of the merchants to charge exorbitant prices for food and supplies added to the resentments. In 1865 the merchants raised the price of flour from $27 to $150 per hundred pounds. An orderly armed invasion of homes and businesses stopped this abuse. The constant flow of gold from the hard working miners to the merchants, the gamblers, the banker, the barkeep, the killer, the robber and the whore kept a high level of resentment running at all times. The anger and resentment hovered, just waiting for an act of extreme violence such as a beating, shooting a Chinaman's back or a lynching through which to relieve their unmanly fear by expressing anger and resentment.

Law for a Lawless Land

Then add to that the difficulty of establishing a structure of law in the unstructured Territories. In the first days of the existence of Bannock, a charter and legal structure were created by the miners and merchants (lawyers being specifically excluded). This was one of several attempts to establish some semblance of law and safety in the midst of lawlessness, violence and danger. A more serious problem with "law and order" was the simple fact that from time to time the United States Congress (involved in fighting a war) simply neglected to enact laws for the territories they were creating. There were times when there simply was no law in Idaho and Montana Territories. That means that while a specific act of violence might be a terrible thing to do from the perspective of some personal moral standard, you would have a perfect right to murder anyone you chose. It means that anyone had the freedom to do anyone else any harm they chose, take away possessions or burn your house down.

Of course it made little difference because violence and abuse was rampant even when it was against the law. If you abused a woman (other than a wife or daughter) you would be soundly thrashed by the miners, but that was whether there was a law or not. The occasional lack of law simply added to the lax attitude toward behavior, the constant expression of violence and the general danger to everyone, especially families. Violence was a part of everyday life in Bannack and Virginia City. Shootings occurred regularly, and often the only ones hit were innocent bystanders. Montaña was not a safe place to bring your family. And Edgerton found that Montaña was an impossible place to govern. When the secessionists came to vote they selected people who would not possibly go along with Edgerton's Union loyalties and made laws that the United States Congress would then nullify. Edgerton and his associates had another tactic, which he had seen in effective operation by the time he set out for Washington on snow shoes and a horse to separate out Montaña as a territory.

Paris Pfouts, Nick Wall, Wilbur F. Sanders, Alvin V. Brookie and John Nye held a secret meeting and determined to form a Vigilance Committee modeled on those in California during the '49 gold rush. They agreed to another meeting the next night, each man bringing another of known trustworthiness. All swore to secrecy. After three or four such meetings the Committee grew to about fifty members. By ten days the organization had extended to over a thousand members from an extensive area of the mining country. Paris Pfouts, with a naive complete faith in his Masonic associates, was elected Chief and immediately caused to be written up an obligation to which each man had to swear and remain silent on pain of death. He selected an Executive Committee which then conducted investigations of wrong doing and began to sentence men to death and then strangle them. Their first actions were not entirely popular. Pfouts and other members were individually threatened. They continued to create enemies for themselves until the terror of more lynchings gave the Vigilantes the power to simply order such critics, and the lawyers who defended them, out of town.

Union Soldier Graffito written secretly

The composition of the Vigilance Committee was almost entirely Republican Masons from the North. Their victims were almost entirely Democrat secessionists who were non-Masons from the South. Paris Pfouts is a good example of "exception". He was an outspoken secessionist and a Democrat, but part of the Union strategy. His belief in his Executive Committee as honest fellow Masons permitted them to do as they wished while keeping Pfouts in the dark. Paris Pfouts the secessionist presided over one of Abraham Lincoln's most important war efforts that of preserving the vital flow of gold for the Union cause. For example, when Deputy Sheriff Jack Gallagher was brought before Pfouts to be sentenced to death, Pfouts assumed that a trial had been held and that he was found guilty. In fact, there was not a shred of evidence against this good man, who had personally offended a Vigilante, and he was not even on "the list" of people to be hit. Gallagher was strangled and struggled in agony there on Wallace Street that fateful day because Paris Pfouts was reliably naive. Edgerton could rely on this process as a tool with which to govern his unruly Territory.

Sidney Edgerton had initiated a strategy of terror before his epic journey to Washington. He had at hand his naive Chief of the Vigilance Committee, Paris Pfouts. He had an able strong arm in the person of X. Beidler, whose cruelty could be relied upon to avoid breaking the necks of the victims but to see to it that the strangulation was slow and agonizing. He had an ambitious field leader, Sergeant James Williams, who pursued those whom the Vigilance Committee or he himself labeled "Villains". Then, in addition to horribly painful lynchings, the Vigilance Committee created the myth that the problem the area was having was the result of a "secret society of road agents". They used secret signs and the password, "I'm Innocent". They spied out gold shipments and then passed the word to the agents out of town who would rob the stage, wagon or traveler. Since Henry Plummer, with personal conflicts with some Vigilantes, was a Democrat and spoke with a strange accent (Maine), he and his deputies were easily included, with Plummer having the honor to be named the secret leader. The Vigilantes represented the whole series of lynchings as necessary punishment for robbers and murderers bound into a dangerous secret society. The result was a wave of terror among all. Everyone feared they might be accused. This strategy resulted in the great movement of support for the Vigilante activities that followed.

Swift Terror

Accusation was as good as conviction. The citizenry was moved as a frightened mob and supported the lynchings[91]. The lynchings were carried out with a cruelty that appears to have been designed to promote dread and terror. With few exceptions, the hangings were all strangulations. The last desperate behaviors of the victims included one who wrapped his legs around a nearby post. He thus kept himself alive for about ten excruciating minutes of torture and pain. Another choked out, "You're choking me" and desperately clutched at the rope. Still another, whose toes touched the floor, did a desperate tap dance to try to relieve the agony of his torturous death. Others struggled and suffered and died in the usual eight minutes of excruciating pain. These scenes added to the

---

[91] The general public, when manipulated into believing that death can come at any moment will sanction events that would be thought reprehensible at any other time.

terrorism of secrecy imposed by the Vigilantes in order to control the populace. The torture also pleased and relieved the vengeful and frightened emotions of such men as X. Beidler.

The victims were absolutely not who the Vigilantes said they were. A variety of individuals were involved in the Vigilance Committee for several different purposes. Their motivations were personal enmity and vengeance, political adversity, racism, elimination of a danger to the community and punishment for robbery or murder. Some were political enemies of the "solid citizens", the Republican merchants, bankers and lawyers. One was the wrong victim. Boone Helm, an escaped murderer from the East, one of the five victims who were strangled in the hangman's building in January, 1864, cried out, "Hooray for Jeff Davis" and leapt off his box to his death. That was hardly the exit line of a road agent. Another victim was a popular rowdy who couldn't behave. The deputy, Jack Gallagher, was not on the "list" of bad men, and there was absolutely no evidence against him. However, some, like Helm, were actually robbers and murderers in other locations.

One thing is clear. There was not an organized secret society of road agents controlled by the sheriff. That myth was created and, together with the terror of the secrecy of the Vigilance Committee and the agony of strangulation, the myth effectively worked to galvanize the citizens in support of the series of lynchings. It was an effective way to fight the Civil War in Montana Territory.

The terrorism worked. Overall the effect was striking. A new degree of safety prevailed. The secessionist cause was very quiet and the Territory with its remarkable and vital flow of gold was secure for Abraham Lincoln. The result was the absolute and terrorizing control of the community by a secret, arbitrary and autocratic government, the Vigilantes. Outsiders who recognized this were able to speak out against the Vigilantes, who ruled the land. When the votes were counted, though, the Democrats and secessionists always won, often by more than the number of registered voters. Ironically, the Democratic candidate for mayor was none other than Paris Pfouts, and he easily became the town's first mayor. His own person characterizes the work of the Vigilantes. Although it was Northerners killing Southerners and Republicans killing Democrats for the most part, Paris Pfouts was a southern Democrat and a secessionist, and he was the Chief and founder of the Vigilantes. Thanks to his naiveté he believed the veracity of the completed convictions when the condemned were brought to him by his fellow Masons. He was deceived and used by them. The five victims strangled in the Hangman's Building were all presented to Pfouts as "tried and convicted", while in fact there were no trials and no evidence against at least one victim. Pfouts then ordered their "execution". He could not know whether there was any evidence against the victims. Several Vigilante actions were, as Langford himself stated, worse than anything the victims were accused of.

Viewing these actions in the context of being a strategy in a vital battle of the Civil War, the terror and tortures of the Vigilante lynchings in Montana were a picnic. Just place it for a moment alongside battlefields strewn with decaying putrid bodies, wounded crying out for water and being bayoneted so that they would not have to be tended as prisoners, or even dying Indian women being raped by soldiers of the United States Army. Seen in context, the strategy concluded successfully by Sidney Edgerton in Virginia City, Montana Territory, on behalf of the Union cause was as humane as any in this inhuman struggle called the "Civil War".

Epilogue

Over time, the Vigilantes themselves became worried about what they had done and how they had done it. They had murdered and lynched many people without trial or authority. They knew that under some circumstances they could be convicted of murder, while at other times there had been no law. They took steps to prevent that possibility. They had Thomas Dimsdale write his famous book describing how it was that they had to execute these members of the secret criminal gang. The Plummer Myth was at the core of the book and was as carefully documented as any lie could be.

In Defense of the Vigilantes

Then they met together for another purpose. They formed the Montana Historical Society. This would permit them to have some continued control over what evidence would be saved for posterity.

But the secessionists had their day. The South won the war in Montana and continued to express that victory for many years, often at their own great cost. Citizens of Virginia City celebrated the assassination of President Lincoln. Paris Pfouts, the Mayor of Virginia City, reluctantly led a town memorial for the assassinated President.

The secesh had the vote. The Republican Party ruled through the appointed officers of Montana Territory, but all over Montana the Rebels enjoyed their ability to disrupt Sidney Edgerton's government. They outnumbered and outvoted him on all kinds of issues. They could turn out six hundred Democratic votes in towns of one hundred. They didn't need to flaunt their ability to flood the ballot boxes, they had the plurality anyway, but they loved being able to do it. Rather than honor the "will of the people" the Republican minority found numbers of ways to take control. This angered the citizens and simply led to more violence.

Paris Pfouts, mayor of Virginia City, left town as he came to realize that his fellow Masons had deceived him in his role as "Chief" of the Vigilantes. Sidney Edgerton left Montana Territory in frustration as the secessionists opposed his every move. Montanans took the Territorial Legislature into ridiculous directions (such as disenfranchising Negroes, Chinese and Indians and granting legislator salary increases for which there was no money). These were later nullified by the United States Congress and then still later reenacted by Territorial legislatures. Over all, the Rebel victory in Montana disrupted many of

Montana's possibilities and, through Republican spite, led to the postponement of statehood for several years.

In 1916, the Daughters of the Army of the Confederacy erected a beautiful stone fountain in the Women's Park, directly across from the Civic Center in Helena Montana. This is the furthest north monument to the Confederate Army. With this, the Civil War in Montana came to an end. As an important battle in the Civil War, the Vigilante action was a relatively painless victory for the Union, a success, it can be argued, that won the war for them.

Secret Socieities

As might be expected, a number of secret societies took part in the build up to the civil war. One of these was the Knights of the Golden Circle, a secret order of Southern sympathizers in the North during the Civil War. Its members were known as Copperheads[92].

Dr. George W. L. Bickley, a Virginian who had moved to Ohio, organized the first "castle," or local branch, in Cincinnati in 1854 and soon took the order to the South, where it was enthusiastically received. Its principal object was to provide a force to colonize the northern part of Mexico and thus extend proslavery interests, and the Knights became especially active in Texas. The Knights of the Golden Circle was a secret antebellum organization that sought to establish a slave empire encompassing the southern United States, the West Indies, Mexico, and part of Central America, an area some 2,400 miles in diameter-hence the name Golden Circle. The Knights hoped to control the commerce of the area and have a virtual monopoly on the world's supply of tobacco, sugar, and perhaps rice and coffee. Secession and the outbreak of the Civil War prompted a shift in its aims from filibustering in Mexico to support of the new Southern government. Appealing to the South's friends in the North, particularly in areas that were suffering economic dislocation, the order soon spread to Kentucky, Indiana, Ohio, Illinois, and Missouri.

In the spring of 1860 the group made the first of two attempts to invade Mexico from Texas. A small band reached the Rio Grande, but Bickley failed to show up with a large force he claimed he was assembling in New Orleans, and the campaign dissolved. In April some KGC members in New Orleans, disgusted by Bickley's inept leadership, met and expelled him, but Bickley called a convention in Raleigh, North Carolina, in May and succeeded in having himself

---

[92] In the American Civil War, the term Copperhead was a reproachful term for those Northerners sympathetic to the South, mostly Democrats outspoken in their opposition to the Lincoln administration. They were especially strong in Illinois, Indiana, and Ohio, where Clement L. Vallandigham was their leader. The Knights of the Golden Circle were a Copperhead secret society. The term was often applied indiscriminately to all Democrats who opposed the administration. It afforded an opportunity for impugning the loyalty of those who opposed Lincoln's policies, either military or civil (e.g., the suspension of habeas corpus), and it was not until years after the Civil War that the Democratic party succeeded in living down the association.

reinstated. He attempted to mount a second expedition to Mexico later in the year, but with Abraham Lincoln's election he and most of his supporters turned their attentions to the secessionist movement. Bickley served for a time as a Confederate surgeon and was arrested for spying in Indiana in July 1863. He was never tried but remained under arrest until October 1865 and died, broken and dispirited, in August 1867[93].

Its membership in these states, where it became strongest, was largely composed of Peace Democrats, who felt that the Civil War was a mistake and that the increasing power of the federal government was leading toward tyranny. They did not, however, at this time engage in any treasonable activity. In late 1863 the Knights of the Golden Circle was reorganized as the Order of American Knights and again, early in 1864, as the Order of the Sons of Liberty, with Clement L. Vallandigham, most prominent of the Copperheads, as its supreme commander. Only a minority of its membership was radical enough, in some localities, to discourage enlistments, resist the draft, and shield deserters. Numerous peace meetings were held. A few extreme agitators, some of them encouraged by Southern money, talked of a revolt in the Old Northwest, which, if brought about, would end the war. Southern newspapers wishfully reported stories of widespread disaffection, and John Hunt Morgan's raid (1863) into Kentucky, Indiana, and Ohio was undertaken in the expectation that the disaffected element would rally to his standard. Gov. Oliver P. Morton of Indiana and Gen. Henry B. Carrington effectively curbed the Sons of Liberty in that state in the fall of 1864. With mounting Union victories late in 1864, the order's agitation for a negotiated peace lost appeal, and it soon dissolved.

The Rothschild Influence

Evidence shows that in addition to the home grown secret societies, there were also a number of European based organizations pulling strings and agitating for the War. It would also be extraordinarily naive to even consider the possibility that a family as ambitious, as cunning and as monopolistically minded as the Rothschilds could resist the temptation of becoming heavily involved on the American front. Following their economic conquest of Europe early in the 1800s, the Rothschilds cast their covetous eyes on the most precious gem of them all -- the United States.

America was unique in modern history. It was only the second nation in history that had ever been formed with the Bible as its law book. Its uniquely magnificent Constitution was specifically designed to limit the power of government and to keep its citizens free and prosperous. Its citizens were basically industrious immigrants who 'yearned to breath free' and who asked nothing more than to be given the opportunity to live and work in such a wonderfully stimulating environment. The results -- the 'fruit' -- of such a unique experiment were so indescribably brilliant that America became a legend around

---

[93] http://www.tsha.utexas.edu/handbook/online/articles/KK/vbk1_print.html

the globe. Many millions across the far flung continents of the world viewed America the Beautiful as the Promised Land.

The Big Bankers in Europe -- the Rothschilds and their cohorts -- viewed the wonderful results borne by this unique experiment from an entirely different perspective; they looked upon it as a major threat to their future plans.

The establishment Times of London stated: *"If that mischievous financial policy which had its origin in the North American Republic [i.e. honest Constitutionally authorized no debt money] should become indurated down to a fixture, then that government will furnish its own money without cost. It will pay off its debts and be without a debt [to the international bankers]. It will become prosperous beyond precedent in the history of the civilized governments of the world. The brains and wealth of all countries will go to North America. That government must be destroyed or it will destroy every monarchy on the globe."*

The Rothschilds and their friends sent in their financial termites to destroy America because it was becoming "prosperous beyond precedent." The first documentable evidence of Rothschild involvement in the financial affairs of the United States came in the late 1820s and early 1830s when the family, through their agent Nicholas Biddie, fought to defeat Andrew Jackson's move to curtail the international bankers. The Rothschilds lost the first round, when in 1832 President Jackson vetoed the move to renew the charter of the 'Bank of the United States' (a central bank controlled by the international bankers). In 1836 the bank went out of business.

The Plan

In the years following Independence, a close business relationship had developed between the cotton growing aristocracy in the South and the cotton manufacturers in England. The European bankers decided that this business connection was America's Achilles Heel, the door through which the young American Republic could be successfully attacked and overcome.

The Illustrated University History, 1878, p. 504, tells us that the southern states swarmed with British agents. These conspired with local politicians to work against the best interests of the United States. Their carefully sown and nurtured propaganda developed into open rebellion and resulted in the secession of South Carolina on December 29, 1860. Within weeks another six states joined the conspiracy against the Union, and broke away to form the Confederate States of America, with Jefferson Davis as President.

The plotters raided armies, seized forts, arsenals, mints and other Union property. Even members of President Buchanan's Cabinet conspired to destroy the Union by damaging the public credit and working to bankrupt the nation. Buchanan claimed to deplore secession but took no steps to check it, even when a U.S. ship was fired upon by South Carolina shore batteries.

Shortly thereafter Abraham Lincoln became President, being inaugurated on March 4, 1861. Lincoln immediately ordered a blockade on Southern ports, to cut off supplies that were pouring in from Europe. The 'official' date for the start of the Civil War is given as April 12, 1861, when Fort Sumter in South Carolina was bombarded by the Confederates, but it obviously began at a much earlier date.

In December, 1861, large numbers of European Troops (British, French and Spanish) poured into Mexico in defiance of the Monroe Doctrine. This, together with widespread European aid to the Confederacy strongly indicated that the Crown was preparing to enter the war on the side of the Confedderacy. The outlook for the North, and the future of the Union, was bleak indeed.

The Russian Connection

In this hour of extreme crisis, Lincoln appealed to the Crown's perennial enemy, Russia, for assistance. When the envelope containing Lincoln's urgent appeal was given to Czar Alexander II, he weighed it unopened in his hand and stated: "Before we open this paper or know its contents, we grant any request it may contain."

Unannounced, a Russian fleet under Admiral Liviski, steamed into New York harbor on September 24, 1863, and anchored there. The Russian Pacific fleet, under Admiral Popov, arrived in San Francisco on October 12. Of this Russian act, Gideon Wells said: "They arrived at the high tide of the Confederacy and the low tide of the North, causing England and France to hesitate long enough to turn the tide for the North" (Empire of "The City," p. 90). History reveals that the Rothschilds were heavily involved in financing both sides in the Civil War.

Lincoln put a damper on the Rothschild activities, and profits, when, in 1862 and 1863, he refused to pay the exorbitant rates of interest demanded by the Rothschilds for their loans and issued constitutionally-authorized, interest free United States notes instead. For this and other acts of patriotism Lincoln was shot down in cold-blood by John Wilkes Booth on April 14, 1865, just five days after Lee surrendered to Grant at Appomattox Court House, Virginia.

However, in final analysis, adjitators on both sides, in conjunction with outside interests, did much to bring about the American Civil War. The Abolitionists tried to foment a slave uprising and the foreign bankers tried to profit from the entire mess. The mere fact that hundreds of thousands died and a way of life ceased to be was small price to pay for banking profits.

CHAPTER EIGHTEEN
THE SPANISH AMERICAN WAR

The next real war fought by the United States is referred to as the Spanish American War. For a number of years, American interests had been urging that the Spanish Trading Empire be removed as an impediment to US interests. When the war came, it found everyone exept the military chomping at the bit to take on the Spanish Army.

Spanish rule in Cuba had become progressively harsh, and revolution broke out in 1895. President William McKinley was under tremendous public pressure to defend U.S. interests on the island. "The media", at this point in history the newspaper chains of Joseph Pulitzer and William Randolph Hearst, had a field day stirring up outrage against the Spanish colonial government's "atrocities." For many years the world believed that the Spanish American War began with a cowardy attack on the USS Maine. However, there are more and more who question that story.

U.S.S. Maine (BB-2)

President McKinley could have selected no finer ship from the US Naval fleet to display the colors in Havana than the vessel he dispatched from Key West on January 25th. The U.S.S. Maine was an impressive battleship, at 319 feet long and displacing 6,682 tons it was the largest ship ever to enter the harbor at Havana. Though only a second class battleship, the nine-year-old vessel was among the most impressive of the U.S. Naval fleet. One of our country's first steel warships, the Maine was unique in the fleet due the fact that it had been totally designed and built by Americans. It was the largest ship ever actually constructed in a U.S. Navy yard. Painted the bright white of a peace-time US Naval Vessel, the impressive battleship boasted four of the huge 10-inch breech-loading rifles in additional to its smaller battery armaments.

Most of Captain Charles D. Sigsbee's 24 naval officers were graduates of the Academy at Annapolis. At least 20% of the 290 sailors they commanded were foreign born men who sought now to serve their adopted country. Even into the late 20th century, American Navy officers considered foreign born members of the armed forces as just a few steps above servants.

A 40-man Marine guard brought the ship's total strength to 355 American servicemen. The leathernecks, under the leadership of five non-coms, were commanded by First Lieutenant Albertus W. Catlin who had graduated from the US Naval Academy with the class of 1890. (Sixteen years later as a major, Catlin would earn the Medal of Honor in the engagement at Vera Cruz, Mexico.) Nearly a fourth of the Marines were foreign-born, American immigrants.

Upon arrival in Havana on Tuesday, January 25th, the U.S.S. Maine anchored at Bouy #4, a space reserved for war ships. Despite this, the potential for the unrest in Cuba to turn violent, and the Maine's impressive array of military power, the mission was a peaceful one. Captain Sigsbee informed his crew that there would be no shore liberty while in Cuba, but for the most part the men were content to spend a brief time riding peacefully at anchor under the tropical sun of the Caribbean. After this short visit they would return to New Orleans...in time for Mardi Gras.

The Spanish welcomed, though somewhat nervously, the arrival of the Maine, and sent a case of sherry to the officer's mess along with an invitation to a bull fight at the "plaza de toros". Captain Sigsbee and a few of his officers dutifully accepted the invite, attending in civilian attire. On his visit ashore the commander of the Maine was at one point handed an anti-American propaganda pamphlet by someone in the crowd. Scrawled across it was the message, "Watch out for your ship." Beyond the scrawled message at plaza de toros however, there was little more to indicate that the crew of the Maine was facing any undue danger. None-the-less, as a matter of prudence, Sigsbee ordered Lieutenant Catlin to keep his Marines at a careful state of alert.

The Maine, simply by her presence, seemed to have a reassuring effect upon the American Foreign Minister. General Fitzhugh Lee[94] noted this in a communication to President McKinley and requested that when the Maine's tenure in Havana expired, another naval vessel be dispatched to replace her. By Tuesday, February 15th the Maine had been at anchor for three weeks without incident. Though Lieutenant Catlin dutifully kept his Marines at a high state of alert, the crew of the Maine's biggest problem became boredom[95].

By the artificial light in his cabin that evening, Captain Sigsbee began was writing a letter to his family when Marine fifer C.H. Newton began playing "Taps" to signal the end of the day. "*I laid down my pen to listen to the notes of the bugle, which were singularly beautiful in the oppressive stillness of the night,*" he wrote. "*The marine bugler, Newton, who was rather given to fanciful effects, was evidently doing his best. During his pauses the echoes floated back to*

---

[94] Former Confederate Major-General Fitzhugh Lee was the consul-general of the United States to Havana, Cuba at the outbreak of the Spanish-American War. During the war he commanded the VII Army Corps.

[95] Adding to the uncertainty in Cuba was the prospect of a growing German influence in the Caribbean

the ship with singular distinctness, repeating the strains of the bugle fully and exactly."

It was a dark, moonless night as the Maine sat idly on the smooth waters of the Caribbean harbor, anchored at peace between the the Spanish cruiser Alfonso XII and the American passenger ship City of Washington.

It was ten minutes after nine when Newton blew his haunting version of "Taps", and when the last note had sounded, all was quiet. Newton returned below deck where most of the enlisted men were billeted. In his cabin, Captain Sigsbee picked up his pen to finish his letter. On deck, Lieutenant John Hood was finishing the day with a fine cigar. As he relished the smoke he noticed someone walking to the starboard side of the ship. Approaching, Hood recognized the familiar face of Lieutenant John Blandon as the latter leaned against the railing to peer off at the lights of Havana. It was 9:40 P.M.
"You asleep?" Hood had asked with a slight laugh.
"No, I'm on watch," Blandon had answered and then, the U.S.S. Maine Exploded!

"I was enclosing my letter in its envelope when the explosion came," Captain Sigsbee later testified. *"It was a bursting, rending, and crashing roar of immense volume, largely metallic in character. It was followed by heavy, ominous metallic sounds. There was a trembling and lurching motion of the vessel, a list to port. The electric lights went out. Then there was intense blackness and smoke. The situation could not be mistaken. The Maine was blown up and sinking. For a moment the instinct of self-preservation took charge of me, but this was immediately dominated by the habit of command."*

Marine Private William Anthony was on the weather deck when the Maine literally erupted. Captain Sigsbee's orderly, his first concern was for his captain. Though the darkness of the harbor was now awash with flame, the passageways inside the ship had been plunged into total darkness, save for flames here and there that flickered amid a heavy pall of smoke. With no concern for his own safety, Anthony search the passage ways until he found his Captain, moving towards the deck of the listing and rapidly sinking battleship.

In the dim flicker of the flames, Anthony calmly saluted his captain and reported, "*Sir, I have to inform you that the ship has blown up and is sinking.*" Both men then quickly proceeded to the weather deck, where Captain Sigsbee directed Lieutenant Commander Richard Wainwright to immediately post sentries around the ship. The first inclination was that the Maine was under attack.

Lieutenant Catlin later testified that he heard the sound like the "crack of a pistol and (then) the second (was) a roar that engulfed the ship's entire forward section." Indeed the entire forward section of the Maine had broken almost entirely in half.

On the weather deck the officers began to organize the survivors. All but two officers survived the explosion, their quarters being located aft on the battleship. The enlisted seamen and Marines were quartered below deck, most of them in the forward section where the explosion had occurred and just two decks above the powder magazines. Lieutenant Hood had witnessed the explosion from his vantage point on the deck with Lieutenant Blandon. He later described the scene. *"The whole starboard of the deck, with its sleeping berth, burst out and flew into space, as a crater of flame came through, carrying with it missiles and objects of all kinds, steel, wood, and human. (After the explosion) all was still except for the cries of the wounded, the groans of the dying, and the crackling of flame in the wreckage."*

Lieutenant Blandon foggily remembered an explosion from the port side, followed by "a perfect rain of missiles of all descriptions, from huge pieces of cement to blocks of wood, steel railings, fragments of gratings, and all the debris that would be detachable in an explosion." A block of cement struck Blandon in the head, but he recovered quickly and joined Lieutenant Hood on the poop deck, now ankle-deep in water, to begin lowering boats.

There were no Marine guards for Lieutenant Commander Wainwright to post about the ship per his Captain's orders. Nearly three-fourths of the Marines were killed in the explosion. The U.S.S. Maine was beyond hope, almost severed at the bow, and sinking badly. Reluctantly, Captain Sigsbee ordered the few survivors on the decks to abandon ship. As the waters of the harbor continued to reach out to claim the body of the American battleship, Sigsbee directed its evacuation. When no one else was left alive, the Captain was the last to depart.

By the time gigs from the nearby City of Washington and Alfonso XII could be dispatched to the scene of the disaster, little of the Maine remained above water. Through the darkness of the night the small boats searched the debris-covered waters of the harbor for survivors, Captain Sigsbee standing in one of them calling into the blackness: *"If there is anyone living on board, for God's sake say so!"* His desperate cries met only silence.

As morning dawned across the harbor, only 103 members of the crew of the U.S.S. Maine had survived. Two of the ship's 26 officers went down with the ship, along with 222 sailors and 28 Marines. Of the 103 survivors, 59 were wounded, 8 of them so severely that they later died as a result of their wounds. Total losses for the once proud battleship reached 260 dead or missing, a casualty rate of 75%. Among the missing was Fifer Newton whose last, memorable rendition of "Taps" had been played not only for his comrades now at rest in the deep, but for himself. In a sense, it had been his own haunting eulogy.

Across the waters of the harbor little remained of the 319-foot battleship. Only a small pile of twisted metal and the protruding mast of the U.S.S. Maine, still proudly "displaying the Colors" were visible.

In the hours after the explosion aboard the Maine, the small gigs from the American passenger steamer and the Spanish warship Alphonso XII had given good account of themselves in braving the darkness, fires and secondary explosions of the sinking American battleship in search of survivors. Having witnessed this first-hand, Captain Sigsbee was reluctant to immediately blame the Spanish. In his first telegram to Washington he reported details of the event then closed with the observation that "Public opinion should be suspended until further report."

There would indeed be further reports, both officially and unofficially. Two days after the explosion the Navy created the "Sampson Board", an official inquiry into the cause of the disaster. On February 21 the Naval Court of Inquiry began their 4-week investigation in Havana. Simultaneously, the Spanish began their own inquiry into the matter.

It would not be an easy process. Captain Sigsbee remembered "a bursting, rending, and crashing roar of immense volume... followed by heavy, ominous metallic sounds." Lieutenant Blandon remembered a single explosion on the port side, followed by "a perfect rain of missiles of all descriptions." Lieutenant Hood, who had been next to Blandon to witness the explosion first hand remember the explosion on the starboard side.

Marine Lieutenant Catlin reported what he thought to be TWO explosions, the first sounding like the "crack of a pistol and the second a roar that engulfed the ship's entire forward section." Some survivors heard one explosion, others a deep rumble followed by one loud explosion, still others a series of explosions. Reaching any kind of reasonable determination as to what caused the destruction of the Maine would be a challenge not only to the official Board of Inquiry, but to historians for the following century.

Back in the United States there were few questions about what had caused the Maine to suddenly explode in the darkness of night, killing 260 American men. Two days after the indicent the headline in the New Your World[96] read: "MAINE EXPLOSION CAUSED BY BOMB OR TORPEDO?"

The New York Journal was more specific: "THE DESTRUCTION OF THE WAR SHIP MAINE WAS THE WORK OF AN ENEMY." Artists created renditions showing how Spanish saboteurs had fastened an underwater mine to the hull of the Maine then detonated it from shore. Randolph Hearst offered a $50,000 reward for "Conviction of the Criminals" and announced that "Naval Officers (were) Unanimous That the Ship Was Destroyed on Purpose[97]".

On March 6th the Spanish government requested the recall of U.S. Cuban Consul Fitzhugh Lee. In the United States citizens gathered solemnly at Capitol Hill and outside the White House to mourn the loss of 260 lives. Tensions continued to mount while the Navy conducted its official inquiry. In a Broadway bar in New York City a patron lifted his glass and said, "Gentlemen, remember the Maine!" A reporter from the Journal happened to be in the bar and wrote about the incident. When it was published America had a new slogan..."*Remember The Main*". Spaniards were burned in effigy in cities and

---

[96] Though the military on the scene really were unclear on what had happened, the news reporters were absolutely certain of what had taken place.

[97] In reality, the Naval officers were not unanimous about anything that had to do with the explosion.

town across America and soon the slogan became a war cry: "*Remember the Maine, and To Hell with Spain!*"

To be sure there were cooler heads, even as the tensions mounted. Amid the cries of the firebrands and the warhawks, U.S. Speaker of the House Thomas B. Reed said, "A war will make a large market for gravestones." Popular author Samuel Clemmens (Mark Twain) continued to speak out against any possible war, urging the United States not to become embroiled in the affairs of distant nations.

Ten days after the explosion, Under Secretary of the Navy Theodore Roosevelt cabled Commodore George Dewey with the U.S. Pacific fleet in Hong Kong. "Keep in full coal," the communiqué stated. "In the event of declaration of war with Spain, your duty will be to see that the Spanish squadron does not leave the Asiatic coast and then offensive operations in Philippine Islands." Itching for a fight and convinced of the truth of his earlier remarks about the glory of war to the Naval War College, Roosevelt went so far as to refer to President McKinley as a "milquetoast"[98].

McKinley, who had served in the Civil War and participated at the tragic battle at Antietam in the earliest days of that war, told one visitor to the White House: "I have been through one war; I have seen the dead piled up; and I do not want to see another."

But the makings of war could not be avoided. As a matter of preparedness, President McKinley requested a $50 million dollar war fund. On March 8th the U.S. Congress stunned Spanish observers when it unanimously approved the request. In San Francisco on the western coast, the battleship Oregon was dispatched for the Caribbean. On March 14 the Spanish fleet under Admiral Cervera began steaming for the Cape Verde Islands. Throughout the period the yellow journalism of competing newspapers inflamed the public with more and more stories. (During the period the New York Journal printed an unprecedented 8 pages each day related to the U.S.S. Maine disaster.)

Late in March the Spanish concluded its official inquiry and delivered the findings to the U.S. government on March 25. On the same day the Spanish government informed Washington that their investigators had determined the Maine had been destroyed by "internal combustion", the President announced the results of his recently received Sampson Inquiry. When he announced to the American public that the Naval Board of Inquiry had determined that the Maine was destroyed "by an external explosion (presumably a mine)", the war cries hit a feverish pitch.

Two days later President McKinley sent these findings to Spain. He also issued Spain his final terms[99]:

---

[98] There is always glory in war to those in command positions or who have political aspirations, but to the grunt in the trenches, there is little glory, only mud, death and pain.

[99] This wold not be the last time that an American President would make demands on a foreign nation that would be impossible for the foreign nation to meet.

- Declare an armistice

- End the reconcentration policy in Cuba initiated by General Weyler

- Begin the process of granting Cuba independence

Meanwhile, Navy Secretary John Davis Long ordered the peacetime white hulls of American warships to be painted with a dull battle gray. A song titled "My Sweetheart Went Down With the Maine" became the tune-of-the-day. Marine Private William Anthony, who had braved the explosions and fire of the Maine to seek out his Captain, was brought home to a hero's welcome. Honored by both the Navy and Marines, he was promoted to sergeant and hailed as the first true hero of the war that was still looking for an excuse to happen.

The Spanish responded with some concessions, but stopped far short of granting Cuban Independence. From without, the President received pressure from the Ambassadors of England, Germany, France, Italy, Austria and Russia to avoid war with Spain. On April 6th the Pope indicated to the President that he would enter negotiations with Spain, requesting that the President delay any actions pending the outcome. The the cry from within for retaliation and U.S. support for the "freedom fighters" of Cuba continued to push the United States towards war. On April 4th the New York Journal dedicated an edition to the war brewing in Cuba and called upon the U.S. to intervene. The press-run was one million copies.

Finally, bowing to the rapidly deteriorating events in Cuba and the overwhelming cries for war at home, President McKinley asked Congress on April 11th to authorize American intervention to end the revolution in Cuba. Five days later the road to war was cleared in Congress when an amendment offered by Colorado Congressman Henry Teller was ratified. Designed to quiet the fears of those who opposed a war based upon an American imperialistic effort to annex Cuba, the Teller Amendment stated that the United States:

"Hereby disclaims any disposition of intention to exercise sovereignty, jurisdiction, or control over said island (Cuba) except for pacification thereof, and asserts its determination, when that is accomplished, to leave the government and control of the island to its people."

On April 20th, while Congress still debated the request for war, President McKinley[100] signed a Joint Resolution for War with Spain, an ultimatum that was

---

100 William Mckinley: Our 25th President was prompted to seek Masonic membership when he observed the fraternal kindnesses being exchanged among Masons in the Union and Confederate Armies during the Civil War. McKinley, who served from 1897 - 1901, was made a Mason May 3, 1865, in Hiram Lodge No. 21, A.F. & A.M., Winchester, Virginia.

promptly forwarded to Madrid with a call for Cuban independence. The Spanish Minister to the United States promptly demanded his passport and, with his Legation, left Washington for Canada.

The following day McKinley received his answer from Madrid...General Steward Woodford, the U.S. Minister to Spain was handed his passport and told to leave the country. The Spanish government considered McKinley's ultimatum a declaration of war. Though Congress had not yet declared war, President McKinley's unilateral action forced Spain to suspend diplomatic relations. With diplomatic relations suspended, President McKinley ordered a blockade of Cuba while the Spanish forces in Santiago began mining Guantanamo Bay.

The U.S. Naval fleet departed Key West, Florida on April 22nd to carry out the President's order for a blockade of Cuba. The American Navy was well prepared for war, especially against the aging Spanish fleet. But the Spanish had at least 80,000 soldiers stationed in Cuba that would require a ground war. The U.S. Army, with only 25,706 enlisted men and 2,116 officers, was not prepared for a ground war. On April 23 the U.S. President issued a call for 125,000 volunteers. After months of patriotic fervor generated by tales of Spanish sabotage and atrocity[101], the recruiting stations were immediately swamped with eager young American would-be soldiers.

On April 25, 1898 the war that had been looking for an excuse to happen, finally became official. The U.S. Congress passed a resolution declaring the United States to be at war with Spain. The Naval blockade of Cuba already underway, Congress made the declaration of war effective as of April 21, thereby legitimizing military actions undertaken in the previous four days.

Under Admiral William Sampson, who had earlier headed up the inquiry into the cause of the explosion on the U.S.S. Maine, the blockade of Cuba was already successfully underway. On the same day that war was declared, American ships bombarded the Spanish at Matanzaras, Cuba.

On the other side of the globe, the U.S. Pacific fleet under Admiral George Dewey was already prepared for war as per the February 25th communiqué from Navy Undersecretary Roosevelt. Cuba in the Caribbean was not the only vestige remaining of the old Spanish Empire...Spain also held much of the series of 700 islands in the Pacific known as the Philippine Islands...which had been under the rule of Madrid since Ferdinand Magellan discovered the vast Archipelago in 1521.

While few Americans gave little notice or concern to events in the Pacific Islands, and even President McKinley confessed that he could not locate the Philippine Islands "within 2000 miles", American Naval planners had long considered the value of the natural port at Manila on Luzon, the largest of the islands. War with Spain was destined to become a global conflict, and while Admiral Sampson's ships conducted their blockade in the Caribbean, on April 27th Admiral Dewey sailed his ships out of Mirs Bay, China and set their course

---

101 That are said to have been 10% truth and 90% imagination.

for Manila. The Spanish-American war would become a battlefield on two, widely separated fronts.

Back home Marine Sergeant William Anthony struggled with his new role as an American hero. On a horrible night in Havana harbor he had, as the public would loudly proclaim, been a brave and daring young leatherneck. Anthony didn't think about his heroics too often, instead his nights and his nightmares were filled with the agonizing cries of his fellow Marines and sailors as they perished in a moment of terror. Those nightmares, and the pressures of an adoring public that could never understand the true horror of war, pushed him to drink. He may have been the first "hero" of the Splendid Little War but he would not be the LAST.

By the time the brief war ended, William Anthony would be discharged from service and overcome by his past as well as his present. Despondent and unemployed, his body was found in Central Park on November 24, 1899. He committed suicide at the age of 46. For the politicians who fought their wars from comfortable desks, there might be something SPLENDID in war. For the young men who fight in the field, WAR is HELL.

Spanish rule in Cuba had become progressively harsh, and revolution broke out in 1895. President William McKinley was under tremendous public pressure to defend U.S. interests[102] on the island. "The media", at this point in history the newspaper chains of Joseph Pulitzer and William Randolph Hearst, had a field day stirring up outrage against the Spanish colonial government's "atrocities."

Two events in early 1898 helped justify U.S. involvement, the publication of a stolen private letter[103] from the Spanish Minister to the United States to a friend in Havana characterizing McKinley as "a weakling...a bidder for the admiration of the crowd", and the sinking of the U.S.S. Maine in Havana harbor on February 15, with a loss of 260 men. The Maine was there on a "goodwill visit", and although a board of American naval officers determined the cause to be a submarine mine, a modern-day National Geographic investigation showed that a fire in a coal bunker could have caused the explosion as well.

However, popular opinion was clearly building against Spain, and war frenzy was breaking out. In their own words- Senator Thurston of Nebraska: *"War with Spain would increase the business and earnings of every American railroad, it would increase the output of every American factory, it would stimulate every branch of industry and domestic commerce."*

On April 19 Congress passed a joint resolution proclaiming Cuba "free and independent", and when signed by McKinley the next day, this resolution

---

[102] In place of the phrase "U.S. Interests" read private investments by the wealthy.

[103] The first of these was the publication by Hearst of a stolen letter (the de Lôme letter) that had been written by the Spanish minister at Washington, in which that incautious diplomat expressed contempt for McKinley. A Cuban agent intercepted this letter and gave it to Hearst to use against the Spanish Crown. No one questioned its authenticity.

amounted to a declaration of war[104]. The first military action of the war was the Battle for Manila in the Philippines. At the eve of the war, a squadron of six vessels immediately departed for the Spanish possession of the Philippines. The Spanish fleet and the batteries surrounding Manila were destroyed May 1 without a single U.S. casualty. However, the conquest of Manila itself became as much a political as a military one; the U.S did not want the Filipinos to gain control, and was negotiating a separate surrender with the Spanish. The Spanish fleet in the Caribbean, after successfully crossing the Atlantic, managed to trap itself in Santiago Bay, and was decimated by the U.S. Navy. On July 17 the Spanish army surrendered. The President reportedly called this imperialist maneuver a "glorious little war."

The Battle for the Philippines

Manila, in the Philippines, provided the front and back covers for the Spanish-American War. It was in this harbor that the opening shots of the 106-day war were fired by the ships of Commodore Dewey on May 1st. On August 13th Admiral Dewey's ships fired the closing volley that signaled the end of the Spanish Empire. In the 104 days between, almost all of the combat was waged half-a-world away in the Caribbean.

When the sun set on the evening of May 1, 1898 Manila Harbor was still filled with smoke--all that remained of a once mighty Spanish Naval squadron. The defeat was unprecedented, Dewey accomplishing what few could have dreamed possible, and all without the loss of a single life (save for the heat stroke victim). It would be however, a full week before officials in Washington, DC would hear the details of the American victory.

Early on, the Spanish Governor-General mistakenly thought the smoke of battle near Cavite in Manila Bay signified a Spanish victory, and cabled this welcome news to Madrid via the underwater telegraph that was Manila's only link to the outside world. On the morning of May 2nd, Commodore Dewey notified this Spanish official that, since that cable was INDEED the only way communications could be sent from Manila, it should be considered NEUTRAL so that he could use it as well. When the Governor-General refused, Dewey dispatched his sailors to dredge up and cut the cable, ending the direct flow of information out of the Philippines. It was the first step in what would have been, but for the later loss of American lives, a comedy of errors.

The USS McCulloch became the bearer of good news to America, steaming towards Hong Kong to telegraph reports of Commodore Dewey's smashing victory at Manila. Aboard were Chicago Tribune reporters Edward Harden and John McCutcheon, and the New York Herald's Joe Stickney, all eager to be first to file their stories. They departed Manila with Commodore Dewey's conditional blessing...

---

104 This was direct interference in the internal affairs of another country by the U.S. Congress and left the Spanish no choice but to go to war.

1) None would file their stories until Lieutenant Brumby FIRST filed his official reports to Washington, and
2) None would speculate on Dewey's post-victory plans in Manila in their stories.

Upon arrival in Hong Kong, Consul General Wildman took a steam launch to the McCulloch to ferry the new arrivals to shore. Even before the launch could tie up at the docks, Harden and Stickney were leaping ashore and racing for the telegraph office. The younger Harden took a shortcut, arriving only minutes before Stickney. While the clerk protested the lengthy (3,000 word) dispatch, Stickney arrived and went directly to the manager's office.

Stickney's observance of office protocol earned the loyalty of the manager, who ruled that the first dispatch would the the Herald's. Harden protested, ordering dispatches to the general manager of the telegraph lines in London requesting the immediate dismissal of the Hong Kong office manager. The clerk refused to send Harden's complaint to the general manager after noting that it was NOT a WAR DISPATCH.

The crafty Harden finally resorted to bribery, informing the office manager he would pay for his dispatches in cash...at a rate THREE TIMES the commercial rate and NINE TIMES the press rate. The bribe worked, and the office manager ruled that Harden's dispatch to the Tribune would go first, followed by Stickney's dispatch, and finally McCutcheon's.

In keeping with the conditions imposed by Commodore Dewey, Harden advised the clerk that Lieutenant Brumby's dispatches must preceded them all, and specified that these official dispatches must be repeated. Harden's instructions were in keeping with the LETTER of the conditions, though not the spirit. In requiring that Dewey's dispatches be repeated, it meant delays at each of the six relay stations between Hong Kong and the U.S. Capitol. At the first relay station, Harden's report of the battle passed the official report of Lieutenant Brumby, arriving between 3 and 4 A.M. (hours ahead of everyone else), just in time to make the morning editions.

"*(Commodore) Dewey, with six fighting ships, operating 7,000 miles from a home base, boldly entered an unfamiliar harbor, sailing past modern, powerful, Krupp-equipped shore batteries, and destroyed an enemy fleet of ten fighting ships and two torpedo-boats fighting from anchorage (which overbalanced the American fleet's advantage of superior speed) at a place in the bay selected by the Spanish Admiral as presumably giving him an advantage over the attacking fleet.*"

Within days of Dewey's victory in Manila Bay, the harbor was crowded with the vessels of several foreign nations, most conspicuously those of Britain, Germany, France, and Japan. These came under the pretext of guarding the safety of their own citizens inside the city of Manila, but with a keen eye on the methods and activities of the American Naval commander. The foremost question in the minds of these observers was what the Commodore would do next. Back in the United States the media had given the impression that Dewey had conquered Manila, and that the Philippines were now under American control. The truth of the matter was far different.

While Commodore Dewey had indeed utterly destroyed the Spanish fleet, his control extended only across the harbor. More than 15,000 Spanish soldiers still garrisoned the city itself. For the next three months, Dewey was contented to blockade the harbor, cutting this force off from the rest of the world. Ironically, Dewey's own blockade placed him in a similar position...cut off 7,000 miles from home and with not means of immediate communications (after having destroyed the only telegraph cable out of Manila).

On May 11th, the same day that the first and only Naval officer to die in the war was killed at Cienfuegos, Cuba, Dewey was promoted to rear admiral. Two days later, as Commodore Schley's "Flying Squadron" departed Hampton Roads for Cuba Admiral Dewey informed Washington, DC that he would require 5,000 ground troops to capture Manila. The Army was quick to respond, marshalling a force near San Francisco that would become the Eighth Army under Major General Wesley Merritt.

The Eighth Army commander was a West Point graduate who had seen distinguished action in the Civil War and then served on the frontiers of the American West. In 1882 he returned to the Academy to serve as its superintendent, until called back into active duty to command the ground forces in the Philippine Islands.

While awaiting the arrival of ground troops, Admiral Dewey contented himself with his impressive Naval blockade of the city. On the deck of his flagship USS Olympia, he welcomed aboard members of the media clamoring for interviews, and watched the goings on aboard the numerous vessels of other foreign nations as they arrived almost daily. He also encouraged the return to the islands of a revered local freedom fighter, a man author Mark Twain would call The George Washington of the Philippines.

Emilio Aguinaldo y Famy

Born in Cavite, Aguinaldo grew up among the elite, the son of the Mayor of Kawit (Cavite viejo). In 1895, twelve years after his father's death, Emilio Aguinaldo became mayor of Kawit.

The following year a major revolt against Spanish rule erupted in the Philippines, and Emilio Aguinaldo joined the secret, nationalist brotherhood Katipunan founded by revolutionary leader Andres Bonifacio. Ultimately, Bonifacio and Aguinaldo clashed and, in 1897 Aguinaldo ordered the arrest and eventual execution of Bonifacio.

As the revolt against Spanish rule faltered, Aguinaldo entered into an agreement with the Spanish rulers whereby he allowed himself to be exiled to Hong Kong in exchange for a payment of 400,000 pesos. Aguinaldo was in Hong

Kong, reportedly using that money to purchase arms for future battles against the Spanish, when Commodore Dewey sailed out on his own conquest. Aguinaldo returned to his homeland with encouragement from Dewey, even meeting with the Admiral aboard his flagship shortly after his return.

Years later in U.S. Senate hearings, Admiral Dewey testified, "*I never treated him (Aguinaldo) as an ally, except to assist me in my operations against the Spaniards.*" That assistance came very close to ending the Spanish rule in the Philippines ahead of Admiral Dewey's schedule.

Emilio Aguinaldo returned to his native island on May 19th, and quickly began assembling a force of patriotic insurgents to roust the Spaniards. The 29-year old freedom fighter believed that the American Naval forces in Manila Bay provided him a tenuous ally that would finally enable his people to rid their country of Spanish rule. Though Admiral Dewey refused to provide either arms or support for the ground campaign, Aguinaldo believed the Americans were his friends and allies in the effort to win Philippine Independence. Towards that end, he was determined to do his part.

Dewey had Manila blockaded by sea, and within two weeks Aguinaldo's insurgent force of 20,000 Filipinos moved within a few miles of the city to surround it with 14 miles of well placed trenches and fortifications. On June 12th Aguinaldo declared Philippine Independence and proclaimed himself President.

Planning for the ground offensive Admiral Dewey had requested against Manila began at the Palace Hotel in San Francisco, where Major General Merritt was building his Eighth Army. Like the forces that were preparing for battle in the Caribbean, his own force would be composed of four separate elements that would depart for combat in the Philippines over a 5 week period. In contrast to the deployments on the east coast, the departures from San Francisco were orderly and with great fanfare from the local populace.

On May 25th Brigadier General Thomas Anderson steamed out of San Francisco with the First Philippine Expeditionary Force, 117 officers in command of 2,382 men. En route to Manila, the convoy made a brief detour when Commander Glass entered the harbor at Apra to claim the Island of Guam for the United States. Following the bloodless conquest, the six transport ships continued towards Manila.

Meanwhile, on June 1st, Civil War hero Arthur MacArthur was promoted to Brigadier General and placed in command of several volunteer regiments training near San Francisco. It was a force numbering nearly 5,000 soldiers.

On June 15th the Second Philippine Expeditionary Force, more than 3,500 men under Brigadier General Francis Green, departed San Francisco. MacArthur's Third Philippine Expeditionary Force followed twelve days later, just ahead of General Merritt and his staff.

While awaiting the arrival of General Merritt's Eight Army, the greatest problem Admiral Dewey faced was in keeping Aguinaldo and his insurgent forces from taking control of Manila[105]. Though the insurgents saw the Americans as allies in their dream of Philippine Independence, political factions were at work to thwart them. Admiral Dewey referred to them as "the Indians" and promised Washington, D.C. that he would "enter the city and keep the Indians out." In its imperial wisdom, the United States began to see itself more and more as a force bent on protecting the Philippine people from themselves, than as a liberating force. Aguinaldo in his optimism, failed to see the shifting tide against him. On June 27th Admiral Dewey cabled Secretary Long to report:

"Consistently I have refrained from assisting him (Aguinaldo) in any way with the force under my command, and on several occasions I have declined requests that I should do so, telling him the squadron could not act until the arrival of the United States troops. At the same time I have given him to understand that I consider insurgents as friends, being opposed to a common enemy...My relations with him are cordial, but I am not in his confidence. The United States has not been bound in any way to assist insurgents by any act or promises, and he is not, to my knowledge, committed to assist us. I believe he expects to capture Manila without my assistance, but (I) doubt (the insurgent's) ability, they not yet having many guns."

In truth, the 15,000 Spanish soldiers now trapped inside Manila were almost as eager for the arrival of American ground forces as was Admiral Dewey. They knew the American forces to be civilized, even generous to their enemies. After the Battle of Manila Bay Commodore Dewey had wired President McKinley to announce, "*I am assisting in protecting the Spanish sick and wounded. Two hundred and fifty sick and wounded are in hospital within our lines.*" For centuries the Spanish had ruled the Philippines with a heavy--often deadly--hand. They considered the Filipino people to be ruthless, uncivilized, and sub-human. There was great fear that if the city fell to Aguinaldo and his insurgent forces, there would be hell to pay. Dewey himself took note of it, writing:

"*Soon after the victory of May 1...General Don Basilio Augustin Davila (the Spanish Commander), through the British consul, Mr. Rawson-Walker, had intimated to me his willingness to surrender to our squadron. But at that time I could not entertain the proposition because I had no force with which to occupy the city, and I would not for a moment consider the possibility of turning it over to the undisciplined insurgents, who, I feared, might wreak their vengeance upon the Spaniards and indulge in a carnival of loot.*"

Spanish officials in Madrid had reached the same conclusion as had Admiral Dewey regarding General Don Basilio Augustin Davila's leanings toward surrender, and replaced him with General Firmin Jaudenes during the

---

[105] In a preview of the War in Vietnam, it was not politically correct for the insurgents to occupy Manila. This would certainly not be the last time that a political agenda ditated military actions.

period when the American ground forces were en route to Manila. Despite this effort to save the city, defeat was inevitable. General Jaudenes was nearly as predisposed to the inevitable surrender as had been his predecessor. Manila was cut off by sea to the west, and surrounded by insurgent forces landward.

General Anderson arrived to unload his nearly 2,500 soldiers at the captured Spanish arsenal on Cavite early in July. On July 17th General Green arrived with the Second Philippine Expeditionary Force of Merritt's Eight Army, deploying his 3,500 soldiers near a peanut field just south of Manila at a site named Camp Dewey. His position was within range of the Spanish guns, but the enemy withheld its fire, fearing that any offensive action would bring swift and devastating return fire from Admiral Dewey's ships, just off shore.

General Merritt arrived on July 25th, just ahead of the MacArthur's Third Expeditionary Force which had been delayed in transit by rough weather. He promptly took command of the ground war, planning with Admiral Dewey for the fall of Manila. Neither gave recognition to Aguinaldo, or included him in the military preparations.

General Merritt noted: "*My instructions from the President fully contemplated the occupation of the islands by the American land forces, and stated that 'the powers of the military occupant (American Army) are absolute and supreme and immediately operate upon the political conditions of the inhabitants.*[106]

"*I did not consider it wise to hold any direct communication with the insurgent leader (Aguinaldo) until I should be in possession of the city of Manila, especially as I would not until then be in a position to issue a proclamation to enforce my authority, in event that his pretensions should clash with my designs. For these reasons the preparations for the attack on the city were pressed and military operations conducted without reference to the situation of the insurgent forces.*"

In the closing days of July, General MacArthur's Brigade joined the rest of Merritt's force, bringing the total American troop strength to more than 10,000 soldiers, amassed only a few miles south of the Walled City of Manila at Camp Dewey. To the east, Aguinaldo waited impatiently with his force of 20,000 insurgents, eager to attack and lay claim to the Philippine Capital. General Jaudenes and his 15,000 Spanish defenders were completely cut off, surrounded, and running out of food and supplies. It was reported that some in the city resorted to eating rats to fill their empty bellies. General Jaudenes knew that defeat was eminent, but the Spanish were proud traditionalists at warfare, and the beleaguered commander was determined NOT to surrender his city to the "savage and uncivilized forces" under Aguinaldo.

---

106 In otherwords, we were taking control of the Philippines just as the Spanish had done. This would certainly make it appear that we were empoire building, not fighting to free the residents of the islands.

Between Manila and General Merritt's three brigades at Camp Dewey sat the seaside guardhouse of Fort San Antonio de Abad, just two miles south of the city. The Spanish trenches stretched eastward towards Blockhouse #4, with the insurgent forces in full command to the east. The arriving American soldiers moved into some of the insurgent positions between Camp Dewey and the Spanish lines in the closing days of July, bringing them directly under the enemy guns. There was only sporadic fire from the Spanish artillery as the newly arrived American forces came ashore to dig trenches and prepare for the coming assault. On the night of July 31st, the American forces could restrain their fire no longer.

The one-and-a-half hour battle that followed pitted the infantry and artillery fire of the two opposing forces against each other in what became the deadliest battle in the Pacific. When the Americans returned fire, their positions were exposed and the Spanish adjusted their fire, resulting in 10 Americans killed and 33 wounded. The following day, Admiral Dewey suggested that the Americans hold their fire in the coming days as General Merritt continued to deploy his forces for a final assault. *"(It is) Better to have small losses, night after night, in the trenches, than to run the risk of greater losses by premature attack,"* he cautioned.

In the days that followed, Merritt's forces continued to land and take up positions. The First Colorado Volunteer Infantry moved their own lines eastward to the Pasay Road approaching Manila from the east. Their work was arduous, fighting swamps, monsoon rains, and intermittent enemy fire. At night the Spanish guns continued to fire on American positions, resulting in 5 more deaths and 10 Americans wounded. On August 7th Admiral Dewey sent a message to General Jaudenes warning that unless he orderd his soldiers to stop firing on American positions, the U.S. Naval commander would turn the big guns of his ships on the city within 48 hours.

General Jaudenes realized that the message from the American Admiral was tantamount to a demand for surrender. He also realized that defiance of Dewey's ultimatum would be suicide for himself and his forces. With Aguinaldo and his Filipino force arrayed to the east, Merritt and his 3 divisions to the south, and the U.S. Naval squadron in the harbor, time had run out for the Spanish empire in the Philippines. What followed was five days of negotiations creating an unusual scenario for surrender. It would pit allies against each other, create a strange alliance between enemies, script one of the strangest battles in military history, and set the stage for a sequel war. It would become known as:

The Mock Battle of Manila

In the annuals of military campaigns there have beena few conducted simply for the drama of war. However, none was as unnecessary as the Battle of Manila. It took place on August 13, 1898.

"Intermittent rain had fallen throughout the night as the soldiers at Camp Dewey shook off the early morning chill and prepared to move north. It was 7:30 A.M. and the battle for Manila had commenced. During the darkness of the previous night, American engineers had crept through the area cutting holes in the enemy's barbed wire to permit passage. Now, General MacArthur's 1st Brigade began its movement towards the enemy positions on the road leading to Pasi. The terrain was swampy, the roads muddy, but by 8:05 that morning most of the elements had reached their forward positions and taken shelter for the opening volley.

Less than a mile to the west, General Greene's 2nd Brigade was making its advance along the beach. Leading the way was the 1st Colorado Volunteer Infantry, followed by volunteers from California, Nebraska, Utah, Pennsylvania, and Oregon. Ahead lay the enemy fortification at Malate, Fort San Antonio de Abad.

At 8:45 the nervous young soldiers, about to face their first test of offensive combat actions, noted the movement of Admiral Dewey's ships in the harbor to their left. The large war ships began positioning themselves for the attack. At 9:45 the big guns boomed, and large shells began raining down on the Fort at Malate. There was only sporadic and light return fire, and the young Americans advanced nervously to capture the fort. As they neared its now badly scarred walls, the naval bombardment stopped.

Cautiously approaching, the young soldiers of the 1st Colorado found Fort San Antonio de Abad deserted, save for two dead and one wounded Spaniard. Quickly the Americans took control of the abandoned enemy stronghold, looking off towards the east where at 10:30 General MacArthur's brigade had noted the end of the naval bombardment and begun moving again towards Manila. At 10:35 Captain Alexander M. Brooks of Denver, Colorado raised the Stars and Stripes over the captured fort.

It seemed that the long awaited assault to capture the city of Manila was going to be an easy task. So far, there were no American casualties. It was an unqualified victory...but then it should have been. This was a battle that, unknown to but a few of the higher ranking commanders, had been carefully scripted. Before the first shot had been fired, the events had already been scripted, and the outcome determined.

Inside the walled city of Manila, General Jaudenes listened to the sound of the naval gunfire. He wasn't concerned. He had already agreed with Admiral Dewey as to how the scenario would play out. On his desk was a piece of paper, the only printed document related to the unfolding events. It sketched out a series of signal flags that, when seen flying from Admiral Dewey's ship, would indicate that it was time for the Spanish commander to order his men to hoist the while sheet over the city that would signify the final act in the mock battle for Manila.

From August 8th to 12th, the opposing commanders had hammered out the details. First, Jaudenes had requested a 48 hour delay in the threatened bombardment in order to obtain permission from Madrid to surrender the city. Granted the delay by Dewey, Madrid refused to permit the surrender. His fate all but sealed, Jaudenes was still more than willing to surrender but for two important details:

It would be a disgraceful act for the Spanish commander to give up his city without a fight. Such an act would be received with derision and probably court martial upon his return to his homeland. The Spanish were still quite fearful of the consequences if the city fell to Aguinaldo and his band of Filipino insurgents.

The resolution of such matters was carefully crafted through the Belgium consul Edouard Andre. In its final draft, the carefully choreographed sequence of events called for the initial shelling of the fort at Malate, which would be promptly abandoned by its defenders. As the Americans then began their ground advance, Admiral Dewey would bring his ships before the city and hoist the signal flags demanding surrender. Upon seeing these, General Jaudenes would order the while flag raised and the Americans would enter. As had been the case in Cuba, the word "surrender" was avoided to be replaced by the term "capitulation".

The capitulation of Manila would transfer control to the invading American forces, which would then secure the city and deny entrance to the insurgent forces under Aguinaldo. The brief, bloodless battle at San Antonio de Abad would save face for the Spanish soldiers and their commander, demonstrating that they had capitulated ONLY after a devastating attack. It was an unusual strategy by two opposing forces, one which would not only save face for the Spaniards, but would also save lives for BOTH sides.

In the swamps and jungles to the east of the city, the guerilla fighters of Emilio Aguinaldo could hear the sounds of the early morning naval bombardment, and greeted the sound with optimism and hope. For weeks they had been poised to take the city and end Spanish rule of their homeland, held in check only at the insistence of the American commanders. As the bombardment ended and the American forces continued north in two columns the insurgents raced to join the battle.

The 1st Colorado lead General Greene's brigade along the beach and past Malate. Meanwhile, in the east, MacArthur's brigade moved through the Spanish trenches, past Blockhouse #4, and towards the Spanish position at Blockhouse #20 near Cingalon. When the 13th Minnesota approached, the Spanish defenders fired a few rounds in a token resistance. It was met by a similarly light return fire from the Americans. Hearing the sound of the skirmish, the guerillas could restrain no longer, rushing into the foray. A pitched battle ensued, the soldiers of the 13th Minnesota caught in a cross-fire between the Spaniards ahead of them and the insurgent forces behind them. Before the battle ended, five American soldiers lay dead. Thirty more were wounded.

It was an unpredictable situation in the scenario, for the Filipinos had not been appraised of the script. They thought there was a REAL battle going on that would liberate their capitol. To make matters worse, they didn't want to be left out.

For the rest of the afternoon the insurgents would be the wild card in the unfolding events for as General Merritt later stated: *"We purposely gave the insurgents no notice of the attack on Manila, because we did not need their cooperation.*" Indeed, the biggest challenge facing the advancing American army was not routing the enemy from the city, but keeping Aguinaldo and the supposed Filipino allies OUT of the city. It mattered little to them that, on the eve of the battle, General Anderson had warned Aguinaldo that any of the insurgents attempting to enter Manila would be fired on by the Americans.

When the skirmish at Cingalon ended, the wounded were moved into a small church for treatment, while the remainder of MacArthur's troops continued towards Manila. At 11 o'clock, as the two columns converged on the city, Admiral Dewey hoisted his signal flags to demand the Spanish surrender. Over the following tense minutes, nothing appeared to be happening. General Greene entered the city with some of his troops, riding into the Luneta...the city promenade. There he was confronted with a heavily defended barricade, and a group of Spanish soldiers who, like the insurgents, apparently were not privy to the unfolding script. Both sides faced off in a tense situation that could have turned deadly with one, mistaken pull of a trigger. In the bay, Admiral Dewey watched the minutes tick by without seeing the white flag of surrender.

The periodic sniping from the insurgents at the outskirts made the Spanish wary of an American double-cross, while Admiral Dewey wondered if the Spanish were about to pull some kind of quick trick when the surrender flag failed to rise over the city. Tension was reaching the flashpoint when, at 11:20, Admiral Dewey at last saw the white sheet flying over Manila. Quickly he dispatched word to his ground forces to enter and negotiate the surrender terms. (The Spanish had actually hoisted their surrender flag shortly after the signal from Admiral Dewey. It had blended into the background of the sky from the Dewey's vantage point, masking the response. Only when the wind shifted, had the surrender been noticable.)

In the hours that followed, the Spanish and American commanders hammered out the final details of the surrender while the foot soldiers took up defensive positions in the suburbs. The 1st Colorado crossed the Pasig River to occupy the districts around San Sebastian and Sampaloc. Some small skirmishes continued from time to time during the afternoon, often precipitated by attempts from insurgent guerillas to enter the city. In the process, the Second Brigade suffered one additional soldier killed in action, 38 men wounded. By 5:30 in the evening, the fighting was over and the United States Flag flew over the capitol city of the Philippine Islands.

There were no Medals of Honor awarded for heroism in the last battle of the Spanish-American war...the battle had been a staged event, a sham to save face for the Spanish and deny victory to Aguinaldo and his guerillas. The day-long drama cost 6 American soldiers their lives, and resulted in 92 wounded. The Spanish suffered 49 killed in action, 100 wounded.

It could have been worse.......Then again, it didn't even have to happen......

The mock battle for Manila occurred on August 13, 1898...more than 24 hours after the signing of the peace protocol in Washington, D.C. at 4:30 P.M.

(5:30 A.M. Manila Time) on August 12th. Because Admiral Dewey had cut the only cable that linked Manila to the outside world, news of the war's end reached neither General Jaudenes nor Admiral Dewey until August 16th. By that time, the United States Army occupied the city and had become the protectors of their former enemy, and the enemy of their former ally.

CHAPTER NINETEEN
Mexican General "Pancho" Villa's Raid on Columbus, NM, 1916

About the only thing for certain about the raid of Mexican General Pancho Villa on Columbus, New Mexico is that it took place. There has always been much speculation concerning General Villa's motivation behind the Columbus raid. No one knows his reason for ordering the attack and Villa wold never talk about the matter. One theory suggests it was an act of retaliation for the American government breaking is word to Villa. Embroiled in a civil war, Mexico searched for leadership. A dispute broke out between Pancho Villa and Venustiano Carranza when Villa refused to acknowledge the authority of the new president, Carranza. Others say that Villa was paid to attack Columbus, NM.

To add insult to injury, President Wilson aided Carranza in defeating Villa by allowing Mexican troops to be transported on the El Paso- Southwestern Railroad through Texas and New Mexico to a campaign in Mexico against Villa. These additional troops helped defeat Villa and his army in the Battle of Agua Prieta, across from Douglas, Arizona on November 1, 1915. Possibly the attack on Columbus occurred as retaliation for the shipment of troops, since the village had an El Paso - Southwestern depot. Amazingly enough however, the depot only sustained light damage from flying bullets.

Looking at where and what the Villistas raided, historians have pointed out that little beyond the business district of Columbus received any real damage. Perhaps Villa raided Columbus to correct a business deal gone bad. This theory contends that Villa bought guns and ammunition from the Ravel Brothers of Columbus. Although he paid for the armaments, Villa never received the weapons and ammunition. During the raid, Villistas captured Arthur Ravel and tried to force him to open the business's safe. Fortunately, the Villistas believed Ravel, when he stated he did not know the combination. Arthur Ravel eventually escaped the Villistas when gunfire, possibly from the machine gun in front of the Hoover Hotel, killed the two men holding his arms.

A final theory concerns the need by the Villistas to secure not just arms and ammunition but food, clothing, and other supplies to continue the civil war. As Villa's army roamed through northern Mexico in the winter of 1915-1916, it needed these supplies to revitalize its dwindling numbers. Despite the U.S. Army garrison at Columbus, the town must have been one of the more inviting targets on the border.

What is known for certain is that on March 9, 1916, at 4:15 am, a Mexican raiding force of approximately 484[107] men attacked Columbus, New Mexico, southwest United States, shouting "Viva Villa" and "Viva Mexico". These raiders wore sombreros and khaki-colored uniforms with criss-cross bandoliers over their chests. Leader of the attack was Mexican revolutionary General Francisco "Pancho" Villa.

Villa strung his men out in a long line just south of Columbus hidden in an arroyo or ditch within a hundred yards of an army outpost where a sentry paced his beat. From their positions in the arroyo, the Villistas silently watched their leader and when he raised his arm they sprung up and attacked. The assault was a complete surprise to American forces.

The evening before, when they went to bed, the 300 or so Columbus residents in 1916 felt quite safe from attack from Mexico. They had the protection of soldiers of the 13th US Cavalry stationed at an outpost across the railroad tracks, south of town. That evening, no one knew that on March 8, the previous day, Lieutenant Colonel Cipriano Vargas of General Villa's staff had scouted Columbus including the military garrison. No one knew that evening that Colonel Vargas had reported back to his General Villa that there were only about 30 soldiers at the post, wrongly underestimating the camp's true strength of 120 soldiers.

There was so much confidence in their safety that, on the evening before the attack, Colonel Herbert Slocum, Army Chief at Columbus, together with other officers, had gone 30 miles north to Deming to attend a polo match playoff.

Columbus in 1916 consisted of a cluster of adobe houses and frame buildings, a railroad station, two hotels, an army outpost, several stores, and a few other buildings. Broadway, the main street, ran from east to west and on it was a hardware store operated by J. L. Walker, a grocery owned by J. T. Dean, and C. Dewitt Miller's drug store. On Taft Street, near the railroad station, was the two-story Commercial Hotel, operated by Mr. and Mrs. W. T. Ritchie. Across was a movie theater and over the tracks was the Customs House with an arroyo (a natural ditch) running nearby and parallel to the road to the Mexico border 3 miles south.

One of the largest stores was the Ravel Brothers Mercantile on Boulevard Street. Sam and Louis Ravel handled bolt goods, cooking utensils, boots, overalls, sundries and--rifles, pistols and ammunition. Arthur, their 12-year-old brother, worked as chore boy. The Ravels encouraged Mexican

---

[107] Thompkins, Frank Col., <u>Chasing Villa</u>, Military Service Publishig Company, Harrisburg, PA, 1934 .

customers to shop as long as they paid in American dollars. And when Mexicans ordered arms, the Ravels never asked embarrassing questions about what use was to be made of them. The Ravels had been a good friend to Villa in the past.

On one arms deal, it's said, General Villa paid cash in advance for a large quantity of rifles and ammunition, but after his order arrived he found he'd been cheated out of $2,500 worth of arms that he'd paid for in advance. Some say this sour deal added to General Villa's growing hatred of Americans, but no one knows for sure.

The Attack--March 9, 1916

The attack began with the thunder of Villistas' rifles dropping the sentry. Then in a hostile wave, Villa and his men rose from the arroyo, some afoot and some mounted, swarming across the town, shooting, yelling, smashing windows and doors, looting, destroying, burning, and killing.

Deans' grocery store went up in flames. The Commercial Hotel was a roaring holocaust. Miller, the druggist, died trying to protect his store. Among the first to die were Dr. H. M. Hart, W. A. Davidson, J. J. Moore, and N. H. Walker.

The raiders broke down the doors of Ravel's Mercantile Store. Once inside they searched every nook for Sam Ravel, stealing and destroying as they went. They tore into a pile of cowhides stopping when they were down to the last few not finding Mr. Ravel who was flattened out beneath the very last hide. Two of Villa's men caught young Arthur Ravel on the street, in his underwear. Lieutenant Castleman saw them manhandling Arthur and shot and killed both of the Villistas. It's said that 12-year-old Arthur broke loose and ran four miles before stopping for breath.

At the army encampment, in the absence of Colonel Slocum, Lieutenant Castleman, the officer of the day, took charge. He found the guard house locked with no way to reach the rifles and ammunition stored inside. Soldiers were forced to fight with whatever they could find. There was one machine gun, which, after a single splendid burst, jammed.

By sunrise, about 2 hours later, General Villa finally realized that the American forces were greater than his scouts had reported, and ordered retreat. By 7:30 the withdrawal of Villa's men was complete.

The Casualties

The raid cost Americans 18 lives while 90 Villistas were killed. Official records list in detail the quantity of food and supplies the raiders stole from Columbus, including 80 fine-bred horses, 30 mules, and an assortment of military equipment including some 300 Mausers. Abortive as the Columbus raid was, Villa succeeded in terms of booty.

Whatever the reasons for the attack, its outcome was the same. Columbus residents experienced a boom in their village. General John J. "Black Jack" Pershing arrived in Columbus to lead a punitive expedition into Mexico to find and capture Pancho Villa. Columbus became the home base of this expedition and a beehive of activity. By March 10, just one day after the raid, the first of several thousand troops began to arrive in Columbus. By late 1916, due to the growth of camp personnel, Columbus held the largest population of any city in the state of New Mexico.

In Pershing's search for Pancho Villa, he conducted an extensive campaign into Mexico. Two columns of soldiers ventured south, one from Columbus and the other from Culberson Ranch in the southwest corner of New Mexico. Several thousand troops, at times going 300 miles into Mexico, were supported by trucks and airplanes, the first such aid in American warfare. Indeed, the punitive expedition saw the end of nineteenth-century warfare and the beginning of twentieth-century combat. Historians also point out that with the use of airplanes the military began its development of modern intelligence.

The two columns of troops marched south. They meet about 100 miles into Mexico in a town called Casas Grandes. Later, when hearing that Villa was ahead of them, they divided and meet up again 50 to 60 miles further south. Pershing also sent three cavalry units after Villa. The master plan contended that a combination of mounted troops and infantry units would trap and capture Villa. Despite the best efforts of Pershing and the U.S. Army, this never came to pass.

The Punitive Expedition prepared not only the troops, but also Pershing and his officers for World War I. The expedition lasted eleven months, pitting American troops against Villistas and Carranza's troops. Although the American government supported Carranza, the Mexican president did not like American troops in his country. Carranzistas attacked and repelled American troops just like Villa's troops. Pershing failed all attempts to capture Pancho Villa and eventually the Army retreated to the United States. The Punitive Expedition was called to a halt in early 1917. Villa was assassinated in Parrall, Mexico in 1923.

Speculation

There are those who find the story of the raid on Columbus, New Mexico to be very odd sounding. First, Villa had no real military reason to attack Columbus and in fact, it actually caused him more problems than he was ready to undertake. Additionally, Villa accomplished absolujtely nothing of value during the attack. It seemed to be an attack just for the sake of attacking.

It should also be kept in mind that all but one officer of the 13th Cavalry was conveniently out of town and, though he was the officer of the day, he did not have the keys to the armory. Thus, in the event of an attack, the garrison and as a result, the town was defenseless. So what really was taking place? Well, I have a theory that I would ask the reader to consider carefully before discarding.

First, history does not make much mention of it, but Pancho Villa and General John Joseph Pershing (Black Jack) were good friends. Villa spent many a night as a guest at the Pershing House (Quarters #1) at Fort Bliss, Texas. There are a number of photos that confirm this association. There have long been stories told by old soldiers who rode with Pershing that during the Punitive Expedition, in the evening, Villa would come into Pershing's camp and they would play cards until dawn when Villa would rejoin his troops and the chase would begin once more.

John Pershing was living in Quarters #1 at Fort Bliss, Texas even though he had no military duties at Fort Bliss. Contrary to public opinion, Pershing was not the commander of Fort Bliss, he actually commanded the Eighth Brigade, with headquarters at the Presidio in San Francisco[108]. However, due to a great deal of unrest along the Mexican border he soon was called to take command of a large mobile force guarding the border under the general supervision of General Frederick Funston. Living conditions were hard and General Pershing left his family in the comfort of the Presidio. In fact, his wife and children were living in quarters at the Presidio and all of them, except for one child, were killed in a fire that broke out in their quarters in 1915. So why was one of America's foremost Generals sitting on his hands, far from his command? The answer, I believe, is that from late 1914, he was preparing for the Punitive Expedition that he would lead into Mexico.

In spite of Wilson's promise to keep the United States out of World War I, there was a great deal of determination in various quarters to get us into the war. In fact, in 1916, shortly before Villa's Raid the Battle of Verdun, the longest and one of the bloodiest engagements of World War I began. Over two million men were engaged in this epic battle. It began on Feb. 21, 1916, when the Germans, commanded by Crown Prince Frederick William, launched a massive offensive against Verdun, an awkward salient in the French line. The outlying forts of Douaumont and Hardaumont soon fell, but the French rallied under General Pétain (with the cry "They shall not pass") and resistance stiffened. A British offensive on the Somme relieved the pressure on Verdun in July, 1916, and by December the French had recovered most of the ground lost. The intention of the Germans had been a battle of attrition in which they hoped to bleed the French army white. In the end, they sustained almost as many casualties as the French; an estimated 328,000 to the French 348,000.

The Big Picture

The events that led up to the attack on Columbus, New Mexico by Pancho Villa actually began in 1914. In that year Archduke Ferdinand of Austria and his wife were assassinated on June 28, 1914 in Sarajevo, Bosnia. The assassination of the heir to the Austrian throne caused several unsteady alliances to erupt into war as Russia and France, two of Serbia's allies, began to mobilize their military forces.

Germany, Austria's ally responds by declaring war on Russia and France on August 1, 1914. Although guaranteeing Belgian neutrality, the German Army marched through Belgium into France. In August of 1914 Bulgaria and Turkey join Germany and Austria-Hungary in the Central Powers. France, England, and Russia (later Japan and Italy) join the Allied Powers

---

[108] He actually took command in January of 1914.

In the face of a major isolationist movement in America, Wilson declared U.S. neutrality August 4, 1914 Washington, D.C. Reflecting strong public opinion, Wilson states that U.S. will not join the war. However, a number of major U.S. businesses began to supply war materials to England. In response, Germany declared the waters around British Isles a war zone on February 15, 1915. Neutral vessels are warned of potential u-boat attacks. Wilson responded by warning Germany that it would be accountable for any loss of American life

The passenger liner, the Lusitania, was sunk by a German U-Boat on May 7, 1915 off coast of Ireland. Torpedoed without warning, the Lusitania sank in 18 minutes, killing 1198 (128 Americans). In spite of the German intent to wage unrestricted warfare, the Kaiser had to be concerned with public opinion. Following the sinking of an unarmed British liner called the Arabic, Berlin signed the Arabic Pledge on September 1, 1915 Berlin in which Germany promised not to sink unarmed liners. However, this was not sufficient for some parties. The Sussex Pledge was signed on May 31, 1916 in Berlin following sinking of French steamer Sussex. In this pledge, Germany again agreed to "visit and search" rules, but insists that Great Britain should also agree to obey international laws regarding freedom of the seas

Woodrow Wilson won the 1916 presidential election on November 1916, based on the platform that "he kept us out of war." Wilson and Democrats barely defeat Hughes and Republicans (277 to 254 in the Electoral College). However, Wilson certainly had his eye on the war and many felt that he fully intended on getting the U.S. involved. On January 22, 1917, Wilson calls for "peace without victory". Frustrated with his efforts to mediate a peace, Wilson became convinced that both sides needed to cease hostilities. Almost as an insult to President Wilson's call for peace, Germany resumed unlimited submarine warfare on January 31, 1917.

Confident that if the U.S. did declare war on the Great powers, that any help given to the allies would be too late, Germany decided to starve England into submission. At about the same time, British Code Breaking Specialists in the secret Room 40's ensured ensured the entry of the US into the war in the spring of 1917. This story begins with a telegram transmitted on 16th January 1917 from the German Foreign Minister, Arthur Zimmermann, to Count Johann von Bernstorff, his Ambassador in Washington, warning them that the Kaiser's Supreme Command had just decided as a point of grand strategy to intensify the U-Boat campaign in the Western Atlantic.

This broke previous German undertakings to the US, and risked bringing the US into the war on the side of France, Britain, and Russia. Von Bernstorff was accordingly instructed to try to persuade the Mexicans to attack the US from the south. What Zimmermann did not know was that the trans-Atlantic telegraph cable was being routinely tapped by a British black chamber[109], and so the "Zimmermann intercept" was soon in Room 40.

---

109 Secret Code Breaking Center.

The British had hoped that the restart of the U-Boat attacks would convince Wilson to enter the war, but it soon became apparent that President Wilson was still vacillating. In mid-February, therefore, with British shipping losses starting to mount, British officials finally took matters into their own hands[110]. Using diplomatic contacts at the US Embassy in London, they passed the Americans the transcript of the Mexico City version of the telegram, wherein German Foreign minister Zimmermann asked Mexico to join Germany in exchange for return of southwest U.S. President Wilson duly made the matter public, and the story hit the streets in the morning papers on 1st March 1916, causing such a violent swing of public opinion against the Kaiser that the US declared war on Germany just over a month later.

Wilson asked Congress for greater powers February 1917 however, the U.S. Senate, led by La Follette, of Wisconsin, refused to grant Wilson power to wage an undeclared naval war against Germany. The Russian Revolution deposed Czar Nicholas March 15, 1917[111]. Instability in Europe encouraged Wilson to act and on April 2, 1917, Wilson asked for a formal declaration of war claiming that "The world must be made safe for democracy."

Various Theories

Was Pancho Villa a German Agent?

In light of the Zimmerman Telegram, the US entered World War I. Wilson had long fought to get the two sides to cease hostilities, but both sides rejected the idea. Subsequently, Wilson with the obsession of peace allowed the Germans to use the American communications systems to transmit messages not known to U.S. officials. Wilson allowed this to proceed under protest from his senior aids.

The German actions were later viewed as treacherous as the American system was used to notify the German Ambassador of the Zimmerman Plan. Giving the U.S. less than eight hours notice, the German ambassador delivered the message about the U-boat war. Washington was taken by surprise. In Berlin everyone asked the question, "What will the United States do?"

On February 3rd. after vacillating for three days, diplomatic relations with Germany were broken off. But it was not war yet and the allies were discouraged at Wilson's ongoing reluctance. At this point, the British furnished the U.S. with a copy of the decoded Zimmerman Telegram. Wilson was astounded at its contents and became angry at what he saw as a great betrayal.

It was later released to the press and caused a storm of protest. But there were many in high levels in the US who called the telegram a fake. What if the Germans denied the telegram? When confronted, Zimmerman inexplicably

---

110 The British are old hands at manipulating U.S. leaders for their own ends.
111 As I will show, U.S. interests orchestrated the Russian Revolution and protected the Communist economy for decades.

admitted his authorship and settled the question in American minds. He also threw away an opportunity to find out how America had obtained the message.

The fall-out from the authenticity of the telegram was great. The pacifists were routed and the German-American lobby retreated in disgrace. The president reconvened Congress for April 2, 1917. Packed into the chamber, the members of both Houses, the Supreme Court, The Cabinet, the diplomatic corps, the press, and the visitors who filled the gallery listened with every nerve to the words as the President declared the "The German government was a 'natural foe of liberty'..."

How could the man who made the April 2 speech be the same man who wished to settle for peace without victory in January and who refused to believe that the Germans were hostile to America in February? Was the Zimmerman Telegram an actual fake and used to push America into the war?

Is it possible that the American people were tricked into declaring war? There is no doubt that the U.S. military had been preparing for war since 1915. The evidence is fairly conclusive on this point. This would also explain the peclair timing of the various incidents along the Southern Border. As the Punitive Expedition withdrew from Mexico, having accomplished its purpose, America learned that Arthur Zimmerman, the German Foreign minister, had sent a telegram to the Mexican government proposing an alliance between the two countries against the US. Germany offered to give New Mexico, Texas and Arizona back to Mexico in exchange for the partnership. The telegram, intercepted by British intelligence, outraged Americans and was one of the decisive factors for the US' entry into WWI. Pancho Villa's exploits, while never forgotten, receded into the background.

Not being one that believes in coincidences, the timing of these two incidents raises a number of questions in this author's mind. First and foremost of these would be the affiliations of Pancho Villa and the reasons for his raid on Columbus, New Mexico. Could it be that, at least in so far as the raid on Columbus, New Mexico was concerned, could Pancho Villa have been working for the Germans?

There is strong circumstantial evidence that Villa was not only financed by the German imperial government, but that some of his military actions were explicitly designed to aid the Kaiser's cause. Before going into further detail, it is useful to examine the sequence of events that propelled Villa toward wishing to do maximum damage to the United States, and therefore being susceptible to German blandishments.

In the early days of the revolution, Villa had very good relations with Americans. On Christmas Eve of 1912 he escaped from the military prison of Santiago Tlatelolco in Mexico City. He had been imprisoned after being reprieved from a death sentence handed down by General Victoriano Huerta, the usurper who would overthrow Francisco Madero in February 1913.

That same month, Villa found himself in El Paso, living there in complete freedom and enjoying countless friendships with gringos. On March 9 he crossed the border with just 15 men and began a rising against the Huerta dictatorship. As noted, Villa has always liked Americans and the feeling was mutual. Among the many that swelled his ranks was a "foreign legion" composed of as colorful a group of adventurers as has ever been assembled under one standard.

Among them was the legendary John Reed (whose book, *Insurgent Mexico*, was about his service with the villistas), Oscar Creighton, a San Francisco bank robber called the "Dynamite Devil," Sam Drebben a/k/a "the fighting Jew," a Spanish-speaking machinist named Ben Turner, and Edward S. "Tex" O'Reilly, a hard-bitten rancher turned soldier-of-fortune, who would later serve in the Philippine Insurrection and the First World War.

Americans also manned Villa's primitive air force, made up of four planes. The pilots, ex-barnstormers and every bit as colorful as their compatriots on the ground, answered to names like Mickey McQuire, Wild Bill Heath and Farnum T. Fish. It has even been claimed that the legendary Hollywood cowboy Tom Mix served with Villa's forces, though this was denied by El Paso Journalist Dale L. Walker. According to Walker, the version of Mix being a "villista" was the invention of a flack in his studio's public relations office.

With the aid of these volunteers, Villa was able to team up with Venustiano Carranza and Alvaro Obregón and drive Huerta into exile in July 1914. But the fall of Huerta did nothing to solve the turbulence plaguing Mexico. Before the end of 1914 Villa had fallen out with Carranza and Obregón. Mexico was again plunged into civil war.

Finally, Carranza was installed in Mexico City as provisional president but it was Obregón who furnished the muscle. Obregón, a self-made but highly skilled general, had studied the trench warfare tactics then prevailing on the Western Front of France. Armed with this expertise, he inflicted a series of defeats on Villa, driving him from central Mexico back into the northern sierra of Chihuahua. On October 19, 1914, the United States extended de facto recognition to Carranza. To Villa, this was the vilest sort of betrayal. He had always been a friend to the gringos and this is how they were repaying him. A simple man, he didn't understand the realpolitik which mandates that you recognize whoever seems to be more effectively in control of a country in chaos.

Villa's anti-Americanism was further inflamed on November 2, 1915, when carrancista troops were allowed to cross U.S. soil to attack him in the rear at Agua Prieta, across the border from Douglas, Arizona. To add insult to injury, U.S. searchlights were deliberately focused on the villistas to make them easier targets for their enemies.

At least one influential American sympathized with Villa and understood his feelings. General Hugh L. Scott, who had many dealings with Villa, wrote that "The recognition of Carranza had the effect of solidifying the power of the man who had rewarded us with kicks and making an outlaw of the man who helped us." Villa sent Scott[112] a telegram saying that he was the one honest man north of the border, however, that didn't stop the villistas from killing 16 American mining engineers captured when they held up a train near Santa Isabel, Chihuahua, on January 10, 1914.

It is clear from history that Germany did not want the US to become involved in WWI. German agents had previously tried to destabilize the Mexican government by offering $10,000,000 to a few Mexicans to engineer an overthrow of the government. When that didn't happen, an arms buyer for Villa suggested to the Germans that they should use him to create a war with the US to divert US attention from Europe. The Germans were, in fact, delighted with Villa's raid, and he may have been encouraged by the promise of German military aid, but there's no evidence suggesting that the Germans funded his project.

Others said that the attack was paid for by a U.S. business consortium. US businesses slobbered over Mexico's natural resources and the fact that "Mexico was an almost virgin outlet for extension of the market of our overproducing civilization" as the Chicago Tribune put it. The Mexican Revolution which started in 1910 and would see the demise of three Mexican Presidents was in many ways a reaction to the fact that most of their economy was foreign-owned. Americans owned 85% of the mines and much of the oil, railroad and timber industries.

Even though Villa wanted to redistribute land from the wealthy to give to the poor, he also took care to not offend the US businesses in his region by not taxing them or seizing their assets. He did not support movements like the International Workers of the World (IWW) or Mexican labor unions. This made him popular with US businessmen while his Robin Hood rhetoric made him appealing to US liberals, though some did criticize him as a "tool for Wall Street."

Wilson expressed admiration for Villa. He wanted someone to modernize and democratize Mexico, but not touch US interests, to stabilize the country without furthering revolutionary potential. Sounds a lot like how the US tried to blunt and cut off the challenge of socialism during this time by instituting progressive "reform." The US had watched the Mexican Revolution with a wary eye. Their pattern was to lend support to a dictator and then help to overthrow him whenever he did something to harm American companies, like collect taxes. Certain American businessmen wanted a full-scale occupation of Mexico instead of leaving their investments up to the whims of Mexican politicians. As this conspiracy tale tells the story, by hiring Villa to invade the US, US companies hoped to force Wilson into a massive intervention in Mexico and thus protect

---

112 General Hugh L. Scott was assistant chief of general staff of the army, April 22, 1914. Settled by diplomacy the impending conflict on the Mexican border at Naco, Ariz., as well as on two other occasions at El Paso; settled Piute Indian trouble at Bluff, Utah, March 1915; he recovered property of foreigners confiscated by Villa, 1915. He was chief of staff of the U. S. Army from November 17, 1914 to September 22, 1917. Retired by operation of law September 22, 1917, but retained on active duty to May 12, 1919 At the time of Villa's raid, he wold have been in a position to organize paying off Villa..

their big-money interests. There are a number of stories that Villa was paid approximately $250,000.00 by the U.S. Government, to carry out the attack and the money was delivered to the Mexican Bandit leader by two U.S. Army officers who later disappeared.

Whatever may have been Villa's motivation, his actions certainly gave substance to the Zimmerman Telegram. The American people were told (and believed) that these troubles of the spring and summer of 1916 were perpetrated by a German government dead-set on embroiling the U. S. in difficulties closer to home so as to distract this country from the battles raging on the European continent. Wilson may also have been harboring some hidden agenda against Mexico that had little to do with Germany. Like most violent conflicts, this one has root causes that sit deep, but such an in-depth discussion remains outside the scope of this series on OAC history.

The German plan, or so it was explained by the Wilson administration, called for the use of two Mexican leaders, President Venustiano Carranza and Francisco "Pancho" Villa, to take action against the U. S. for the purpose of "insulting and defying your great northern neighbor," acts which began to manifest on January 11, 1916. Without warning, Villa seized a train in the Mexican state of Chihuahua and took into custody 19 United States citizens who were immediately shot to death. The reaction north of the border was instant outrage, mixed with loud cries for strong retaliation. Wilson, mad as hell, hesitated to call out the Army, preferring rather to see what Villa's next move might be.

It came on March 9th. Villa, with 484 well-armed troops, attacked the town of Columbus, New Mexico, killing 11 civilians. The town was plundered almost beyond recognition. Now Wilson acted. United States Army troops in the vicinity rushed to the scene, causing Villa's army (referred to as "bandits" by U. S. military officials) to flee. A skirmish ensued and 30 of Villa's men and nine American soldiers were killed.

Wilson and the rest of America, incensed by the bad news now pouring from the border, called on President Carranza to do something decisive. Carranza promised to punish the Villistas, provided the United States would agree not to interfere. Wilson agreed but patience began to run thin as Carranza, according to the American public's perception of the matter, seemed to balk at doing anything significant. Therefore, the president, possibly in a momentary fit of impatience, ordered General Frederick Funston, the U. S. commander along the border, to send a strong American column into Mexico to pursue Villa and to capture him "alive-or-dead[113]."

General John Pershing, who would later lead the famed American Expeditionary Force (AEF) that went "over there" in 1917 to fight the German Army in Europe, was placed as overall commander of the border operation. Among his youngest officers on this campaign was future World War II icon

---

113 Legally, the U.S. invaded a foreign country.

George Patton Jr., at this time a young lieutenant on the front-end of his military career.

Pershing's force, numbering 4,000 men, entered (legally or illegally) Mexico on March 15th to find and punish Villa (he was never captured), remaining there until early 1917. On March 29, bullets began flying in a small-scale battle near the town of Parral in Chihuahua between about 400 U. S. soldiers and a larger force of Villistas. The latter were defeated at the cost of one American dead. Villa immediately dispersed his men in different directions, most taking refuge in the inaccessible mountains of the region.

Other small fire fights erupted over the next several months (April 12th, June 24th), inflicting more U. S. casualties. War between Mexico and the United States, according to reports of the time, "trembled in the balance." Wilson now made a decision that would place the nation on a war footing. Fearing the "Mexican difficulty," as he put it, was far too important to be left to such a small force of Army regulars, the president mobilized various National Guard units from around the country. The date was June 18th.

Does it make sense to mobile the National Guard and disrupt the lives of thousands of American citizens because of bandit raids along the Mexican Border? It is more likely that he called up the National Guard because he planned on getting the country into the war in Europe in spite of his promises to the American people. The Villa Raid was merely his excuse.

Did We Really Try To Capture Villa?

Much has been written over the years about our diligent efforts to capture Pancho Villa during the Punitive Expedition. However, what really happened was that a call to arms was issued by the the Government, who sent a well equipped army into Chihuahua to try and chase Villa down. According to reports, Villa managed to elude Pershing's forces by allegedly *following them around* and hiding behind the huge cloud of dust that they kicked up with their mule trains and motorized vehicles. The U.S. Military, on the other hand, was taking this opportunity to test all of their fancy, modernized military equipment in preparation for our entry in WW1. In an event that presaged our chase of Osama Bin Laden, we never caught up with Villa, however.

Legend has it that Villa, disguised as a peasant, actually walked right up to Pershing and had extensive conversations with him. General Pershing, who has a reputation for being one of our smarter general officers, carried out these talks with a man who was his friend[114], but alleged did not recognize him. Wilson sent this man to lead our forces in World War I? Pershing eventually withdrew his forces from Mexico, but Villa managed to stay in the field for four more years before finally surrendering to the Mexican government.

---

[114] Villa had even visited Pershing's Home at fort Bliss.

German Involvement

Germany had made great inroads in Mexico in defiance of he Monroe Doctrine. No one expected a revolution in 1910, least of all the Germans. According to a former German ambassador, the Mexicans were a little more than a "teeming, bestial mass of humanity" that had no chance of toppling President Porfirio Diaz. When the unthinkable happened, Berlin then assumed his replacement, Francisco Madero, would turn out to be another Diaz who would once again rule Mexico with an iron grip.

Even though Madero attempted to follow a generally pro-German foreign polic, Berlin found his domestic policies extremely disturbing. The problem was that Madero insisted on promoting democratic freedoms instead of following the example of Porfirio Diaz by suppressing Mexico's unrest. According to Hintze, "The cardinal error lies in his ... belief that he can rule the Mexican people as one would rule one of the more advanced German nations. This raw people of half-savages without religion, with its small ruling stratum of superficially civilized mestizos can live with no regime other than enlightened despotism." Hintze, however, never divulged his political opinions to Madero, knowing it would only turn him away from his otherwise pro-German policies. What Hintze hoped for most was a military coup that would establish a dictatorship aimed at reversing Madero's revolution.9 He did not have long to wait.

In February 1913 the conspiracy that overthrew Madero began to take shape, one of its chief figures being the American amabssador to Mexico, Henry Lane Wilson. From the beginning Wilson enjoyed the strong support of Hintze, although they differed on the question of who should succeed Madero. Wilson favored Felix Diaz, nephew of the former dictator, while Hintze viewed Diaz as both incompetent and pro-American. Their most serious split occured during the Decena Tragica, when Wilson arranged for a ceasefire to evacuate foreigners caught in the crossfire. But since he feared that removing all the foreigners would weaken his other objective, an armed American intervention, he didn't tell the rest of the diplomatic corps about the ceasefire. Already upset by Wilson's effort to install Diaz, Hintze decided to press for his own candidate, General Victoriano Huerta, without bothering to consult Wilson.

He arranged a meeting with Madero's foreign minister, Pedro Lascurain, where he proposed the "Installation of General Huerta as Governor-General of Mexico, with full powers to end the revolution according to his own judgment." Lascurain passed on the proposal to Madero, who initially agreed, according to Hintze's later account. To the ambassador's chagrin, however, Madero then changed his mind.

Shortly thereafter, the Mexican president and his government were prisoners of the conspirators, prompting Hintze to launch his final campaign against the rise to power of Felix Diaz. In this he was successful, helping to forge a compromise whereby Huerta was given "temporary" control of the government and Diaz was promised that he would be his successor. However, he was less successful in his campaign to persuade Huerta to exile Madero, whom he hoped would be useful as a potential counterweight to the Huerta government in case it took a pro-American stance. Ignoring Hintze's offer to send Madero to Europe, Huerta had the ex-president murdered two days later.

So, let's get back to our discussion about the part that the Germans played in Villa's actions. At this point we must focus on the shadowy figure of Felix A. Sommerfeld, described by the prize-winning German historian Friedrich Katz as "one of the most interesting members of the shadowy army of agents, double agents, and lobbyists who swarmed like locusts over Mexico once the revolution had begun."

Sommerfeld was a con man extraordinaire. Though he had fought against the revolutionary Boxers in China, he came to Mexico and convinced Madero that he was a revolutionary democrat. At the same time he was establishing close relations with the German government and certain U.S. business interests.

The latter were represented by a shady lobbyist name Sherbourne Hopkins, who was closely allied with Carranza. In what was undoubtedly a union of kindred spirits, Sherbourne befriended Sommerfeld, gave him money, and told him to go to Mexico and place himself at Carranza's disposal. In Mexico, the fast-talking Sommerfeld so completely won Carranza's trust that the latter delegated him to go to Chihuahua and spy on Villa.

This he did, but not for Carranza. All information gained on Villa went directly to the German government. In addition, he so ingratiated himself with Villa, that Villa game him an exclusive concession to import dynamite for his forces. For this activity, Sommerfeld pulled down a commission of 5,000 dollars a month.

In late 1915, a few months before the attack on Columbus, the U.S. Justice Department ascertained that 340,000 dollars had been paid into an account that Sommerfeld maintained in a St. Louis bank. The money came from an account in New York in the name of the German government. Shortly after these transactions came to light, Sommerfeld closed the account. Where did the money go? Treasury sleuths learned that every penny of it had been paid to the Western Cartridge Company - arms suppliers for Villa.

When confronted by agents of the Justice Department, Sommerfeld demonstrated that he'd lost none of his gift of gab. Piously insisting that he had severed all relations with Villa after the U.S. recognized Carranza, he even sent Villa a telegram protesting the massacre of the 16 mining engineers.

At the same time, he was unable to explain why 340,000 dollars deposited in his account by the German government had ended up in the hands of Villa's arms supplier. In addition, according to Carranza's agents in the U.S., Sommerfeld continued to buy arms for Villa even after his interrogation by Justice Department agents. The question inevitably arises as to who was using whom.

Pancho Villa was a revolutionary first and foremost and the fact that he may have received arms and financial aid from the Germans doesn't transform him into an adherent of Kaiserism. Between the dominant Carranza-Obregón forces and the now hostile United States, Pancho Villa was in a very difficult spot. And if somebody offered to help him, he wasn't about to require the would-be benefactor to submit to an ideological litmus test. On at least one occasion he resisted the blandishments of the Germans. The German consul in Torreón, which Villa had recently captured, gave a lavish banquet for him and urged him to march on the Tampico oil fields. With the capture of Tampico, German ships would land in the port and bring him money and arms. Villa appeared to consider the offer - then changed his mind and marched on Chihuahua.

So in final analysis, did the U.S. or U.S. interests promote the raid by Pancho Villa on Columbus, New Mexico? I don't think that anyone who reads this with an open mind could doubt that someone was orchestrating the situation. Too many people benefited from this action for it to have come about by pure chance.

CHAPTER TWENTY
WORLD WAR I

What we call World War I was never intended to become a world war, nor was it intended to upset the status quo of Europe. It was also one of the first wars where a Secret Society was openly involved in instigating the war. In order that the reader thoroughly understand the situation in Europe at the time this war eruptred, it is necessary that some preliminary information be given regarding the participants.

The True Cause of World War 1

History books record that World War I started when the nations went to war to avenge the assassination of the Archduke Francis Ferdinand, the heir to the Habsburg throne, on June 28, 1914. This is the typical explanation. But the "revisionist historian" knows just what caused and what the purpose was of the conflagration of World War I.

Up until America's entry into this war, the American people had followed the wise advice of President George Washington given in his farewell address, delivered to the nation on September 17, 1796. President Washington said: "*It is our true policy to steer clear of permanent alliance with any portion of the foreign world.... Why, by interweaving our destiny with that of any part of Europe, entangle our peace and prosperity in the toils of European ambition, rivalship, interest, humour or caprice?*"

President Washington attempted to warn the American people about getting embroiled in the affairs of Europe. But in 1914, it was not to be. There were those who were secretly planning America's involvement in World War I whether the American people wanted it or not.

The Plan to Involve America in World War 1

The pressure to involve the American government started in 1909, long before the actual assassination of the Archduke. Norman Dodd, former director of the Committee to Investigate Tax Exempt Foundations of the U.S. House of

Representatives, testified that the Committee was invited to study the minutes of the Carnegie Endowment for International Peace as part of the Committee's investigation. The Committee stated: "*The trustees of the Foundation brought up a single question. If it is desirable to alter the life of an entire people, is there any means more efficient than war.... They discussed this question... for a year and came up with an answer: There are no known means more efficient than war, assuming the objective is altering the life of an entire people. That leads them to a question: How do we involve the United States in a war. This is in 1909.*"

So the decision was made to involve the United States in a war so that the "life of the entire people could be altered." This was the conclusion of a foundation supposedly committed to "peace."

The Players

It is also quite beneficial to look at the primary parties involved in the war. First, the historic "bad guys" of this war have long been the Germans and the Austro-Hungarian Empire. The union between Austria and Hungary took place in 1867. Both states had unelected upper houses and elected lower houses of parliament, but the overall political authority was held by Emperor Franz Josef. Over 51 million people lived in the 675,000 square kilometres of the empire. The two largest ethnic groups were Germans (10 million) and Hungarians (9 million). There were also Poles, Croats, Bosnians, Serbians, Italians, Czechs, Ruthenes, Slovenes, Slovaks and Romanians. Overall, fifteen different languages were spoken in the Austro-Hungarian empire.

The Austro-Hungarian government had long feared attack from Russia, which under the Czar was considered a powerful Empire. In 1879 Austro-Hungary and Germany agreed to form a Dual Alliance, which became the Triple Alliance when in 1882 it was expanded to include Italy. The three countries agreed to support each other if attacked by either France or Russia. Both of these countries were known for being aggressive against smaller countries.

The Triple Alliance was renewed at five-yearly intervals. The formation of the Triple Entente in 1907 by Britain, France and Russia, reinforced the belief in the minds of the Austro-Hungarian Empire, Germany and Italy that they needed a military alliance for their mutual protection.

The Austro-Hungarian Imperial Army was officially under the control of the Commander-in-Chief, Emperor Franz Josef[115], but by 1914, the Emperor was 84 years old and the Army chief of staff, Count Franz Conrad, had more power over the armed forces. Conrad favoured an aggressive foreign policy and

---

115 Franz Josef was born in 1830. At the age of eighteen he became Hapsburg Emperor and in 1867, ruler of Austria-Hungary. Over the next few years his army subdued revolts in Hungary and Lombardy. Franz Josef suffered several personal tragedies. His brother Maximilian was shot by revolutionaries in Mexico and his only son, Rudolf, committed suicide in 1889. Nine years later, his wife, Elizabeth of Bavaria, was assassinated by an anarchist in Geneva.

advocated the use of military action to solve Austro-Hungary's territorial disputes with Italy and Serbia.

The Austro-Hungarian Navy was fairly small. By 1914 it had 16 battleships, 5 cruisers, 18 destroyers and 5 submarines. Austro-Hungary neglected military aviation and in 1914 the Austro-Hungarian Air Service only had 35 aircraft and one airship.

Bosnia-Herzegovina became part of the Turkish Ottoman Empire in 1389. Over the years Serbs living in the area made several attempts to obtain independence from Turkey. Revolts in 1821, 1831 and 1837 ended in failure. Armed insurrection against Turkish rule in 1874 was also unsuccessful. However, the Serbs living in Bosnia now had a powerful supporter in Russia. When Russia defeated Turkey in 1877, it forced the Turkish government to promise independence to Serbia and Rumania, autonomy to Bulgaria and reforms to Bosnia-Herzegovina.

Other European powers became concerned about the growth of Russian influence and in 1878 held the Congress of Berlin. The settlement reached at the conference resulted in independence for Serbia and Rumania and autonomy for Bulgaria. However, Bosnia-Herzegovina came under the control of Austria-Hungary and in 1908 this was consolidated when the territory was added to the Austria-Hungarian Empire.

The population of Bosnia and Herzegovina at this time was about two million. Over 40 per cent were of the Serb-Orthodox faith, 30 per cent were Moslems and about 25 per cent were Roman Catholics. The remainder was Jews and Protestants. Most of the Serb-Orthodox group was Serbs who favoured union with the state of Serbia. Unhappy with Austria-Hungarian rule, some joined terrorist organizations such as the Black Hand group.

The Black Hand

In 1911 Bogdan Zerajic attempted to assassinate General Varesanin, the Austrian governor of Bosnia. Zerajic failed and so did Muhamed Mehmedbasic when he tried to kill General Oskar Potiorek, Governor of the Austrian provinces of Bosnia-Herzegovina in 1914. However, later that year, another member of the Black Hand group, Gavrilo Princip, assassinated Archduke Franz Ferdinand, Inspector of the Austro-Hungarian Army and heir to the throne.

Conquered by the Turks in 1389, Serbia did not regain independence until 1878, and established a monarchy in 1882. Geographically a land-locked state, Serbia had the Austro-Hungarian Empire on its borders in the north, and Romania and Bulgaria in the east. To the south lay Macedonia and the northern shores of Greece, including the major port of Salonika.

Serbia was an overwhelmingly rural society. It had few mineral or industrial resources and had less than 10,000 people employed in manufacturing. The economy relied heavily on the exports of food to Germany, Turkey and Austria-Hungary.

In 1903 Dragutin Dimitrijevic, Voja Tankosic and a group of junior officers planned the assassination of the the autocratic and unpopular King Alexander of Serbia. The group stormed the royal palace and killed both the king and his wife, Queen Draga. Soon afterwards, Peter Karadjordjevic was elected king of Serbia by the Serbian parliament and Nikola Pasic became prime minister. The new National Assembly was elected by all civilian male tax payers.

Serbian encouragement of Slav separatist movements in Bosnia-Herzegovina and Croatia angered the government of Austria-Hungary. Serbia received support from Russia in this policy but the two countries were unable to prevent the Austro-Hungarian Army from seizing Bosnia in 1908.

In May 1911, ten men in Serbia formed the Black Hand Secret Society. Early members included Colonel Dragutin Dimitrijevic, the chief of the Intelligence Department of the Serbian General Staff, Major Voja Tankosic and Milan Ciganovic. The main objective of the Black Hand was the creation, by means of violence, of a Greater Serbia. Its stated aim was: "To realize the national ideal, the unification of all Serbs. This organisation prefers terrorist action to cultural activities; it will therefore remain secret."

Dragutin Dimitrijevic, who used the codename, Apis, established himself as the leader of the Black Hand. In 1911 he sent a member to assassinate Emperor Franz Josef. When this failed, Dimitrijevic turned his attention to General Oskar Potiorek, Governor of the Austrian provinces of Bosnia-Herzegovina. Dimitrijevic recruited Muhamed Mehmedbasic to kill Potiorek with a poisoned dagger. However, Mehmedbasic returned to Belgrade after failing to carry out the task.

In 1912, during the Balkan War, Serbia, Greece, Bulgaria and Montenegro won a series of comprehensive military victories over Turkish forces. The following year, Bulgaria, disappointed by the terms of the Treaty of London, attacked Greek and Serbian forces, but was quickly defeated when invaded by Romania. The subsequent peace treaty doubled the size of Serbia and gave Greece control over most of the Aegean coast.

After the war Serbia had a population of 4.5 million. All males aged between 21 and 46 were liable for compulsory military service and by 1914 the Serbian Army contained about 260,000 men.

The main objective of the Black Hand was the creation, by means of violence, of a Greater Serbia. Its stated aim was: "To realize the national ideal, the unification of all Serbs. This organisation prefers terrorist action to cultural activities; it will therefore remain secret."

By 1914 there were around 2,500 members of the Black Hand. The group was mainly made up of junior army officers but also included lawyers, journalists and university professors. About 30 of these lived and worked in Bosnia-Herzegovina.

Three senior members of the Black Hand group, Dragutin Dimitrijevic, Milan Ciganovic, and Major Voja Tankosic, decided that Archduke Franz Ferdinand should be assassinated. Dimitrijevic was concerned about the heir to the Austro-Hungarian throne, Ferdinand's plans to grant concessions to the South Slavs. Dimitrijevic feared that if this happened, an independent Serbian state would be more difficult to achieve.

When Dragutin Dimitrijevic heard that Archduke Franz Ferdinand[116] was planning to visit Sarajevo in June 1914, he sent three members of the Black Hand group, Gavrilo Princip, Nedjelko Cabrinovic and Trifko Grabez from Serbia to assassinate him. Nikola Pasic, the prime minister of Serbia, Pasic heard about the plot and gave instructions for the three men to be arrested. However, his orders were not implemented and Archduke Franz Ferdinand was assassinated.

Several members of the Black Hand group interrogated by the Austrian authorities claimed that three men from Serbia, Dragutin Dimitrijevic, Milan Ciganovic, and Major Voja Tankosic, had organised the plot. On 25th July, 1914, the Austro-Hungarian government demanded that the Serbian government arrest the men and send them to face trial in Vienna. On 25th July, 1914, Nikola Pasic, the prime minister of Serbia, told the Austro-Hungarian government that he was unable to hand over these three men as it "would be a violation of Serbia's Constitution and criminal in law". Three days later the Austro-Hungarian Empire declared war on Serbia.

The Spark

The spark that lit the flame that became the First World War was ignoted with the assassination of the Archduke Franz Ferdinand, the heir to the throne of the Austro-Hungarian Empire. During the first two years of the First World War the Serbian Army suffered a series of military defeats. Nikola Pasic blamed the Black Hand for the war, and in December 1916 decided to disband the organisation. Dragutin Dimitrijevic and several of the Black Hand leaders were arrested and executed the following year. With these deaths ended the earliest incarnation of the Secret Society that started a World War.

It is interesting to note that every phase of the events that led to the assassination of the Archduke was an internal family squabble. None of this should have led to a war that encompassed the globe and resulted in the deaths of millions. Even the naming of Franz Ferdinand as the heir to the throne was never anticipated. In 1889, Crown Prince Rudolf, the actual son of Franz Josef, shot himself at his hunting lodge[117]. The succession now passed to Franz Ferdinand's father, Carl Ludwig. When Carl Ludwig died in 1896, Franz Ferdinand became the new heir to the throne.

Franz Ferdinand's wife died in the car with him, and she too was never supposed to have been the wife of the Archduke. Franz Ferdinand had first met

---

116 Franz Ferdinand, eldest son of Carl Ludwig, the brother of Emperor Franz Josef, was born in 1863. Educated by private tutors, he joined the Austro-Hungarian Army in 1883. His military career included service with an infantry regiment in Prague and with the hussars in Hungary. While in the army Ferdinand received several promotions: captain (1885), major (1888), colonel (1890) and general (1896).

117 History reports the death of Prince Rudolf as a suicide, but there are a number of unanswered questions regarding this death.

Sophie von Chotkovato[118] at a dance in Prague in 1888. Shortly thereafter, the couple fell in love but although Sophie came from a noble Bohemian family, she was not considered a suitable woman to marry Franz Ferdinand who would one day sit on the throne of the Austro-Hungarian Empire. To be an eligible partner for a member of the Austro-Hungarian royal family, you had to be descended from the House of Hapsburg[119] or from one of the ruling dynasties of Europe.

Just as the Duke of Windsor and Prince Charles of England have done, Franz Ferdinand insisted he would not marry anyone else if he could not marry the woman he loved. Emperor Wilhelm II of Germany, Tsar Nicholas II of Russia and Pope Leo XIII all made representations to Franz Josef on Franz Ferdinand's behalf arguing that the the disagreement over Ferdinand's marriage was undermining the stability of the monarchy.

In 1899 Emperor Franz Josef agreed a deal with Franz Ferdinand. He was allowed to marry Sophie von Chotkovato but it was stipulated that her descendants would not be allowed to succeed to the throne. It was also pointed out that Sophie would not be allowed to accompany her husband in the royal carriage nor could she sit by his side in the royal box.

Franz Josef did not attend the wedding, nor did his brothers or their families. The only people of the royal family who went to the ceremony were Franz Ferdinand's stepmother, Maria Theresia, and her two daughters. Over the next few years the couple had three children: Sophie (1901), Maximilian (1902) and Ernst (1904).

In 1913 Franz Ferdinand was appointed Inspector General of the Austro-Hungarian Army. A promoter of naval expansion and military modernization, Ferdinand was popular with the armed forces and in the summer of 1914 General Oskar Potiorek, Governor of the Austrian provinces of Bosnia-Herzegovina, invited the Inspector of the Armed Forces, to watch his troops on maneuvers. When Potieoek[120] made it clear that his wife, Dutchess Sophie would also be made welcome, Franz Ferdinand agreed to make the visit.

Franz Ferdinand knew that the journey would be dangerous. A large number of people living in Bosnia-Herzegovina were unhappy with Austro-Hungarian rule and favoured union with Serbia. In 1910 a Serb, Bogdan Zerajic, had attempted to assassinate General Varesanin, the Austrian governor of Bosnia-Herzegovina, when he was opening parliament in Sarajevo.

Zerajic was a member of the Black Hand (Unity or Death) who wanted Bosnia-Herzegovina to leave the Austro-Hungarian Empire. The leader of the group was Colonel Dragutin Dimitrijevic, the chief of the Intelligence Department of the Serbian General Staff. Dimitrijevic considered Franz

---

118 Sophie Chotek von Chotkova was the daughter of the chief equerry at the Imperial Court in Vienna.

119 The Hapsburg family is one that still wields a great deal of influence to this day.

120 There have been rumors that Potiorek knew that there was a great danger of assassination, but was a supporter of the next in line for the throne. In the normal course of events, the assassination of the Archduke would have merely meant that the next in line would assume he title. This would have solved a number of political problems for the Empire.

Ferdinand a serious threat to a union between Bosnia-Herzegovina and Serbia. He was worried that Ferdinand's plans to grant concessions to the South Slavs would make an independent Serbian state more difficult to achieve.

When it was announced that Franz Ferdinand was going to visit Bosnia in June 1914, Dimitrijevic began to make plans to assassinate the heir of the Austro-Hungarian throne. Dimitrijevic sent three members of the Black Hand group based in Belgrade, Gavrilo Princip, Nedjelko Cabrinovic and Trifko Grabez, to Sarajevo to carry out the deed.

Unknown to Dragutin Dimitrijevic, Major Voja Tankosic, a senior member of the Black Hand group, informed Nikola Pasic, the prime minister of Serbia, about the plot. Although Pasic supported the main objectives of the Black Hand group, he did not want the assassination to take place, as he feared it would lead to a war with Austro-Hungary. He therefore gave instructions for Gavrilo Princip, Nedjelko Cabrinovic and Trifko Grabez to be arrested when they attempted to leave the country. However, his orders were not implemented and the three men arrived in Bosnia-Herzegovina where they joined forces with fellow conspirators, Muhamed Mehmedbasic, Danilo Ilic, Vaso Cubrilovic, Cvijetko Popovic, Misko Jovanovic and Veljko Cubrilovic

The Last Trip for the Royal Couple

Just before 10 o'clock on Sunday, 28th June, 1914, the royal couple arrived in Sarajevo by train. General Oskar Potiorek, Governor of the Austrian provinces of Bosnia-Herzegovina, was waiting to take the royal party to the City Hall for the official reception. In the front car was Fehim Curcic, the Mayor of Sarajevo and Dr. Gerde, the city's Commissioner of Police. Franz Ferdinand and Sophie were in the second car with Oskar Potiorek and Count von Harrach. The car's top was rolled back in order to allow the crowds a good view of its occupants.

At 10.10, when the six car possession passed the central police station, Nedjelko Cabrinovic hurled a hand grenade station at the archduke's car. The driver accelerated when he saw the object flying towards him and the grenade exploded under the wheel of the next car. Two of the occupants, Eric von Merizzi and Count Boos-Waldeck were seriously wounded. About a dozen spectators were also hit by bomb splinters.

Franz Ferdinand's driver, Franz Urban, drove on extremely fast and other members of the Black Hand group on the route, Cvijetko Popovic, Gavrilo Princip, Danilo Ilic and Trifko Grabez, decided that it was useless to try and kill the archduke when the car was going at this speed.

After attending the official reception at the City Hall, Franz Ferdinand asked about the members of his party that had been wounded by the bomb. When the archduke was told they were badly injured in hospital, he insisted on being taken to see them. A member of the archduke's staff, Baron Morsey, suggested this might be dangerous, but Oskar Potiorek, who was responsible for the safety of the royal party, replied, "Do you think Sarajevo is full of assassins?" However,

Potiorek did accept it would be better if Sophie remained behind in the City Hall. When Baron Morsey told Sophie about the revised plans, she refused to stay arguing: "As long as the Archduke shows himself in public today I will not leave him."

In order to avoid the city centre, General Oskar Potiorek decided that the royal car should travel straight along the Appel Quay to the Sarajevo Hospital. However, Potiorek forgot to tell the driver, Franz Urban, about this decision. On the way to the hospital, Urban took a right turn into Franz Joseph Street. One of the conspirators, Gavrilo Princip, happened to be was standing on the corner at the time. Oskar Potiorek immediately realised the driver had taken the wrong route and shouted "What is this? This is the wrong way! We're supposed to take the Appel Quay!"

The driver put his foot on the brake, and began to back up. In doing so he moved slowly past the waiting Gavrilo Princip. The assassin stepped forward, drew his gun, and at a distance of about five feet, fired several times into the car. Franz Ferdinand was hit in the neck and Sophie in the abdomen. Princip's bullet had pierced the archduke's jugular vein but before losing consciousness, he pleaded "Sophie dear! Sophie dear! Don't die! Stay alive for our children!" Franz Urban drove the royal couple to Konak, the governor's residence, but although both were still alive when they arrived, they died from their wounds soon afterwards.

On 28th June, 1914, after Archduke Franz Ferdinand, was assassinated in Sarajevo. Josef accepted the advice given by his foreign minister, Leopold von Berchtold, that Austria-Hungary should declare war on Serbia. On the outbreak of what became known as the First World War, Josef allowed the military to take over the running of the country. Franz Josef died on 21st November 1916 and was succeeded by his great-nephew Karl I[121].

On the 6th day of July, 1914 the German government announced its full support for Austro-Hungary if it decided to take reprisals against Serbia for refusing to hand over the assassins of the Archduke. At this time, due to Serbia''s

---

121 Karl I was born in 1887. He joined the Austro-Hungarian Army and was a cavalry officer until the assassination of his uncle, Archduke Franz Ferdinand, in 1914, left him heir to the throne.

In the First World War Karl commanded a corps on the Italian Front until being sent to Galicia to halt the Brusilov Offensive during the summer of 1916. On the death of Franz Josef on 21st November, 1916, Karl became the Emperor of Austria and King of Hungary. Karl held liberal views and introduced a series of reforms including the abolition of flogging in the army, halting strategic bombing and restricted the use of poison gas. These measures upset his military commanders who felt Karl's reforms were undermining their attempts to win the war.

Unlike his chief of staff, Count Conrad von Hotzendorf, Karl favoured a negotiated peace settlement. He also wanted more personal control over the Austro-Hungarian forces and in March 1917 he sacked Conrad and replaced him with Arz von Straussenberg. Approaches made by Karl's diplomats offering peace negotiations were rejected by the Allies. Nationalistic unrest in the Imperial & Royal Army intensified after the Allied victory at Vittorio Veneto. Karl accepted the inevitable and on 31st October he permitted his soldiers to join the individual national armies. On the defeat of the Central Powers in November, 1918, Karl abdicated and fled to Switzerland. Karl died in 1922.

actions, many felt that the Serbian government has been involved in the assassination.

On the 9th day of July, 1914 the Austro-Hungarian government sent Friedrich von Wiesner to Sarajevo to investigate the claims that the Serbian government was involved in a plot to kill Archduke Franz Ferdinand.

On the 13th of July, Wiesner reports to the Austro-Hungarian government that members of the Serbian Army were involved in the assassination of Franz Ferdinand. As far as the Austro-Hungarian government was concerned this was the same as Serbian government involvement.

On the 21st of July, Conrad von Hotzendorf[122] convinced Emperor Franz Josef that Austro-Hungary could punish Serbia without the other major countries taking action.

On the 23rd of July, the Austro-Hungarian government maked fifteen demands on the Serbian government. This includes the demand they arrest the leaders of the Black Hand group based in Serbia and send them to face trial in Vienna.

On the 24th of July, Nikola Pasic and the Serbian government appealled to Russia for help against the proposed attack by the Austro-Hungarian Army.

On the 25th of July, Nikola Pasic told the Austro-Hungarian government that he is unable to accept their fifteen demands, as it "would be a violation of Serbia's Constitution and criminal in law[123]".

On the 26th day of July, Russia promised that it would help Serbia if it is attacked by Austro-Hungary.

On the 28th day of July, Austro-Hungarian declared war on Serbia.

On the 31st day of July, Russia mobilized its armed forces in support of Serbia. This included the sending of troops to its borders with Germany and Austro-Hungary.

On the 1st day of August, Germany declared war on Russia.

On the 2nd day of August, Italy declared that it does not intend to honour its Triple Alliance obligations and will remain neutral.

On the 3rd day of August, Germany declared war on France. Belgian neutrality was guaranteed by Britain under a treaty signed in 1839. Sir Edward

---

122 Conrad von Hotzendorff was born in 1852. A close friend of Archduke Franz Ferdinand, in 1906 he became chief of staff to the Austro-Hungarian Army. Hotzendorff was a strong supporter of an aggressive foreign policy and after favoured surprise attacks on Serbia and Italy.

123 There may have been other, more practical reasons, for refusing to hand over the assassins. According to Fisher on the Great War: [Paul A. Fisher [1988] Behind the Lodge Door] "Not mentioned by the Scottish Rite journal [New Age] was the fact that the alleged assassins of the Archduke were members of the "Black Hand," a South Slav revolutionary organization which was a progeny of Freemasonry.

"During the trial, Princep (the actual assassin) testified that his colleague, Ciganovitch, 'told me he was a Freemason;' and, on another occasion, 'told me that the Heir Apparent [Franz Ferdinand] had been condemned to death by a Freemason's lodge.'

"Moreover, another of the accused assassins, Chabrinovitch, testified that Major Tankositch, one of the plotters, was a Freemason." (ibid, pp. 217-218).

Grey, Britain's foreign secretary, warned Germany that Britain would go to war if Belgium was invaded.

On the 4th day of August, the German Army marched into Belgium. Britain declared war on Germany.

On the 5th day of August, Austro-Hungary declared war on Russia.

On the 10th day of August, France declared war on Austro-Hungary.

On the 12th day of August, Britain declared war on Austro-Hungary.

On the 14th day of August, France invaded Lorraine.

By the end of 1914, all of the European participants were involved in the War. This was a purely European war being waged over the assassination of the heir to the throne of Austro-Hungary. If there were any "bad guys" involved in this war, it was the Serbians for refusing to take action against the assassins. A suitable compromise could have been worked out to satisfy all parties rather than going to war.

In fact, as shown above, Karl I, upon assuming the throne, approached the Allies, suggesting a negotiated settlement. His efforts were rebuffed. What is the most interesting point is that one of the major powers involved in this war was France. From 1877 to the eve of the Second World War, Freemasons dominated the French government[124]. Their domination earned them bitter enemies.

In the 1880's, at the height of this political conflict, Joseph Alexandre St. Yves d'Alveydre[125], "the supreme Hermeticist of his epoch,"(1) proposed a new idea for injecting moral values into governing society. He called it "synarchy" and claimed it was the method used by the Knights Templar to change medieval society. An elect band of initiates would influence groups representing different aspects of society. Those groups would influence their spheres and ultimately the entire social order.

By the turn of the century, the royalist faction came to fear synarchy, whose influence had spread beyond esoteric groups. By the 1920s, Masonic groups with distinctly synarchist policies were a reality in France. In the 1930s, even a leftist group, called the X-Cruise Club, advocated a technocracy with synarchist ideas.

In this era, the French far right formed its own seemingly esoteric groups. But they were actually front organizations, pretending to have Masonic and esoteric affiliations in order to draw support away from the Masons. As anti-semitism spread across Europe in the 1930s, the French far right denounced

---

124 Abraham asserts that one of the primary reasons these Illuminati (Masons) worked behind the scenes to foment WWI was to create in its aftermath a world government to control resources of the world. The selling point is peace. Professor Carroll Quigley, Mr. Clinton's own professor at Georgetown University, in his book Tragedy and Hope (MacMillan, New York, 1966) informs us that the secret Round Table was created for Rothschild, to be headed by Lord Milner, using Cecil Rhodes' money. (Is it accidental that Rhodes scholarship fund was created and a Rhodes scholar, Bill Clinton, was nominated and elected President of the U.S.?) The Round Table worked behind the scenes at the highest levels of British government, influencing foreign policy and England's involvement and conduct of WWI.

125 Joscelyn Godwin, "The Creation of a Universal System: St.-Yves d'Alveydre and his Archaeometer," in Alexandria 1 (1991), p. 230.

Masons and Jews in the same breath. When fourteen initiatic orders created a federation called FUDOSI to promote peace and positive ideals, the far right increased its formation of pseudo-Masonic groups.

U.S. Entry Into World War I

As we have shown above, World War I, which began in 1914, was primarily a family affair, involving various countries with their own agendas. The spark was the assassination of Archduke Franz Ferdinand in Sarajevo by members of the Masonic connected secret society the Black Hand. Serbia refused to turn the plotters over to the Austro-Hungarians for trial and punishment. So what was the U.S.'s purpose in entering this war?

In 1915, the United States, who were not yet involved in the war, lent France and Great Britain $500 million through American banks. In 1916, a single French loan totaled $750 million. In all, the total amount of the loans to these allied countries amounted to $3 billion, plus another $6 billion for exports, none of which were repaid. This was just one of the reasons for America's entry into the war. Had Germany won the war, those bonds held by American bankers would have been worthless. J. P. Morgan (who served as England's financial agent in the U.S.), Rockefeller (who made more than $200,000,000 on the war), Warburg, and Schiff, were instrumental in pushing America into the war so they could protect their loans to Europe.

The Masonic-controlled newspapers publicized, and played-up the sinking of the British auxiliary cruiser, the Lusitania, which was torpedoed by a German U-Boat on May 7, 1915. The Germans said they had the right to attack an allied ship, even though the United States, up to that time, had been neutral. The Lusitania, which had been converted into an ammunition war ship early in the war, was armed with guns, and was carrying six million pounds of ammunition, which were to be sold to England and France for use in the war against Germany. During 1916 and early 1917, there was a continual barrage of propaganda directed at the American people urging entry into the War. Against this backdrop, it would seem imminently reasonable for the Hawks to be the one to fund Pancho Villa's attack on Columbus, New Mexico and the Zimmerman Telegram to be forged to incite the American people to go to war.

In regard to the so called U-Boat atrocities, it was illegal for American passengers to be on board a ship carrying munitions, and on May 1, 1915, the German embassy in Washington, D.C., ran ads in the New York papers, in addition to verbal announcements, warning Americans that the ship would be attacked. Three months earlier, Germany had issued a proclamation that the waters around the British Isles were part of the war zone, In addition, it was later revealed, that on December 14, 1914, British Intelligence broke the German war code, which meant that the First Lord of the Admiralty, Winston Churchill, knew the location of every U-Boat in the English Channel area.

When the ship was sunk off the coast of Ireland, 1201 people were killed, including 128 Americans. The Masonic interests used the incident to create a war fever in the United States, portraying the Germans as being barbaric. Because of President Wilson's handling of the Lusitania affair, William Jennings Bryan, his Secretary of State, resigned. There is no doubt that the British government sacrificed those passengers in order to get the United States into the war.

At the same time that President Wilson was claiming that he was opposed to our involvement in World War I, Colonel Edward House, President Wilson's "alter ego" was already in England, making firm commitments that America would enter the war; and on April 6, 1917, Congress declared war, selling it to the American public as a "war to end all wars," and a war "to make the world safe for democracy."

When the war was finally over, over 63,000 American soldiers had been killed in the fighting. A year later, in 1919, Lenin offered four-fifths of Soviet territory, in exchange for the formal recognition of his communist government, and economic aid from the United States. He offered to accept the creation of allied-sponsored non-communist states in the Baltic region, in the area of Archangel, Western Byelorussia, half of the Ukraine, Crimea, the Caucasus, the Ural Mountains, and all of Siberia. Wilson rejected the offer for "patriotic reasons[126]," because the Masonic Orders had big plans for that country. Had he accepted the offer, Russia would have never have become a world power.

The League Of Nations

The League of Nations is forever linked with President Wilson. However, while most believe that it was an international organization founded after the First World War at the Paris Peace Conference in 1919, it was actually proposed before World War I. In the years immediately before the war, certain masonically controlled organization, using various influential groups in the United States and Great Britain, urged the creation of an organization to promote world peace, even though George Washington warned against involvement with foreign nations.

President Wilson favored the idea, and echoed those sentiments in his famous "Peace Without Victory" speech before the Senate. He proposed his idea of a League of Nations to the Senate in 1917, seeing it as a means of preventing another World War. It would provide "collective security," or in other words, an attack on one, would be considered an attack on all[127]. The League would also help in the arbitration of international disputes, the reduction of armaments, and the development of open diplomacy.

The League's stated goals included disarmament; preventing war through collective security; settling disputes between countries through negotiation and

---

126 Acceptance would have left the Russians in no position to be a threat to world peace. Thus a major moneymaking "cold war" would have been impossible.

127 There is much evidence that the League of Nations, as originally proposed would actually function as a world government with countries being states within the larger whole.

diplomacy; and improving global welfare. The diplomatic philosophy behind the League represented a fundamental shift in thought from the preceding hundred years. The old philosophy, growing out of the Congress of Vienna (1815), saw Europe as a shifting map of alliances among nation-states, creating an equilibrium of power maintained by strong armies and secret agreements. Under the new philosophy, the League was a government of governments[128], with the role of settling disputes between individual nations in an open and legalist forum. The impetus for the founding of the League came from Democratic U.S. President Woodrow Wilson, but, along with many other countries, the United States never joined the League of Nations.

Like the United States, the League lacked an armed force of its own and so depended on the Great Powers to enforce its resolutions, which they were often very reluctant to do. After a number of notable successes and some early failures, the League ultimately proved incapable of preventing aggression by the fascist Axis Powers in the 1930s. The onset of the Second World War made it clear that the League had failed in its primary purpose—to avoid any future world war. The United Nations effectively replaced it after World War II and inherited a number of agencies and organizations founded by the League.

The Treaty of Versailles

The armistice ending World War I on November 11, 1918, was negotiated on the basis of Wilson's "Fourteen Points" and on June 28, 1919, was included in the Treaty of Versailles, a 20-year truce which divided up Europe, setting the stage for World War II. It demanded that Germany pay war reparations to the victorious countries. The Allies maintained that "since Germany was responsible for the War she was liable for the costs and damages incurred by the victors[129]." This amount was set at $32 billion, plus interest; which called for annual payments of $500 million, plus a 26% surcharge on exports. The agreement forced Germany to forfeit some of her prime provinces, colonies, and natural resources. They signed away their rights, had to make trade concessions, and lost what property they had in those foreign countries.

The Treaty was widely criticized. David Lloyd George, the Prime Minister of England, said: "We have written a document that guarantees war in 20 years ... *When you place conditions on a people (Germany) that it cannot possibly keep you force it to either breech the agreement or to war. Either we modify that agreement, and make it tolerable to the German people, or when the new generation comes along they will try again.*" Lord Curzon, the British Foreign Secretary, said: "This is no peace; this is only a truce for twenty years!" Even President Wilson was reported to have said: "If I were a German, I think I should never sign it."

---

128 In otherwords, a one world government.

129 Germany was not responsible for the war, it was merely honoring a treaty with Austro-Hungarian Empire after the assassination of archduke Franz Ferdninand.

The League of Nations was signed and sealed at the Paris Peace Conference. Even though the United States was represented by Wilson, Col. House was calling the shots. Bernard Baruch, who, as head of the War Industries Board made about $200,000,000 for himself, was also in the American delegation at the Paris Conference; as well as, Waiter Lippman (who later became a syndicated newspaper columnist), Allen Dulles (who was appointed Director of the CIA in 1951), John Foster Dulles (brother of Allen, who later became the Secretary of State under Eisenhower), and Christian Herter (who became Secretary of State after the death of Dulles). English Prime Minister George was accompanied by Sir Philip Sassoon, a member of the British Privy Council and a direct descendant of Amschel Rothschild. Georges Clemenceau, the French Prime Minister, had at his side, his advisor, Georges Mandel, also known as Jeroboam Rothschild.

The citizens of the United States refused to accept the League of Nations, because they felt it would draw them into future European conflicts. Frank B. Kellogg (who in 1925 became Secretary of State under Coolidge), inspired by the American "outlawry of war" movement, and supported by those who were disappointed at the failure of the United States to enter the League, proposed a pact to the French Foreign Minister, Aristide Briand in the spring of 1927. Its purpose was to create alliances directed against a possible resurgence of German aggression. This Pact of Paris was signed on August 27, 1928, by 65 nations, who promised to settle all international disputes by peaceful means.

Because of the efforts of Sen. Henry Cabot Lodge, who saw through Wilson's plan, the United States didn't join the League, and in 1921, made a separate peace treaty with Germany and Austria.

The League of Nations, headquartered in Geneva, Switzerland, throughout the 1920's, gained new members, and helped settle minor international disputes. However, weakened by the failure of the United States to join, and the restlessness of nations who were not satisfied, such as Japan, Italy and Germany, the Mason's second attempt at establishing a one-world government failed. The League had little impact on international affairs, and ceased to exist in 1946 when the United Nations was established.

What the League of Nations did do, was allow the Masonic Orders to get more of a grip on world finances. Countries which belonged to the League, sought financial aid from the United States, wherein Rockefeller said that no country could get a loan unless the International Bankers controlled the Central Bank of the borrowing country. If they had no bank, they were able to set one up. Through the Bank for International Settlement, established in 1930, the Masonic Orders were able to control more of the world's money.

So from these facts it is clear that the United States as a country had nothing to gain and everything to lose in getting involved in the First World War. The ones with much to lose were the Bankers who had loaned so much money to France and Britian. Only our involvement in the war would guarantee that their investment would be safe. So to ensure they would not lose money, 65,000 Americans had to die.

Made in America

As pointed out above, a number of millionaires and billionaires were created as a result of the U.S.'s entry into World War I. The individuals who benefited the most were names well known to history.

For the first time, government tried to place monopoly controls over the every day necessities of life. The Food Administration, formed May 1917, and headed by Herbert Hoover controlled food resources and began to dictate to farmers what they could and could not grow.

The Creel Committee, formed in May of 1917, issued official propaganda Daily "Official Bulletins" to convince Americans of the crusade for freedom and democracy and the bestial nature of the "Huns." The mere fact that the Germans were not in the war to conquer the world was never mentioned.

Bernard Baruch became an industrial dictator as the head of the War Industries Board (WIB). The WIB set prices and determined what goods should be produced by private industry. No one ever commented on the fact that patriotic Bernard Baruch just happened to make over $200,000,000 for himself while serving in his position. Rockefeller was also another of a group of "patriotic" bankers who made more than $200,000,000 on the war.

As is always the case, the members of the special clique who seem to run this country, never have to be endangered by going to war and profit no matter who wins or is in office. This, I believe, is highly curious and certainly most revealing.

CHAPTER TWENTY-ONE
AN AMERICAN COUP D'ETAT

The next war on our agenda is World War II, however, there are a large number of factors that have been hidden in the mists of time that had a direct impact on the U.S. and the decision by our leaders to get us involved in that war.

Durng the time that the situation in Europe was heating up and Hitler was dominating the political scene, President Franklin D. Roosevelt was being fored to deal with the unthinkable, a plot by leading Americans to overthrown the Presidency. There was a small but influential group who felt that America has lost its way and needed a strong leader other than Roosevelt.

Franklin D. Roosevelt[130] holds an unusual place in American history. He is not only the longest sitting president in history, but he is also, at the same time, the most hated as well as the most admired man to hold this office. He assumed the Presidency at the depth of the Great Depression, when many were about to give up hoping for better days. Franklin D. Roosevelt helped the American people regain faith in themselves. He brought hope as he promised prompt, vigorous action, and asserted in his Inaugural Address, "the only thing we have to fear is fear itself."

Following the example of his fifth cousin, President Theodore Roosevelt, whom he greatly admired, Franklin D. Roosevelt entered public service through politics, but as a Democrat. He won election to the New York Senate in 1910. President Wilson appointed him Assistant Secretary of the Navy, and he was the Democratic nominee for Vice President in 1920.

In the summer of 1921, when he was 39, disaster hit- he was stricken with poliomyelitis. Demonstrating indomitable courage, he fought to regain the use of his legs, particularly through swimming. At the 1924 Democratic Convention he dramatically appeared on crutches to nominate Alfred E. Smith as "the Happy Warrior." In 1928 Roosevelt became Governor of New York.

---

130 Born in 1882 at Hyde Park, New York--now a national historic site--he attended Harvard University and Columbia Law School. On St. Patrick's Day, 1905, he married Eleanor Roosevelt.

He was elected President in November 1932, to the first of four terms. However, by March there were 13,000,000 unemployed, and almost every bank was closed. In his first "hundred days," he proposed, and Congress enacted, a sweeping program to bring recovery to business and agriculture, relief to the unemployed and to those in danger of losing farms and homes, and reform, especially through the establishment of the Tennessee Valley Authority.

By 1935 the Nation had achieved some measure of recovery, but businessmen and bankers were turning more and more against Roosevelt's New Deal program. They feared his social experiments, were appalled because he had taken the Nation off the gold standard and allowed deficits in the budget, and disliked the concessions to labor[131]. Roosevelt responded with a new program of reform: Social Security, heavier taxes on the wealthy, new controls over banks and public utilities, and an enormous work relief program for the unemployed.

In 1936 he was re-elected by a top-heavy margin. Feeling he was armed with a popular mandate, he sought legislation to enlarge the Supreme Court, which had been invalidating key New Deal measures. Roosevelt lost the Supreme Court battle, but a revolution in constitutional law took place. Thereafter the Government could legally regulate the economy.

Roosevelt had pledged the United States to the "good neighbor" policy, transforming the Monroe Doctrine from a unilateral American manifesto into arrangements for mutual action against aggressors. He also sought, through neutrality legislation, to keep the United States out of the war in Europe, yet at the same time he worked to strengthen nations threatened or attacked. When France fell and England came under siege in 1940, he began to send Great Britain all possible aid short of actual military involvement.

Feeling that the future peace of the world would depend upon relations between the United States and Russia, he devoted much thought to the planning of a United Nations, in which, he hoped, international difficulties could be settled. Many, however, saw the United Nations as another attempt to form a League of Nations type one world government.

A Coup Against A Tyrant

As might be expected, a large number of influential, wealthy, conservatives viewed Roosevelt and his programs with a great dal of suspicion. There was so much unrest that, for the third time in U.S. history, a plan was put into motion to overthrow the United States Government[132]. However, due to the influential people involved in this attempt, the very existence of this attempted coup d'etat has been censored out of our history books, courtesy of corporate America. Fortunately, this coup was not supported by the military, so European fascism didn't happen that time. Fascism has to have the support of both

---

[131] Many of those who disliked Roosevelt were from the old line families who had formed this country and who had manipulated government for their own benefit for many years.

[132] The first was the Whiskey Rebellion and the Second was the Civil War.

corporate power and will and military/police power and obedience together or it doesn't happen[133].

Had this coup taken place, at a minimum, there would have been another Civil War and it could well have resulted in the overthrow of the duly elected President, Franklin D. Roosevelt. What kept this coup from becoming a reality was the integrity of one man, a retired Marine Corp Major General, Smedley Darlington Butler[134].

MG Butler was the sort of person for whom the word "colorful" is woefully inadequate. Butler won America's highest military award for bravery (the Congressional Medal of Honor) twice. His style of warfare was unusual not only for his personal courage, but for the energy he put into avoiding bloodshed when it was possible to achieve his aims in other ways. Not surprisingly, this engendered a remarkable loyalty among the men who served under him -- and that loyalty was why certain very highly placed men asked Butler to lead a military attack on Washington, D.C., with the goal of capturing President Roosevelt.

Butler was more than a remarkable soldier. He served as police commissioner of Philadelphia during 1924-25 (on loan from the Marines), in an attempt to enforce Prohibition. While the effort was a failure, his insistence on enforcing the law against wealthy partygoers as well as poor immigrants established his reputation as a man of high integrity. He was not universally loved, but he was widely respected. Butler is best remembered today for his oft-quoted statement in the socialist newspaper Common Sense in 1935:

"I helped make Mexico and especially Tampico safe for American oil interests in 1914. I helped make Haiti and Cuba a decent place for the National City Bank boys to collect revenues in. I helped in the raping of half a dozen Central American republics for the benefit of Wall Street. The record of racketeering is long. I helped purify Nicaragua for the international banking house of Brown Brothers in 1909-12. I brought light to the Dominican Republic for American sugar interests in 1916. I helped make Honduras "right" for American fruit companies in 1903. In China in 1927 I helped see to it that Standard Oil went its way unmolested.... Looking back on it, I felt I might have given Al Capone a few hints. The best he could do was to operate his racket in three city districts. We Marines operated on three continents."

In <u>War Is A Racket</u>[135], Butler argued for a powerful navy, but one prohibited from traveling more than 200 miles from the U.S. coastline. Military aircraft could travel no more than 500 miles from the U.S. coast, and the army

---

133 Gary G. Kohls, MD 1306 E. 8th St, Duluth, MN 55805 Ph/fax 218-728-9756, for Every Church A Peace Church http://www.ecapc.org

134 http://home.iprimus.com.au/korob/fdtcards/Butler.html

135 Butler, Smedley D. and Adam Parfrey, <u>War is a Racket</u>, Feral House; Reprint edition (April, 2003)

would be prohibited from leaving the United States. Butler also proposed that all workers in defense industries, from the lowest laborer to the highest executive, be limited to "$30 a month, the same wage as the lads in the trenches get." He also proposed that a declaration of war should be passed by a plebiscite in which only those subject to conscription would be eligible to vote.

From 1935 through 1937, Butler was a spokesman for the League Against War and Fascism, a Communist-dominated organization of the time. He also participated in the Third U.S. Congress Against War and Fascism, sharing the platform with well-known leftists of the era, including Langston Hughes, Heywood Broun, and Roger Baldwin. When the Spanish Civil War (1936-39) threatened the collapse of the Soviet-supported Spanish government, the League's pacifism evaporated, and they supported intervention. Butler, however, remained true to his belief in non-interventionism, stating publically, "*What the hell is it our business what's going on in Spain?*" But before Butler became involved in these causes, he had already exposed a fascist plot against his own government.

The Plot

Butler had friends in the press and Congress, so he could not be ignored when he came forward in late 1934 with a tale of conspiracy against President Roosevelt, in which he had been asked to take a leading role. At first glance, Butler seems an unlikely candidate for such a position. While Butler was a Republican, in 1932 he campaigned for Roosevelt, calling himself a "Republican-for-Ex-President Hoover." (Butler had a poor relationship with Hoover going back to their time together during the Boxer Rebellion.)

But there were good reasons why someone seeking to overthrow the U.S. government would have wanted Butler involved. Butler was a powerful symbol to many American soldiers and veterans -- an enlisted man's general, one that spoke out for their interests while on active duty, and after retirement. Butler would have attracted men to his cause that would not otherwise have participated in a march on Washington.

Butler would have been a good choice also because of his military skills. His personal courage and tactical skill would have made him a powerful commander of an irregular army. Finally, his ties of friendship to many officers still on active duty might have undermined military opposition to his force, as friends and colleagues sought to avoid a direct confrontation with him.

Another reason that the plotters might have approached such an unlikely candidate was that Butler was not regarded as a great intellect. After World War I, the Marine Corps had begun to emphasize a new college-educated professionalism. Butler, one of the less educated "bushwhacker" generals, might have seemed easy to manipulate.

Butler testified that bond trader Gerald MacGuire had approached him in the summer of 1933. MacGuire claimed to represent wealthy Wall Street broker Grayson Murphy, Singer sewing machine heir Robert Sterling Clark, and other unnamed men of wealth. They asked Butler to speak publicly on behalf of the gold standard, recently abandoned by President Roosevelt. MacGuire's rationale for why Butler should ally himself with the gold standard cause was that the veterans of World War I were due a bonus in 1945. As MacGuire told Butler, "We want to see the soldiers' bonus paid in gold. We do not want the soldier to have rubber money or paper money."

It appears that the plotters underestimated Butler's intelligence and character. When this explanation failed to persuade Butler, MacGuire and Clark offered him money, abandoning any pretense of civic mindness. Butler's sense of honor prevented him from speaking in favor of any policy for mercenary reasons.

MacGuire eventually told Butler their real goal. MacGuire asked Butler to lead an army of 500,000 veterans in a march on Washington, D.C. The stated mission was to protect Roosevelt from other plotters, and install a "secretary of general welfare" to "take all the worries and details off of his shoulders." But Butler saw through their supposed concern for Roosevelt. He testified before Congress that he told MacGuire:

> *"[M]y interest is, my one hobby is, maintaining a democracy. If you get these 500,000 soldiers advocating anything smelling of Fascism, I am going to get 500,000 more and lick the hell out of you, and we will have a real war right at home.."*

Yes; and then you will put somebody in there you can run; is that the idea? The President will go around and christen babies and dedicate bridges, and kiss children. Mr. Roosevelt will never agree to that himself.

Butler eventually deduced that the real goal was a coup d'état to take Roosevelt captive, and force reinstatement of the gold standard, the loss of which many wealthy Americans feared would lead to rapid inflation. The plotters would keep Roosevelt as a figurehead until he could be "encouraged" to retire.

That MacGuire had significant financial backing behind him seems clear, considering the substantial bank savings books he showed to Butler. What remains unclear is whether the names MacGuire dropped (other than Robert Sterling Clark) were really involved, or whether MacGuire was a con man.

MacGuire's claims and financial resources alone did not convince Butler that such a conspiracy actually existed. The fulfillment of a series of startling predictions by MacGuire did finally persuade Butler that there was more than just hot air involved. MacGuire knew in advance of significant personnel changes in the White House. He correctly predicted the formation of the American Liberty League (the major conservative opposition to Roosevelt), and the principal players in it. Especially disturbing was that many of the supposed backers of the plot were also members of the League. MacGuire's claim that the League ("villagers in the opera" of the scheme, in MacGuire's words) was part of the plot could not be easily dismissed.

The American Liberty League was a successor to the highly successful Association Against the Prohibition Amendment, the lobbying organization responsible for the repeal of the "Noble Experiment." From its formation in 1918 until 1926, the AAPA made little progress, at least partly because it had little money. But in 1926, money poured into the AAPA from some of America's wealthiest men, including Pierre, Irenee, and Lammot du Pont, John J. Raskob, and Charles H. Sabin. The AAPA spent its new found wealth on distribution of literature, and on the formation of a bewildering number of associated organizations. These associated organizations gave the impression of a grassroots movement, rather than a collection of millionaires feeding press releases to friendly newspapers. The AAPA also rapidly took control of the Democratic Party, with one of their supporters, Al Smith, receiving the 1928 Democratic Presidential nomination. While AAPA had powerful friends within the Republican Party, they never achieved control of it.

The AAPA's motivations were a mixture of idealism and pragmatism. The stated concern was that Prohibition had done serious damage to the principle of federalism -- that the federal government's authority did not include the police powers used to enforce Prohibition. But it appears that this was not the only motivation, or even the reason most important to the men who funded the AAPA. Like many other Americans, these business leaders "found themselves unable to gratify what seemed a natural, more or less innocent, desire without breaking a law" (i.e., the consumption of alcoholic beverages). To suddenly find themselves among the criminal classes was not pleasant to a group who had always thought of themselves as law-abiding and respectable members of American society. There is also strong evidence that the backers of the AAPA saw Repeal as a method of reducing income and corporate taxes, by taxing alcoholic beverages instead.

The AAPA went out of business at the end of 1933, with the end of Prohibition. But within a year, from the same offices, with most of the same backers, many of the same employees, and much of the same style, it reappeared as the American Liberty League. Throughout the next six years, it led the fight against the New Deal, arguing that much of Roosevelt's program was contrary to the letter and spirit of the Constitution. In an age when Hitler and Mussolini had commandeered extraordinary economic powers, the fears that the American Liberty League expressed about Roosevelt's vaguely similar gathering of economic power could not be summarily dismissed.

The League, in spite of its impressive resources, was rapidly made to appear "ridiculous or dangerous" or both by the Roosevelt Administration. Most importantly, the leadership of the League was largely rich men. The Depression-era gap between rich and poor had become too wide, too obvious, and too painful for the League to be credible to the majority of Americans.

Butler's testimony before Congress claimed that some of the people associated with the League were the very ones that had approached him -- including Grayson Murphy, the League's treasurer.

In the depths of the Great Depression, in that nadir of despair before Roosevelt gave his stirring first inaugural address in 1933, America was awash in political groups identifying in greater or lesser degrees with communism or fascism. Rep. Samuel Dickstein (D-NY), concerned about the threat of such groups, persuaded the House of Representatives to create the Special Committee to Investigate Nazi Propaganda Activities in the United States. This committee investigated Butler's charges in late 1934.

MacGuire, not surprisingly, denied that such a plot existed. Instead, he claimed his activities had been political lobbying to preserve the gold standard, but he quickly destroyed his credibility as a witness by giving contradictory testimony. While the final report agreed with Butler that there was evidence of a coup d'état plot against Roosevelt, no further action was taken on it. The Committee's authority to subpoena witnesses expired at the end of 1934, and the Justice Department started no criminal investigation.

Part of the reason for the lack of prosecution of the alleged plotters may have been the untimely death of the only man who could have testified against the rest: Gerald MacGuire. He died at age 37 from complications of pneumonia, less than a month after the Committee released its report. MacGuire's physician claimed that his death was partly the result of the stress of the charges made by Butler, but there is no reason to assume that MacGuire's death was in any way suspicious.

The Committee's report excluded many of the most embarrassing names given by MacGuire, and repeated by Butler. MacGuire had claimed that some of those he represented included the 1928 Democratic President candidate Al Smith; General Hugh Johnson (head of Roosevelt's National Recovery Administration); as well as General Douglas MacArthur, and a number of other generals and admirals currently on active duty.

Since Butler had no evidence of their involvement, other than MacGuire's claims, it was certainly reasonable for the Committee to exclude these details from the final report as "certain immaterial and incompetent evidence." But in conjunction with MacGuire's apparent advance knowledge of the details of internal White House staff activities; it certainly suggests that if a coup was planned, it had significant support within the Roosevelt Administration.

The News Media Downplays The Plot

The news media of the day, gave an inappropriately small amount of attention to the report[136]. Time Magazine ridiculed Butler's claims. The week following Butler's testimony, Time described it as a "Plot Without Plotters," simply because the alleged plotters claimed innocence. But Time also admitted that Veterans of Foreign Wars commander James Van Zandt confirmed that he, too, had been approached to lead such a march on Washington.

The leftist magazine *New Masses* carried an article by John Spivak that included wild claims of "Jewish financiers working with fascist groups." Spivak's article spun an elaborate web involving the American Jewish Congress, the

---

[136] Perhaps this was a result of Joe Kennedy and his friends calling in favors.

Warburg family, "which originally financed Hitler," the Hearst newspaper chain, the Morgan banking firm, the Du Ponts, a truly impressive list of prominent American Jewish businessmen, and Nazi spies! Spivak's article raised some disturbing and legitimate questions about why much of Butler's testimony was left out of the final committee report. But these important concerns were seriously undermined by Spivak's paranoid ravings. The left-of-center magazines *Nation* and *New Republic* were unconcerned about it, since in their view "fascism originated in pseudoradical mass movements," and therefore could not come from a wealthy cabal.

Newspaper descriptions of the final report are also astonishing for how lightly most treated it. A New York Times article about subversion and foreign agitators started on the front page, but gave only two paragraphs to the coup plot inside the paper. "It also alleged that definite proof has been found that the much publicized Fascist march on Washington... was actually contemplated." It was not a major story.

The San Francisco Chronicle took the story more seriously. The only headline with a larger type size that day concerned the recent fatal crash of the airship Macon. The Chronicle carried an Associated Press story headlined, "*Justice Aids Probe Butler Fascist Story*." The first five paragraphs were devoted to Butler's allegations. The Chronicle quoted the Committee report that it "was able to verify all the pertinent statements by General Butler, with the exception of the direct statement suggesting creation of the organization."

A third newspaper sampled showed an even more astonishing lack of interest than the New York Times: the Sacramento Bee used a substantially different Associated Press wire story that emphasized propaganda efforts by foreign agents. Another AP wire story, at the bottom of page five, described Butler's allegations, taking the Committee's report at face value. This wire story includes the comforting knowledge that the committee found "no evidence to show a connection between this effort" and any foreign government.

An apparently serious effort to overthrow the government, perhaps with the support of some of America's wealthiest men, largely substantiated by a Congressional committee, was mostly ignored. Why? Roosevelt's Secretary of the Interior, Harold Ickes, wrote a book in 1939 about the concentration of American journalism. He claimed that, "In 1934, 82 per cent of all dailies had a complete monopoly in their communities." Newspaper chains, in Ickes' view, "*control a dangerously large share of the national daily circulation and in many cities have no competition*."

Ickes' book was largely devoted to proving that the major newspapers of the United States were intentionally distorting the news, and in some cases, directly lying. Ickes argued that newspaper editors did so in the interests of both their advertisers and in defense of the capitalist class. Ickes mentioned the Liberty League as one of the "propaganda outfits" who were allied with the major newspapers. Indeed, the New York Times, one of the papers that had downplayed the Committee's report, had editorialized in favor of the Liberty League's formation.

Did newspapers and magazines consciously play down the plot, because it represented an embarrassment to people of influence? Or did editors simply give it low visibility because they regarded it as an absurd story?

We must consider another disturbing possibility. Butler was associated with the loose alliance of progressive and populist forces that were dragging Roosevelt towards the left. It is easy to forget that for much of Roosevelt's first term as President from 1932-36, he was the rope in a tug of war between conservative and progressive forces in America. The popularity of men such as Senator Huey Long (D-Louisiana) and the nationally known radio priest Father Coughlin-and the need to short-circuit their rising political power-appears to have caused Roosevelt's increasingly leftward movement in 1935-36.

Is it possible that Butler concocted this story as a way of creating animosity towards conservatives by Roosevelt? If Butler had lied to the Committee, and no such conspiracy was ever planned, why did MacGuire apparently perjure himself before the Committee? Or, alternatively, could leftward leaning members of the Roosevelt Administration have manipulated Butler into believing that such a plot actually existed as a way of creating animosity towards conservatives, thus dragging Roosevelt to the left? Either theory could explain why MacGuire, Murphy, Clark, or the other supposed plotters were never prosecuted.

Yet another possibility (though less likely) is that there was no prosecution because Roosevelt's own advisors had taken part in the plot, as MacGuire claimed. A criminal prosecution would have washed the Roosevelt Administration's dirty laundry in public.

Why Is The Plot So Poorly Known?

Butler's account of the MacGuire plot was a very serious accusation. If MacGuire had told Butler the truth, a large number of wealthy men had made serious plans to overthrow representative government in the United States -- though their concern that Roosevelt was creating a government in the style of Mussolini or Hitler, might provide some legitimate reason for their actions. Why doesn't this plot appear in history books? That conservatives might discount the plot is not unexpected; that liberals have tended to ignore the plot is a little more surprising.

It is hard to imagine how different American politics was in the 1930s. The collapse of the world economy had shaken the faith of many Americans in individualism and free market capitalism. Many traditionalists, here and in Europe, toyed with the ideas of Fascism and National Socialism; many liberals dallied with Socialism and Communism. Prominent populists such as Huey Long and Father Coughlin sided with progressives in support of isolationism, redistribution of wealth, and a federal government that would play a more active role in the American economy.

In hindsight, the moral and economic deficiencies of these various collectivized systems are now clear. In 1934, however, people of good will persuaded themselves that Hitler, Mussolini, and Stalin were doing good, and ignored the great evils that were already underway. To turn over the rock exposing MacGuire's plot raises unpleasant questions about the political sensibilities of both right and left in 1930s America.

Another reason that things were kept so quiet was that two of the prominent backers just happened to be members of the DuPont family and the Morgan banking interests. Although the House Committee to Investigate Un-American Activities found MG Butler's allegations credible, it failed to call major conspirators to testify, and the Committee deleted crucial testimony from its final report to the public. The press relegated the story to the back pages, and discredited those, including Major Butler, who tried to alert the public to the threat against republican government. No prosecutions were forthcoming from the Justice Department, in part because the main witness who would have substantiated Butler's claims died suddenly from pneumonia at the age of 37. In short, there was a cover-up, maybe worse.

In 1934, two events aroused the wrath of the DuPonts and the Morgans. First, there were rumors that pressure was being exerted to open a Senate investigation into the munitions industry's alleged role in America's entry into WWI. The DuPonts were the leading armament producers in the world. They had already earned the title "Merchants of Death" because of the huge profits they made during the Civil War and the War of 1812. The DuPonts always tried to bury this fact in carefully crafted public relations euphemisms such as" DuPont - Better things for better living through chemistry." The DuPonts have always remained reticent about revealing the extent of their wealth, corporate holdings and armament productions.

Certainly, a Senate investigation revealing their irregular dealings and huge profits during a time of national hardship when many Americans were already questioning whether financiers really had the national interest at heart could be disastrous for industrialists like the DuPonts. It could only lead to more popular support for the reforms Roosevelt was trying to implement.

The second event that alarmed the big financiers, striking directly at the heart of the Morgan Empire, was the passage of the Securities Acts of 1933 and 1934. This legislation proposed federal supervision of securities traded over state boundaries, and established the Securities and Exchange Commission empowered to enforce the regulations. Some of the abuses that the commission was to address were insider trading, bear raiding, and manipulating stocks to create the illusion of activity. One of the most alarming propositions was that companies selling stocks would have to reveal their financial histories to the public.

In choosing a chairman for the Securities and Exchange Commission, Roosevelt needed a man who would strike a balance between the more radical, anti-business theorists of the New Deal, and the entrenched business interests whose support Roosevelt needed. Confiding to his advisors with the cavalier phrase "I'll set a thief to catch a thief," Roosevelt appointed Joseph P. Kennedy as the first Chairman of the Securities and Exchange Commission.6 With this appointment Kennedy became responsible for drafting legislation which would regulate the business dealings of his former Wall Street colleagues. Furthermore, an alliance between the Roosevelt and Kennedy families was indelibly printed upon the minds of reactionary elements of business. I will return to this Kennedy-Roosevelt alliance and its repercussions later.

How Secure Are The Institutions of Legal Government In America?

How secure, indeed? It would be tempting to write off this entire matter as a group of con men separating wealthy conservatives from their money by pretending to hatch a plot against the Roosevelt Administration. But there are too many disturbing pieces of evidence in this tale that suggest that the Zeitgeist of the 1930s was not limited to Europe.

If MacGuire's claims to Butler were true, some U.S. military commanders were prepared to stand aside while 500,000 veterans marched on Washington and took Roosevelt captive. (Between the World Wars, the United States Army was so small that 500,000 veterans might have given them a serious fight – even if every officer remained loyal to Roosevelt.)

But unlike many European countries, American government was highly decentralized in 1934, and this would have worked against any serious military action against the legitimate government. Every state governor had control of state militia units, armed with out of date, but still serviceable military weapons.

In addition to the regularly organized state militias, the population of the United States, then as now, was heavily armed with the sort of weapons well suited to military operations. Whatever the advantages of the plotters' army of 500,000 veterans, they would have been far outnumbered by the unorganized militia of the United States -- then as now, consisting of every U.S. citizen between 18 and 45, and legally obligated by state laws to fight at the order of the governor in the event of insurrection, invasion, or war.

But in a nation that was suffering from the ravages of the Great Depression, another model exists for what might have happened: the Spanish Civil War. The divisions over religion in America were not as dramatic as those that ripped apart Spanish society. But many Americans were beginning to lose their faith in American institutions -- as evidenced by the growth of American Nazi and Communist movements during the 1930s. It is frightening to think of what might have happened if a general as capable as Butler had become the man on a white horse.

In the words of U.S. Supreme Court Justice Hugo Black, delivered at New York University in 1960 concerning the protections of the U.S. Bill of Rights:

I cannot agree with those who think of the Bill of Rights as an 18th century straitjacket, unsuited for this age.. The evils it guards against are not only old, they are with us now, they exist today. Experience all over the world has demonstrated, I fear, that the distance between stable, orderly government and one that has been taken over by force is not so great as we have assumed.

Indeed, the plot that Butler exposed -- if what MacGuire claimed was true -- is a sobering reminder to Americans. We were not immune to the sentiments that gave rise to totalitarian governments throughout the world in the 1930s. We make a serious mistake when we assume, "*It can't happen here!*"

Some Other Details

In the working out of a great national program seeking the primary good of the greater number, the toes of some very powerful people are going to be stepped on. But these toes belong to the comparative few who seek to retain or to gain position or riches or both by some short cut that is harmful to the greater good.

Roosevelt did step on some very sensitive toes. Roosevelt and the New Dealers were determined to eliminate the abuses of the national financial system by subjecting it to federal regulation. Threatened by prospects of government regulation and taxation of individual wealth as well as corporate profits to fund relief programs and public works, industrialists and old line money took up the offensive.

Up until that time the dollar was backed by gold, meaning the US Treasury could only print as much money as there was gold reserve backing that money in Fort Knox. Going off the Gold standard allowed for more money to printed and pumped into the economy, partially to fund the proposed relief programs. Those who had a lot of money were opposed to going off the Gold standard for fear their money would have less value. So Butler was asked to convince the veterans, who were due a second bonus payment, that if they were not paid in money backed by gold, their bonuses would be compromised. Butler became suspicious. Who was trying to use him in this way? Where did MacGuire get all this money and for whom was he really working? And wasn't the Gold Standard argument merely a means to alienate the veterans from Roosevelt by convincing them his policies would render their money worthless?

Feigning interest in order to learn more about the purpose of the intrigue, and who was behind it, Butler said he might be interested, but he needed to know the plan was foolproof. Butler also said he wanted to talk to the top man, and not intermediaries. After some hesitation MacGuire revealed that Singer Sewing Machine heir Robert Sterling Clark was instrumental, as was Grayson M.P.

Murphy. Murphy ran a Wall Street brokerage house, was a director of Guaranty Trust, Morgan Bank, and also had interests in Anaconda Copper, Bethlehem Steel and Goodyear Tire.

Other meetings followed. At one point MacGuire took out his wallet and threw down 18 $1000 bills saying he wanted to pay Butler for his help. Robert Sterling Clark himself paid Butler a visit, and hinted at such things as Butler's mortgage payments. Finally MacGuire revealed their real plans: he wanted Butler to lead an insurrection army to march on the White House, "force" Roosevelt to resign, and install a Secretary of General Affairs to take Roosevelt's place and reinstate the Gold Standard.

Why would the plotters choose Butler? Butler, a two-time Congressional Medal of Honor winner was one of the few well-loved military men. Only Butler could induce veterans, who would ordinarily have nothing to do with insurrection to follow him. The plotters felt they could seduce Butler with money and power. They misjudged him.

Butler was an extraordinary man. Of Quaker stock, he served for thirty years in the Marines and enjoyed great popularity among the men he commanded as well as among the rank and file veterans. His military experiences in China, Nicaragua, Haiti, and Cuba eventually led him to suspect that these interventions were nothing more than scouting expeditions for big business. He felt that the lives of American boys were being sacrificed for the profits of United Fruit. In retirement Butler become very outspoken about this. He went on speaking engagements, and even penned a book entitled "War is a Racket".10 He was also one of the few military men to support the Bonus Marchers. These veterans had camped outside the capital demanding the money owed them, only to have their tents burned down by the likes of Generals MacArthur, Patton, and Eisenhower acting on orders from President Hoover.

Butler was still unconvinced that there was a real plot; however, MacGuire made some starling predictions. He predicted there would be an announcement in the press about the formation of a new organization, the American Liberty League. The American Liberty League, funded by the DuPonts, was to complement the coup by functioning as a propaganda organ to discredit the overthrown Roosevelt in the public's mind (a technique which should be all too familiar to students of the character postmortem on JFK).11 MacGuire was also able to predict, well in advance, important personnel changes in the White House. This apparent forecasting ability indicated to Butler that conspirators were even within the New Deal administration. Butler, now taking the conspiracy seriously, approached some of his friends in Congress and the media. The House Committee to Investigate Un-American Activities, chaired by Congressmen John McCormack and Samuel Dickerstein, agreed to hear Butler's testimony.

What The Committee Revealed

Not surprisingly, when called as a witness, MacGuire denied any plot. He claimed he was part of The Committee For Sound Dollar and Sound Currency, Inc., which was spearheading a lobbying effort on behalf of the Gold Standard. However, his contradictory testimony and his inability to satisfactorily explain the large amounts of money which were deposited in several of his accounts compromised his credibility as a witness. At one point he said he was acting as purchasing agent of securities for Clark, but he never produced any evidence that he ever purchased any securities at all. It was also revealed that Clark had sent MacGuire on a trip to Germany, Italy, Spain, and France allegedly to study 'economic' conditions. But records of the Committee for a Sound Dollar, where MacGuire filed his reports, indicated he was studying something more. In each of the countries he met with veterans in paramilitary groups. These were the types of groups that carried out coups and assassinations in Germany and Italy on behalf of Hitler and Mussolini. A similar group operated in France, the Croix de Feu, about which MacGuire wrote this glowing report: "... *this French super organization is composed of about 500,000 men, and each of them was the leader of 10 others, and that is the kind of organization that we should have in the United States.*"

Finally, Butler's story was corroborated by Commander James Van Zandt of the Veterans of Foreign Wars who claimed he was also approached to lead an insurrection army. It was also alleged by Butler that MacGuire had guaranteed arms on credit from the Remington Arms Company. Investigation by the committee revealed that the DuPonts had just bought the controlling interest in Remington Arms.

The committee stated in its final report that it found credible evidence of a contemplated plot to overthrow the elected government with a military coup. Nevertheless, some alleged co-conspirators (supposedly revealed to Butler by MacGuire) such as General Hugh Johnson, (who was head of FDR's National Recovery Administration), former NY Governor Al Smith and General Douglas MacArthur were never subpoenaed.

Aftermath And Beyond

Although the coup never materialized the unrelenting propaganda attack against Roosevelt and the New Deal reforms continued, spearheaded by the American Liberty League. The League listed as its main contributors the DuPont family, representatives of the Morgan interests, Robert Sterling Clark, the Pew Family (Sun Oil), and Rockefeller Associates. Its Treasurer was Grayson M.P. Murphy, MacGuire's immediate boss. The League itself was ostensibly dedicated to the virtues of the Constitution, individual freedom and free market capitalism. But it claimed that all New Deal reforms were inspired by Communists within the Roosevelt administration.

In the election of 1936, the League spent twice as much money as the Republican Party spent in trying to defeat Roosevelt. Although the League disbanded after Roosevelt won his second term, it spawned a series of extreme right-wing groups and paramilitary bands which constituted a network that endured through the 1960s, and whose descendants are with us today. Their propaganda was anti-Communist and anti-Semitic; their tactic was violence.

Some groups which the League financed were the Sentinels of the Republic (which labeled the New Deal "Jewish Communism"), the Minutemen and the Minutewomen. Another group, the Southern Committee to Uphold the Constitution, was associated with the Silver Shirt Squad of the American Storm Troopers. The goals of this organization, headed by a Texas oil magnate, were to create a mass movement of whites in the South to dilute Roosevelt's Dixie vote, and to stir up anti-black racism in order to attack organizing drives by the unions from the North. Significantly, these same hate sentiments were being stirred up against JFK, and for the same reasons. These groups formed the dark underside to the League, which tried to present a polite public face. But some industrialists, like Henry Ford, had no qualms about explicitness. American Fascists groups hawked his anti-Semitic tracts like "The International Jew."

The main function of these hate groups was to enforce the will of right-wing corporate America, seeking to regain the political power it lost in the 1932 election. On the grassroots level, this intention translated into supporting the efforts of management to stop workers from unionizing. The most glaring example of this is the struggle at the General Motors plants (General Motors was owned by the DuPonts). The DuPonts employed the Black Legion, a sort of Northern Klux Klux Klan, which would terrorize workers, bomb union halls, and torture and murder organizers. The Legion was organized into arson squads, execution squads, and anti-Communist squads. Discipline within its own ranks was maintained with the weapons of torture or death and was strictly enforced. The LaFollette Committee found that the Legion had penetrated police departments, high government offices, and the Michigan Republican Party.

These groups also acted as intelligence networks. They infiltrated unions, leftwing groups, and universities, and they sold their information to industry. One example of such an intelligence agency was the American Vigilant Intelligence Federation, headquartered in Chicago and operated by Harry Jung. Jung later relocated to New Orleans where he was an associate of Guy Bannister, who also hailed from Chicago. Banister's Detective Agency was spying for right-wing businesses as well. Some believe it may have been in Jung's hotel in New Orleans that the famous Congress of Freedom meeting took place in the Spring of 1963. At this meeting, with Edwin Walker and Joseph Milteer in attendance, a police informant reported there was talk of murdering national leaders.

In the Thirties, corporate America's fear of government regulation threatened by Roosevelt's New Deal, ("Socialism" in their minds), gave them a reason to embrace Fascism. It justified their financing of paramilitary hate groups to carry out violent, anti-government and anti-union campaigns exploiting the vehicles of racism, anti-Semitism and anti-Communism. By the Sixties these groups had become entrenched in the grassroots landscape.

The institutionalization of the military industrial complex and the national security state, with which corporate America would meld, developed during World War II and its aftermath. The DuPonts, as well as other industrialists, implicated in the attempted coup against FDR played a major role in these developments.

The Nye Committee Hearings to investigate the munitions industry were finally held in 1935. Committee findings revealed that the DuPonts were heavily invested in fascist Italy, and had played a major role in the rearming of Germany. According to the Versailles Treaty, which ended WWI, it was illegal to sell arms to Germany, but the DuPonts lobbied State Department delegates to the Paris Peace Conference. They finally obtained assurance from one of the delegates that their business with Germany would be "winked at." That delegate was Wall Street lawyer Allen Dulles. In addition, the Wall Street lawyer who represented the DuPonts at the hearings was William Donovan, who went on to head the Office of Strategic Services (the OSS was the forerunner of the CIA) during WWII.

In spite of the DuPonts' illegal dealings, no prosecutions were forthcoming as a result of the Nye committee either. The DuPont family interests represented the largest holdings in the military industrial complex. DuPont built and operated the plant for the Manhattan project. They built all the facilities for atomic bomb production including the facility at Oak Ridge Tennessee. DuPont technicians and engineers ran the show; and by the Sixties the DuPonts effectively had control of the whole atomic energy industry.

Payback Is Hard To Do

When Franklin Delano Roosevelt appointed Joseph Kennedy as Chairman of the Securities and Exchange Commission, it was payback time. For it was Joseph Kennedy as chair of the Roosevelt election committee who helped put together that winning "Roosevelt coalition" of urban ethnic groups and the Catholic votes of the Northeast. Kennedy and his family had a powerful legacy in the urban political wards and could deliver that vote. They also elicited the support of some businessmen who were otherwise suspicious of FDR (Kennedy even managed to get William Randolph Hearst to support FDR's first bid for the Presidency).

The Roosevelts and the Kennedys cooperated on other levels as well. James Roosevelt, the President's son, was instrumental in securing British liquor franchises for Joseph Kennedy. Elliot Roosevelt, another son, served alongside Joseph Kennedy Jr. in WWII. In fact, he was flying the escort plane when Joseph was shot down[137].

The relationship between Kennedy and Roosevelt was not always cordial, but Kennedy's isolationism vs. Roosevelt's internationalism is beyond the scope of this article. Kennedy nevertheless remained a loyal Roosevelt

---

[137] Certainly a convenient situation.

supporter even after most businessmen abandoned the New Deal ship. By the time Roosevelt sought his third term, Kennedy had become more critical of FDR, fostering hope in the business community that he might endorse Wendel Wilkie. Robert E. Woods of the right-wing America First Committee encouraged Kennedy to support Wilkie. Kennedy apparently led Woods, and the Luces, to believe he would shift allegiances. Remember, in 1940 Kennedy was a well-known public figure, and the nation anxiously awaited his radio address to announce whom he supported for President. In spite of his contrary posturing, Kennedy finally supported Roosevelt. Years later, he told Claire Booth Luce, "*I simply made a deal with Roosevelt. We agreed that if I would endorse him for President in 1940, then he would support my son Joe for Governor of Massachusetts in 1942*[138]."

So Joseph Kennedy gained the enmity of FDR's enemies; he was said to be perceived as a traitor to his own class by many. In spite of his support, however, Roosevelt continued to be very suspicious of Kennedy and considered him a silent member of the Coup d'Tate.

---

138 Of course Roosevelt was excused from having to keep his promise when Joe Kennedy was killed. Convenient wasn't it?

CHAPTER TWENTY-TWO
DESPERATE DECEPTION: BRITISH COVERT OPERATIONS IN THE UNITED STATES, 1939-44

At the same time that President Franklin D. Roosevelt was dealing with a potential Coup d'Tate orchestrated by very wealthy members of his own class, the British Intelligence Services were conducting covert operations in the United States designed to involve the U.S. in the growing war in Europe.

Unfortunately for the American people, Roosevelt saw that the defeat of the Axis was necessary to save the world. He firmly believed that only American entry into the war could secure this goal. The President accordingly had to resort to deception to inveigle America into the conflict. While publically promising peace, he set out to provoke war. Roosevelt's policy, it is claimed, was vindicated by the Allied defeat of Germany and Japan in 1945.

Not everyone convinced that isolation from war in 1941 was wrong adopts this bold line. Some historians, such as Dexter Perkins, reluctant to embrace Machiavelli so openly, argue that Roosevelt and the American public were not so far apart as first appears. True, the great majority of the public opposed entry into the war, but the public also favored aid to Britain of a sort that risked war. Roosevelt thus acted to secure what the public "really" wanted.

As Louis D. Rubin, Jr., has expressed this position: "*But public opinion was overwhelmingly on the side of Britain; an opinion poll taken in July 1940 indicated that seven out of ten Americans believed a Nazi victory would place the United States in danger, and so were in favor of assistance to the embattled British.*"

An obvious problem with this interpretation is that it ascribes to the public views that quickly generate tension, if not outright inconsistency. People believed, it is claimed, both that the United States should stay out of the war and that the country should adopt policies liable to produce just the undesired outcome. Given this tension, would not people be apt to revise their beliefs to restore equilibrium? That is to say, would they not either reject unneutral policies or abandon the resolve to stay out of the war? Certainly, people sometimes hold beliefs that ill comport together, but this problem was glaringly obvious. Were we that stupid? The polls that showed American support for violations of neutrality were rigged by British agents. "British intelligence had 'penetrated' the Gallup organization.... British intelligence officer David Ogilvy later wrote about his days at Gallup: '*I could not have had a better boss than Dr. Gallup. His confidence in me was such that I do not recall his ever reading any of the reports I wrote in his name*'". By careful manipulation of the questions asked, results could be contrived to order. "*In 1940 and 1941, BSC [British Security Coordination] rigged a series of polls...to project the notion that the members of prominent organizations were pro-British, avidly in favor of intervention, and intensely antagonistic toward America First*".

What exactly were the questions asked in the various polls? Had they been phrased differently, would the respondents have answered in a way more consistent with non-intervention? The balance of evidence suggests strongly that they would have done so. Although a Gallup poll taken August 1940 showed an "astounding figure" of 70 percent in favor of conscription, Congressional mail "overwhelmingly" opposed the draft. Further, a poll sponsored by Robert Hutchins, a strong opponent of the war, showed that only 34 percent of the public favored entry into the war, even if Britain was defeated. (Incidentally, one wonders whether polls still are rigged. A careful examination of the polls that showed a rise in popularity for President Clinton whenever a new act of his malfeasance was disclosed seems warranted.)

Professor Mahl offers a comprehensive account of British intelligence activities designed to involve the United States in war. The single most striking example of the effectiveness of the British effort is this. Before the Office of Strategic Services (OSS) was established, a presidential directive in July 1941 set up a preliminary group called The Coordinator of Information (COI). Not only was this group, which devised the plans for the OSS, organized at the behest of British Intelligence; its head was a British agent. Colonel Charles Howard "Dick" Ellis, an assistant to the principal British intelligence agent in America, Sir William Stephenson, "actually ran [William] Donovan's COI office and produced the blueprint for the American OSS" (p. 194).

I cannot describe in detail the vast range of episodes which Mr. Mahl discusses. Rather, I shall confine myself to two additional examples of British influence. The first relates to the crucial US election of November 1940. In order to win the war, Britain needed the support of the United States as a fighting ally. But, if the Republicans ran a strong noninterventionist campaign, not even the machinations of Franklin Roosevelt would suffice to accomplish this. "The first peacetime draft law in American history, Burke-Wadsworth, and the Destroyer Deal would not have received Roosevelt's endorsement had a genuine opposition candidate stood ready to make it a political issue in the 1940 election" (p. 164).

To secure the British goal, then, the Republican candidate had to be solidly in the interventionist camp. How could this be achieved? Mr. Mahl answers his question by pointing to an anomaly: the unexpected surge of support for Wendell Willkie in the months before the Republican convention, and at the convention itself.

The stampede toward Willkie, the quintessential dark horse candidate, puzzled informed contemporaries. H.L. Mencken "wrote, after watching the nomination: 'I am thoroughly convinced that the nomination of Willkie was managed by the Holy Ghost in person'" (p. 156). Our author essays a more down-to-earth explanation. The boom for Willkie was contrived with heavy British support; the banker Thomas W. Lamont played a key role in the endeavor. Whether Mr. Mahl's account is successful must be left for readers to judge.

In any event, once nominated Willkie enabled the British strategy to proceed apace. Mr. Mahl cites in this connection a telling remark of Walter Lippmann, himself an ally of British intelligence: "Second only to the Battle of Britain, the sudden rise and nomination of Wendell Willkie was the decisive event, perhaps providential, which made it possible to rally the free world when it was almost conquered" (p. 164). Willkie was if anything more interventionist than Roosevelt; non-interventionist voters in 1940 were in effect shut out of the presidential election. The other incident selected for discussion will, I fear, evoke memories of The Starr Report. (May I reiterate what is said elsewhere in these pages: The Mises Review has no connection with that salacious document.) Again the key issue involves the paralysis of isolationist opposition to British plans. Senator Arthur Vandenberg of Michigan, a protégé of the isolationist William Borah, ranked among the foremost non-interventionists during the 1930s. He executed a sudden volte-face in July 1940 and supported the crucial Lend-Lease Bill in March 1941.

Mr. Mahl attributes the change of heart to the influence of Mitzi Sims, Vandenberg's mistress, who had strong ties to British intelligence, and of another woman, Betty Thorpe Pack ("Cynthia"), also romantically linked with him. Our author admits he cannot prove that Vandenberg's relationship with those women changed the senator's views; but his conjecture certainly helps us understand Vandenberg's otherwise inexplicable behavior.

But is Vandenberg's changing in fact a strange phenomenon that requires special explanation? One might object that it is not: if the interventionist view of the wartime situation is accepted, then Vandenberg's support for Lend-Lease responded realistically to grave threats to America's interests. Perhaps, to echo A.J.P. Taylor on Lord Halifax, Vandenberg "heard the call of conscience in the watches of the night." More generally, why need we invoke British intrigues to explain American policy? Once more, will not the national interest suffice?

The imagined rejoinder fails. It begs the question by assuming the correctness of interventionism. No doubt, Lend-Lease was in the national interest-but only if one accepts the interventionist account of that interest. The point at issue is that only a minority of people in the United States held this view before Pearl Harbor. On the isolationist position, Lend-Lease and similar measures did not serve our interests. Why then were these policies instituted? Mr. Mahl's study gives us indispensable aid in answering this question.

CHAPTER TWENTY-THREE
WORLD WAR II

For years, I have read various books that maintain that Franklin D. Roosevelt did everything in his power to force the Japanese to attack the United States. Allegedly, this was not because he wanted war with Japan, rather because he wanted war with Germany.

In hind sight, a number of informational sources have opened up that were not available to researchers earlier. To my surprise, the information newly released does support the premise that Roosevelt was aware of the pending attack and wanted it to happen.

In 1944, The Army Board stated that "...everything that the Japanese were planning to do was known to the United States..." President Roosevelt (FDR) provoked the attack, knew about it in advance and covered up his failure to warn the Hawaiian commanders. FDR needed the attack to sucker Hitler to declare war on the United States, since the public and Congress were overwhelmingly against entering the war in Europe. It was his backdoor to war. FDR blinded the military commanders at Pearl Harbor and set them up by denying intelligence to Hawaii (HI) on November 27 and later, misleading the commanders into thinking negotiations with Japan were continuing to prevent them from realizing the war was on having false information sent to HI about the location of the Japanese carrier fleet.

A Short History Lesson

Like any good soldiers, the Japanese high command believed in the value of the surprise attack. In 1904 the Japanese destroyed the Russian navy in a surprise attack in an undeclared war. In 1932 in the U.S. Military Grand Joint Army-Navy Exercises, a force of 152 aircraft carrier planes caught the defenders of Pearl Harbor completely by surprise. This mock attack also took place on a Sunday. In 1938 Admiral Ernst King led a carrier-born airstrike from the USS Saratoga successfully against Pearl Harbor in another exercise.

In the face of this solid proof that the United States Pacific Fleet was not safe in Pearl Harbor, in 1940 President Roosevelt ordered the U.S. Pacific Fleet transferred from the safety of the West Coast to its exposed position in Hawaii. He was adamant about this order that the fleet remain stationed at Pearl Harbor even over complaints by its commander, Admiral Richardson, that there was inadequate protection from air attack and no protection from torpedo attack. Richardson felt so strongly that he twice disobeyed orders to berth his fleet there and he raised the issue personally with FDR in October of 1940. As a result of his protests over the well being of the Americans under his command, he was soon after replaced. His successor, Admiral Kimmel, also brought up the same issues with FDR in June 1941 and was also threatened with being replaced[139].

The McCollum Memo

On 7th of October 1940, Lieutenant Commander Arthur H. McCollum, head of the Far East desk of the Office of Naval Intelligence, wrote the eight-action memo at Roosevelt's specific request. This memo outlined eight different steps the United States could take that he predicted *would lead to an attack by Japan on the United States*. The day after this memo was given to Franklin D. Roosevelt, Roosevelt began to implement these steps. By the time that Japan finally attacked the United States at Pearl Harbor on 7 December 1941, all eight steps had been implemented by Roosevelt.

The eight steps consisted of two main subject areas; the first being a sign of United States military preparedness and threat of attack, the second being a forceful control on Japan's trade and economy. The main subject area of the eight-action memo was a discussion of the United States' military preparedness and threat of attack. McCollum called for the United States to make arrangements with both Britain (Action A) and Holland (Action B), for the use of military facilities and acquisition of supplies in both Singapore and Indonesia.

He also suggested for the deployment of a division of long-range heavy cruisers (Action D) and two divisions of submarines (Action E) to the Orient. The last key factor McCollum called for was to keep the United States Fleet in the vicinity of the Hawaiian Islands (Action F). Roosevelt personally took charge of Action's D and E; these actions were called "pop up" cruises. Roosevelt had this to say about the cruises, "*'I just want them to keep popping up here and there and keep the Japs guessing.*"

With the fleet located around Hawaii and particularly based out of Pearl Harbor a double-sided sword was created; it allowed for quicker deployment times into South Pacific Water, but more importantly it lacked many fundamental military needs, and was vulnerable due to its geographic location. To understand the true vulnerability of Pearl Harbor one must look at Oahu, the Hawaiian Island

---

[139] Roosevelt was either foolhardy about the safety of the American military or he had another reason to risk so many lives. Why would he refuse to listen to his military commanders?

that the military base is located. The North part of the island is all mountains which hinder the vision of military look out points, making an attack from the North virtually a surprise until the sound of fighter planes are over head by the defenders.

There were many key military needs of the U.S. military forces stationed in Hawaii that were missing from Pearl Harbor, and they were a;
- lack of training facilities;
- lack of large-scale ammunition and fuel supplies;
- lack of support craft such as tugs and repair ships; and
- lack of overhaul facilities such as dry-docking and machine shops.

Commander in Chief, United States Fleet Admiral James O. Richardson, was outraged when he was told by President Roosevelt of his plans on keeping the fleet in Hawaiian Waters. Richardson knew of the problems and vulnerability of Pearl Harbor, the safety of his men and warships was paramount in his mind. In a luncheon with Roosevelt, Richardson confronted the President, and by doing so ended his military career. Four months later Richardson was removed as commander-in-chief, and replaced by Rear Admiral Husband Kimmel.

Kimmel by many top Naval personal was looked down upon on for taking orders from Roosevelt and not considering the immediate dangers he was putting the fleet in. The second part of McCollum's eight-action memo was an outlined for a forceful control on Japan's trade and economy. He urged that the Dutch refuse to grant Japanese demands for oil (Action G), and that a complete embargo of all trade with Japan (Action H), by instituted by the United States. This embargo closely resembled a similar embargo that was being imposed by the British Empire.

McCollum also knew that if Japan established controlled of the sea in the Pacific, it would put a strain on America's resources for copper, rubber, tin, and other valuable goods. These imports from the Pacific were all essential to America's Economy, and to protect these trading routes McCollum urged that all possible aid to be given to the Chinese government of Chiang Kai-shek (Action C).

As further proof of the danger to which Roosevelt had exposed the Pacific Fleet by sending them to Pearl Harbor, on November 11, 1940, 21 aged British planes completely destroyed the Italian fleet, including 3 battleships, at their homeport in the harbor of Taranto in Southern Italy by using technically innovative shallow-draft torpedoes.

On February 11, 1941 FDR proposed deliberately sacrificing 6 American cruisers and 2 carriers at Manila to get the American people to support America getting into war. Navy Chief Stark objected: "*I have previously opposed this and you have concurred as to its unwisdom. Particularly do I recall your remark in a previous conference when Mr. Hull suggested (more forces to Manila) and the question arose as to getting them out and your 100% reply, from my standpoint,* was that you might not mind losing one or two cruisers, but that you did not want to take a chance on losing 5 or 6[140]."

In March of 1941 FDR sold munitions and convoyed them to belligerents in Europe -- both acts of war and both violations of international law – under the provisions of the Lend-Lease Act. On Jun 23, 1941 Advisor Harold Ickes wrote FDR a memo the day after Germany invaded the Soviet Union, *"There might develop from the embargoing of oil to Japan such a situation as would make it not only possible but easy to get into this war in an effective way. And if we should thus indirectly be brought in, we would avoid the criticism that we had gone in as an ally of communistic Russia."*

FDR was pleased with Admiral Richmond Turner's report read July 22: *"It is generally believed that shutting off the American supply of petroleum* [to the Japanese] *will lead promptly to the invasion of Netherland East Indies...it seems certain she* [Japan] *would also include military action against the Philippine Islands, which would immediately involve us in a Pacific war."*

On July 24 FDR told the Volunteer Participation Committee, *"If we had cut off the oil of, they probably would have gone down to the Dutch East Indies a year ago, and you would have had war."* The next day FDR froze all Japanese assets in the US, cutting off their main supply of oil and forcing them into war with the US. Intelligence information was withheld from Hawaii from this point forward.

On August 14, at the Atlantic Conference, Churchill noted the "astonishing depth of Roosevelt's intense desire for war." Churchill cabled his cabinet "(FDR) obviously was very determined that they should come in." On the 18th of October - diary entry by Secretary of Interior Harold Ickes: *"For a long time I have believed that our best entrance into the war would be by way of Japan."*

CODES

Another indication that President Roosevelt knew about the attack on Pearl Harbor in advance was that the Japanese Purple Code[141] had previously been cracked by the Army Signal Intelligence Service. J-19 was the main Japanese diplomatic code book. This columnar code was also cracked. The Coral Machine Cipher or JNA-20 was a simplified version of Purple used by Japanese Naval attaches. Only one message deciphered prior to Pearl Harbor has been declassified. However, make no mistake we knew everything the Japanese planned as soon as its Embassies knew.

JN-25[142] was a very simple old-type code book system used by the American Army and Navy in 1898 and abandoned in 1917 because it was

---

140 Beard, Charles PRESIDENT ROOSEVELT AND THE COMING OF WAR 1941, p 424

141 The top Japanese diplomatic machine cipher which used automatic telephone switches to separately and differently encipher each character sent.

142 The Japanese Fleet's Cryptographic System, a.k.a. 5 number code (Sample). JN stands for Japanese Navy, introduced 1 June 1939.

insecure. Version A has a dictionary of 5,600 numbers, words and phrases, each given as a five figure number. These were super-enciphered by addition to random numbers contained in a second code book. The dictionary was only changed once before Pearl Harbor on Dec 1, 1940, to a slightly larger version B but the random book was changed every 3 to 6 months- last on Aug 1.

The Japanese blundered away the code when they introduced JN25-B by continuing to use, for 2 months, random books that had been previously solved by the Allies. That was the equivalent of handing over the JN-25B dictionary. It was child's play for the Navy group OP-20-G (738 men whose primary responsibility was Japanese naval codes) to reconstruct the exposed dictionary. In 1994 the NSA published that JN-25B was completely cracked in December 1940. In January 1941 the US gave Britain two JN-25B code books with keys and techniques for deciphering.

Churchill wrote "*From the end of 1940 the Americans had pierced the vital Japanese ciphers, and were decoding large numbers of their military and diplomatic telegrams.*" The official US Navy statement on JN-25B is the NAVAL SECURITY GROUP HISTORY TO WORLD WAR II prepared by Captain J. Holtwick in June 1971, page 398: "By *1 December 1941 we had the code solved to a readable extent.*" Chief of Navy codebreaking Safford reported that during 1941 "*The Navy COMINT team did a thorough job on the Japanese Navy with no help from the Army.*"(SRH-149)

The first paragraph of the Congressional Report Exhibit 151 says the US was "currently" (instantly) reading JN-25B and exchanging the "translations" with the British prior to Pearl Harbor. The top Navy codebreaker wrote in Cryptologia, July 1982: "*So far as inherent security was concerned, JN-25B was little better than the ciphers used by Julius Caesar and Augustus Caesar. The vocabulary was in Japanese - supplemented by Chinese characters - and the difficulties of written Japanese afforded more security and occasioned more difficulty than the crypto-system.*"

The entire Pearl Harbor scheme was laid out in this coded message. In 1979 the NSA released 2,413 JN-25 orders of the 26,581 intercepted by US between Sept 1 and Dec 4, 1941. The NSA says "*We know now that they contained important details concerning the existence, organization, objective, and even the whereabouts of the Pearl Harbor Strike Force.*"

Of the over thousand radio messages sent by Tokyo to the attack fleet, only 20 are in the National Archives. All messages to the attack fleet were sent several times, at least one message was sent every odd hour of the day and each had a special serial number. Starting in early November 1941 when the attack fleet assembled and started receiving radio messages, OP-20-G stayed open 24 hours a day and the "First Team" of codebreakers worked on JN-25. In November and early December 1941, OP-20-G spent 85 percent of its effort reading Japanese Navy traffic, 12 percent on Japanese diplomatic traffic and 3 percent on German naval codes. FDR was personally briefed twice a day on JN-25 traffic by his aide, Captain John Beardell, and demanded to see the original raw messages in English. The US Government refuses to identify or declassify any pre-Dec 7, 1941 decrypts of JN-25 on the basis of national security, a half-century after the war.

Magic was the security designation given to all decoded Japanese diplomatic messages. It's hard not to conclude with historians like a number of historians that "*Magic standing alone points so irresistibly to the Pearl Harbor attack that it is inconceivable anybody could have failed to forecast the Japanese move.*" The NSA reached the same conclusion in 1955.

Other Warnings

So it is now clear the President Roosevelt had briefings on coded intercepts from the Japanese High Command that made it clear that an attack was being planned against Pearl Harbor. This makes it amazing that neither Roosevelt nor the Army or Navy senior staff warned the commanders in Hawaii of the danger of an attack. However, in order to be fair, let us assume that perhaps the briefings were in military speak and Roosevelt did not understand what he was told.

Assuming that this was true, however, it now turns out that there were a number of warnings from other countries that the Japanese were planning a surprise attack. On January 27, 1941, Dr. Ricardo Shreiber, the Peruvian envoy in Tokyo told Max Bishop, third secretary of the US Embassy in Tokyo that he had just learned from his intelligence sources that there was a war plan involving a surprise attack on Pearl Harbor[143].

On March 31, 1941 a Navy report by Bellinger and Martin predicted that if Japan made war on the US, they would strike Pearl Harbor without warning at dawn with aircraft from a maximum of 6 carriers. For years Navy planners had assumed that Japan, on the outbreak of war, would strike the American fleet wherever it was - it was the greatest danger from Japan.

The U.S. Pacific fleet was the only real threat to Japan's plans of conquest. Logically, Japan couldn't engage in any major operation with the American fleet on its flank. Initial seriously crippling attacks on the US fleet in Hawaii would be the only chance the Japanese military would have for eventual victory. The strategic options for the Japanese were not unlimited.

On July 10, 1941 US Military Attache Smith-Hutton at Tokyo reported that the Japanese Navy was secretly practicing aircraft torpedo attacks against capital ships in Ariake Bay. The bay closely resembles Pearl Harbor.

In July of 1941, the US Military Attache in Mexico forwarded a report that the Japanese were constructing special small submarines for attacking the American fleet in Pearl Harbor, and that a training program then under way included towing them from Japan to positions off the Hawaiian Islands, where they practiced surfacing and submerging.

---

143 Assuming for a moment that this was the earliest warning, it was still almost 11 months prior to the actuall attack.

On the 10th of August, 1941, the top British agent, code named "Tricycle[144]", told the FBI of the planned attack on Pearl Harbor and that it would be soon. The FBI told him that his information was "*too precise, too complete to be believed. The questionnaire plus the other information you brought spell out in detail exactly where, when, how, and by whom we are to be attacked. If anything, it sounds like a trap.*"

He also reported that a senior Japanese naval person had gone to Taranto to collect all secret data on the attack there and that it was of utmost importance to them. The info was given to Naval IQ.

Early in the fall of 1941, Kilsoo Haan, an agent for the Sino-Korean People's League, told Eric Severeid of CBS that the Korean underground in Korea and Japan had positive proof that the Japanese were going to attack Pearl Harbor before Christmas. Among other things, one Korean had actually seen the plans. In late October, Haan finally convinced US Senator Guy Gillette that the Japanese were planning to attack. Gillette alerted the State Department, Army and Navy Intelligence and FDR personally.

On the 24th of September, 1941, the "bomb plot" message in J-19 code from Japan Naval Intelligence to Japan's consul general in Honolulu requesting grid of exact locations of ships pinpointed for the benefit of bombardiers and torpedo pilots was deciphered. There was no reason to know the EXACT location of ships in harbor, unless to attack them - it was a dead giveaway.

Chief of War Plans, Turner, and Chief of Naval Operations, Stark, repeatedly kept this intelligence and warnings based on it prepared by Safford and others from being passed to Hawaii. The Chief of Naval Intelligence, Captain Kirk, was replaced because he insisted on warning the senior military commanders at Pearl Harbor of the pending attack by the Japanese. It was lack of information like this that led to the exoneration of the Hawaii commanders and the blaming of Washington for unpreparedness for the attack by the Army Board and Navy Court. At no time did the Japanese ever ask for a similar bomb plot for any other American military installation.

Why the Roosevelt administration allowed flagrant Japanese spying on Pearl Harbor has never been explained, but they blocked two Congressional investigations in the fall of 1941 to allow it to continue. The bomb plots were addressed to "Chief of 3rd Bureau, Naval General Staff", marked Secret Intelligence message, and given special serial numbers, so their significance couldn't be missed. There were about 95 ships in port. The text was of the "Bomb Plot Message was:

"*Strictly secret.*

"*Henceforth, we would like to have you make reports concerning vessels along the following lines insofar as possible:*

---

144 Dusko Popov

"1. The waters (of Pearl Harbor) are to be divided roughly into five subareas (We have no objections to your abbreviating as much as you like.)

"Area A. Waters between Ford Island and the Arsenal.
"Area B. Waters adjacent to the Island south and west of Ford Island. (This area is on the opposite side of the Island from Area A.)
"Area C. East Loch.
"Area D. Middle Loch.
"Area E. West Loch and the communication water routes.

"2. With regard to warships and aircraft carriers, we would like to have you report on those at anchor (these are not so important) tied up at wharves, buoys and in docks. (Designate types and classes briefly. If possible we would like to have you make mention of the fact whenthere are two or more vessels along side the same wharf.)"

Simple traffic analysis of the accelerated frequency of messages from various Japanese consuls gave a another identification of war preparations, from Aug-Dec there were 6 messages from Seattle, 18 from Panama, 55 from Manila and 68 from Hawaii.

In October of 1941, Soviet top spy Richard Sorge, the greatest spy in history, informed Kremlin that Pearl Harbor would be attacked within 60 days. Moscow informed him that this was passed to the US. Interestingly, all references to Pearl Harbor in the War Department's copy of Sorge's 32,000 word confession to the Japanese were deleted[145].

On the 16th of October President Roosevelt grossly humiliated Japan's Ambassador and refused to meet with Premier Konoye in order to help engineer the war party, lead by General Tojo, into power in Japan.

On the 1st day of November the JN-25 Order was intercepted and translated that instructed recipient units to continue drills against anchored capital ships to prepare to "*ambush and completely destroy the US Enemy.*" The message included references to armor-piercing bombs and 'near surface torpedoes.'

On the 13th day of November the German Ambassador to the US, Dr. Thomsen, an ardent anti-Nazi, told US IQ that Pearl Harbor would be attacked.

On the 14th day of November the Japanese Merchant Marine was alerted that wartime recognition signals would be in effect as of December 1.

On the 22nd day of November Tokyo said to Ambassador Nomura in Washington about extending the deadline for negotiations to November 29: *"...this time we mean it, that the deadline absolutely cannot be changed. After that things are automatically going to happen."*

---

145 NY Daily News article, 17 May 1951.

Central Intelligence Agency Director Allen Dulles told people after the war that US was warned in mid-November 1941 that the Japanese Fleet had sailed east past Tokyo Bay and was going to attack Pearl Harbor[146].

On the 23rd day of November, a JN25 order was intercepted and translated that stated "The first air attack has been set for 0330 hours on X-day[147]." (

On the 25th day of November, British decrypted the Winds setup message sent Nov. 19. The US decoded it Nov. 28. It was a J-19 Code message that there would be an attack and that the signal would come over Radio Tokyo as a weather report - rain meaning war, east (Higashi) meaning US.

On the 25th of November Secretary of War Stimson noted in his diary "*FDR stated that we were likely to be attacked perhaps as soon as next Monday.*" FDR asked: "*the question was how we should maneuver them into the position of firing the first shot without too much danger to ourselves. In spite of the risk involved, however, in letting the Japanese fire the first shot, we realized that in order to have the full support of the American people it was desirable to make sure that the Japanese be the ones to do this so that there should remain no doubt in anyone's mind as to who were the aggressors.*"

On the 25th of November the Navy Department ordered all US trans-Pacific shipping to take the southern route[148]. ADM Turner testified "*We sent the traffic down to the Torres Straight, so that the track of the Japanese task force would be clear of any traffic[149].*"

Also on the 25t of November Japanese Admiral Yamamoto radioed this order in JN-25: " *(a) The task force, keeping its movements strictly secret and maintaining close guard against submarines and aircraft, shall advance into Hawaiian waters and upon the very opening of hostilities, shall attack the main force of the United States Fleet in Hawaii and deal it a mortal blow. The raid is planned for dawn on X-day -- exact date to be given by later order. (b) Should the negotiations with the US prove successful, the task force shall hold itself in readiness forthwith to return and reassemble. (c) The task force will move out of Hitokappu Wan on the morning of 26 November and advance to the standing-by position on the afternoon of 4 December and speedily complete refueling[150].*"

This was decoded by the British on November 25 and the Dutch on November 27. When it was decoded by the US is a national secret, however, on November 26 Naval Intelligence reported the concentration of units of the Japanese fleet at an unknown port ready for offensive action.

---

146 CIA FOIA

147 Tokyo time or 8 A.M. Honolulu time.

148 PHH 12:317 (PHH = 1946 Congressional Report, vol. 12, page 317)

149 PHH 4:1942

150 Order to sail - scan from the PHA Congressional Hearings Report, vol 1 p 180, transcript p 437-8)

At 3 AM on the 26th of November Churchill sent an urgent secret message to FDR, probably containing the above message. This message caused the greatest agitation in DC. Of Churchill's voluminous correspondence with FDR, this is the only message that has not been released (on the grounds that it would damage national security). Stark testified that "*On November 26 there was received specific evidence of the Japanese intention to wage offensive war against Great Britain and the United States.*"

C.I.A. Director William Casey, who was in the OSS in 1941, in his book The Secret War Against Hitler, p 7, wrote "*The British had sent word that a Japanese fleet was steaming east toward Hawaii.*" Washington, in an order of Nov 26 as a result of the "first shot" meeting the day before, ordered both US aircraft carriers, the Enterprise and the Lexington out of Pearl Harbor "as soon as practicable." This order included stripping Pearl of 50 planes or 40 percent of its already inadequate fighter protection.

In response to Churchill's message, FDR secretly cabled him that afternoon "*Negotiations off. Services expect action within two weeks.*" Note that the only way FDR could have linked negotiations with service action, let alone have known the timing of the action, was if he had the message to sail. In other words, the only service action contingent on negotiations was Pearl Harbor.

On the 26th of November "*The "most fateful document*" was Hull's ultimatum that Japan must withdraw from Indochina and all China. Roosevelt's Ambassador to Japan called this "*The document that touched the button that started the war.*"

On the 27th of November Secretary of War Stimson sent a confused and confusing hostile action possible or DO-DON'T warning. The Navy Court found this message directed attention away from Pearl Harbor, rather than toward it. One purpose of the message was to mislead Hawaii into believing that the negotiations with the Japanese were continuing. The Army units stationed in and around Pearl, which did not have the resources to conduct reconnaissance was ordered to do so and the Navy, which did have the resources to conduct reconnaissance, was ordered not to do so.

The Army units were ordered on sabotage alert, which specifically precluded attention to outside threat. Navy attention was misdirected 5000 miles from Hawaii. Washington DC repeated, no less than three times as a direct instruction of the President, "*The US desires that Japan commit the first overt act Period.*" It was unusual that FDR directed this warning, a routine matter, to Hawaii which is proof that he knew other warnings were not sent. A simple question--what Japanese "overt act" was FDR expecting at Pearl Harbor? He ordered sabotage prevented and subs couldn't enter, that leaves air attack. The words "overt act" disclose FDR's intent - not just that Japan be allowed to attack but that they inflict damage on the fleet. This FDR order to allow a Japanese attack was aid to the enemy - explicit treason.

On the 29th of November Hull sat in Layfayette Park across from the White House with ace United Press reporter Joe Leib and showed him a message stating that Pearl Harbor would be attacked on December 7. This could well have been the Nov. 26 message from Churchill. The New York Times in its 12/8/41 Pearl Harbor report on page 13 under the headline "Attack Was Expected" stated the US had known that Pearl Harbor was going to be attacked the week before. Perhaps Leib wasn't the only reporter Hull told.

On the 29th day of November the FBI embassy wiretap made an intercept of an uncoded plain-text Japanese international telephone conversation between Ambassador Kurusu in Washington and the Chief Foreign Officer in Tokyo K. Yamamoto in which an Embassy functionary asked *'Tell me, what zero hour is. Otherwise, I won't be able to carry on diplomacy.'* The voice from Tokyo said softly, *'Well then, I will tell you. Zero hour is December 8 at Pearl Harbor*[151].*'*

On the 30th day of November[152] the Japanese fleet was radioed this Imperial Naval Order (JN-25): "JAPAN, UNDER THE NECESSITY OF HER SELF-PRESERVATION AND SELF-DEFENSE, HAS REACHED A POSITION TO DECLARE WAR ON THE UNITED STATES OF AMERICA.[153]" US ally China also recovered it in plain text from a shot-down Japanese Army plane near Canton that evening. This caused an emergency Imperial Conference because they knew the Chinese would give the information to both Great Britian and the United States. In a related J-19 message the next day, the US translated elaborate instructions from Japan dealing in precise detail with the method of internment of American nationals in Asia "on the outbreak of war with England and the United States"

On the 1st day of December the Office of Naval Intelligence, ONI, Twelfth Naval District in San Francisco found the missing Japanese fleet by correlating reports from the four wireless news services and several shipping companies that they were getting strange signals west of Hawaii. The Soviet Union also knew the exact location of the Japanese fleet because they asked the Japanese in advance to let one of their ships pass[154]. This info was most likely given to them by US because Sorge's spy ring was rolled up November 14. All long-range PBY patrols from the Aleutians were ordered stopped on Dec 6 to prevent contact.

On the 1st day of December Foreign Minister Togo cabled Washington Ambassador Nomura to continue negotiations *"to prevent the U.S. from becoming unduly suspicious."*

On the 1st day of December the tanker Shiriya, which had been added to the Striking Force in an order intercepted Nov 14, radioed "proceeding to a position 30.00 N, 154.20 E. Expect to arrive at that point on 3 December." (near Hawaii) The fact that this message is in the National Archives destroys the myth

---

151 US Navy translation 29 Nov 41 - remember Dec 8 Tokyo time is December 7 US time
152 US Time (or 1 Dec. Tokyo time)
153 Congress Appendix D, p 415.
154 Layton, And I Was There p 261

that the attack fleet maintained radio silence. The Striking Force orders[155] were that all 31 ships were to use longwave radio and the Battleship Hiei was ordered to communicate with Tokyo and other fleets by shortwave.

Serial numbers prove that the Striking Force sent over 663 radio messages between Nov 16 and Dec 7 or about 1 per hour. The NSA has not released all raw intercepts because the headers would prove that the Striking Force did not maintain radio silence nor have they released all Direction Finding reports for the same reason. On Nov 29 the Hiei sent one message to the Commander of the 3rd fleet; on Nov 30 the Akagi sent several messages to its tankers[156]. There is evidence found of over 100 messages being sent from the Striking Force in the National Archives. All Direction Finding reports from Hawaii have been crudely cut out. Reports from Dec 5 show messages sent from the Striking Force picked up by Station Cast, P.I.

From traffic analysis, Hawaii reported that the carrier force was at sea and in the North. THE MOST AMAZING FACT is that in reply to that report, General Douglas MacArthur's command sent a series of three messages, Nov 26, 29, Dec 2, to Hawaii lying about the location of the carrier fleet. MacArthur's was adamant that the carrir fleet was in the South China Sea. This false information, which the NSA calls inexplicable, was the true reason that Hawaii was caught unawares. A former member of MacArthur's command, Duane Whitlock, who is still alive in Iowa, sent those messages to Hawaii.

There were a large number of other messages that gave the location of the Striking Force by alluding to the Aleutians, the North Pacific and various weather systems near Hawaii.

On the 1st day of December FDR cut short his scheduled ten day vacation after 1 day to meet with Hull and Stark. The result of this meeting was reported on 2 Dec. by the Washington Post: "*President Roosevelt yesterday assumed direct command of diplomatic and military moves relating to Japan.*" This politically damaging move was necessary to prevent the mutiny of the conspirators involved in the brewing coup against Roosevelt.

On the 1st day of December 3:30 P.M. FDR read Foreign Minister Togo's message to his ambassador to Germany: "*Say very secretly to them that there is extreme danger between Japan & Anglo-Saxon nations through some clash of arms, add that the time of this war may come quicker than anyone dreams.*" This was in response to extreme German pressure on November 29 for Japan to strike the US and promises to join with Japan in war against the US. The second of its three parts has never been released. The message says it contains the plan of campaign. This is 1 of only 3 known DIPLOMATIC intercepts that specified Pearl Harbor as a target for a surprise air attack. It was so interesting, FDR kept a copy.

---

155 Strike Force order # 820

156 See page 474 of the Hewitt Report. Stinnett in DAY OF DECEIT (p 209)

On the 2nd day of December 2200 Tokyo a typical JN-25 ships-in-harbor report was sent to the attacking fleet, words in parenthesis were in the original: "Striking Force telegram No. 994. Two battleships (Oklahoma, Nevada), 1 aircraft carrier (Enterprise) 2 heavy cruisers, 12 destroyers sailed. The force that sailed on 22 November returned to port. Ships at anchor Pearl Harbor p.m. 28 November were 6 battleships (2 Maryland class, 2 California class, 2 Pennsylvania class), 1 aircraft carrier (Lexington), 9 heavy cruisers (5 San Francisco class, 3 Chicago class, 1 Salt Lake class), 5 light cruisers (4 Honolulu class, 1 Omaha class)"

On the 2nd day of December the Commander of the Combined Imperial Fleet, Admiral Yamamoto radioed the attack fleet in plain (uncoded) Japanese "Climb Niitakayama 1208[157]". Thus the US knew EXACTLY when the war would start. Mount Niitaka was the highest mountain in the Japanese Empire.

On the 2nd day of December General Hein Ter Poorten, the commander of the Netherlands East Indies Army gave the Winds setup message to the US War Department. The Australians had a center in Melbourne and the Chinese also broke JN-25. A Dutch sub had visually tracked the attack fleet to the Kurile Islands in early November and this info was passed to DC, but DC did not give it to Hawaii. The intercepts the Dutch gave the US are still classified.

Also on the 2nd day of Dececember Japanese order No. 902 specified that old JN-25 additive tables, version 7, would continue to be used alongside version 8 when the latter was introduced on December 4. This means the US read all messages to the Striking Force through the attack.

On the 4th day of Dececember in the early hours, Ralph Briggs, at the Navy's East Coast Intercept station, received the "East Winds, Rain" message, the Winds Execute, which meant war. He put it on the TWX circuit immediately and called his commander. This message, Japanese Dispatch # 7001, was deleted from the files. One of the main coverups of Pearl Harbor was to make this message disappear because why would Roosevelt not warn Hawaii when he knew war was certain? The Winds message makes treason too easily proved. In response to the Winds Execute, the Office of US Naval IQ had all Far Eastern stations (Hawaii not informed) destroy their codes and classified documents including the Tokyo Embassy.

On the 4th day of December the Dutch invoked the ADB joint defense agreement when the Japanese crossed the magic line of 100 East and 10 North. The U.S. was at war with Japan 3 days before they were at war with us.

On the 4th day of December General Ter Poorten sent all the details of the Winds Execute command to Colonel Weijerman, the Dutch military attache' in Washington to pass on to the highest military circles. Weijerman personally gave it to Marshall, Chief of Staff of the War Department.

---

[157] Dec 8 Japanese time, Dec 7 our time.

On the 4th day of December US General Thorpe at Java sent four messages warning of the Pearl Harbor attack. Washington ordered him to stop sending warnings.

On the 5th day of December all Japanese international shipping had returned to home port.

Also on the 5th day of December, at a Cabinet meeting, Secretary of the Navy Knox said, "*Well, you know Mr. President we know where the Japanese fleet is?*" "*Yes, I know*" said FDR. "*I think we ought to tell everybody just how ticklish the situation is. We have information as Knox just mentioned...Well, you tell them what it is, Frank.*" Knox became very excited and said, "*Well, we have very secret information that the Japanese fleet is out at sea. Our information is...*" and then a scowling FDR cut him off[158].

Also on the 5th day of December Washington Star reporter Constantine Brown quotes a friend in his book <u>The Coming of the Whirlwind p 291</u>, "*This is it! The Japs are ready to attack. We've broken their code, and we've read their ORDERS.*"

On the 6th day of December this 18 November J19 message was translated by the Army:

"*1. The warships at anchor in the Harbor on the 15th were as I told you in my No.219 on that day. Area A -- A battleship of the Oklahoma class entered and one tanker left port. Area C -- 3 warships of the heavy cruiser class were at anchor.*

2. On the 17th the Saratoga was not in harbor. The carrier Enterprise, or some other vessel was in Area C. Two heavy cruisers of the Chicago class, one of the Pensacola class were tied up at docks 'KS'. 4 merchant vessels were at anchor in area D.

3. At 10:00 A.M. on the morning of the 17th, 8 destroyers were observed entering the Harbor..."

Of course this information was not passed to HI.

On the 6th day of December a Dec 2 request from Tokyo to Hawaii for information about the absence of barrage balloons, anti-torpedo nets and air recon was translated by the Army.

Also on the 6th day of December at 9:30 P.M FDR read the first 13 parts of the decoded Japanese diplomatic declaration of war and said "*This means war.*" When he returned to his 34 dinner guests he said, "*The war starts tomorrow.*"

Also on the 6th day of December the war cabinet: FDR, top advisor Hopkins, Stimson, Marshall, Secretary of the Navy Knox, with aides John

---

158 Infamy, Toland, 1982, ch 14 sec 5

McCrea and Frank Beatty *"deliberately sat through the night of 6 December 1941 waiting for the Japs to strike*[159]*."*

On the 7th day of December, the following message was received from the Japanese Consul in Budapest to Tokyo:

"On the 6th, the American Minister presented to the Government of this country a British Government communique to the effect that a state of war would break out on the 7th."

The communique was the December 5th War Alert from the British Admiralty. It has disappeared. This triple priority alert was delivered to FDR personally on December the 5th. The Mid-East British Air Marshall told Col. Bonner Fellers on Saturday that he had received a secret signal that America was coming into the war in 24 hours. Churchill summarized the message in GRAND ALLIANCE page 601 as listing the two fleets attacking British targets and *"Other Japanese fleets...also at sea on other tasks."* There only were three other fleets- for Guam, the Philippines and Hawaii. 2 paragraphs of the alert, British targets only, are printed in At Dawn We Slept, Prange, p 464. There is no innocent purpose for our government to hide this document.

On the 7th of December 1941, very early Washington time, there were two Marines, an emergency special detail, stationed outside the Japanese Naval Attache's door.

At 9:30 AM Aides begged Stark to send a warning to Hawaii. He did not.

At 10:00 AM FDR read the 14th part of the Declaration of War, then at 11:00 A.M. FDR read the accompanying 15th part setting the time for the declaration of war to be delivered to the State Department at 1:00 PM, about dawn Pearl Harbor time, and did nothing.

Navy Secretary Knox was given the 15th part at 11:15 A.M. with this note from the Office of Naval IQ: *"This means a sunrise attack on Pearl Harbor today."* Naval IQ also transmitted this prediction to Hull and about 8 others, including the White House[160].

At 10:30 AM Bratton informed Marshall that he had a most important message (the 15th part) and would bring it to Marshall's quarters but Marshall said he would take it at his office. At 11:25 Marshall reached his office according to Bratton. Marshall testified that he had been riding horses that morning but he was contradicted by Harrison, McCollum, and Deane. Marshall who had read the first 13 parts by 10 PM the prior night, perjured himself by denying that he had even received them. Marshall, in the face of his aides' urgent supplications that he warn Hawaii, made strange delays including reading and re-reading all of the 10 minute long 14 Part Message (and some parts several times) which took an hour and refused to use the scrambler phone on his desk, refused to send a warning by the fast, more secure Navy system but sent Bratton three times to

---

159 (Infamy ch 16 sec 2)

160 PHH 36:532

inquire how long it would take to send his watered down warning - when informed it would take 30 or 40 minutes by Army radio, he was satisfied (that meant he had delayed enough so the warning wouldn't reach Pearl Harbor until after the 1 PM Washington time deadline). *The warning was in fact sent commercial without priority identification and arrived 6 hours late.* This message reached all other addressees, like the Philippines and Canal Zone, in a timely manner.

The 7th day of December, 1941, 7:55 A.M. Hawaii time - AIR RAID PEARL HARBOR. THIS IS NOT DRILL.

Also on the 7th of December at 1:50 P.M. Washington time. Harry Hopkins, who was the only person with FDR when he received the news of the attack by telephone from Knox, wrote that FDR was unsurprised and expressed "great relief." Eleanor Roosevelt wrote about December 7th in *This I Remember* [161] that FDR became "in a way more serene." In the NY Times Magazine of October 8, 1944 she wrote: "*December 7 was...far from the shock it proved to the country in general. We had expected something of the sort for a long time.*"

On the 7th of December at 3:00 PM "*The (war cabinet) conference met in not too tense an atmosphere because I think that all of us believed that in the last analysis the enemy was Hitler...and that Japan had given us an opportunity*[162]." Harry Hopkins[163].

MacArthur Was In On The Plot

Also on the 7th of December about 9 hours later, MacArthur's entire air force was caught by surprise and wiped out in the Philippines. MacArthur's reaction to the news of Pearl Harbor was quite unusual - he locked himself in his room all morning and refused to meet with his air commander General Brereton, and refused to attack Japanese forces on Formosa even under orders from the War Department. MacArthur gave three conflicting orders that ensured that all of his planes were on the ground most of the morning. MacArthur used radar tracking of the Japanese planes at 140, 100, 80, 60, down to 20 miles to time his final order and ensure his planes were on the ground.

Strategically, the destruction of half of all US heavy bombers in the world was more important than naval damage in Pearl Harbor. Either MacArthur had committed the greatest blunder in military history or he was under orders to allow his forces to be destroyed. If it were the greatest blunder in history, it is remarkable how he escaped any reprimand, kept his command and got his fourth star and Congressional Medal of Honor shortly later. Prange argued, "*How could the President ensure a successful Japanese attack unless he confided in the commanders and persuaded them to allow the enemy to proceed unhindered?*"

---

161 p 233

162 Dec. 7 Memo (Roosevelt and Hopkins R Sherwood, p. 431)

163 Top KGB agent and FDR's alter ego

Also on the 7th of December at 8:30 PM, FDR said to his cabinet, "*We have reason to believe that the Germans have told the Japanese that if Japan declares war, they will too. In other words, a declaration of war by Japan automatically brings...*" at which point he was interrupted, but his expectation and focus is clear.

Mrs. Frances Perkins, Secretary of Labor, observed later about FDR: "*I had a deep emotional feeling that something was wrong, that this situation was not all it appeared to be.*" Mrs. Perkins was obsessed by Roosevelt's strange reactions that night and remarked particularly on the expression he had:" *In other words, there have been times when I associated that expression with a kind of evasiveness.*"

FDR met with CBS newsman Edward R. Murrow at midnight. Murrow, who had seen many statesmen in crises, was surprised at FDR's calm reaction. After chatting about London, they reviewed the latest news from Pearl Harbor and then FDR tested Murrow's news instincts with these 2 bizarre giveaway questions: "*Did this surprise you?*" Murrow said yes. FDR: "*Maybe you think it didn't surprise us?*"

FDR gave the impression that the attack itself was not unwelcome. This is the same high-strung FDR that got polio when convicted of perjury; the same FDR that was bedridden for a month when he learned Russia was to be attacked by Germany; the same FDR who couldn't eat or drink when he got the Japanese order to sail.

On the 8th day of December in a conversation with his speech writer Rosenman, FDR "emphasized that Hitler was still the first target, but he feared that a great many Americans would insist that we make the war in the Pacific at least equally important with the war against Hitler."

Later, Jonathan Daniels, administrative assistant and press secretary to FDR said, "The blow was heavier than he had hoped it would necessarily be...But the risks paid off; even the loss was worth the price..."

FDR reminisced with Stalin at Tehran on November 30, 1943, saying "*if the Japanese had not attacked the US he doubted very much if it would have been possible to send any American forces to Europe.*"

Compare this statement with what FDR said at the Atlantic Conference 4 months before Pearl: "*Everything was to be done to force an 'incident' to justify hostilities.*" Given that a Japanese attack was the only possible incident, then FDR had promised he would do it.

CHAPTER TWENTY-FOUR
COMMISSIONS AND COVERUPS

Two and only two courts of law have decided the issue of whether President Franklin D. Roosevelt and Washington or the commanders in Hawaii were responsible for the Pearl Harbor disaster. Both the Navy Court and the Army Board found Washington guilty.

There was a NAVY Court of Inquiry as well as a Top Secret Army Board convened to look into this matter. In October of 1944, the Army Board wrote: "*Now let us turn to the fateful period between November 27 and December 6, 1941. In this period numerous pieces of information came to our State, War, and Navy Departments in all of their Top ranks indicating precisely the intentions of the Japanese including the probable exact hour and date of the attack.*"

In response to this report, General George C. Marshall offered his resignation - the sign of a guilty conscience. Marshall testified at the MacArthur hearings that he considered loyalty to his chief superior to loyalty to his country.

JOINT CONGRESSIONAL COMMITTEE

A Joint Congressional Committee was convened to conduct an Investigation of the Pearl Harbor Attack. This Committee, which sat from Nov 15, 1945 to May 31, 1946, proved that there had been so much reversion of testimony, coverup and outright lies that the truth would have to wait until all Pearl Harbor records were declassified.

Most of the conspirators were military men, all men of FDR's own choice, men who only followed orders and FDR never delegated authority. Stark, in answer to charges that he denied IQ to Hawaii, publicly offered a Nuremberg defense in August 1945 that everything he did pre-Dec 7, 1941 was on FDR's orders. The handful of military men in DC responsible for the disaster at Pearl Harbor were directly under the control of FDR and were later promoted and protected from investigation; promoted with FDR's full knowledge that they were responsible for not warning Hawaii. On the record, Intelligence tried to warn Hawaii scores of times but was prevented by FDR's men.

Internal army and navy inquiries in 1944 held Stark and Marshall guilty of dereliction of duty for keeping the Hawaiian commanders in the dark. But the military buried those findings. As far as the public knew, the final truth was uncovered by the Roberts Commission, headed by Justice Owen Roberts of the Supreme Court, and convened eleven days for the attack. The Roberts Commission appeared to have identified its culprits in advance and gerrymandered its inquiries to make the suspects appear guilty. The scapegoats were Kimmel and Short, who were both publicly crucified, forced to retire, and denied the open hearings they desired. One of the Roberts Commission panelists, Admiral William Standly, would call Robert's performance, "Crooked as a snake."

There were eight investigations of Pearl Harbor altogether. The most spectacular was a joint House-Senate probe that reiterated the Roberts Commission findings. At those hearings, Marshall and Stark testified, incredibly, that they could not remember where they were the night the war declaration came in. But, a close friend of Frank Knox, the secretary of the Navy, later revealed that Knox, Stark, and Marshall spent most of that night in the White House with Roosevelt, awaiting the bombing of Pearl Harbor and the chance for America to join World War II.

A widespread cover-up ensued. A few days after Pearl Harbor, reports Historian John Toland, Marshall told his top officers, "*Gentlemen, this goes to the grave with us.*" General Short once considered Marshall his friend, only to learn that the chief of staff was the agent of his frame-up. Short once remarked that he pitted his former pal because Marshall was the only general who wouldn't be able to write an autobiography.

The Results of the Roosevelt Plan

STATISTICS - ROOSEVELT WAS DIRECTLY RESPONSIBLE FOR THE FOLLOWING:
American
Deaths: 2403; Wounded 1,178.
Eighteen ships were sunk or seriously damaged including 5 battleships.
188 planes were destroyed and 162 were damaged.

Japanese
Out of an attack force of 31 ships and 353 raiding planes the Japanese lost:
64 deaths,
29 planes,
5 midget submarines.

Conclusion

The US was warned by, at least, the governments of Britain, Netherlands, Australia, Peru, Korea and the Soviet Union that a surprise attack on Pearl Harbor was coming. All important Japanese codes were broken.

Franklin D. Roosevelt and Marshall and others knew the attack was coming, allowed it and covered up their knowledge. It's significant that both the the chief of OP-20-G Safford and Friedman of Army SIS, the two people in the world that knew what we decoded, said that FDR knew Pearl Harbor was going to be attacked.

Pearl Harbor was not about war with Japan - It was about war with GERMANY Most important was the promise FDR had made to the American people - solemnly given and repeated--not to send their sons into foreign war unless attacked. He did not mind violating that pledge. He merely feared the political effect of the violation. Alsop and Kintner, White House columnist pets, had written a short time before that "*He (Roosevelt) does not feel he can openly violate them (his pledges). But he can get around them the smart way.*" They explained this meant getting the Germans to shoot first. Then he could shoot back. But it was clear to him by November that the Germans were not going to shoot first. But FDR knew that he could force the Japanese to do so.

How do you bait Hitler to declare war on you?

You don't get it by looking unbeatable! Direct provocation by US forces in the Atlantic had failed Hitler didn't bite. FDR knew from Magic that if Japan attacked, Germany would declare war as required by its treaties with Japan. Therefore: the problem was how to maneuver Japan into firing the first shot or make the first overt act.

Japan must succeed or Hitler would renege.

War with Japan was a given because they had to attack the Philippines. If Japan's fleet were destroyed, it would defeat the purpose. It would have been obvious suicide for Hitler to declare war if Japan were crippled, it would allow the US to attack him without even the possibility of a two-front war. That was what he had just been avoiding for months. The plan could only work if Japan's attack succeeded. The lure of a weakened US in a two-front war focused on Japan seemed to make a German war declaration cost-free. But it was all a trap, FDR was always going to ignore Japan and go after Hitler, for his ultimate goal was to save his beloved Soviet Communism.

Behind the Scenes

In November FDR ordered the Red Cross Disaster Relief director to secretly prepare for massive casualties at Pearl Harbor because he was going to let it be attacked. When he protested to the President, President Roosevelt told him that "the American people would never agree to enter the war in Europe unless they were attack [sic] within their own borders[164]."

Churchill wrote that President Roosevelt that the Japanese were going to attack Pearl Harbor. Did FDR know that Pearl Harbor was a Japanese target?

---

[164] See U.S. Naval Institute - Naval History - Advance Warning? The Red Cross Connection by Daryl S. Borgquist

Answer: FDR planned Pearl Harbor to be their target. He ordered the ships in and the carriers out. Co-conspirator Churchill wrote about the Pearl Harbor attack that FDR and his top advisers "knew the full and immediate purpose of their enemy[165]." Churchill's entire discussion of Pearl Harbor was a justification of treason, e.g.: "*A Japanese attack upon the U.S. was a vast simplification of (FDR's and advisors') problems and their duty. How can we wonder that they regarded the actual form of the attack, or even its scale, as incomparably less important than the fact that the whole American nation would be united...?*" Now why would Churchill bother to defend treason unless it happened?

J. Edgar Hoover told his friends in early 1942 that FDR had known about the Pearl Harbor plan since the early fall. It was totally in character for FDR to concoct such a plan. Not only had the US Senate already censured FDR for utterly lacking moral perspective, but as Walter Lippmann wrote: "his purposes are not simple and his methods are not direct."

Old, Slow Ships

FDR had to do coverup the Japanese plan to attack Pearl Harbor in order to get into the war, as he himself later told Stalin. He needed massive public outrage and that required big sacrifice. Would he do it? Did he "love the Navy too much?" He was sacrificing ships in the Atlantic for the same purpose. Of course he would do it - he was doing it.

He saved all the important elements of the fleet. In the spring he had sent many ships to the Atlantic. He kept the aircraft carrier Saratoga on the West Coast. And his sending of the two carrier groups out of harbor meant that not only they but also their fast escort ships would be saved - all the new ships stationed at Pearl Harbor were saved. Only WWI junk was left in harbor. Here is a list of all the ships saved - Ships saved at Pearl December 7

FDR's attitude is best summed up by co-conspirator Admiral Bloch's testimony to Congress, "*The Japanese only destroyed a lot of old hardware. In a sense they did us a favor.*"

This was obviously FDR's view as well, because on 7 December at 2:15 PM, minutes after hearing of the attack and before any damage reports were in, FDR called Lord Halifax at the British Embassy and told him "*Most of the fleet was at sea...none of their newer ships were in harbour.*" He had protected the new ships, the important elements of the fleet, and that fact was at the forefront of his mind in relation to the attack. First, it means FDR didn't care about the old ships. Secondly, it means he knew before the attack that only old ships were in harbor for the attack. Therefore, Pearl Harbor was "*the first shot without too much danger to ourselves*" he sought. FDR was the architect of the attack plot from the oil embargo to the ultimatum to the final touches of deciding who would live and who would die.

---

165 Churchill, Winston, GRAND ALLIANCE, p 603.

Continuing Coverup

Why does the government refuse to release all the messages to the attack fleet, or any JN-25 messages decoded before Dec 7? There is absolutely nothing about national security to hide in JN-25B. It is a trivial and worthless 19th century code. The techniques for cracking it had been published world-wide in 1931. The US government has proudly showed how they used JN-25B decrypts after December 8 to win the Battle of Midway which occurred 7 months after Pearl Harbor. Therefore, there is nothing intrinsic about the code itself, the means of cracking it, or the fact that we cracked it, that has any national security implications of any nature. What is the difference between decrypts from the Purple machine and decrypts from JN-25? The answer is simply that the JN-25 messages contained the final operational details of the Pearl Harbor attack, whereas the Purple did not.

Why won't they let the truth out? Such secrecy breeds mistrust in government. The only thing that is left to hide are JN-25 decrypts and worksheets showing that the US and Britain monitored the Japanese attack fleet all the way to Pearl Harbor. That is the scandal. That is the big secret. It raises the issue of whether the NSA is accessory after the fact to treason. However, the secrecy and misdirection by the NSA about our capabilities with JN-25B and pre-war messages proves there is something very wrong. The NSA has systematically lied about the size of the JN25 books by a factor of 4 and about how many codebreakers worked on the code in 1941 by a factor of 22. More than one quarter of even the encrypted JN-25 messages sent in November and early December 1941 are still classified! The NSA refuses to release Registered Intelligence Publication 79, the complete JN-25B codebook the US Navy published 11 July 1941 because it would destroy their lies. The NSA is an evil Gestapo that is committed neither to truth nor open government nor the rule of law. We live an Orwellian history in which treason is honored, in which FDR's murder of thousands of young innocent men is good. In a word, we are no different from the tyranny we decry. A self-governing people must have truth to make proper decisions. By subverting the truth, the National Security Agency is subverting our Democracy.

He who controls the past, controls the future. He who controls the present, controls the past. - Orwell

Tokyo had to send the daily bomb-plots, cabled from its Honolulu consulate, to the attack fleet by JN-25 radio messages. The pilots had to get their target information. *"The news of the position of enemy ships in Pearl Harbor comes again and again."* - Lt. Cmdr. Chigusa, executive officer of the attack fleet's Akigumo in his diary, December 4, 1941[166]. FDR got it, too. FDR knew the Japanese pilots' targets as well as they did, because he got their bomb-plots

---

166(At Dawn We Slept, G. Prange, page 453)

when they did. He had their specific targets, ship by ship, in his hands at the White House. These messages would prove absolutely that FDR knew that the attack fleet's target was Pearl Harbor and therefore are not released. The unnecessary and illogical secrecy about pre-December 7, 1941, JN-25 decoding is conclusive evidence that there was wrongdoing at the highest levels.

FDR was a traitor for maneuvering Japan into war with US - and that is known and admitted - FDR was a traitor for sacrificing American lives, for putting America in danger, for usurping the Constitutional power of Congress to make war. Day of infamy, indeed; he chose his words precisely with a hidden double-meaning. Four days before the attack, FDR could have sent telegrams of condolence to the families of the sailors he was going to allow to be killed.

Even today there is a coverup, based on a transparently bogus excuse of national security that shows that our government cannot face the truth about what happened a half-century ago. The Air Corps in the Philippines and the Navy at Pearl were FDR's bait, the oil embargo was his stick, the end of negotiations was the tripwire in FDR's game of shame - a game of death for so many. Roosevelt aided and abetted the murder of thousands of Americans.

CHAPTER TWENTY-FIVE
POINTS TO PONDER

Why did Roosevelt want to enter into World War II? Was it to defeat the tyranny of Hitler? Stalin, who was our partner during the war, was even more vicious and tyrannical than Hitler. Was it to stop the aggression of the Japanese? Before the war, this country did everything it could to give Japan no choice and goaded them into waging war.

Roosevelt was a 33rd degree mason. That is the highest level one can attain in the Masonic Order. Allegedly, one of objectives of the Masonic order is to establish a one world government. After World War I these people tried, and failed, to start a one world government organization, The League of Nations. Realizing they would need another world war to finally create such an organization, they manipulated world events, started and won World War II, and created the United Nations, the tool for the final phase of one world government.

Roosevelt's 'Secret Map' Speech[167]

Franklin Roosevelt often lied to further his goals. In a radio address broadcast to the nation on 23 October 1940, for example, he gave "this most solemn assurance" that he had not given any "secret understanding in any shape or form, direct or indirect, with any government or any other nation in any part of the world, to involve this nation in any war or for any other purpose." But American, British and Polish documents proved that this "most solemn assurance" was a bald-faced lie. Roosevelt had, in fact, made numerous secret arrangements to involve the U.S. in war.

Of all his speeches, perhaps the best example of Roosevelt's readiness to lie is his 1941 Navy Day address broadcast over nationwide radio on 27 October. A lot had happened in the months preceding that address. On 11 March 1941 Roosevelt signed the Lend-Lease bill into law, permitting increased deliveries of military aid to Britain in violation of U.S. neutrality and international law. In April Roosevelt illegally sent U.S. troops to occupy Greenland. On 27 May he

---

167 This section was attributed to Mark Weber.

proclaimed a state of "unlimited national emergency," a kind of presidential declaration of war that circumvented a power constitutionally reserved to Congress. Following the Axis attack against the USSR in June, the Roosevelt administration began delivering enormous quantities of military aid to the beleagured Soviets. These shipments also blatantly violated international law. In July Roosevelt illegally sent American troops to occupy Iceland.

The President began his Navy Day address by recalling that German submarines had torpedoed the U.S. destroyer *Greer* on 4 September 1941 and the U.S. destroyer *Kearny* on 17 October. In highly emotional language, he characterized these incidents as unprovoked acts of aggression directed against all Americans. He declared that although he had wanted to avoid conflict, shooting had begun and "history has recorded who fired the first shot."

What Roosevelt deliberately failed to mention was the fact that in each case the U.S. destroyers had been engaged in attack operations against the submarines, which fired in self-defense only as a last resort. Hitler wanted to avoid war with the United States, and had expressly ordered German submarines to avoid conflicts with U.S warships at all costs, except to avoid imminent destruction. Roosevelt's standing "shoot on sight" orders to the U.S Navy were specifically designed to make incidents like the ones he so piously condemned inevitable. His provocative efforts to goad Hitler into declaring war against the U.S. had failed and most Americans still opposed direct involvement in the European conflict.

And so, in an effort to convince his listeners that Germany was a real threat to American security, Roosevelt continued his Navy Day speech with a startling announcement: "Hitler has often protested that his plans for conquest do not extend across the Atlantic Ocean. I have in my possession a secret map[168], made in Germany by Hitler's government-by the planners of the new world order. It is a map of South America and a part of Central America as Hitler proposes to reorganize it." This map, the President explained, showed South America, as well as "our great life line, the Panama Canal," divided into five vassal states under German domination. "That map, my friends, makes clear the Nazi design not only against South America but against the United States as well."

Roosevelt went on to reveal that he also had in his possession "another document made in Germany by Hitler's government. It is a detailed plan to abolish all existing religions -- Catholic, Protestant, Mohammedan, Hindu, Buddhist, and Jewish alike" which Germany will impose "on a dominated world, if Hitler wins."

"The property of all churches will be seized by the Reich and its puppets. The cross and all other symbols of religion are to be for- bidden. The clergy are to be ever liquidated. In the place of the churches of our civilization there is to be

---

168 Bratzel, John F., and Leslie B. Rout, Jr., "FDR and The 'Secret Map'," The Wilson Quarterly (Washington, DC), New Year's 1985, pp. 167-173.

set up an international Nazi church, a church which will be served by orators sent out by the Nazi government. And in the place of the Bible, the words of Mein Kampf will be imposed and enforced as Holy Writ. And in the place of the cross of Christ will be put two symbols: the swastika and the naked sword."

Roosevelt emphasized the importances of his "revelations" by declaring: "*Let us well ponder these grim truths which I have told you of the present and future plans of Hitlerism*" All Americans, he said, "*are faced with the choice between the kind of world we want to live in and the kind of world which Hitler and his hordes would impose on us.*" Accordingly, "*we are pledged to pull our own oar in the destruction of Hitlerism.*"

The German government immediately responded to Roosevelt's speech by denouncing his "documents" as preposterous frauds. The Italian government declared that if Roosevelt did not publish his map, "*within 24 hours, he will acquire a sky high reputation as a forger.*" At a press conference the next day, a reporter rather naturally asked the President for a copy of the "secret map." But Roosevelt refused, insisting only that it came from "a source which is undoubtedly reliable."

As has often happened, the truth about the map did not emerge until many years after the war: It was a forgery produced by the British intelligence service, most probably at its technical laboratory in Ontario, Canada. William Stephenson (code name: Intrepid), chief of British intelligence operations in North America, passed it on to U.S. intelligence Chief William Donovan, who gave it to Roosevelt. In a memoir published in late 1984, war-time British agent Ivar Bryce[169] claimed credit for thinking up the "secret map" scheme. Of course, the other "document" cited by Roosevelt, purporting to outline German plans to abolish the world's religions, was just as fraudulent as the "secret map."

Some U.S. officials were concerned about British wartime ef- forts to deceive the American government and people. In a 5 September 1941 memorandum forwarded to Secretary of State Cordell Hull, Assistant Secretary of State Adolf Berle warned that British intelligence agents were manufacturing phony documents detailing supposed German conspiracies. Americans should be "on our guard" against these British-invented "false scares," Berle concluded.

It's doubtful if any of Roosevelt's great contemporaries, including Stalin, Hitler and even Churchill, ever delivered a speech as loaded with falsehoods as brazen as those in his 1941 Navy Day address. On at least one occasion, Roosevelt privately admitted his willingness to lie to further his goals. During a conversation on 14 May 1942 with his close Jewish adviser, Treasury Secretary Henry Morgenthau, Jr., the President candidly remarked: "*I may have one policy for Europe and one diametrically opposite for North and South America. I maybe*

---

169 "Ex-British Agent Says FDR's Nazi Map Faked," Foreign Intelli- gence Literary Scene (Frederick, MD: University Publications of America), December 19-84, pp. 1-3.

entirely inconsistent, and furthermore, I am perfectly willing to mislead and tell untruths if it will help us win the war."

CHAPTER TWENTY-SIX
KOREAN WAR

Now we come to a war that really was not a war. Rather it was a police action, designed to prove to the world that the United Nations could function as a political entity. The conflict that some call the Korean War and others the Korean Conflict was actually an episode in the Cold War. The Korean War was the time when the Cold War became a global conflict.

In 1945, Korea was freed from the Japanese. US troops stayed in Korea until 1946. The country was split in half at the 38th parallel. On the surface, it seemed to be a war between South and North Korea, but America and Russia were using it to fight a war without having a 'hot war'. Both countries wanted to fight for territory, but since both had nuclear weapons, neither wanted a nuclear war. So a number of "brushfire wars" were fought.

The United States went to war in Korea for three reasons. The first reason was because of a fear that the 'Domino Theory' was correct and that one after another Southeast Asian countries would turn Commnist. China turned Communist in 1949 and Truman feared that the next 'domino' would be Japan, which was very important to U.S. trade.

The second reason for American participation in the Korean War was to undermine Communism and protect the American way of life. President Truman believed that capitalism, freedom and the American way of life were in danger of being overrun by Communism. The Truman Doctrine had been one of 'containment' – stopping the Communists gaining any more territory. In April 1950 the American National Security Council issued a report[170] recommending that America abandon 'containment' and start 'rolling back' Communism. This led Truman to consider driving the Communists out of North Korea.

---

170 NSC 68

Thirdly, Truman realised the USA was in a competition for world domination with the USSR and it would not do for the USSR to become more powerful that the United States.

Russia went to war because Stalin wanted Communism to grow. In 1949, North Korean strongman Kim Il Sung persuaded Stalin and Mao Tse Tung to support an invasion of South Korea. Stalin did not think that America would get involved, so he gave his agreement. In 1950, Syngman Rhee threatened to attack North Korea. It was an excuse – the trigger for war: the NKPA invaded South Korea

The War
On 25 June 1950, the North Koreans attacked South Korea. They were very successful and the North Korean People's Army (NKPA) easily defeated the Republic of Korea's army (the ROKs). They captured most of South Korea. U.S. leaders were very alarmed by the happenings in Korea.

On 27 June they persuaded the United Nations to pass a resolution supporting South Korea. The Americans sent troops to Korea to reinforce the South Korean Army at Pusan.

On 15 September, the American General MacArthur led a UN amphibious landing at Inchon (near Seoul) behind the NKPA. Out of the 300,000 UN troops, 260,000 were Americans.

In danger of being cut off, the NKPA had to retreat. The Americans drove them back and recaptured South Korea. 125,000 NKPA prisoners were taken.

On 7 October 1950 MacArthur invaded North Korea. He advanced as far as the Chinese border. He boasted that the Americans would be 'home by Christmas'.

Now the Chinese were alarmed by MacArthur's success against the North Korean Army.

On 25 November, 200,000 Chinese troops ('People's Volunteers') attacked MacArthur. They had modern weapons supplied by Russia, and a fanatical hatred of the Americans. Then, on 31 December, half a million more Chinese troops entered the war and attacked the Americans. They drove the Americans back (using 'human wave tactics'). They recaptured North Korea, and advanced into South Korea.

The Americans landed more troops and began to use bombers. The Chinese admitted to losing 390,000 men dead - UN sources put the figure at up to a million Chinese and half a million North Koreans dead. The Americans drove the Chinese back, but lost 54,000 American soldiers dead doing so.

MacArthur reached the 38th parallel in March 1951. Truman told MacArthur to stop moving north. MacArthur was sacked when he publicly criticised Truman's order.

In 1953, Eisenhower became American president.

The Americans threatened to use the atomic bomb if China did not stop fighting. The Chinese agree to a truce, which was signed on 27 July 1953.

It is estimated that 10 million people died in the war - as many as died in the First World War.

Hidden Reasons

However, as with every war in which the United States has engaged, behind the scenes there are a number of hidden reasons for our involvement in the first Southeast Asian War. To understand these hidden reasons, you must first know something of the history leading up to the war.

In 1948 the United Nations (U.N.) approved the establishment of the Republic of Korea in the South, held elections in which Rhee won an overwhelming majority as president, and promptly recognized his government. In September 1948, with strong Soviet encouragement, Kim refused U.N.-sponsored elections and proclaimed the Democratic People's Republic of Korea, a Soviet ally and client which the United Nations declined to recognize. Both Korean governments shared at least one objective: the elimination of their rival and their country's eventual reunification under their own control.

The question of which state was responsible for beginning the Korean War has given rise to much historiographical and political debate. For many years the Chinese argued that South Korea, in collaboration with the United States, invaded the North in June 1950, and that North Korean, Chinese, and Soviet policy was entirely reactive. In 1991 Bruce Cumings suggested that responsibility for the war remained unclear, that South Korea was as eager as the North to reunify the country, and South Korean troops probably initiated the actual hostilities. A still more conspiratorial theory suggested that the United States deliberately provoked the Korean War in order to win congressional and public support for the enormous three- to four-fold increases in American defense spending envisaged in the 1950 policy planning staff paper NSC-68. According to this theory, U.S. officials lured North Korea and the Soviet Union into war by publicly stating that they considered South Korea extraneous to United States security interests in Asia.

Foremost among the evidence cited to support this thesis was a 12 January 1950 speech to the National Press Club in which U.S. Secretary of State Dean Acheson declared that neither Korea nor Taiwan fell within the Asian "defensive perimeter" of vital strategic interests that the United States would defend. The U.S. government had launched a major reassessment of its defense policies, supposedly intended to match the country's vast and growing post-Second World War military commitments to its limited capabilities. Although Acheson suggested these countries could rely upon the United Nations to defend them, apparently many among the wider audience, including leaders of the

Communist states, simply assumed that the United States had completely abandoned Taiwan and South Korea[171].

On the Communist side, it appears that Kim Il Sung, whose forces in 1950 enjoyed substantial military superiority over those of the South, initiated the invasion in the hope that he could unify Korea. It is also clear that the Soviet Union knew well in advance Kim's intentions, which he advocated enthusiastically from the spring 1949 forward. In late January 1950, Soviet leader Joseph Stalin finally endorsed Kim's plans for the invasion of South Korwa and promised him military and economic aid essential to the enterprise's success, but he refused to commit Soviet troops. In all likelihood, Communist China's supreme leader Mao Zedong had some foreknowledge of Kim's intentions, though Kim did not then seek his assistance. Apparently all three Communist leaders considered the United States unlikely to intervene to defend South Korea, interpreting Acheson's speech as confirmation that the United States would not do so.

This miscalculation by the Communist leaders need not imply that the United States deliberately entrapped them into opening hostilities. Most historians now agree that, although U.S. intervention in the Korean War undoubtedly brought massive long-term enhancements of both American defense spending and military commitments around the world, U.S. officials failed to anticipate the war's outbreak and cannot be held guilty of manipulating their opponents into opening hostilities. Moreover, until the September 1950 Inchon landing there was a real likelihood that North Korean forces might emerge victorious, driving United States forces from Korea and annexing all of South Korea's territory. It was highly improbable that American or South Korean leaders would have risked so much deliberately. It seems clear that the outbreak of war surprised both the United States and South Korea; the South Koreans only possessed sufficient resources to wage a defensive war for fifteen days (10).

The question then remains: why, given American officials' distinct distaste for the South Korean government and their previous dismissal of its strategic significance, did they almost immediately decide to intervene to restore the status quo and energetically persuade the United Nations to endorse this stance? Certainly, broader Cold War preoccupations intersected with a fluid Asian situation to dissuade U.S. officials from acquiescence in any North Korean takeover. They feared that inaction would lead other United States allies to doubt American resolve to fulfill its commitments to them, while Communist states would learn that, faced with a hostile army the United States would not back its pledges with military force. U.S. leaders essentially perceived the Korean conflict as a test of American credibility and their commitment to the strategy of "containing" Communism, which by 1950 had become an entrenched dogma of American foreign relations[172].

---

171 This was much as the US Ambassador to Iraq stated to Saddam Hussein that the US would not oppose his policies vis a vis Kuwait.

172 Basically, it appeared to be a situation of the U.S. did not want Korea, but also did not want the Communists to have it either.

Moreover, virtually all American policy makers of this period were strongly influenced by the lessons of the 1930s. In their view, "appeasement" of dictators simply encouraged them to escalate their demands, whereas firm initial resistance to such aggression would lead them to yield and withdraw. Perceiving Stalin as a second Hitler and Kim merely as his puppet, American officials believed there was no alternative to intervention in Korea. Besides having basically "suckered" Kim into invading, the U.S. could not very well stand by and watch the country be overrun as we did with Vietnam.

In the early 1980s several American scholars suggested that the Korean War marked a "lost chance in China," that without the military confrontation between Communist Chinese and U.S. troops and the revitalized American commitment to Taiwan that the war precipitated, there existed a strong possibility of a rapprochement between the new PRC and the United States. Moreover, in late 1949 and early 1950, Acheson, influenced by the emergence in 1948 of Yugoslavia's independence Titoist Communist regime, believed in the potential of driving a "wedge" between the Soviet Union and mainland China.

Subsequent scholarship, however, suggests that the prospects for such a Sino-American understanding ranged from slim to nonexistent[173]. Several historians, particularly Chinese, have noted the centrality of Communist ideology and revolutionary fervor in contemporary Chinese leaders' international political outlook, impelling them to distrust the United States and favor the Soviet Union. U.S. opposition to the emergence of a Communist state on the Chinese mainland, and American incomprehension of the deep resentment that a century of Western exploitation and humiliation had generated in China's new leaders, compounded the problem.

This is not to deny that China's intervention in Korea in late 1950, which precipitated direct combat between Chinese and American troops, intensified and hardened existing deep-seated Sino-American antagonisms. Two decisions contributed to this situation: that of the United States in September 1950 to permit U.N. forces to cross the 38th parallel, and that of China to intervene in Korea in October 1950.

U.S. officials originally restricted their war aims to the restoration of the "status quo," namely, the expulsion of North Korean forces from the South and the recovery of all former southern territory. Following the spectacular Inchon landing and recapture of Seoul, Washington and the United Nations Command were tempted to expand their aims to include the North's conquest, the overthrow of its government, and Korea's reunification under a southern-dominated (and presumably Western-oriented) regime. The momentum of victory was difficult to resist, generating a sense of "hubris" (16).

In September and October 1950 American officials, therefore, ignored successive Chinese warnings that, should U.N. forces cross the 38th parallel, Chinese forces would intervene. Allen Whiting's classic work *China Crosses the*

---

[173] It was just a liberal day dream.

Yalu took these messages at face value. Historians Jian Chen and Shu Guang Zhang believe that by early October the decision was already made. However, William Stueck argues that immediately before Chinese intervention the situation remained fluid, and a decision to permit only South Korean forces to move north of the parallel might well have persuaded the PRC to reverse its decision to join the conflict (17). Stueck contends that, even at this late date, Mao was still uncertain whether to intervene. The 1993 work Uncertain Partners suggests that in autumn 1950 Stalin, eager to prevent the extension of Western power to Russia's land border with Korea, pressed a somewhat reluctant Mao to enter the Korean War.

Historians have noted the extent to which Mao dominated Chinese decision-making on Korea (19). Several have posited that his thinking was shaped by "military romanticism," a sense that war, conflict, and battle were the measure and proving ground for nations. Relations between China and North Korea were close, and from the war's beginning Mao believed Chinese intervention might be necessary—though he hoped the North Korean forces would triumph completely before any outside power could intervene.

Chinese antagonism toward the United States further intensified in late June 1950, when President Harry S. Truman sent the U.S. 7th Fleet to patrol the Taiwan Strait, thereby precluding a mainland takeover of the island. Then, when the United States committed troops to Korea in July 1950, Mao began mobilizing units on the Chinese-Korean frontier as the Northeast Border Defense Army.

Meanwhile, discussions on intervention began within the Chinese Communist Party's Central Committee. Although several committee members disapproved of intervention, Mao overrode their objections. While admitting that its economic price might well be high, he argued that intervention would demonstrate that the new China was finally "standing up" for itself in the world. Despite the misgivings of some cadres (notably PRC Premier Zhou Enlai, and his top general, Lin Biao, who declined to command China's Korean forces), in late September and early October 1950 Mao succeeded in winning over the majority of his colleagues.

The Chinese stance benefitted Stalin, a cautious leader who was unwilling to risk direct confrontation with the United States. In September 1950, Stalin refused Kim's request for Soviet intervention and recommended instead that Kim seek Chinese help. Kim quickly followed this advice, while on 1 October Stalin himself suggested that China send "volunteers".

At this juncture, Mao, in messages to Stalin that may have reflected either his genuine doubts or a calculated effort to persuade Russia to offer China more generous military assistance, appeared at least tentatively to decide against intervention in Korea. In response, Stalin coaxed him to enter the war, stressing the potential dangers to China of an American satellite Korean state on its border. Initially, his arguments appeared unsuccessful, and on 13 October Stalin issued provisional orders that North Korean forces and government should abandon the Korean peninsula entirely and retreat to the Soviet Union or China. Within a day he rescinded this order, once Mao informed him of the Chinese politburo's ultimate decision to intervene in Korea, a choice for which he had apparently lobbied forcefully.

On 19 October 1950, massed units of the Northeast Border Defense Army began to cross China's Yalu River border into North Korea, where they quickly turned the tide of battle, forcing United Nations troops back beyond the 38th parallel. After initial sweeping Chinese gains, U.N. forces recovered lost ground, and from late spring 1951 the war settled into a stalemate, with each side holding approximately the territory under its control in June 1950. Armistice negotiations opened in July 1951, dragging on inconclusively until a settlement was reached in July 1953.

How did the Korean War affect its protagonists domestically, and how did it alter the Cold War's international aspects? Internally, it undoubtedly brought a hardening of attitudes within the United States, China, and North and South Korea, reinforcing demands for conformity and the suppression of dissent (25). Internationally, the Korean War represented a turning point in the extension of the Cold War to Asia and in United States commitments to that region, greatly enhancing American support for Taiwan, South Korea, and the French and non-Communist elements in Indochina. It also brought a massive and sustained enhancement of American military spending, the much increased United States contribution of troops to NATO, and the proliferation of American global strategic alliances and undertakings, effectively implementing NSC-68.

One must doubt whether, without the Korean War, the United States would have signed security treaties with South Korea and Taiwan, or for that matter the ANZUS (1950) and SEATO (1953) Pacts with Australia and New Zealand and the Southeast Asian nations respectively. The United States assumed the role of patron to a variety of Asian, Middle Eastern, Latin American, and eventually African client-states. In this role it effectively replaced the European colonial powers dispossessed in the Second World War's aftermath by creating a new form of international empire, based on indirect and informal controls rather than outright colonialism.

In the broad sense, this war was another one that was instigated by interests within the U.S. government for very obtuse reasons. As shown above, one of the reasons for the invasion of the South was the Soviet belief that the United States had no interest in honoring its commitments to South Korea.

In this sense the impact of the Korean War was undoubtedly global, converting the Cold War into a truly worldwide struggle in which both the United States and the Soviet Union would regard all international developments as potentially related to their all-embracing rivalry. It set the character of international relations for decades to come.

CHAPTER TWENTY-SEVEN
VIETNAM WAR

"A lie is a lie. It is a misrepresentation of fact." – Senator J. William Fulbright referring to President Johnson's official statements concerning the Tonkin Gulf "incidents" in "Hearts and Minds" (1974)

Most American wars have obvious starting points or precipitating causes: the Battles of Lexington and Concord in 1775, the capture of Fort Sumter in 1861, the attack on Pearl Harbor in 1941, and the North Korean invasion of South Korea in June 1950, for example. But there was no fixed beginning for the U.S. war in Vietnam. The United States entered that war incrementally, in a series of steps between 1950 and 1965.

In May 1950, President Harry S. Truman authorized a modest program of economic and military aid to the French, who were fighting to retain control of their Indochina colony, including Laos and Cambodia as well as Vietnam. When the Vietnamese Nationalist (and Communist-led) Vietminh Army defeated French forces at Dienbienphu in 1954, the French were compelled to accede to the creation of a Communist Vietnam north of the 17th parallel while leaving a non-Communist entity south of that line. The United States refused to accept the arrangement. The administration of President Dwight D. Eisenhower undertook instead to build a nation from the spurious political entity that was South Vietnam by fabricating a government there, taking over control from the French, dispatching military advisers to train a South Vietnamese army, and unleashing the Central Intelligence Agency (CIA) to conduct psychological warfare against the North.

President John F. Kennedy rounded another turning point in early 1961, when he secretly sent 400 Special Forces-trained (Green Beret) soldiers to teach the South Vietnamese how to fight what was called counterinsurgency war against Communist guerrillas in South Vietnam. When Kennedy was assassinated in November 1963, there were more than 16,000 U.S. military advisers in South Vietnam, and more than 100 Americans had been killed. Kennedy's successor, Lyndon B. Johnson, committed the United States most fully to the war. In August 1964, he secured from Congress a functional (not actual) declaration of war: the Tonkin Gulf Resolution. Then, in February and March 1965, Johnson authorized the sustained bombing, by U.S. aircraft, of targets north of the 17th parallel, and on 8 March dispatched 3,500 Marines to South Vietnam. Legal declaration or no, the United States was now at war.

The multiple starting dates for the war complicate efforts to describe the causes of U.S. entry. The United States became involved in the war for a number of reasons, and these evolved and shifted over time. Primarily, every American president regarded the enemy in Vietnam--the Vietminh; its 1960s successor, the National Liberation Front (NLF); and the government of North Vietnam, led by *Ho Chi Minh--as agents of global communism. U.S. policymakers, and most Americans, regarded communism as the antithesis of all they held dear. Communists scorned democracy, violated human rights, pursued military aggression, and created closed state economies that barely traded with capitalist countries. Americans compared communism to a contagious disease. If it took hold in one nation, U.S. policymakers expected contiguous nations to fall to communism, too, as if nations were dominoes lined up on end. In 1949, when the Communist Party came to power in China, Washington feared that Vietnam would become the next Asian domino. That was one reason for Truman's 1950 decision to give aid to the French who were fighting the Vietminh,

Truman also hoped that assisting the French in Vietnam would help to shore up the developed, non-Communist nations, whose fates were in surprising ways tied to the preservation of Vietnam and, given the domino theory, all of Southeast Asia. Free world dominion over the region would provide markets for Japan, rebuilding with American help after the Pacific War. U.S. involvement in Vietnam reassured the British, who linked their postwar recovery to the revival of the rubber and tin industries in their colony of Malaya, one of Vietnam's neighbors. And with U.S. aid, the French could concentrate on economic recovery at home, and could hope ultimately to recall their Indochina officer corps to oversee the rearmament of West Germany, a Cold War measure deemed essential by the Americans. These ambitions formed a second set of reasons why the United States became involved in Vietnam.

As presidents committed the United States to conflict bit by bit, many of these ambitions were forgotten. Instead, inertia developed against withdrawing from Vietnam. Washington believed that U.S. withdrawal would result in a Communist victory--Eisenhower acknowledged that, had elections been held as scheduled in Vietnam in 1956, "Ho Chi Minh would have won 80% of the vote"--and no U.S. president wanted to lose a country to communism. Democrats in particular, like Kennedy and Johnson, feared a right-wing backlash should they give up the fight; they remembered vividly the accusatory tone of the Republicans' 1950 question, "Who lost China?" The commitment to Vietnam itself, passed from administration to administration, took on validity aside from any rational basis it might once have had. Truman, Eisenhower, and Kennedy all gave their word that the United States would stand by its South Vietnamese allies. If the United States abandoned the South Vietnamese, its word would be regarded as unreliable by other governments, friendly or not. So U.S. credibility seemed at stake.

Along with the larger structural and ideological causes of the war in Vietnam, the experience, personality, and temperament of each president played a role in deepening the U.S. commitment. Dwight Eisenhower restrained U.S. involvement because, having commanded troops in battle, he doubted the United States could fight a land war in Southeast Asia. The youthful John Kennedy, on the other hand, felt he had to prove his resolve to the American people and his Communist adversaries, especially in the aftermath of several foreign policy blunders early in his administration. Lyndon Johnson saw the Vietnam War as a test of his mettle, as a Southerner and as a man. He exhorted his soldiers to "nail the coonskin to the wall" in Vietnam, likening victory to a successful hunting expedition.

When Johnson began bombing North Vietnam and sent the Marines to South Vietnam in early 1965, he had every intention of fighting a limited war. He and his advisers worried that too lavish a use of U.S. firepower might prompt the Chinese to enter the conflict. It was not expected that the North Vietnamese and the NLF would hold out long against the American military. And yet U.S. policymakers never managed to fit military strategy to U.S. goals in Vietnam. Massive bombing had little effect against a decentralized economy like North Vietnam's. Kennedy had favored counterinsurgency warfare in the South Vietnamese countryside, and Johnson endorsed this strategy, but the political side of counterinsurgeny--the effort to win the "hearts and minds" of the Vietnamese peasantry-- was at best underdeveloped and probably doomed. Presidents proved reluctant to mobilize American society to the extent the generals thought necessary to defeat the enemy.

As the United States went to war in 1965, a few voices were raised in dissent. Within the Johnson administration, Undersecretary of State George Ball warned that the South Vietnamese government was a functional nonentity and simply could not be sustained by the United States, even with a major effort. Antiwar protest groups formed on many of the nation's campuses; in June, the leftist organization Students for a Democratic Society decided to make the war its principal target. But major dissent would not begin until 1966 or later. By and large in 1965, Americans supported the administration's claim that it was fighting to stop communism in Southeast Asia, or people simply shrugged and went about their daily lives, unaware that this gradually escalating war would tear American society apart.

Gulf of Tonkin

On August 5, 1964, a NY Times headline read, "President Johnson has ordered retaliatory action against gunboats and 'certain supporting facilities in North Vietnam' after renewed attacks against American destroyers in the Gulf of Tonkin," (Solomon & Cohen, 1994). The previous day, the Pentagon announced that North Vietnamese boats stationed in the Gulf of Tonkin had unleashed an unprovoked torpedo attack against a U.S. destroyer ship on routine patrol, and two days later, continued the "deliberate attack" on U.S. ships. For American journalists, the truth seemed immaterial. By reporting government claims as immutable facts, the media virtually set the stage for the longest and undoubtedly one of the most controversial wars in American history. By its conclusion, the Vietnam War had resulted in nearly 60,000 American deaths and 2 million Vietnamese deaths.

The Cold War period consumed America during the 1960s. Any aggressive Communist move was perceived as a threat to democracy. Responding to these Gulf of Tonkin reports, nearly all of America jumped to the same conclusion. The overwhelming majority incontrovertibly believed the "nefarious" North Vietnamese had been the aggressors, and the U.S. was not only entitled, but had a duty as a democratic nation, to seek retaliation. Throughout this time of national tension and angst, it would take quite a courageous and valiant figure to seek out the truth and express peaceful aspirations. This man was Senator Wayne Morse of Oregon, and in doing so, he absolutely proved to be one of the most heroic Americans in the twentieth century.

The truth behind the Gulf of Tonkin incident was quite different from what had been reported. Rather than on routine patrol, the U.S. destroyer Maddox was actually conducting an aggressive espionage mission, collecting intelligence about North Vietnamese defenses. In addition, despite the proposal of Captain John Herrick that the ambiguous circumstances surrounding the situation — including darkness, stormy seas and nervous, inexperienced crewmen – warranted a "through investigation", Secretary of defense Robert McNamara told Congress there was "unequivocal proof" of the second "unprovoked attack" on U.S. ships (Ford, 1997). As a result, on August 7, 1964, within hours of McNamara's dogmatic assertions, Congress passed the Gulf of Tonkin Resolution by an astonishing margin of 416-0 in the House and 88-2 in the Senate (Kim, 1999). This resolution, which essentially served as a green light for the Vietnam War, authorized President Lyndon Johnson to engage American troops without a formal declaration of war. Eventually, more than eight million U.S. military personnel would serve and fighting would spread from North and South Vietnam to Laos and Cambodia. Morse, who was one of the two Senators to vote nay, was "unalterably opposed" to this belligerence. He dubbed the conflict "McNamara's War," and declared "I believe that within the next century, future generations will look with dismay and great disappointment upon a Congress which is now about to make such a historic mistake" (Ford, 1997).

Under the Gulf of Tonkin Resolution, Morse believed, Congress had surrendered its power, and in doing so, had surrendered the power of the people that it was elected to represent. In Morse's words, Congress had given the president and the military a "blank check," to be paid with taxpayer's money and citizens' lives (Brooks, 1999).

CHAPTER TWENTY-EIGHT
THE GULF WARS

It would be improper to speak only of the Gulf War as there have been many wars fought over this area since the discovery of oil. In almost each case of conflict, Iraq had been involved to some extent.

Iraq, as we know it today, did not exist prior to World War One. For several hundred years prior to the First World War, the mostly Arab region known as Mesopotamia lay within the Turkish Ottoman Empire. During that war, the British invaded Ottoman Mesopotamia, finally conquering the area and overthrowing Turkish Rule. The peace treaty that ended Turkey's part in World War One caused the Turks to give up control of Mesopotamia, which became known by the older name of Iraq.

The new Iraq was under British control at first, a fact which caused a great deal of unrest among the Iraqi people. The current borders of Iraq and most Middle Eastern nations, such as Syria and Palestine/Israel, were drawn by the conquering Europeans, often with little regard to the preferences of the people who were to live in these newly created nations. Thus, Iraq became a nation with three large demographic groups; the Sunni Kurds in the north, the Sunni (Sunna) Arabs in the middle of the country, and the Shiite (Shia) Arabs in the south. The Kurds wanted a nation of their own, as did the Kurds living in neighboring Turkey and Iran. Though the British eventually granted full independence to Iraq, it was not without much bloodshed and hard feelings in Iraq about the long occupation.

Below is a list, with some details, on the wars and conflicts of Iraq.
- World War One — 1914-1918 - Also known as the Great War, this conflict brought about the end of the Turkish Ottoman Empire, which had aligned itself with the German-led Central Powers. The Turks fought largely against the British Empire forces mostly in Ottoman Palestine, and Ottoman Mesopotamia, and the Russian Empire in the Caucasus region and neighboring Iran. In November, 1914, British forces landed at Basra, in what is now southern Iraq. Despite a serious British defeat at al-Kut in 1916, Baghdad fell to the British army in March, 1917. By

November, 1918, the British had gained control over most of the Ottoman vilayets (provinces) that formed Iraq.

- The next conflict was known as the Great Iraqi Revolution (known in Iraq as Ath Thawra al Iraqiyya al Kubra and by the British as the Arab Revolt of 1920)—May 1920-Feb. 1921-Rebellion by Iraqi Arabs against the rule of the British Mandate. The rebellion was suppressed by the British military. This can be considered the First Anglo-Iraqi War.

The immediate causes of this conflict arose out of the results of the British conquest of the Mesopotamian region from the Ottoman Turks during World War I. Following that war, the British established, with League of Nations approval, a colonial-style Mandate over the region now named "Iraq." Many Iraqi nationalists, who believed independence would result from the ejection of the Turks, were severely disappointed with the establishment of the British Mandate. Other, related events and issues also inflamed Iraqi Arab opinion against the British. The Mandate government almost completely excluded Iraqis, as the British imported experienced civil servants from India (also ruled by Britain) to help administer the country. In northern Iraq, the British allowed thousands of Christian refugees escaping persecution in Turkey, to settle in mostly Muslim Iraq.

- Next there was the Kurdish Revolt—1922-1924 – This was a general uprising by Iraqi Kurds against the British Mandate. Kurdish tribesmen, led by Sheik Mahmud, a powerful Kurdish leader, attempted to establish an independent Kurdish nation. British forces, primarily using airpower, suppressed the rebellion. This turned out to be the first of many Kurdish rebellions against the British Mandate and later, against the Iraqi government. As with many of the later Kurdish uprisings, the rebels were put down with some aid from rival Kurds.

It should be noted that many similar and often related Kurdish uprisings took place in neighboring Turkey and Iran. Government forces always succeeded in defeating the rebels in Iraq, Turkey and Iran. Though Kurds in Iraq and Iran did enjoy some successes, they almost always came with the aid of foreign nations. When the foreign aid eventually is withdrawn, the Kurds' success, historically, also fades away.

- Then there was the Assyrian "Revolt" and Massacre-- August, 1933-- The Iraqi military, using a supposed revolt as an excuse, massacre at least 600 Iraqi Assyrian Christians.

- Next there was the Shia Tribal Revolt-1935, which was a Shiite uprising against the Iraqi government.

- Anglo-Iraqi War of 1941 (Rashid Ali Coup)--During World War Two, Iraqi politician Rashid Ali seized power in Iraq and aligned himself with the German-led Axis Powers. British forces invaded Iraq and quickly defeated the Iraqi military.

- Taking advantage of the general confusion brought about by World War II, there was another Kurdish Revolt in 1943 (July to October). This rebellion was led by Mullah Mustafa Barzani and suppressed by the Iraqi Army and the British RAF.

- There was another Kurdish Revolt in 1945 (August 10 to October). The rebellion was suppressed by the Iraqi Army and the British RAF. This revolt was again led by Mullah Mustafa Barzani, who escaped into Iran after breaking through an Iraqi Army force. Once in Iran, Mustafa Barzani and his forces joined the army of the new "Mahabad Republic," the first independent, though in this case, (short-lived) Kurdish state. After Mahabad was crushed by the Iranian Army, Barzani led his forces back into Iraq on April 28, 1947.

- In what is called the Kurdish Campaign of 1947 (May 27 to June 15),- after returning to Iraq from the failed Mahabad Republic, Iraqi government actions (arrests, executions, etc.) caused Mustafa Barzani and 496 followers to begin a fighting retreat from the Barzan region in northern Iraq through Turkey and into Iran in an attempt to reach the Soviet Union. They reached the U.S.S.R. on June 15, 1947, followed by the Iranian Army.

- The Al-Wathbah Uprising- (Jan. to May, 1948) – This was an anti government uprising led by Iraqi leftists. This revolt was sparked by the Treaty of Portsmouth, in which Iraq agreed to let Britain keep military bases in Iraq and maintain continued influence in Iraqi foreign affairs. The imposition of martial law in May, 1948 allowed the government to crush the rebellion, just in time for the Iraqi army to travel to Palestine for the First Arab-Israeli War.

- The first Arab-Israeli War was in 1948-1949-Israel declared independence from the British Mandate Authority on May 1, 1948, and was subsequently invaded by the armies of Egypt, Syria, Lebanon, Transjordan, Iraq, and Saudi Arabia. This is actually a continuation of the violence between Jewish (Israeli) militias and Palestinian Arab militias in the leadup to the British withdrawal. The war concluded on July 20, 1949 with the last Israeli armistice with the Arab nations. A legal state of war continued to exist, despite the temporary end of conventional combat. A legal state of war between Iraq and Israel continues to this day.

- Army Revolt/Coup of July 14, 1958--Brigadier General Abdul Karim el Qassim overthrew the royal government of King Faisal II. Both the king and Prime Minister Nouri al Said were killed. Qassim soon withdrew Iraq from the pro-Western Baghdad Pact and established friendly relations with the Soviet Union.

- Mosul Revolt--March, 1959--Pro-Qassim communist militia, called the People's Resistance Force, violently suppressed an anti-Qassim Sunni Army faction made up mostly of junior officers.

- Kirkuk Violence-1959--Pro-Qassim (pro-Communist) Kurds and People's Resistance Force killed ethnic Turkomen in Kirkuk.

- Kurdish Revolt—1961-1970 –After a period of relative calm, Iraqi government promises of Kurdish autonomy, or self-rule, went unfulfilled, sparking discontent and eventual rebellion among the Kurds in 1961. Mullah Mustafa Barzani is again a leader of the Kurdish forces. Beginning in 1963, Syrian Army and Air Force units aid the Iraqi military in fighting against the Kurds. A cease-fire in 1964, lasting until April of 1965, can be seen as a dividing point between two separate conflicts, though this web site interprets this rebellion as one continuous conflict. This prolonged period of Kurdish-Iraqi fighting ends in 1970 with a cease-fire and a government guarantee of Kurdish autonomy.

- Six-Day War (3rd Arab-Israeli War) 1967--Israel launched a pre-emptive attack on Egypt, Jordan, and Syria, fearing they were preparing to launch their own attack. The Israeli air force also attacked Iraqi airfields. Iraq sent ground forces to support the Jordanians and the Syrians.

- Ramadan (Yom Kipper) War -1973-1974 -Egypt and Syria launched a surprise attack on Israel during the Jewish Yom Kippur holiday. The attack also fell on the Muslim holiday of Ramadan. Iraq sent army and air forces to support Syria.
- Kurdish Revolt -March, 1974 --In March, 1974, Kurdish rebels led by Mullah Mustafa Barzani (having survived an assassination attempt) rebelled against the government. The Kurds felt that the government was not living up to the agreement which ended the previous revolt. The Iraqi Kurds were supported by the Shah (King) of neighboring Iran, who sought to put pressure on the Iraqi government over a border dispute. The Kurds were also assisted by the American Central Intelligence Agency (CIA), who opposed the Iraqi government due to its friendly

relations with the Soviet Union. After an agreement between the Shah of Iran and Iraqi leader Saddam Hussein in 1975, (which temporarily settled the border dispute until the Iran-Iraq War began in 1980), the Kurds collapsed under intense Iraqi military pressure. The CIA, allied to the Shah, also suspended aid. Kurds cite this betrayal by two key allies as evidence supporting their future distrust of American attempts to incite them to fight Saddam Hussein's forces in the 1990s and in the early years of the 21st Century.

- Intra-Kurdish warfare 1978-1979 --In 1975, Jalal Talabani formed the Patriotic Union of Kurdistan (PUK)-urban-based and leftist) in opposition the Barzani-led Kurdish Democratic Party (KDP).

- Shia unrest in Karbala -February, 1979--Suppressed by the Saddam regime. Under Saddam Hussein, the Shiites (Shia) were a persecuted religious group, both despite the fact, and because of, their numerical majority in the country.

- The First Persian Gulf War (also known as the Iran-Iraq War)—1980-1988 - In 1975, Iraq and Iran came to an agreement on the disputed Shatt al-Arab waterway which provides Iraq's only outlet to the sea. In exchange for Iran stopping support for Kurdish rebels, Iraq agreed to share the Shatt al-Arab with Iran. This and other disputes over their common border, plus the belief that the 1979 revolution had weakened Iran, led Iraqi leader Saddam Hussein to launch an invasion of Iran on September 22, 1980. After initial successes, the Iraqi army ground to a halt and soon retreated under repeated assaults by the numerically larger Iranian Army and Revolutionary Guards. After the Iranians pushed the war into Iraq, Saddam's forces began using chemical weapons. By 1988, both nations faced exhaustion and, after nearly a million casualties between them, agreed to end the conflict.

- Osiraq Reactor Raid—June 7, 1981 –Fearing the consequences of a successful Iraqi nuclear weapons program, Israel launched a pre-emptive air strike on the Osiraq nuclear reactor (under construction) in June, 1981. One of the pilots (the youngest) in that raid was Ilan Ramon, who later became Israel's first astronaut, and who died in the Space Shuttle Columbia tragedy on February 1, 2003.

- Kurdish Revolt—1983-1988 –During the Iran-Iraq War (1980-1988), Iraqi Kurds, aided by Iran, fought against Iraqi government forces. In 1987 and 1988, the Iraqi military used chemical weapons to kill thousands of Kurds (including many civilians) in a successful effort to break the back of the resistance.

Iraq-Kuwait Relations

1961- Iraq threatened Kuwait, claiming that it belonged to Iraq because of old Ottoman territorial claims. The British supported Kuwait by sending military forces to Kuwait. Saddam Hussein used similar excuses for his 1991 invasion of Kuwait.

1973 (March)- Iraq occupied as Samitah, a border post on Kuwait-Iraq border. Dispute began when Iraq demanded the right to occupy the Kuwaiti islands of Bubiyan and Warbah. Saudi and the Arab League convinced Iraq to withdraw.

The Second Persian Gulf War (known in the U.S. as "Operation Desert Storm"—Aug. 2, 1990-Feb. 1991 – On August 2, 1990, Iraqi forces invaded and quickly conquered the small, oil-rich emirate of Kuwait. Almost immediately, an international coalition of nations gathered a powerful military force under the authority of the United Nations and the leadership of the United States, first to defend the United States, first to defend the oil-rich kingdom of Saudi Arabia, and secondly, to force Iraq to withdraw from occupied Kuwait. From the beginning of the crisis, the United Kingdom, led by Prime Minister Margaret Thatcher, worked very closely with the U.S. in assuming a determined posture against Saddam Hussein's territorial ambition.

- Kurdish Revolt—1991 –Encouraged by the stunning defeat of Saddam's forces in Kuwait and spurred by appeals by President George H. W. Bush of the U.S., Kurds rose up against the Iraqi government. With the bulk of his elite forces having escaped from the fighting in Kuwait and southern Iraq, Saddam was able to quell the revolt, causing hundreds of thousands of Kurdish refugees to flee into neighboring Turkey and Iran to escape.

- Shiite Revolt—1991 – Encouraged by the stunning defeat of Saddam's forces in Kuwait and spurred by appeals by President George H. W. Bush of the U.S., the Shiites of southern Iraq rose up against the Iraqi government, only to be crushed by Saddam's forces. Sporadic guerrilla resistance continued, with the bulk of the Shiite fighting forces seeking refuge in neighboring Shiite Iran.

- The "No-Fly Zone War" --1991-2003--Following the cease-fire ending the Gulf War, the Allies, (U.S., U.K., and France) had the right to conduct air patrols over parts of Iraq to ensure Iraqi compliance with the cease-fire terms. France soon left the Coalition, but U.S. and British planes continued to patrol Iraqi skies, often drawing anti-aircraft fire from the ground. Several major bombing campaigns were launched to punish the Baghdad regime. This conflict officially ended when the Third Gulf War began in March, 2003.

- Intra-Kurdish warfare --1996 – Combat between various Kurdish militias.

- The Third Persian Gulf War (known in the U.S. as "Operation Iraqi Freedom")—March 19, 2003- Present– The current war can be seen in at least two distinct phases: The Invasion and the Occupation. Though Saddam's regime fell fairly quickly, the insurgency was able to gain strength in large part because the U.S. and Coalition leadership was slow to recognize that they had a nascent guerrilla movement underfoot. Though the Iraqi people have voted, and now have an elected government (featuring a Kurdish president!), the situation is now changing from a war against the occupier, to becoming more of a civil war among Iraqis.

The Second Persian Gulf War
ALTERNATE NAMES: The Gulf War (US), Operation Desert Storm (US)

The first major conflict involving the United States since Vietnam proved to be a catharsis of sorts for the American military and public. Just as the Spanish-American War of 1898 gave the nation a "short victorious war" following the angst of the Civil War, the Gulf War lifted the U.S. out of a self-conscious, post-Vietnam malaise. However, just as the short war of 1898 quickly led to the bloody Philippine-American War, the Gulf War's dark legacy soon reared it's ugly head; the Gulf War Syndrome plagues veterans and the No-Fly Zone War, kept alive the violence and confrontation as a lead-in to the current Third Persian Gulf War, also known in the U.S. as the Iraq War.

There are nearly as many links dealing with Gulf War Syndrome as there are on the war itself. This is not really a surprise, considering the relative brevity of the war compared to the serious long-term consequences of the disease from which many veterans suffer.

Lebanese Civil War (1975-1991)
SUCCESSOR: (Related conflicts that occur later)
Iraqi Shiite Revolt of 1991
Iraqi Kurdish Revolt of 1991
No-Fly Zone War (1991-2003)

The Third Persian Gulf War (2003-Present)--AKA "The Iraq War"

CHAPTER TWENTY-NINE
THE "NEW" ENEMY

WHO WERE THE PERPETRATORS?

In a normal terrorist scenario, the terrorists immediately contact the media and announce who they are and generally why they carried out the attack that they are taking credit for. However, in regard to the attacks on the World Trade Center, the Pentagon and the aborted attack on the White House (or Camp David depending on which news broadcast the reader may have listened to on that black day) the announcement that it was Osama Bin Laden and Al-Qaeda actually came from the United States Government.

In fact, according to Richard A. Clarke, the former Counter-terrorism Czar who had served under Presidents Ronald Reagan, George H.W. Bush, William Jefferson Clinton and George W. Bush, there was never any doubt in anyone's mind that the attacks of September 11, 2001 were the work of Al-Qaeda. In fact, in the foreword, he even went to far as to partial out the blame for this attack to:

• Ronald Reagan, who did not retaliate for the murder of 278 United States Marines in Beirut and who violated his own terrorism policy by trading arms for hostages in what came to be called the Iran-Contra Scandal.

• George H.W. Bush, who did not retaliate for the Libyan murder of 259 passengers on Pan Am 103, who did not have an official counter-terrorism policy and who left Saddam Hussein in place, requiring the United States to leave a large military presence in Saudi Arabia.

• William Jefferson Clinton, who identified terrorism as the major post-Cold War threat and acted to improve our counter-terrorism capabilities; who (little known to the public) quelled anti-American terrorism by Iraq and Iran and defeated an Al-Qaeda attempt to dominate Bosnia; but who weakened by continual political attack, could not get the CIA, the Pentagon and FBI to act sufficiently to deal with the threat.

- George W. Bush, who failed to act prior to September 11 on the threat from Al-Qaeda despite repeated warnings and then harvested a political windfall for taking obvious yet insufficient steps after the attacks; and who launched an unnecessary and costly war in Iraq that strengthened the fundamentalist, radical Islamic terrorist movement worldwide.

Of course, no one should criticize Richard Clark for leaving during this period of danger in order to write a tell-all book and make a lot of money. I would also point out that that he criticizes George W. Bush for doing what he criticized George H.W. Bush for not doing. As for the presence of US troops in Saudi Arabia, we have had personnel stationed there since mid-1964 under a secret deal between the Saudi Royal Family and Lyndon Baines Johnson. He also overlooks the fact that George W. Bush had a military force that had been gutted by William Jefferson Clinton's anti-military policies. I would also point out that William Jefferson Clinton, a President that had never served in the military, used US military force more than any previous president. However, this book is not intended to be a critique of Mr. Clarke's literary efforts.

Returning to the question of the profit that the terrorists realized through their attacks on September 11, 2001, it would appear at first blush, the only ones that truly profited from this attack were the terrorists. This stateless band of freedom fighters had shown America that no one was safe anytime, anywhere. This is the simple answer that satisfied the majority of the American people. The television news and the newspapers made it clear that this dastardly attack was planned and executed by a terrorist group that no one had ever heard of before, Al-Qaeda and its leader Osama Bin Laden.

However, I believe that we should consider what the terrorists actually gained from this attack. Now, to be sure, a terrorist attack is not an act of war, in the classic sense of the word, but rather a political statement. The terrorist groups involved in this attack certainly had a political agenda and have long felt that they are disenfranchised. But was this political statement worth the deaths of over twenty of their members?

Of course, every success brings with it a price, the response of the United States against this terrorist attack was to declare a war on terrorism and seek out the Al-Qaeda leadership where it was hiding. This war on terrorism has resulted in the destruction of the governments of Afghanistan and Iraq and the deaths of thousands of terrorist rank and file. So in the final analysis, did the terrorists profit?

WHAT IS TERRORISM?

To the average American, more concerned with the latest football or basketball scores, a terrorist is a bad guy that we need to kill before he or she kills us. The problem is that with a terrorist, there is no real definable enemy, unlike Nazism or Communism. In the latter cases, there were identifiable countries that housed the enemy. With a terrorist, he or she can be anyone, from any background. It is very hard to gather public opinion to go to war with a ghost. Having given the local definition of terrorism let me now give some more formal definitions, of which there are several.

• The Federal Bureau of Investigation defines terrorism as "The unlawful use of force or violence against persons or property to intimidate or coerce a government, civilian population or any segment thereof, in furtherance of political or social objectives."

• The State Department defines terrorism as "The premeditated, politically motivated violence perpetrated against non-combatant targets by sub-national groups or clandestine agents, usually intended to influence an audience."

• The Department of Defense defines terrorism as "The calculated use of violence or threat of violence to inculcate fear, intended to coerce or to intimidate governments or societies in the pursuit of goals that are generally political, religious or ideological."

• Department of Defense Directive 2000.12H defines terrorism as: "The calculated use of violence or threat of violence to attain goals, political, religious or ideological in nature, by instilling fear or using intimidation or coercion. Terrorism involves a criminal act, often symbolic in nature, intended to influence an audience beyond the immediate victims."

• The United States Code defines terrorism as "Premeditated, politically motivated violence perpetrated against non-combatant targets by sub-national groups or clandestine agents."

The point that I wanted to make with these definitions is that no matter how the issue is examined, terrorism is a federal crime and punishable by our courts. Thus, it would seem logical that those who carried out a terrorist act in this country would be hounded until captured. In the face of such a devastating attack on this country, every law enforcement procedure would be followed to the letter in order to apprehend those responsible. Well, this is not necessarily so.

THE EXCEPTION TO THE RULE

As was mentioned earlier, in the aftermath of the attacks of September 11, 2001, every civilian flight, both commercial as well as private was grounded. Everyone except one, that is. Due to the rapid identification of the individual behind the attack as being Osama Bin Laden, I think that is interesting to consider this one exception to the grounding of all flights within the continental United States.

A very complete discussion of the grounding of all flights within the United States is found in Craig Unger's book House of Bush/House of Saud. When even medical flights were being cancelled, Prince Bandar Bin Sultan ibn

Abdul Aziz, the Saudi Arabian Ambassador to the United States was taking steps to fly over 140 Saudis out of the country. This group of very special people consisted of members of two prominent families, the Saudi Royal Family and members of the family of Osama Bin Laden.

In other circumstances and with less wealthy people, this exodus might have seemed suspicious. Just because the majority of the terrorists were identified as coming form Saudi Arabia and Osama Bin Laden was immediately identified as their leader, this was not sufficient reason to see anything odd about this immediate flight and the special permission given by the White House for this flight to take place.

Immediately after the attacks of September 11, 2001, the Federal Aviation Administration sent out a NOTAM to airports across the country ordering every plane then in the air to land at the nearest airport and further prohibiting planes on the ground from taking off. This order was specific and contained no exceptions. However, in the face of this order, flights did take off bringing the scattered members of the Saudi Royal Family and the Bin Laden Family to Washington so that they could be flown out of the country. The orders for these exceptions came from the White House.

The most interesting thing about these flights that was reported by Mr. Unger in his well written book was that the FAA apparently knew nothing about these exceptions. There were no airport records found confirming any of the flights to ferry the Saudis to a selected gathering place in Kentucky nor were there any records of the flight out of the country. Even the White House denies that such flights ever took place.

The Federal Bureau of Investigation, supposedly diligently looking for terrorists in the aftermath of 9/11 denied knowing anything about the flights. In fact, in Craig Unger's book, FBI Special Agent John Innarelli was quoted as specifically stating that "I can say unequivocally that the FBI had no role in facilitating these flights one way or the other." However, Prince Bandar told CNN that "With coordination with the FBI, we got them all out." It would be interesting to know who is telling the truth.

Now with the knowledge that Osama Bin Laden was the mastermind of the 9/11 attacks, surely the FBI at least questioned his relatives who were being spirited out of the country in the wake of 9/11, right? Well, not necessarily. For some reason, the FBI seemed unbelievably reluctant to do anything that might inconvenience the Saudis. Eventually, over the objections of Prince Bandar, the FBI was only able to check papers and ascertain the identity of those on the flights. To have conducted an investigation into the flights and who was on them would have meant violating standing rules that the FBI may not launch an investigation without a strong reason to believe the suspect had engaged in a crime. Though the circumstances were certainly suspicious, the FBI later said that it was not a crime for these foreign nationals to leave the country.

It was clear that special flights, White House involvement in the breaking of rules and clandestine movements of people related to and/or associated with the leader of a terrorist group that had just attacked this country were not enough to arouse the suspicions of the FBI. However, I wonder what would have happened had the terrorist group been a domestic militia, would the FBI have been as polite in its handling of the relatives of the terrorist leader? Why was Timothy McVeigh not given the same consideration?

Of course, the mere fact that many of those on the plane had connections with the known leader of a terrorist group that had just attacked the country should have been a sufficient legal basis for at least questioning the Saudis. However, the White House forbade the detaining of the special flights. When airport authorities in Massachusetts tried to get FBI involvement, the FBI counter terrorism team had better things to do than to question suspicious Saudis. Clearly, the Saudis had a great deal of influence with the Bush White House; or was it something more than mere influence?

THE SEVEN SISTERS

Another player that is widely talked about in the world of conspiracy theories and who certainly profited as an indirect result of the attacks of September 11th were the Oil Companies. There are many who call both the original war in the Middle East to free Kuwait from Iraqi occupation and this current war on terrorism as wars fought over oil. Certainly, the history of Standard Oil, the first multinational corporation to be able to influence US policy would tend to support such a theory.

Standard Oil

Standard Oil was an oil refining company founded by John D. Rockefeller and partners in 1863. Borrowing heavily to expand his business, he drew five big refineries including the business concern of Henry Morrison Flagler into one firm, Rockefeller, Andrew & Flagler. By 1868 he headed the world's largest oil refinery. On January 10, 1870 he formed the Standard Oil Company of Ohio and started his strategy of buying up the competition and consolidating all oil-refining under one company. By 1878 Standard Oil held about 90% of the refining capacity in the U.S. In 1881 the company was reorganized as the Standard Oil Trust. The three main men of "Standard Oil" were Henry H. Rogers, William Rockefeller, and, the most important, John D. Rockefeller.

This attracted attention from antitrust authorities in the 1890s, the Ohio Attorney General filed and won an antitrust suit in 1892 and the company was broken up after the United States Supreme Court declared the company to be an "unreasonable" monopoly under the Sherman Antitrust Act on May 15, 1911. However, the owners remained in charge of the smaller companies which made up four of the Seven Sisters.

Standard Oil was not a well-loved company. Through a series of dubious business practices it either subdued competitors or engaged in illegal transportation deals with the railroad companies to ensure it could undercut its competitors' prices. Standard Oil, formed well before the discovery of Spindletop and a demand for oil other than for heat and light, was well placed to control the growth of the oil business. It did this by ensuring it owned and controlled all aspects of the trade.

During a massive strike by employees of the Rockefeller-owned Colorado Fuel and Iron Company, what was referred to as the Ludlow Massacre occurred on April 20, 1914. The state militia fired on a tent city inhabited by workers and their families, causing numerous deaths and a public relations disaster. John D. Rockefeller Jr. was forced to take action to bolster his public image to avert large-scale market losses.

Perhaps the most infamous action of Standard Oil was its involvement with IG Farben. The two organizations worked together to build a plant for the manufacture of synthetic rubber in Nazi Germany, using slave labor from Auschwitz.

The following quotation (from journalist Thomas Lawson's 1905 book, Frenzied Finance) perhaps epitomizes the company as perceived by the public. "Standard Oil" has from its birth to present writing been responsible for more hell than any other trust or financial thing since the world began. Because of it the people have sustained incalculable losses and have suffered untold miseries.

There were eight distinct groups of individuals and corporations which made up the big "Standard Oil":

1. The Standard Oil, seller of oil to the people, which was made up of many sub-corporations either by actual ownership or by ownership of their stock or bonds;
2. Henry H. Rogers, William Rockefeller, and John D. Rockefeller, active heads, and included with them their sons;
3. A large group of active captains and first lieutenants, men who conducted the affairs of the different corporations or sections of corporations in which some or all of the "Standard Oil" were interested;
4. A large group of captains retired from active service in the Standard Oil army;
5. The estates of deceased members of the wonderful "Standard Oil" family, which were still largely controlled by some or all of the prominent "Standard Oil" men;
6. "Standard Oil" banks and banking institutions, and the system of national banks, trust companies, and insurance companies, of which "Standard Oil" had, by ownership and otherwise, practically absolute control;
7. The "Standard Oil" army of followers, capitalists, and workers in all parts of the world;
8. The countless hordes of politicians, statesmen, lawmakers and enforcers -- political structure -- and judges and lawyers.

Standard Oil, though nominally a US Company was actually a law unto itself. This mind set is what led to many of its anti-US actions. The Standard Oil governing rules were rigid and yet simple as shown below.

- Keep your mouth closed, as silence is gold, and gold is what we exist for;
- Collect our debts today. Pay the other fellow's debts tomorrow;
- Keep the seller waiting; the longer he waits, the less he'll take. Hurry the buyer, as his money brings us interest;
- Make all profitable bargains in the name of "Standard Oil," chancy ones in the names of dummy corporations;
- Never forget our Legal Department is paid by the year, and our land is full of courts and judges;
- As competition is the life of trade (our trade), and monopoly the death of trade (our competitor's trade), employ both judiciously;
- Never enter into a "butting" contest with the Government. Our Government is by the people and for the people, and we are the people, and those people who are not us can be hired by us;
- Always do "right." Right makes might, might makes dollars, dollars make right, and we have the dollars.

The success of "Standard Oil" was largely due to two things -- to the loyalty of its members to each other and to "Standard Oil," and to the punishment of its enemies. Each member before initiation knew its religion to be reward for friends and extermination for foes. The "Standard Oil" man was constantly reminded in a thousand and one ways that punishment for disloyalty is sure and terrible, and that in no corner of the earth where can he escape it, nor can any power on earth protect him from it. Standard Oil also helped to pioneer the use of advertising to create brand loyalty. Even though its products were not particularly romantic or otherwise conducive to advertising, Standard Oil became known for its bright red packaging.

"Standard Oil" was never loud in its rewards nor its punishments. It did not care for the public's praise nor for its condemnation, but endeavored to avoid both by keeping its "business" to itself. Of course, as a result of the crime busting efforts of the Attorney General of Ohio, such a cruel taskmaster has ceased to be. Or has it? Actually, Standard Oil has merely changed its name, just as the American Telephone and Telegraph did when the baby bells were created a few years ago. The crime busting efforts of the Ohio Attorney General actually increased Standard Oil's profits and control.
Successor companies to Standard Oil include:

- Standard Oil of Ohio - or Sohio now part of BP (British Petroleum)
- Standard Oil of Indiana - or Stanolind, renamed Amoco - now part of BP

- Standard Oil of New York - or Socony and merged with Vacuum - renamed Mobil, now part of ExxonMobil
- Standard Oil of New Jersey - or Esso (S.O.) - renamed Exxon, now part of ExxonMobil
- Standard Oil of California - or Socal - renamed Chevron, now part of ChevronTexaco
- Atlantic and Richfield - merged to form Atlantic Richfield or Arco - now part of BP - Atlantic operations spun off and bought by Sunoco
- Standard Oil of Kentucky - or Kyso was acquired by Standard Oil of California - now part of ChevronTexaco
- Continental Oil Company - or Conoco is now known as ConocoPhillips

Other Standard Oils:
- Standard Oil of Iowa - pre 1911 - became Standard Oil of California
- Standard Oil of Minnesota - pre 1911 - bought by Standard Oil of Indiana
- Standard Oil of Illinois - pre 1911 - bought by Standard Oil of Indiana
- Standard Oil of Kansas - refining only, eventually bought by Indiana Standard
- Standard Oil of Missouri - pre 1911 - dissolved
- Standard Oil of Nebraska - eventually bought by Indiana Standard
- Standard Oil of Louisiana - always owned by Standard Oil of New Jersey (Esso)
- Standard Oil of Brazil - always owned by Standard Oil of New Jersey (now Esso)
- Standard Oil of Colorado - a scam to cash in on the Standard Oil brand in the 1930s
- Standard Oil of Connecticut - A fuel oil marketer in Connecticut not related to the Rockefeller companies

The oil that has become the lifeline of the modern world and that has been the underlying cause of so many wars and revolutions around the world, but especially in the Middle East was discovered by Standard Oil and originally controlled by a group called the Seven Sisters.

Following the break up by the US Government of Standard Oil, several new companies were created, four of which, along with three other major oil companies, were once referred to as the Seven Sisters. These were:
- Standard Oil of New Jersey. This later became Exxon, now ExxonMobil.
- Royal Dutch Shell Anglo-Dutch
- British Anglo-Persian Oil Company. This later became British Petroleum, then BPAmoco following a merger with Amoco (which in turn was formerly Standard Oil of Indiana). It is now known solely by the initials BP.

- Standard Oil of New York. This later became Mobil, which merged with Exxon to form ExxonMobil.
- Texaco. This later merged with Chevron to form ChevronTexaco.
- Standard Oil of California (Socal). This became Chevron, and now ChevronTexaco.
- Gulf Oil. Most of this became part of Chevron, and eventually ChevronTexaco. A network of stations in the northeastern United States now bears this name.

As of 2003, the surviving companies are ExxonMobil, ChevronTexaco, Shell, and BP. If a reader follows the merging and name changes, there is no doubt that the Seven Sisters are still alive and well. With the staggering increases in the price of gasoline since the beginning of this series of "Gulf Wars" the profits to these multinational companies is simply staggering.

Discussing the profits of the oil companies during these troubled times also raises some other interesting questions. According to a story in the Washington Times on August 26, 2003, motorists were warned expect to pay record-high prices at the pump for the Labor Day weekend. Regular-grade gasoline surged 12 cents nationwide, or 7.4 percent, in the week prior to that Labor Day to a record $1.747 a gallon, according to the U.S. Energy Information Administration.

Reasons given to the public for this increase included refineries being shut down for one or two days by the Northeast power outage, rising crude oil prices, a broken gas pipeline in Arizona and increased demand expected for Labor Day. As usual, no one questioned the verbal pabulum given by the Oil Companies for price increases.

In College Park, premium gas sold for $1.84 cents per gallon at the College Park station, up about 9 cents from two weeks prior. In the Washington area, unleaded regular gasoline averaged $1.63 per gallon yesterday. At the same time in 2002, it cost $1.43 per gallon, according to AAA Mid-Atlantic.

"This is quite unusual to see prices rocket up the way they have," said AAA Mid-Atlantic spokeswoman Deborah DeYoung. "It's just been a weird year all around."

The nationwide price in 2003 was the highest since March 17, 2003 just before the start of the U.S.-led war on Iraq, when rates hit a record high of $1.728 a gallon.

The Labor Day 2003 weekend — the unofficial end of summer — put more demands on the nation's gasoline supply. About 33.4 million Americans were expected to travel away from home during the weekend, about 1.8 percent more than the previous year, according to AAA. About 84 percent will drive. The AAA also stated that the gasoline prices could drop as much as 25 cents per gallon after Labor Day if Persian Gulf political tensions ease.

Service station managers are complaining as much as customers about high gas prices. Service stations make only a cent or two per gallon on gasoline

sales. Their prices — and profit margins — are determined by contracts with the oil companies. Some motorists blamed the companies for the rising gas prices.
In support of this feeling on the part of motorists, oil companies reported the highest earnings in the second quarter of 2003 since their record profits in 2001.

Exxon Mobil Corp., the world's largest publicly traded oil company, posted second-quarter profits that rose 58 percent to $4.17 billion (62 cents per share) from $2.64 billion (39 cents) a year earlier. Revenue rose 12 percent to $57.16 billion from $50.8 billion. Profit from the production unit rose 27 percent to $2.84 billion, and rising fuel sales led to a 50 percent jump in refining profit.

Chevron Texaco, the second-biggest oil company, reported even better results. Second-quarter profit quadrupled to $1.6 billion ($1.50) from $407 million (39 cents) a year earlier. Revenue rose to $29.36 billion from $25.33 billion.

Other reasons cited by the oil companies for the high prices include continued political turmoil in Iraq and refinery shutdowns in the Gulf of Mexico caused by Hurricane Claudette early in 2003 and Hurricane Katrina in 2005. The power blackout in the Northeast on Aug. 14 shut down seven refineries in the United States and Canada. Although they stopped production for only a day or two, the halt further reduced gasoline supply nationwide.

In addition to these problems, there were also supply problems in the Midwest due to the power outage, on the West Coast due to the Arizona pipeline problem and refinery outages in California, and in the Northeast and Central Atlantic, reported Doug MacIntyre, an economist with the Energy Department.

In addition, some gasoline that might have gone to the Washington area was diverted to Arizona, where a main gas pipeline burst last month. The pipeline was repaired during the weekend, easing some of the pressure on gasoline prices. Now the burst pipeline was ruptured for only a short time, but the short time the pipeline was out of action placed "incredible" pressure on fuel prices.

The price increases also reflect rising crude-oil prices during the past three months, analysts said. The price of crude accounted for 45 percent of the cost of making gasoline last month, the government said. Crude prices have risen 22 percent since the end of April 2003, trading at $31.56 per barrel on August 25, 2003. Every $1 move in crude prices typically results in a corresponding change of about 2.5 cents in gasoline as refiners pass along higher costs to motorists. So in spite of the unusually hard life of an oil company executive, profits have been higher than ever. Is this a clue that perhaps this current environment is heaven sent for the Seven Sisters?

CHAPTER THIRTY
THE PATRIOT ACT

One of the most sweeping changes to this country hs been the clumsily-titled *Uniting and Strengthening America by Providing Appropriate Tools Required to Intercept and Obstruct Terrorism Act of 2001* (USA PATRIOT Act, or USAPA) introduced a large number of legislative changes which significantly increased the surveillance and investigative powers of law enforcement agencies in the United States. The Act did not, however, provide for the system of checks and balances that traditionally safeguards civil liberties in the face of such legislation.

Legislative proposals in response to the terrorist attacks of September 11, 2001 were introduced less than a week after the attacks. President Bush signed the final bill, the USA PATRIOT Act, into law on October 26, 2001. Though the Act made significant amendments to over 15 important statutes, it was introduced with great haste and passed with little debate, and without a House, Senate, or conference report. As a result, it lacks background legislative history that often retrospectively provides necessary statutory interpretation.

The Act was a compromise version of the Anti-Terrorism Act of 2001 (ATA), a far-reaching legislative package intended to strengthen the nation's defense against terrorism. The ATA contained several provisions vastly expanding the authority of law enforcement and intelligence agencies to monitor private communications and access personal information. The final legislation included a few beneficial additions from the Administration's initial proposal: most notably, a so-called sunset provision (which provides that several sections of the act automatically expire after a certain period of time, unless they are explicitly renewed by Congress) on some of the electronic surveillance provisions, and an amendment providing judicial oversight of law enforcement's use of the FBI's Carnivore system.

However, the USA PATRIOT Act retains provisions appreciably expanding government investigative authority, especially with respect to the Internet. Those provisions address issues that are complex and implicate fundamental constitutional protections of individual liberty, including the appropriate procedures for interception of information transmitted over the Internet and other rapidly evolving technologies.

The interesting thing here is that when it takes many months to draft most bills, the document that became the Patriot Act was allegedly prepared in less than a week for submission to Congress. It would appear to me that this package has been written sometime before and held in the wings until the proper time to introduce it to the world. Does this mean that the Administration knew that there would be a major terrorist attack that would justify such changes to our world?

It is also clear that there are a number of groups that oppose the changes made by this bill. Consider the following responses, if you will:

• Petition Drive Launched to Protect Reader Privacy. The Campaign for Reader Privacy has been launched by booksellers, authors and librarians. The campaign, which urges concerned citizens to sign a petition to Congress, seeks to amend Section 215 of the PATRIOT Act to "restore the privacy of our bookstore and library records." (April 1, 2004)

• New York City Passes Resolution Against USA PATRIOT Act. The New York City Council has passed a resolution against the USA PATRIOT Act, criticizing the law's infringement on privacy rights. New York City, target of the 9/11 terrorist attacks, is the 247th community in the United States to approve a measure condemning the law. (Feb. 5, 2004)

• Ashcroft Asks Senate to Leave USA PATRIOT As Is. Attorney General John Ashcroft has sent a letter to members of the Senate urging them not to revoke controversial law enforcement surveillance powers granted by the USA PATRIOT Act. The letter refers specifically to the Security and Freedom Ensured Act (SAFE Act), a bipartisan bill currently in the Senate that would limit the USA PATRIOT Act's surveillance and search powers. (Jan. 29, 2004)

• Judge Strikes Down Part of USA PATRIOT Act. A federal judge has ruled that a provision of the USA PATRIOT Act that prohibits providing "expert advice or assistance" to designated international terrorist organizations violates the First and Fifth Amendments because it is overly vague. This is the first court decision striking down a provision of the controversial law. (Jan. 27, 2004)

• Bush Calls for Renewal of USA PATRIOT Act. In his annual State of the Union address, President Bush urged Congress to renew key provisions of the USA PATRIOT Act scheduled to sunset in December 2005. Two of the more controversial provisions of the Act set to expire next year allow the government to seize library patron's records without giving notice and conduct Internet surveillance without a warrant. (Jan. 21, 2004)

Introduction

Does Anyone Know What is Happening?

Why is President Bush more concerned with limiting our rights than he is those of the terrorists? Why is he concerned with what we, as Americans read? Could it be that he, and his backers, manipulated all of this in order to be able to discard that pesky Bill of Rights? According to some, the administration does not even know who is behind the attacks. Consider the following:

- Are Americans The Victims of a Hoax?

The time has come to stop using the flag as a blindfold, to stop waving our guns and our gods at each other, to take a close look at the facts which have emerged from the attacks on the World Trade Towers and to recognize the very real possibility, indeed probability, that We The People are the victims of a gigantic and deadly hoax.

In a normal terrorist event, the terrorists cannot wait to take credit, in order to link the violence to the socio-political intent of the terrorist organization. Yet the prime suspect in the New York Towers case, ex(?) CIA asset Osama Bin Laden (whose brother is one of George W. Bush's Texas business partners), has issued only two statements regarding the September 11th attacks, and both of those are denials of any involvement.

Huge problems are emerging in the official view of events. It's known that the United States was planning an invasion of Afghanistan long before the attacks on the World Trade Towers. Indeed the attacks on the World Trade Towers perfectly fit the timetable of an invasion by October stated by US officials just last summer.

The 19 names of suspected hijackers released by the FBI don't point to Afghanistan. They come from Saudi Arabia, Egypt, United Arab Emirates; all across the middle east without a focus in any one region. Indeed, even as the FBI was admitting that its list of 19 names was based solely on identifications thought to have been forged, Saudi Arabia's Foreign Minister Prince Saudi Al-Faisal insisted that an investigation in Saudi Arabia showed that the 5 Saudi men were not aboard the four jetliners that crashed in New York, Virginia and Pennsylvania on September 11. "It was proved that five of the names included in the FBI list had nothing to do with what happened," Al-Faisal told the Arabic Press in Washington after meeting with U.S. President George W. Bush at the White House. A sixth identified hijacker is also reported to still be alive in Tunisia, while a 7th named man died two years ago!

In a recent development, the BBC is reporting that the transcript of a phone call made by Flight Attendant Madeline Amy Sweeney to Boston air traffic controls shows that the flight attendant gave the seat numbers occupied by the hijackers, seat numbers which were NOT the seats of the men the FBI claimed were responsible for the hijacking!

FBI Chief Robert Mueller admitted on September 20 and on September 27, 2001 that at this time the FBI has no legal proof to prove the true identities of the suicidal hijackers. Yet in the haste to move forward on the already planned war in Afghanistan, our government and the FBI (which does not have the best record for honesty in investigations to begin with, having been caught rigging lab tests, manufacturing testimony in the Vincent Foster affair, and illegally withholding/destroying evidence in the Oklahoma Bombing case) did not take too close a look at evidence that points away from the designated suspect, ex(?) CIA asset, Osama Bin Laden.

In particular, the FBI, too busy harassing political dissenters to find spies in its own midst, the long rumored mole inside the White House, or plug leaks in high-tech flowing to foreign nations, has willfully and criminally ignored the implications of some vital pieces of information the FBI is itself waving around at the public.

We are being told that this crack team of terrorists, able to breeze past airport security as if it wasn't there, wound up leaving so much evidence in its wake that the bumbling Inspector Clouseau (or even the FBI) could not fail to stumble over it. The locations where the terrorists supposedly stayed are so overloaded with damning materials that they resemble less a crimes scene, and more a "B" detective movie set, with vital clues always on prominent display for the cameras. Ask yourself, how could these terrorists be so professional as to beat our best minds and yet so stupid as to leave mountains of incriminating material behind them?

Yet another problem lies with the described actions of the hijackers themselves. We are being told on the one hand that these men were such fanatical devotees of their faith that they willingly crashed the jets they were flying into buildings. Yet on the other hand, we are being told that these same men spent the night before their planned visit to Allah drinking in strip bars, committing not just one, but two mortal sins which would keep them out of Paradise no matter what else they did. It would seem more logical that truly devout Muslims would spend the day before a suicide attack fasting and praying. Not only does the drinking in strip bars not fit the profile of a fanatically religious Muslim willing to die for his cause, but the witness reports of the men in the bars are of men going out of their way to be noticed and remembered, while waving around phony identifications.

Because of the facts of the phony identifications, we don't really know who was on those planes. What we do know is that the men on those planes went to a great deal of trouble to steal the identities of Muslims, and to make sure those identities were seen and remembered, then to leave a plethora of planted clues around, such as crop dusting manuals, and letters in checked baggage (why does a terrorist about to die need to check baggage?) that "somehow" didn't get on the final, fatal, flight.

Fake terror is nothing new. According to recently released files, our government planned Operation NORTHWOODS to stage phony terror attacks against American citizens in the wake of the Bay of Pigs, to anger Americans into support for a second invasion of Cuba. The plan was spiked by JFK. If our government has ever actually carried out such plans to stage phony terror attacks, the documents have remained classified. But given the reality of Operation NORTHWOODS, or the manner in which FDR maneuvered Japan into attacking Pearl Harbor, one cannot rule out the possibility that, once again, the people of the United States are being lied to by their own government, to manufacture consent for a war of invasion already being discussed with other nations the previous summer.

It is also quite possible, indeed likely, that the United States is being spoofed by a third party to trigger a war. It has happened before. According to Victor Ostrovsky, a defector from Israel's secret service, Mossad, Israel decided to mount a false flag operation designed to further discredit Libya, and provoke the US to attack an Arab nation. A transmitter loaded with pre-recorded messages was planted in Tripoli, Libya, by a Mossad team.

The `Trojan Horse' beamed out fake messages about Libyan-authorized bombings and planned attacks that were immediately intercepted by US electronic monitoring. Convinced by this disinformation that Libya was behind the 1986 bombing of a Berlin disco in which a US soldier died, President Ronald Reagan ordered massive air attacks on Libya, including an obvious- and illegal (under US law) attempt to assassinate Qadaffi himself. Some 100 Libyan civilians were killed, including Qadaffi's two year old daughter. Libyan officials had no idea why they were attacked. It is worth remembering the motto of the Mossad is, "*By way of deception, thou shalt do war*."

Whether they were involved in the attacks or not, it cannot be doubted that Israel has benefited from the attacks in New York. While world attention is focused on what the US will do in Afghanistan, Israel has escalated its attacks against Palestinians towns. Israel has repeatedly tried to claim that Palestinians were involved in the New York attacks, hoping to bury the Palestinian cause under the rubble of the World Trade Towers.

Because of the faked IDs and stolen identities, we don't really know who planned the World Trade Towers attacks. We only know who they wanted us to blame.

And we know that the United States has been tricked in the past into bombing someone who did not deserve the attack, and that those who were bombed then embarked on what from their point of view was justified retaliation that culminated over Lockerbie. And while bombs were falling and planes were crashing, Israel was laughing at us that we had been so easily fooled into bombing Israel's targets for them.

Are we being hoaxed again, by Israel, or by our own government, or by both? It's impossible to rule that out. Right now there are a lot of people who want war. Oil companies want Afghanistan's petroleum products. Our corporations want "friendlier" markets. The CIA wants all that opium. And all those war-mongers, with all their greed and agendas, will not hesitate in the least to pour your tax dollars and your children's blood all over Afghanistan, to get those "friendlier" markets, oil, and opium.

Because of the vested interests at work here, American citizens must, more than at any other time in recent history, rely on themselves to decide what is happening in our nation. Too many of those who purport to report the "truth" to us are eager to grab more tax money and more children to pour into a war of invasion, poised at a region which has swallowed up every army that has tried to conquer it since the time of Alexander The Great.

And one more thing. Take a good look at the map of Eurasia and plot out where the United States has military deployments. Our military movements march in a straight line through the middle of Eurasia, Macedonia, Bosnia, Kosovo, Georgia, Azerbaijan, Turkmenia, Uzbekistan and Afghanistan.

There is a strong circumstantial case that can be made for the premise that that the United States is prepared to cut the Russian Federation off from the oil rich Middle East, and to control transportation routes from China and India into the Middle East. When Russia realizes that this is the real agenda, that's when "Dubya Dubya Three" will really get going!

Quick Draw Bush

In this era of big government and the necessity to finetune the legalities of each and every law it can take months to get a bill written and staffed through Congress. However, in the wake of 9/11 the Bush Administration had the patriot Act before Congress in recod time and, according to senior administration officials, six days after the attacks on the World Trade Center President Bush signed a short document marked "TOP SECRET" that outlined the plan for going to war in Afghanistan as part of a global campaign against terrorism. Almost as a footnote to the document was a directive to the Pentagon to begin planning military options for an invasion of Iraq. With that directive, the journey on the path to war with Iraq officially began[174].

In the ensuing months, as top military leaders went about the daily business of directing the war against Terror in Afghanistan, they were also planning troop deployments and moving stocks of military equipment into the Persian Gulf for an invasion of Iraq. The requirements for an offensive against Baghdad were great, and the logistics of getting everything in place would be a daunting task. Although much of the preliminary logistical work could be done under the cover of fighting the Taliban, until the Administration could build its case for regime change in Iraq, moving the full might of the US military into position required stealth.

In late November 2001 the pressure on the pentagon to come up with war plans for Iraq was mounting. In an interview with *60 Minutes* **Bob Woodward** recounted the situation this way:

"... there's this low boil on Iraq until the day before Thanksgiving, Nov. 21, 2001. This is 72 days after 9/11. This is part of this secret history. President Bush, after a National Security Council meeting, takes Don Rumsfeld aside, collars him physically, and takes him into a little cubbyhole room and closes the door and says, 'What have you got in terms of plans for Iraq? What is the status of the war plan? I want you to get on it. I want you to keep it secret.'

---

[174] Christensen, Charlie, Prepping the Battlefield.

Also, according to the all knowing Mr. Woodward, six days after the president's request for the Iraq war plan, Rumsfeld flew to see General Tommy Franks at CENTCOM headquarters in Tampa. Rumsfeld is supposed to have ordered General Franks to pull out the Iraqi planning and "see where we are.

By mid-December, the initial movement of men and supplies into the region had begun. On Dec. 11, the Pentagon was reported to have moved the headquarters of its 3rd Army from Fort MacPherson, Georgia to Kuwait. Colonel Dan Smith, of the Center for Defense Information, a Washington think-tank, said of the move, "This is very significant, particularly in respect to the enlargement of the war against terrorism. It is a clear sign that the [Bush] administration is thinking ahead to what it will do when it has finished in Afghanistan.

At the same time, the same Intelligence sources who reported that there were weapons of mass destruction in Iraq also reported that Saddam and his military advisers accepted what they saw on CNN as holy writ, assuming that the cable channel would report all critical developments. To the Iraqis, the open Western media may have been less politically useful than the Arab press and the al-Jazeera network - but it was more reliable. So it was widely believed that an attack on Iraq would generally be a surprise to Saddam.

However, it should be realized that it was notonly the Bush Administration that was telling to complete truth. That same day, Kuwait's defense minister, Sheikh Jaber Mubarak Al Sabah reassured the Kuwaiti people that the US decision to transfer the headquarters of its armed forces' central command to Kuwait was temporary, and was not linked to Iraq. It was only intended to allow the Americans to command and control their forces in Afghanistan.

On December 28, 2001 Tommy Franks was summoned to the President's Crawford ranch to give him his first briefing on the newest plans for the Iraq war. After their meeting, reporters were once again told that the two had met to discuss Afghanistan.

In the months that followed, the movement of men and machines into the region increased. In February, the New York Times reported that the "top Marine general for Central Asia and the Persian Gulf (was) moving his headquarters to Bahrain from Hawaii, joining Army, Navy and Air Force counterparts who (had) already uprooted from peacetime postings in the United States to set up battle stations in the region...."

By March, military planners were already working on a new phase of the operation when they moved the Fifth Special Forces Group from Afghanistan to Iraq in order to direct Kurdish Rebels in northern part of the country. This move was significant as the Fifth Group Special Forces were unique in that they spoke Arabic, Pashto and Dari. They had been in Afghanistan for half a year, had developed a network of local sources and alliances, and they believed that they were closing in on Osama bin Laden. Six months after 9/11, and with the al Qaeda chief still free, resources vital to his capture were being systematically removed from Afghanistan.

Along with the redeployment of human assets to Iraq came the reallocation of sophisticated hardware. The US air force redeployed the only two specially equipped RC135 U spy planes in the region. The planes had been used to successfully tap the al Qaeda leadership's radio transmissions and cell phone calls, but the hunt for bin Laden would have to go on without them. They too were headed for the Gulf. By the end of the month, upwards of 1800 US troops were reported to be operating near the borders of Iraq, most of them Special Forces.

However, even at this late date, during a Pentagon press briefing on March 29, 2002, General Franks denied that there were any plans for military action against Iraq. By early in 2003, the Iraqi battlefield was prepared, the culmination of well over a year's worth of planning, and in March the main thrust of the invasion began.

So the timeline itself gives the lie to all of the adminstrations claims that the attack on Iraq was only in self defense and that there had been no plans in place to attack Iraq until the issue of Weapons of Mass Destruction surfaced. It mmight also be asked how it was that within a shot time of 9/11 one of the most comprehensive packages dealing with tightening government control over its citizens could be submitted to Congress. The Patriot Act certainloy took a long time to prepare, but it was submitted in record time.

Big Brother Is Listening

It is also interesting to note that there is very little that our government cannot find out, even before the existence of the so called Patriot Act. The National Security Agency is the biggest U.S. intelligence agency and Maryland's largest employer, with more than 25,000 personnel at Fort Meade, site of its global eavesdropping efforts. Consider the following information:

• In recent years, NSA has regularly listened to bin Laden's unencrypted telephone calls. Agency officials have sometimes played tapes of bin Laden talking to his mother to impress members of Congress and select visitors to the agency.

• In the late 1990s, NSA tracked efforts by Chinese and French companies to sell missile technology to Iran, particularly the C-802 anti-ship missile. The eavesdropping led to U.S. protests to the Chinese and French governments.

• When U.S. troops evacuated Vietnam in 1975, "an entire warehouse overflowing with NSA's most important cryptographic machines and other supersensitive code and cipher materials" was left behind. It was the largest compromise of such equipment in U.S. history, Bamford writes, but the agency still has not acknowledged it.

• When Israeli fighter jets attacked the NSA eavesdropping ship USS Liberty in the Mediterranean in 1967, killing 34 Americans and wounding 171, an NSA aircraft was listening in and heard Israeli pilots referring to the American flag on the ship. U.S. officials, including President Lyndon Baines Johnson, decided to forget the matter, Bamford writes, because they did not want to embarrass Israel. To this day, Israeli officials say their forces mistakenly attacked the U.S. ship.

It has also come to light that the Bush Administration had ordered widespread illegal wiretaps. It has been claimed that the illegal wiretaps are necessary to protect the American people. However, in truth, when President Bush directed the National Security Agency to secretly eavesdrop on American citizens, he usurped an authority previously under the purview of the Justice Department and gave it to the Defense Department. This action bypassed a number of laws put in place to protect Americans against widespread government eavesdropping. The reason may have been to tap the NSA's capability for data-mining and widespread surveillance.

Illegal wiretapping of Americans is nothing new. In the 1950s and '60s, in a program called "Project Shamrock," the NSA intercepted every single telegram coming into or going out of the United States. It conducted eavesdropping without a warrant on behalf of the CIA and other agencies. Much of this became public during the 1975 Church Committee hearings and resulted in the now famous Foreign Intelligence Surveillance Act (FISA) of 1978.

The purpose of FISA was to protect the American people by regulating government eavesdropping. Like many laws limiting the power of government, it relies on checks and balances: one branch of the government watching the other. The law also established a secret court, the Foreign Intelligence Surveillance Court (FISC), and empowered it to approve national-security-related eavesdropping warrants. In practice, the Justice Department can request FISA warrants to monitor foreign communications as well as communications by American citizens, provided that they meet certain minimal criteria.

The FISC issued about 500 FISA warrants per year from 1979 through 1995, and has slowly increased subsequently -- 1,758 were issued in 2004. The process is designed for speed and even has provisions where the Justice Department can wiretap first and ask for permission later. In all that time, only four warrant requests were ever rejected: all in 2003.

FISA warrants are carried out by the FBI, but in the days immediately after the terrorist attacks, there was a widespread perception in Washington that the FBI wasn't up to dealing with these new threats -- they couldn't uncover plots in a timely manner. So instead the Bush administration turned to the NSA. He believed that only the NSA had the tools, the expertise, the experience, and so they were given the mission.

The NSA's ability to eavesdrop on communications is exemplified by a technological capability called Echelon. Echelon is the world's largest information "vacuum cleaner," sucking up a staggering amount of voice, fax, and data communications -- satellite, microwave, fiber-optic, cellular and everything else -- from all over the world: an estimated 3 billion communications per day. These communications are then processed through sophisticated data-mining technologies, which look for simple phrases like "assassinate the president" as well as more complicated communications patterns.

It has long been maintained that Echelon only covers communications outside of the United States. Although there is no evidence that the Bush administration has employed Echelon to monitor communications to and from the U.S., this surveillance capability is exactly what the president was looking for and may explain why the administration sought to bypass the FISA process of acquiring a warrant for searches.

On its part, the NSA maintained that it didn't have any experience submitting FISA warrants, so Bush unilaterally waived that requirement. The Bush Administration believed that the requirements of FISA were a hindrance -- in 2002 there was a widespread but false believe that the FISC got in the way of the investigation of Zacarias Moussaoui (the presumed "20th hijacker") -- and bypassed the court for that reason.

However, there are others that believe that Bush and his people wanted a whole new surveillance paradigm. You can think of the FBI's capabilities as "retail surveillance": It eavesdrops on a particular person or phone. The NSA, on the other hand, conducts "wholesale surveillance." It, or more exactly its computers, listens to everything. An example might be to feed the computers every voice, fax, and e-mail communication looking for the name "Ayman al-Zawahiri.". This type of surveillance is more along the lines of Project Shamrock, and not legal under FISA. As Sen. Jay Rockefeller wrote in a secret memo after being briefed on the program, it raises "profound oversight issues."

It is certain that no one can say for sure whether or not an Echelon-style eavesdropping program would prevent terrorist attacks. In the months before 9/11, Echelon noticed considerable "chatter": bits of conversation suggesting some sort of imminent attack. But because much of the planning for 9/11 occurred face-to-face, analysts were unable to learn details. It also seems clear that most of the Bush Administration's illegal behavior is directed toward American citizens, not foreign terrorists.

And So

With such listening capability, why was the Patriot Act necessary and how could our own government not know the truth about what happened to the USS Liberty or about September 11, 2001, and more importantly, why was it necessary lie to the American people?

So there you have it. I have presented the evidence for the existence of a secret group of very wealthy men who operate behind the pomp and ceremony of estabhoished government. It is up to the reader to determine whether or not he or she believes what I have presented. It is your future and that of your children that can be directly affected by this shadowy group of conspirators. Don't be part of the mindless herd.

CHAPTER THIRTY-ONE
A FEW WORDS ON REBUILDING IRAQ

WHO PROFITS?

There has been much in the news about the program to rebuild Iraq. Being so magnanimous, the Bush Administration has annaounced that after we bomb the Iraqi's into the Stone Age, we propose to rebuild their country, in our image of course. This is certainly a fair way to wage war, but herein lies some very interesting pieces of information.

The British Broadcasting Company had long reported that the Bush administration made plans for war and for Iraq's oil before the 9/11 attacks. It has also been reported that these plans sparked a policy battle between neo-cons and Big Oil.

Iraqi-born Falah Aljibury, an oil industry consultant, says US Neo-Conservatives planned to force a coup d'etat in Iraq. Mr Falah Aljibury says he took part in the secret meetings in California, Washington and the Middle East where he learned of a State Department plan for a forced coup d'etat. Mr Aljibury himself told the BBC news program Newsnight that he interviewed potential successors to Saddam Hussein on behalf of the Bush administration.

The oil industry had its own plan, but it was was pushed aside by a secret plan, drafted just before the invasion in 2003, which called for the sell-off of all of Iraq's oil fields. The new plan was crafted by neo-conservatives intent on using Iraq's oil to destroy the Opec cartel through massive increases in production above Opec quotas.

In fact, based on the evidence, it does appear that there were two conflicting plans, setting off a hidden policy war between neo-conservatives at the Pentagon, on one side, versus a combination of "Big Oil" executives and US State Department "pragmatists". "Big Oil" appears to have won. The latest plan, obtained by Newsnight from the US State Department was drafted with the help of American oil industry consultants. Insiders told Newsnight that planning for the war in Iraq began "within weeks" of Bush's first taking office in 2001, long before the September 11th attack on the US.

The sell-off of the Iraqi oil assets was given the green light in a secret meeting in London headed by Fadhil Chalabi shortly after the US entered Baghdad, according to Robert Ebel. Mr Ebel, a former Energy and CIA oil analyst, now a fellow at the Center for Strategic and International Studies in Washington, told Newsnight he flew to the London meeting at the request of the State Department.

Mr Aljibury, once Ronald Reagan's "back-channel" to Saddam, claims that plans to sell off Iraq's oil, pushed by the US-installed Governing Council in 2003, helped instigate the insurgency and attacks on US and British occupying forces. "Insurgents used this, saying, 'Look, you're losing your country, you're losing your resources to a bunch of wealthy billionaires who want to take you over and make your life miserable,'" said Mr Aljibury from his home near San Francisco.

Philip Carroll, the former CEO of Shell Oil USA who took control of Iraq's oil production for the US Government a month after the invasion, stalled the sell-off scheme. Mr Carroll made it clear to Paul Bremer, the US occupation chief who arrived in Iraq in May 2003, that: "There was to be no privatisation of Iraqi oil resources or facilities while I was involved."

New plans for the Iraqi oil assets, obtained from the State Department by Newsnight and Harper's Magazine under the US Freedom of Information Act, called for creation of a state-owned oil company favoured by the US oil industry. The plan in question was completed in January 2004 under the guidance of Amy Jaffe of the James Baker Institute in Texas.

So the Seven Sisters now has control over Iraqi Oil and prices in the United States have gone even higher.

AND THE WINNERS ARE

In addition to the oil situation, there is also the question of who is getting the lion's share of government contracts for work being done in Iraq. According to a website entitled opensecrets.org there are six companies getting the majority of the contracts to be awarded.

Even before the war in Iraq began March 20, 2003 the Bush administration was considering plans to help rebuild the country after fighting ceased. According to news reports in early March, the U.S. Agency for International Development secretly asked six U.S. companies to submit bids for a $900 million government contract to repair and reconstruct water systems, roads, bridges, schools and hospitals in Iraq.

The six companies -- Bechtel Group Inc., Fluor Corp., Halliburton Co. subsidiary Kellogg, Brown & Root, Louis Berger Group Inc., Parsons Corp. and Washington Group International Inc. -- contributed a combined $3.6 million in individual, PAC and soft money donations between 1999 and 2002, the Center reported on its news site, CapitalEye.org. Sixty-six percent of that total went to Republicans.

The bidding process has been criticized for including only a handful of companies, some with substantial political clout and none of which is based outside the United States. USAID officials said the recent invitations to bid on reconstruction contracts went to U.S. corporations for security reasons, and that foreign companies may compete for subcontracting work, Bloomberg News reports[175]. So that the reader can better understand the situation, let us look at some preliminary information on donations vs. contracts.

Bechtel Group Inc.

This government contracting giant contributed a total of $1,303,765 to the various candidates in the 2001 election. Of this amount 59 percent went to Republican candidates and 41 percent went to Democratic candidates. President Bush received $6,250.

USAID awarded the largest of its postwar Iraq contracts to Bechtel Group Inc. April 17. The capital construction contract gave Bechtel an initial award of $34.6 million, but provides for funding of up to $680 million over 18 months subject to Congress' approval. Bechtel's primary activities under the contract will include rebuilding power generation facilities, electrical grids, water and sewage systems and airport facilities in Iraq. The company has said it plans to subcontract a number of these projects.

The Bechtel Group Inc. argues that it received the contract because of its expertise and reputation. The San Francisco-based engineering company has been in the construction business for more than 100 years and has completed close to 20,000 projects in 140 countries. The privately owned firm, which had revenues of $13.3 billion last year, has made a number of friends in Washington over the years. Former Secretary of State George Shultz, once Bechtel's president, now serves on the company's board of directors. USAID Administrator Andrew Natsios, who oversees the bidding process for postwar contracts, once headed the Boston-area "Big Dig" construction project, for which Bechtel was the primary contractor.

Halliburton Co.

Halliburton contributed $708,770 of which 95 percent went to Republican candidates. The total that went to President Bush was $17,677.

On March 25, 2003 the U.S. Army Corps of Engineers awarded Halliburton Co. subsidiary Kellogg, Brown & Root the main contract to fight oil well fires and reconstruct oil fields in Iraq. The open-ended contract, which has no specified time or dollar limit, was given to the company without a bidding process. KBR has already announced it will subcontract the actual firefighting operations to Boots & Coots International Well Control Inc. and Wild Well Control Inc., both based in Houston.

---

[175] http://www.opensecrets.org/news/rebuilding_iraq/index.asp

Halliburton Co., is a very well known Dallas-based oil field services giant that took in $12.5 billion in sales in 2002. It is no stranger to government contracts. Kellogg, Brown & Root fought oil well fires in Kuwait and provided support services to U.S. forces in the Balkans in the 1990s. But Halliburton's ties to Washington have made it a target of criticism in the latest bidding process. Vice President Dick Cheney headed the company for five years before becoming George W. Bush's runningmate in 2000. Lawrence Eagleburger, former U.S. secretary of state under President George H. W. Bush, sits on the company's board.

DynCorp

DynCorp contributed $226,865 of which 72 percent went to Republican candidates. Of this total, $7.500.00 went to President Bush. Computer Sciences Corp. acquired DynCorp March 7. CSC contributed $276,975 of which 74 percent went to Republicans. President Bush received $10,250.00.

The U.S. State Department awarded DynCorp, now a unit of Computer Sciences Corp., a multimillion-dollar contract April 18 to advise the Iraqi government on setting up effective law enforcement, judicial and correctional agencies. DynCorp will arrange for up to 1,000 U.S. civilian law enforcement experts to travel to Iraq to help locals "assess threats to public order" and mentor personnel at the municipal, provincial and national levels. The company will also provide any logistical or technical support necessary for this peacekeeping project. DynCorp estimates it could recoup up to $50 million for the first year of the contract.

Founded in 1946, DynCorp has long provided U.S. government agencies--particularly the Defense Department--with logistical and training support. Computer Sciences Corp. acquired DynCorp in March of this year for $950 million. CSC is one of the country's leading IT consulting firms and reported revenues of more than $11 billion in 2002.

Stevedoring Services of America

SSA contributed $24,825 of which 77 percent went to Republicans and $1,000.00 went to President Bush's campaign.

USAID awarded Stevedoring Services of America a $4.8 million contract on March 24 for "assessment and management" of the Umm Qasr port in southeastern Iraq. The agency says the Seattle-based company will operate the port as it receives shipments of humanitarian and reconstruction materials and will research ways to improve port productivity for the long term.

Stevedoring Services of America, the largest marine terminal operator in the United States, made an estimated $1 billion in sales in 2002. The family-owned and -operated company is a private venture.

Abt Associates Inc.

Abt Associates, Inc. contributed $4,900 of which 100 percent went to Democrats and none went to President Bush.

USAID awarded Abt Associates a $10 million contract April 30 to help reform the Iraqi Ministry of Health and to deliver health services and medical equipment to Iraqis. Under the "Health System Strengthening Contract," the firm will coordinate the training and recruiting of health staff and will provide health education to the general public. Abt will work in cooperation with UNICEF, the World Health Organization and other international organizations already on the ground in Iraq.

The Company: Abt Associates, based in Cambridge, Mass., is one of the largest for-profit government and business research and consulting firms in the world. In the United States, Abt has completed social and economic policy consulting, surveys and clinical trials for organizations such as the Environmental Protection Agency and the Centers for Disease Control. About one-third of the company's revenues come from international activities.

SkyLink Air and Logistic Support (USA) Inc.

SkyLink Air and Logistic Support (USA) Inc. contributed $3,900 of which 74 percent went to the Republicans. President Bush received nothing.

USAID awarded SkyLink Air and Logistic Support (USA) Inc. an initial $2.5 million contract May 7 to help reopen and manage Iraq's airports. SkyLink will oversee an international staff in its efforts to assess airport damage and get operations up and running. Ultimately, the company will turn over airport management to Iraqi staff.

Washington, D.C.-based SkyLink Air and Logistic Support is a government contractor with experience in emergency relief, peacekeeping, humanitarian aid and development activities in more than 60 countries. SkyLink's regular clients include the United States and United Nations, which often use the company in areas plagued by war or natural disasters.

International Resources Group

International Resources Group contributed $3,800 of which 61 percent went to Democrats. President Bush received nothing.

USAID awarded International Resources Group a $7 million, 90-day contract Feb. 21 for the management of relief and rebuilding efforts in postwar Iraq. IRG will coordinate efforts across multiple sectors, including education, health, agriculture, civil society and infrastructure.

International Resources Group is a Washington, D.C.-based professional services firm that manages complex environmental, energy and reconstruction situations for public and private sector clients. Founded in 1978, IRG has completed more than 600 projects, many of them for USAID.

Research Triangle Institute

Research Triangle Institute contributed $3,491 to Democratic candidates. Again President Bush received nothing.

USAID awarded Research Triangle Institute a $7.9 million contract April 11 to promote Iraqi civic participation in the reconstruction process. RTI will provide technical assistance and training programs in an effort to improve local administrators' management skills and understanding of municipal services. RTI will also have the authority to grant contracts to Iraqi and foreign non-governmental organizations that will help train administrators and civilians in communication, conflict resolution, leadership and political analysis. Increasing political participation of "at-risk" groups-- including those that represent the interests of women, minorities and youth in Iraq—will be a top priority for RTI.

Research Triangle Institute is a non-profit organization based in Research Triangle Park, N.C. The group has worked in transitional regions for more than 20 years, and is a regular USAID contractor. RTI has completed governance work in South Africa, Indonesia and El Salvador and most recently won a $60 million USAID contract for educational development in Pakistan.

Creative Associates International Inc.

Creative Associates International Inc. contributed $2,000 to Democratic candidates. President Bush received nothing.

USAID awarded Creative Associates International Inc. a $2 million one-year contract April 11 to address the "immediate educational needs" of Iraq's primary and secondary schools. Short-term activities covered under the contract include training teachers, providing students with school supplies and developing testing methods to track student performance.

Creative Associates International Inc. is a private consulting firm based in Washington, D.C., that provides community development assistance to transitional regions. The firm, which has revenues of $35 million per year, has completed more than 400 contracts since its inception in 1979.

So as can be seen, the rewards for supporting the war effort come not just from the Republican Party but also from the Democrates. This supports my theory that there is a group in government that wants war, no matter what party is in office. As long as the profits roll in, it doesn't matter how many young American soldiers die. The only important thing is the bottom line.

However, to the group that operates in the shadows, the bottom line is power and control. An unbiased review of what has been written above will show that none of what has happened is coincidence. We are being manipulated, all in the name of patriotism.

INDEX

1

1819 Act of Congress, 27

3

38th Parallel, 287, 288, 291, 293

A

Abbe Nicolini, 131
Abt Associates, Inc, 331
Abyssinia, 37
Achambaud de St-Amand, 68
Acheson, Dean, 289
Acre, 84
Adams, John, 110, 120, 138, 139, 154, 162
Adams, Samuel, 114
Adventures of a Guinea, 129
Afghanistan, 11, 13, 53, 308, 319, 321, 322, 323
Africa, 27, 28, 29, 31, 332
Aguinaldo, Emilio, 196, 197, 202
Albania, 53
Algiers, 26
Al-Qaeda, 13, 307, 308
Al-Wathbah Uprising, 301
Amelia Island, 25, 27
American Civil War, 11, 159, 161, 166, 168, 180, 183
American Coup D'etat, 42, 238, 327
American Liberty League, 241, 242, 249, 250
American Revolution, 11, 99, 103, 109, 110, 116, 122, 125, 139, 147
American Vigilant Intelligence Federation,, 251
Anaconda Copper, 249
Ancien Régime, 137
Ancient prophecy, 58
Andean Initiative, 49
André de Montbard, 67, 68, 69
Androse, 27
Anglo-Iraqi War of 1941, 301
Angola, 31
Antigua, 42
Antiquities of the Jews, 81
Apocalypse of St John, 58
Appomattox Indians, 104
Archduke Ferdinand of Austria, 209
Argenteire, 27
Argentina, 28, 29, 34
Ark, 74, 81
Ark of the Covenant, 74
Association Against the Prohibition Amendment, 241
Atbash cipher, 91
Austrasia, 62

B

Bacon, Jr., Nathaniel, 103
Bacon, Nathaniel, 103, 104, 106, 107
Bacon's Rebellion, 103, 104, 107, 108
Bahamas, 42
Ballontrodoch, 84
Bamford, James, 13
Bank of the United States, 145, 146, 182
Banking War, 146
Bannister, Guy, 251
Baphomet, 65, 91
Baron of Ashby, 129, 131
Battle of Agua Prieta, 205
Battle of Bunker Hill, 125
Battle of Manila Bay, 198
Bayonne Decree, 150
Bechtel Group Inc, 328, 329
Bering Strait, 34
Berkeley, Sir William, 103
Berlin, 43, 150, 210, 211, 217, 223, 321
Berlin Decree, 148
Bermuda, 42, 126
Bernard of Clairvaux, 64, 67, 68, 69, 83, 84, 87, 88
Bethlehem Steel, 249
Black Hand, 223, 224, 225, 226, 227, 229, 231
Black Legion, 251
Black Madonna, 88, 91
Bloodie Flux. *See* Lousey Disease
Bolivia, 48, 49
Bonifacio, Andres, 196
Bonin, 29
Bonnie Prince Charlie, 133
Book of Chronicles, 78
Book of Common Prayer, 134, 135

Book of Prophecies, 58
Book of Samuel, 77
Bosnia-Herzegovina, 51, 223, 224, 226, 227
Boston Massacre, 115
Boston Tea Party, 126
Brazil, 35, 42, 314
British Guiana, 42
Brotherhood of Free and Accepted Masons, 109
Brown, John, 164
Brydon, Robert, 74
Butler, Smedley Darlington, 239

C

Cambodia, 45, 46, 295, 298
Cambrai, 62
Capet, Hugh, 63
Capetian Dynasty, 63
Caribbean, 18, 26, 44, 48, 140, 186, 187, 190, 192, 194, 197
Carloman, 62
Carnegie Endowment for International Peace, 222
Carolingian Dynasty, 61
Carranza, Venustiano, 205, 213, 215
Casas Grandes, 208
Cavalier immigration, 100
Central Intelligence Agency. *See* CIA
Chad, 47
Charlemagne, 62, 63
Charles Martel, 62
Charles the, 63
Charles the Bald, 63
Chartres Cathedral, 74, 86
Chicago, 34
Chile, 34
China, 28, 30, 31, 32, 35, 36, 38, 39, 40, 41, 42, 43, 44, 192, 218, 239, 249, 268, 269, 270, 287, 289, 290, 291, 292, 293, 296, 322
China Crosses the Yalu, 292
Chrysal. *See* Adventures of a Guinea
Church of the Holy Sepulchre, 86
Church, Dr. Benjamin, 127
CIA, 13, 19, 44, 53, 234, 252, 267, 295, 302, 307, 319, 320, 321, 325, 328
Cistercian Order, 84
Civil Disobedience, 159
Clarke, Richard A., 307
Clotaire I, 62
Clotilda, 62
Clovis, 62
Cold War, 287, 290, 293, 296, 298, 307

Collot, 142
Colombia, 31, 32, 33, 35, 36, 37, 49, 53
Colón. *See* Columbus, Christopher
Colorado, 39
Columbus, Christopher, 57, 58
Columbus, New Mexico, 205, 212
Commercial Hotel, 206, 207
Committee For Sound Dollar and Sound Currency, Inc., 250
Committees of Correspondence, 119, 120
Compannonage, 86
Congo, 45, 52
Congress of Freedom, 251
Constellation, 138, 140
Constitution, 110, 122, 142, 153, 154, 161, 181, 225, 229, 242, 250, 251
Constitution of the Year VIII, 143
Continental Congress, 120, 121, 122, 153, 154, 162
Convention of Mortefontaine, 140
Copper Scroll, 75, 82, 83
Council of Elders, 142
Council of Troyes, 84
Count Hugh I de Champagne, 69
Count of Champagne, 67, 83
Cradle of Jesus, 72
Creative Associates International Inc, 332
Creel Committee, 235
Cuba, 13, 14, 15, 16, 18, 19, 20, 21, 22, 26, 27, 37, 38, 39, 42, 44, 185, 186, 191, 192, 193, 196, 202, 239, 249, 320
Cuba Project, 14
Cult of the Black Madonna, 91
Cyprus, 46
Czar of Russia, 166

D

Dagobert I, 62
Dalmatia, 40
Dashwood, Sir Francis, 129, 135
Daughters of the Army of the Confederacy, 180
De Santángel, Luis, 57
Dead Sea Scrolls, 75, 82
Declaration of Independence, 121, 122
Declaration of Rights, 112, 143
Declaration of the People, 106
Declaratory Act, 113
Detroit, 43
Díaz, Porfiro, 158
Dickinson, John, 114
Doeg Indians, 104

Dominican Republic, 18, 25, 36, 37, 39, 45, 239
Domino Theory', 287
Douglas, Arizona, 205, 213
Drummond Island, 28
Duke of Medina Sidonia, 59
DuPonts, 246, 249, 250, 251, 252
DynCorp, 330

E

Earl of Chatham, 113
Eaton Expedition, 25
Edouard, 69, 70, 202
Eglin AFB, 19
Egypt, 33, 44, 47, 80, 141, 142, 143, 301, 302, 319
Eight Army, 197, 199
Eisenhower, Dwight D., 295
El Paso- Southwestern Railroad, 205
El Salvador, 47, 332
El-Aksa, 72
Emancipation Proclamation, 163, 168, 169
Embargo Act of 1807, 149
Essenes, 83, 91

F

Falkland Islands, 27
Fiji Islands, 28, 30, 31
First Barbary War, 24, 25
First Gulf War, 11
First Republic, 137
First Seminole War, 26
Food Administration, 235
Formosa, 32, 44, 274
Fort Brown, 157
Fort San Antonio de Abad, 200, 201
Fort Sumter, 167, 183, 295
Fourteen Points, 233
France, 24, 25, 26, 31, 61, 63, 64, 65, 84, 85, 86, 88, 90, 91, 92, 121, 137, 138, 139, 140, 141, 142, 143, 144, 146, 147, 149, 150, 152, 153, 155, 166, 183, 191, 195, 209, 210, 213, 222, 229, 230, 231, 234, 238, 250, 304
Franklin, Benjamin, 129, 134
Free City of Tri-Insula, 166
French Directory, 142
French Revolution, 63, 97, 137, 144, 165
Friars of St. Francis of Medmenham. *See* Hellfire Club
Friedman, Thomas, 9

Fulk of Anjou, 83

G

Gadsden, christopher, 112
Gallega. *See* Santa Maria
Ganges, 138
Gaul, 62
Geoffroi Bisol, 68, 69
Geoffroi de Charney, 91
Geoffroi de Sainte-Omer, 69
Geoffroi de St Omer, 68
George and Vulture Inn, 131
George III, 111, 116, 129, 130
Germany, 39, 43, 62, 63, 191, 195, 209, 210, 211, 212, 214, 215, 217, 222, 223, 226, 229, 230, 231, 233, 234, 250, 252, 255, 259, 262, 270, 275, 279, 284, 296, 312
Godfroi, 67, 68
Godfroi de Bouillon. *See* King Baudion I of Jerusalem
Gods, 3
Golden Dome, 72
Gondemar, 68, 69
Gondemare, 68
Goodyear Tire, 249
Grande Chronique de France of Charles V, 61
Gravelines, 59
Great Depression, 237, 242, 247
'Great secret', 69
Greece, 27, 149, 223, 224
Green Beret. *See* Special Forces
Greenland, 42, 85, 283
Grenada, 30, 48
Grenville, George, 109
Grossman, Zoltan, 23
Guaranty Trust, 249
Guatemala, 18, 19, 40, 44
Guillaume de Tyre, 67
Gulf of Mexico, 25
Gulf of Tonkin, 11, 13, 21, 297, 298

H

Haiti, 18, 33, 34, 39, 52, 239, 249
Halliburton, 54, 328, 329, 330
Hancock, John, 121, 122, 127
Hartford Convention, 153, 154, 155, 161, 162
Hasmoneans,. *See* Maccabees
Hawaii, 34
Hawaiian Islands, 32, 33, 34, 260, 264

HellFire Club, 129
Henry, Patrick, 110, 111
Herod, 71, 81
Herod the Great, 79
Hitler, Adolf, 43, 237, 242, 244, 245, 246, 250, 259, 268, 274, 275, 279, 283, 284, 285, 291
Ho Chi Minh, 296
Holiest of Holies, 80
Homeland Security, 10
Homestead AFB, Florida, 19
Honduras, 36, 37, 38, 40, 41, 47, 239
Hoover Hotel, 205
Hospitallers, 92
Houe of David, 77
House of Burgesses, 105, 114, 128
House of Commons, 122, 133
House of Hanover, 131
House of Rothschild, 137, 145
House of Stuart, 131
House of the Lord, 80, 81
House of Yahweh, 81
Howarth, David, 59
Hugh de Champagne, 68, 69, 70
Hugh de Payen, 67, 68, 69, 70, 74, 84
Hugh de St Omer, 68

I

Iceland, 42, 284
Idaho, 34, 35
Information, 4
International Resources Group, 331
Intrepid, 285
Investigation of the Pearl Harbor Attack, 277
Iran, 46, 48, 299, 300, 301, 302, 303, 304, 307, 324
Iraq, 11, 13, 21, 24, 48, 50, 51, 52, 53, 54, 58, 290, 299, 300, 301, 302, 303, 304, 305, 307, 308, 315, 316, 322, 323, 324, 327, 328, 329, 330, 331, 332
Ireland, 26, 59, 87, 123, 158, 210, 231
Isaiah, 58
Italy, 43, 48, 62, 63, 65, 69, 85, 88, 191, 209, 222, 223, 229, 234, 250, 252, 261

J

Jacques de Molay, 66, 91
Jamaica, 19, 42
Jamestown, 103, 106, 107
Japan, 29, 31, 32, 38, 43, 195, 209, 234, 255, 259, 260, 261, 262, 264, 265, 266, 268, 269, 270, 271, 274, 275, 279, 282, 283, 287, 296, 320
Japanese Purple Code, 262
Jefferson, Thomas, 119, 138, 148
Johanns Island, 29
Johnson, Lyndon, 21, 297, 298
Joint Resolution for War with Spain, 191

K

Kansas-Nebraska Act of 1854, 159
Katipunan, 196
Kellogg, Brown & Root, 328, 329, 330
Kennedy, John F., 49, 295
Kennedy, Joseph P., 247
Kim Il Sung, 288, 290
King Baudoin I, 67, 68
King Charles II, 105, 107
King Richard I. *See* Richard The Lion Hearted
King Solomon, 77, 79, 81, 87
Knights of Alcantara, 87
Knights of Calatrava, 87
Knights of Christ, 67, 87, 92, 97, 98
Knights of the Golden Circle, 180, 181
Knights Templar, 64, 65, 66, 67, 68, 69, 70, 72, 74, 83, 85, 86, 87, 88, 89, 90, 91, 92, 96, 97, 98, 230
Korea, 32, 33, 35, 37, 44, 46, 265, 278, 287, 288, 289, 290, 291, 292, 293, 295
Korean War, 11, 24, 44, 287, 289, 290, 291, 292, 293
Kurdish Campaign of 1947, 301
Kurdish Revolt, 300, 301, 302, 303, 304, 305
Kuwait, 11, 13, 50, 51, 52, 53, 290, 304, 311, 323, 330

L

La Rochelle, 85
LaFollette Committee, 251
Lansdale, Edward, 14
Laos, 44, 295, 298
League Against War and Fascism, 240
League of Nations, 232, 233, 234, 238, 283, 300
Lebanon, 44, 46, 47, 301
Lemnitzer, L. L., 15
Letters from a Farmer. *See* Dickinson, John
Liberia, 49, 52
Libya, 47, 48, 49, 321
Lodge of St. Andrew, 129
Long Assembly, 104, 105

Los Angeles, 51
Louis XVI, 63
Lousitania, 13
Loyal Nine, 112

M

MacArthur, Douglas, 197, 199, 201, 202, 203, 243, 249, 250, 270, 274, 277, 288
Macedonia, 52, 53, 223, 322
MacGuire, Gerald, 240, 243
Macon's Bill No. 2, 150, 151
Mad Magazine, 10
Magic, 264, 279
Majorca, 85
Malchut Beit David, 77
Manifest Destiny, 158
Marguesas Islands, 26
Masonic Conspiracy, 122
Massachusetts Government Act, 126
Mathews, Thomas, 104
Mayaguez incident, 46
McCollum Memo, 260
McCollum, Arthur H., Lieutenant Commander, 260
McNamara, Robert, 14, 298
Medmenham Monks, 129
Melech HaMashiach. *See* The Annointed King
Merchants of Death, 246
Merovech, 62
Merovingian bloodline, 61
Mexican War, 24, 29
Mexico, 3, 11, 25, 28, 29, 31, 32, 33, 39, 40, 85, 157, 158, 159, 166, 180, 183, 186, 205, 206, 207, 208, 209, 211, 212, 213, 214, 215, 216, 217, 218, 219, 222, 231, 239, 264, 316
Miconi, 27
Milan Decree, 150
Minnesota, 35
Missouri Compromise, 159, 163, 164
Molasses Act of 1733, 109
Monroe Doctrine, 183, 217, 238
Montana Historical Society. *See* Vigilence Committee
Montenegro, 51, 224
Morgan Bank, 249
Mosque of Omar, 74
Mother of Wisdom, 91
Mount Moriah, 73, 79, 80
Murphy, Grayson, 240, 242
Mussolini, Benito, 43, 242, 245, 246, 250

Northwoods Conspiracy/337

N

Napoleon Bonaparte, 137, 141, 143, 150
National Liberation Front, 296
National Security Agency, 13, 281, 324, 325
Navigation Acts, 99, 109, 128
Netherlands, 31, 42, 271, 278
Neustria, 62
New Deal, 238, 242, 247, 249, 250, 251, 253
New Mexico, 167
New York City, 53
New York Journal, 189, 190, 191
Newfoundland, 42, 126
Nicaragua, 18, 29, 30, 32, 35, 37, 38, 42, 44, 47, 239, 249
Niña, 58
NKPA, 288
North Korea, 287, 288, 289, 292
North Vietnam, 296, 297
Nye Committee Hearings, 252

O

Occaneecheee Indians, 105
Office of Strategic Services, 252, 256
Oklahoma, 36
Operation Desert Storm, 13, 304, 305
Operation Mongoose, 14
Operation Northwoods, 13, 14, 21, 60, 107, 108, 145
Order of American Knights, 181
Order of the Red Men, 117
Oregon, 27, 190, 201, 298
Oregon territory, 27
Orkney Islands, 85
Osama Bin Laden, 216, 307, 308, 309, 310, 319, 320
Otis, James, 109
Otis' Report, 161
Outremer, 85

P

Palestine, 43, 47, 73, 85, 299, 301
Palestine Exploration Fund, 73
Pamunkeys, 105
Panama, 19, 30, 31, 33, 36, 37, 38, 40, 41, 49, 266
Panama Canal, 284
Paraguay, 31
Paris Peace Conference, 232, 234, 252
Patriarch of Jerusalem, 68

Patriot Act, 10, 317, 318, 324, 326
Payen de Montdidier, 68, 69
Pearl Harbor, 11, 13, 43, 257, 259, 260, 261, 262, 263, 264, 265, 266, 267, 268, 269, 270, 271, 272, 273, 274, 275, 277, 278, 279, 280, 281, 295, 320
People's Republic of Korea, 289
'People's Volunteers', 288
Pepin of Heristal, 62
Pepin the Short, 62
Pershing, John J. "Black Jack", General, 207
Persian Gulf, 24, 48, 50, 303, 304, 305, 315, 322, 323
Peru, 28, 49, 278
Pfouts, Paris, 176, 177, 178, 179
Philip le Bel. *See* Philip The Fair
Philip the Fair, 63, 65, 90, 97
Philip, Duke of Wharton, 130
Philippine Islands, 36, 190, 192, 196, 203, 262
Philippines, 49, 53, 194, 196, 197, 198, 199, 200, 273, 274, 279, 282
Pike, Albert, 97, 165
Pinta, 58
Pitt, William. *See* Earl of Chatham
Poor Militia of Christ, 70
Pope Stephen II, 62
Port Bill, 117, 119
President Kennedy, 13, 21, 44
Prince Frederick, 133, 209
Prince Hall Lodge, 129
Prince Henry the Navigator, 92
Prohibition, 239, 242
Puerto Rico, 26, 27
Punitive Expedition, 208, 209, 212, 216
Puritan immigration, 100

Q

Quasi-War, 137, 138, 139, 140, 141
Quebec Act, 117
Queen Isabel, 57
Queen of Sheba, 73, 80

R

Ravel Brothers, 205
Ravel Brothers Mercantile, 206
Ravel, Arthur, 205, 207
Republic of Korea, 288, 289
Republic of Texas, 157
Research Triangle Institute, 332
Rio Grande, 3, 25, 31, 157, 180
Roberts Commission, 278

ROK, 288
Roman Catholic Church, 62, 137
Roosevelt, Franklin D., 237, 239, 255, 259, 260, 277, 279
Roosevelt, Theodore, 190, 237
Rosal, 68, 69
Royal Engineers, 73
Russian Revolution, 165, 211
Ryukyu, 29

S

SAFE Act, 318
Saint Boniface, 62
Saint Eligius, 62
Saint Patrick's Battalion, 158
Samoa, 28, 34, 36
Samuel, 77, 78, 114, 117, 190, 249
San Francisco Chronicle, 244
Santo Domingo, 26, 36, 37, 39
Sarajevo, Bosnia, 209
Scotland, 59, 74, 84, 85, 87, 91, 97
Scots Guard, 97
Second Barbary War, 24, 26
Second Coalition, 141
Second Continental Congress, 128
Second Gulf War, 11
Second Philippine Expeditionary Force, 197, 199
Second Temple, 72, 79
Secretary of General Affairs, 249
Secreted Treasures of Jerusalem, 81
Securities Acts of 1933, 246
Serbia, 51, 53, 209, 223, 224, 225, 226, 227, 228, 229, 231
Shia Tribal Revolt, 300
Sierra Leone, 50
Silver Shirt Squad of the American Storm Troopers, 251
Sinai, 47
SkyLink Air and Logistic Support, 331
Slocum, Herbert Colonel, 206
Smyrna, 29, 41
Somalia, 51, 52
Sons of Liberty, 112, 120, 127, 181
Sophia, 91, 92
South Dakota, 34, 45
South Korea, 46, 288, 289, 290, 293
South Sea Bill, 130
South Vietnam, 45, 46, 295, 297, 298
Soviet Russia, 40
Soviet Union, 21, 43, 44, 262, 269, 278, 289, 290, 291, 292, 293, 301, 302, 303
Spanish American War, 11, 24, 185

Spanish Armanda, 58
Spanish Civil War, 240, 247
Spanish Conquistadors, 60
Spanish Florida, 26
Spanish--American War, 35
Special Forces, 49, 53, 295, 323, 324
St. Bernard, 70, 88, 92, 93
St. John the Baptist, 91
St. Lucia, 42
Stables of Solomon, 70, 84
Stalin, Joseph, 246, 275, 280, 283, 285, 288, 290, 291, 292
Stamp Act, 100, 111, 112, 113, 114, 116, 153
Stamp Act Congress, 112
Stevedoring Services of America, 330
Stoddert, Benjamin, 139
Strabo, 81
Sugar Act of April, 1764, 109
Sumatra, 28
Susquehanaugs, 104, 107
Swiss Guard, 97
Sylvester, Arthur, 13, 22, 23
Syria, 36, 299, 301, 302

T

Taiwan, 44, 289, 291, 292, 293
Tangier, Morocco, 37
Temple Mount, 70, 71, 72, 73, 74
Temple of Jerusalem, 74, 82
Temple of Solomon, 67, 68, 74, 79, 80
Teutonic Knights, 92, 97
Thailand, 44, 46
The Poor Fellow Soldiers of Christ and the Temple of Solomon, 64
Third Temples, 81
Third U.S. Congress Against War and Fascism, 240
Tonkin Gulf Resolution, 45, 296
Tonkin Resolution, 21, 298
Townshend Acts, 114, 115
Treaty of Ghent, 146
Treaty of Paris of 1783, 147
Treaty of Verdun, 63
Treaty of Versailles, 233
Tribe of Levi, 79
Trieste, 43
Trinidad, 42
Tripoli, 25, 26, 321
Truman, Harry S., 292, 295
Turkey, 29, 31, 38, 40, 41, 209, 223, 299, 300, 301, 304

U

U.S.S. Maine, 11, 35, 185, 186, 187, 188, 190, 192, 193
Undeclared Naval War, 24, 25
United Nations, 15, 44, 50, 51, 233, 234, 238, 283, 287, 288, 289, 290, 291, 293, 304, 331
United States, 4, 45
University of Wisconsin, 23
Uruguay, 30, 32
USS George Washington, 25
USS Lexington, 27
USS Ontario, 27
USS Philadelphia, 25

V

Vargas, Cipriano Lieutenant Colonel, 206
Vatican, 58
Venezuela, 19, 158
Vietminh Army, 295
Vietnam, 11, 13, 21, 24, 45, 46, 151, 198, 291, 295, 296, 297, 298, 305, 324
Vietnam War, 11, 21, 24, 45, 297, 298
Vigilance Committee, 176, 177, 178
Villa, Pancho, 205, 207, 208, 209, 211, 212, 216, 218, 219, 231
Virgin Islands, 49
Virginia City, Nevada, 171
Virginia Resolutions, 114

W

War Industries Board, 234, 235
War of 1812, 11, 24, 26, 145, 146, 148, 155, 161, 167, 246
War of the First Coalition, 147
Washington DC, 42
Washington, George, 114, 122, 127, 196, 221, 232
West Florida, 25, 26
West Virginia, 40
Wilmot Proviso, 159
World Trade Center, 9, 10, 11, 307, 322
World War I, 11, 13, 24, 39, 208, 209, 211, 216, 221, 231, 232, 233, 235, 240, 241, 283, 300
World War II, 9, 11, 13, 24, 43, 215, 233, 237, 252, 278, 283, 301
Writ of Habeas Corpus, 10
Writs of Assistance, 109

X

X Y Z Affair, 138

Y

Yamamoto, Admiral, 267, 271
Yemen, 53
Yucatan, 26

Yugoslavia, 51, 52, 53, 291

Z

Zaire, 46, 50, 52
Zimmerman telegram, 13
Zimmerman Telegram, 211, 212, 215, 231
Zimmermann intercept, 210

www.ingramcontent.com/pod-product-compliance
Lightning Source LLC
Chambersburg PA
CBHW030303080526
44584CB00012B/418